Hostages of Fortune
CHILD LABOR REFORM
IN NEW YORK STATE

Hostages of Fortune

CHILD LABOR REFORM
IN NEW YORK STATE

JEREMY P. FELT

SYRACUSE UNIVERSITY PRESS 1965

Manufactured in the United States of America. Composition
and printing by The Heffernan Press Inc. of Worcester, Massachusetts;
binding by Vail-Ballou Press of Binghamton, New York.

For Dorothy and Waldo

Preface

Every society makes a tacit or overt decision regarding its youth. When the industrial revolution struck the United States in the nineteenth century and began to draw thousands of children into its service, the prevailing social consensus was undisturbed. It was not only acceptable but praiseworthy for children to work. They could help to support needy parents, develop qualities of industry, and avoid the vice of idleness. The leader of society was the self-made man. But as the full implications of industrial child labor became evident, society reacted. Here was no benevolent system of practical education for young people but a program of cheap, easily discarded labor that depressed the wages of adults and broke the spirits and bodies of children. Here were children from the age of six working in filthy, jam-packed tenements, operating dangerous machinery, or running about the streets doing everything from selling newspapers and carrying messages to procuring women and narcotics.

Until 1938, the opponents of child labor did most of their work on the state and local level. Two federal laws were in effect briefly, but both were declared unconstitutional by the Supreme Court, and a proposed child labor amendment to the Constitution failed to carry the necessary number of states. Very few critical accounts of the struggle within the states exist, and that is unfortunate, for the story of child labor reform has considerable value for the present. This is particularly true in the case of New York, an industrial state that entered the twentieth century with an extremely serious child labor problem and emerged half a century later with one of the highest legislative standards in the United States. New York became a center for many different social reform organizations. Its Child Labor Committee, the first permanent organized group of its kind, developed into an expert pressure group, studying conditions, drafting bills, lobbying in Albany, publicizing child labor abuses, and setting a standard for other states to follow. The progressive era may have come to an end in 1920, but its impulse remained strong in New York up to the Second World War and, in the effort to regulate agricultural child labor, to the present day. Today few people would argue that the problems of New York's youth have been solved. Juvenile delinquents attack their teachers in the classrooms of the blackboard jungle, murder each other in gang warfare, and sell dope in high-school corridors. Is it better for a child to lose a finger to a machine than to become addicted to narcotics? Ironically unemployment of school dropouts exists because there is little industrial child labor and now the National Child Labor Committee is better known as the Committee on Youth Employment. Occasionally one hears the argument that agricultural child labor is a sure cure for juvenile delinquency, as if delinquency was unknown fifty years ago. Obviously we still have far to go and much to learn from New York's experience in patchwork legislation.

I first became interested in child labor when I read a short commemorative account of the New York Child Labor Committee written by Fred S. Hall, its first secretary. Inquiry established that the complete papers of the committee, comprising over eighty thousand items and covering the forty years of its existence, were in the New York State Library at Albany. This hitherto unexploited collection, standing in the original filing cabinets with the packing cords intact, was of prime importance to my study. A portion of the findings included in this book were presented in my dissertation for the Ph.D. in history at Syracuse University (1959). This book is not a statistical analysis, although I have attempted to reduce the inadequate and contradictory statistical data of the nineteenth century to some kind of common-sense order. This is not a history of organized labor or of social work. My major concern has been the working of New York's child labor laws, for they were successful only to the degree that they prevented child labor. I have also placed some emphasis on the ways in which the reformers reacted to their problems and on the complexities of the cause in which they were engaged—in other words on the nature of reform itself. Where I have carried my account beyond the Second World War, my purpose has been to suggest areas where child labor is still a problem and not to write a history of present-day juvenile delinquency or to present a complete study of New York's migrant labor problem, for both are topics that would require separate volumes.

I am convinced that there is no satisfactory definition of child labor. Sometimes a distinction is made between "child labor" and "children's work." Opponents of the child labor amendment once charged that its advocates wished a law prohibiting children from doing the supper dishes or helping in the family garden. I favor no such restriction. Because of the technological pressures of the present day, I am opposed to full-time employment for children under eighteen and to part-time employment if it deprives young people of health, recreation, or education. "Child labor" in this book refers to all full- and part-time employment under sixteen and to employment in hazardous work under eighteen. While not all part-time work was child labor, the kind that crossed the path of the reformers and official agencies (and hence found its way into this book) usually was. My definition does not necessarily coincide with the law at a particular time. When New York barred thirteen-year-olds from factory work I still refer to fourteen- and fifteen-year-old factory workers as "child laborers." Biases are inherently difficult to define. My own, insofar as I know them, are these: I am in favor of federal child labor legislation and of far more extensive national planning to meet the problems of school dropouts, migrant labor, and poverty than now exists. I view child labor as having been one and only one expression of a much larger cultural problem whose solution was not to be found in legislation by bits and pieces.

Even a book as restricted in scope as this one incurs many obligations for its author. I am heavily indebted to Sol Markoff, formerly Executive Secretary of the National Child Labor Committee, and to Emily Sims Marconnier, formerly Director of the Bureau of Women in Industry and Minimum Wage, New York State Department of Labor, for permitting me to use the New York Child Labor Committee papers. George W. Alger, formerly Chairman of the New York Child Labor Committee, gave freely of his time and memory as did another former Chairman, Frederick A. O. Schwarz. Frances Perkins answered several of the author's queries by letter. Eli E. Cohen, Executive Secretary of the National Child Labor Committee, placed his organization's files at my disposal; Henry B. Herman, formerly President of the New York Consumers' League, extended me every courtesy and permitted me to take a large part of the league files for the 1940's and 1950's to my home in Vermont for further study; Monsignor Gerald S. Kirwin, formerly editor of the Albany *Evangelist,* gave me his recollections of the child labor amendment fight and permitted me to use certain of his diocesan files. Others who were extremely helpful both through personal interviews and correspondence include Mary K. Armbrister, Raymond G. Fuller, Curtis Gatlin, Pauline Goldmark, Helen Gulick, Felice Louria, Anne Montero, Norman Thomas, Anna Strunsky Walling, and Gertrude Folks Zimand. State officials, particularly Murray Janis of the Labor Department and Robert Minnich of the Education Department, contributed much to this book. I am grateful to the staffs of the New York Public Library, the Tamiment Institute, the Columbia University Libraries, the Library of Congress, the Cornell University Library, the Syracuse

University Library, and the New York State Library for their assistance. I am unusually obligated to Miss Juliet Wolohan of the Manuscripts Division, New York State Library, for the unfailing good humor with which she greeted my daily expeditions into the dusty archives of the New York Child Labor Committee. Colleagues at the University of Vermont, notably Harold S. Schultz, Robert V. Daniels, and Milton Nadworney, provided me with insights and encouragement. Numerous other colleagues patiently endured my interest in this subject, as did my students. My friend Ray C. McCraw offered valuable editorial suggestions; Gail and Dena Monahan gave indispensable assistance. The Institutional Grants Committee of the University of Vermont made possible the continuation of my research. The staff of the University of Vermont Library cooperated in arranging extensive interlibrary loans. Mary Bottomley typed the manuscript perfectly under severe time pressure.

I owe a special debt to Professor Oscar T. Barck, Jr., of Syracuse University, who directed my early researches and to Professor Nelson M. Blake of Syracuse who has provided friendly encouragement and advice from my graduate student days.

This book would not have been written without my wife, Kaye, and it is in every way a joint endeavor. Some of the individuals mentioned will disagree sharply with my conclusions and none of them is to be charged with my errors of fact and interpretation; this responsibility is entirely mine.

JEREMY P. FELT

Essex, Vermont
April, 1964

Contents

Illustrations

(following page 116)

Tables

Any system of labor which results in such injury to the physical nature and an ignorance so deplorable as found among these children . . . is not only a disgrace, but will . . . prove dangerous to the prosperity and stability of our free institutions.

—CHARLES F. PECK, *Commissioner of Statistics of Labor, State of New York, 1884*

I. Origins of the Problem (1830-86)

At the turn of the last century New York was the leading industrial state in the nation. With garment centers, flour mills, carpet plants, foundries, machine shops, cotton mills, and shoe factories sprawling from Brooklyn to Buffalo, the Empire State held first place in thirty-six of the country's ninety-nine principal industries.[1] Children helped New York attain this preeminence, though in the course of their labors some fell down elevator shafts, burned to death, were mangled by machinery, worked standing in several inches of water, delivered messages to houses of prostitution, stood on their feet for twelve hours a day, sold newspapers at two o'clock in the morning, or froze to death in delivery wagons. In 1880 the highly conservative *Tenth Census* reported over 60,000 children between the ages of ten and fifteen at work in the state at occupations ranging from agriculture to mining and from manufacturing to personal services. Yet, at the same time, Charles Loring Brace of the Children's Aid Society told the *New York Times* that at least 100,000 children between the ages of eight and sixteen worked in New York City alone. Moreover, only about 35 per cent of the state's youngsters between the ages of five and twenty-one attended public school.[2] Most of the remainder worked.

Of course New York was not the only state with a child labor problem after the Civil War. In 1880, an estimated 6 per cent of the entire nation's children between the ages of ten and fifteen worked in some kind of industry. All of the New England states passed child labor laws in the 1840's, and by 1880 seven states had established a minimum age for employment and twelve had set maximum hours for child workers. Southern states in the 1880's were on the verge of a threefold increase in their cotton mill working force, 25 per cent of whom would be children under sixteen.[3] Because New York had a serious child labor problem yet eventually developed one of the country's most effective labor codes, its struggle to achieve this reform is

1

of particular interest, especially since it reflected so many features of the battles against child labor as carried on in other states.

Between the end of the Civil War and the passage of the state's first factory act in 1886, some of the charitable societies, the state labor organizations, and a few politicians began to realize that New York had a sizable child labor problem. The actions taken by these groups to curb child labor proved ineffective since the number of child workers increased steadily throughout the period. Extremely rapid industrialization occurred in an atmosphere heavily conditioned by puritanical ideas of the virtue of hard work and the vice of idleness. The prevailing social ethic still resembled the idea expressed by the framers of a Virginia statute of 1646 who believed in work "for the better educating of youth in honest and profitable trades and manufactures, as also to avoid sloath and idlenesse wherewith such young children are easily corrupted."[4] The common law regarded the child as a miniature adult. Blackstone's *Commentaries,* for example, contains no chapter on infancy. The child was, in the words of Florence Kelley, "an incidental phenomenon." Pauper children had been apprenticed since at least the time of the Elizabethan Poor Law of 1598, and New York State sanctioned the practice in a law of 1826. Alexander Hamilton's argument that one of the advantages of a manufacturing system would be the opportunity for early employment of children is well known. Less well known is the fact that Hamilton's opponents, in attacking the need for manufacturing, did not reproach him for advocating child labor but sought only to prove that manufacturing was not necessary to provide employment for children.[5] As the Gilded Age began, the puritan ethic reappeared in the Gospel of Wealth with the emphasis shifted to the moral duty of the individual to acquire property and wealth through industry and thrift.[6] It is not surprising that although the 1880's were a time of growing awareness of child labor, the solutions offered were fumbling and naive.

While the puritan heritage enjoined man to work hard and save, it also stressed the importance of education. To some Americans the rise of a large industrial working class, both immigrant and native, in the mid-nineteenth century was cause for uneasiness and alarm. The new urban proletariat had missed the beneficent puritan influences available in small towns. They were uneducated, unassimilated, and to the older middle and upper classes in the Northeast they seemed a frightening incarnation of Hamilton's "Great Beast." Education of the youngest laborers seemed to be the answer and, faced with a practical reason for implementing the puritan injunction, several states passed compulsory education laws.[7] The education laws failed to accomplish their purpose. The very group they were supposed to help—the poverty-stricken lower classes—benefited least. Some poor children were dragooned into school, but school probably influenced them far less than the labor they engaged in after school. In many instances school authorities accepted poverty as a valid excuse for nonattendance. School systems were not anxious to increase their enrollment and their costs by hunting for poor children. Hence already weak laws were often destroyed by lax enforcement on the part of the schools.

An 1853 action of the New York State Senate illustrates the ambiguity, hypocrisy, and confused thinking behind many of the early education laws. Defeating a bill to prohibit children under ten from working in factories, the legislators immediately passed one regulating truancy because they believed it "the imperative duty of the State to enforce, by legal enactment, the proper care, training, and education of its children."[8]

The conviction that education and friendly interest would solve the problems of New York's laboring children found active expression in the work of Charles Loring Brace, founder of the Children's Aid Society of New York City. Alarmed that 4,000 of the 11,000 children between the ages of five and sixteen in the city's tenement-packed Eleventh Ward were not attending school, Brace worked to establish lodging houses, reading rooms, and industrial schools. At first he thought that sending children into the country would be the best solution for homeless and wandering delinquents. He hoped "to be the means of draining the city of these children, by communicating with farmers, manufacturers, or families in the country who have need of them for employment." During 1868 Brace actually placed almost 2,000 children in country homes and provided rooms for over 11,000 more in his five metropolitan lodging houses. By 1871 he estimated that about 2,000 children under fifteen were working in the New York City paper collar industry alone, although the 1870 Federal Census claimed that only 4,269 children under fifteen worked in manufacturing of all kinds in the metropolitan area. Brace saw four-year-olds working in a Manhattan tobacco factory for three dollars a week and was appalled by the twenty to thirty thousand child vagrants he believed were present in the city. Concluding that "the evil is already vast . . . and must be checked" and that it "can only be restrained by legislation," Brace asked Charles E. Whitehead, the legal counsel for the Children's Aid Society, to draft a child labor bill.[9]

The proposed statute, for which the society lobbied unsuccessfully in four legislative sessions (1871-76), would have prohibited children under ten from work in manufacturing. In addition it required that children up to twelve show that they could read "intelligibly" before going to work, and it limited children under sixteen to a sixty-hour week. Every factory worker under sixteen was to file a teacher's certificate with his employer, indicating that he had attended school for at least three months during the year preceding the start of employment. The bill also requested funds for one factory inspector. Although it failed to become law, the Children's Aid Society bill of 1872 foreshadowed later legislation such as the Factory Act of 1886. Clearly visible in the early bill were some potential legislative loop-holes: the loose educational standard implied in the word "intel-ligibly"; the absence of a valid requirement for proof of age; the acceptance of a teacher's certificate, readily obtained in overcrowded schools; and the request for only one factory inspector to cover the entire state. Even the Children's Aid Society approved an exception to the educational requirement stating that it did not apply to any family that had more than one child between twelve and sixteen if the commissioners of the poor certified that the family needed the child's earnings.[10]

The Children's Aid Society was not the only organization groping its way toward a solution for the city's social problems. In the 1860's the Citizen's Association, an anti-Tweed group led by Peter Cooper, August Belmont, William B. Astor, and other prominent New Yorkers, investigated metropolitan health conditions. Under the direction of Dr. Stephen Smith, later Commissioner of the Metropolitan Board of Health, the association's physicians found that the death rate in New York City for the period 1861-66 averaged thirty-eight per thousand, compared to the national rate of sixteen per thousand.[11] Since over half the city's population of 800,000 was jammed into 15,000 tenements in 1864, this high death rate is not surprising. Child labor was only one product of life in overcrowded tenements where garbage and slops oozed down stairwells and children urinated on the walls: disease, death, sweatshop labor, prostitution, drunkenness, and pov-erty contributed to the general decay.

Investigating "Ragpicker's Court," a tenement near Mulberry Street and the Bowery, writers for *Harper's Weekly* were shocked. It was horrifying that "right in the very rooms where their food is cooked and eaten, where their children are born and reared, where they sleep at night—God knows how!— . . . these scavengers of the streets dump the filthy refuse of the city, and assort it for the buyers of such rubbish."[12] Few children were seen, most of them "being away on begging tours, or engaged as boot-blacks or street musicians."[13] In "Gotham Court" on Cherry Street lived Danny Burke, "the youngest newsboy in New York," not quite four years old, who upon being coaxed by a bystander gleefully shouted "Even' Teldram, two cents!"[14] Moving on to "Bottle Alley," near Five Points, the journalists observed a bachelor quarters occupied by five Italians: a carpenter, a shoemaker, and three streetsweepers. "The floor is destitute of carpet, is sunken in one corner, and is covered with grease and dirt," reported one investigator. "The ceiling and walls are more like those of a smoke-house than of a dwelling." In this case, Italian cooking failed to whet the appetite; the food was "gathered principally from the garbage boxes on the streets or from the offal of the markets" and boiled in a pot once a week. Adults might digest garbage, but the children "with their little pinched faces and shivering forms" would hardly thrive on it.[15]

The Citizen's Association was asking a question whose answer was too complicated for the times when it tried to discover why the city government had done nothing and why the City Inspector's department was a "gigantic imposture," most of whose health wardens were "grossly ignorant" liquor dealers.[16] Many reformers were to ask how such things could be. Like the blind men describing an elephant, each saw the solution in the particular part of the problem he happened to be observing. To the Citizen's Association the answer was better health administration and better housing; to C. L. Brace it had been lodging houses and fresh air; to the charitable societies it was piecemeal handouts; and to Elbridge Gerry, the future president of the Society for the Prevention of Cruelty to Children, humane treatment of children. That child labor, slums, crime, poverty, and vice were the results of society's failure to cope with its industrial revolution and not of individual depravity was a concept that rarely penetrated to the working level of reform. Hence the solutions were superficial, the results negligible and short-lived. Like the other community improvement organizations of the era (the State Charities Aid Association, the New York Association for Improving the Condition of the Poor, the New York Charities Organization Society, the Y.M.C.A., and the Children's Aid Society), the Citizen's Association struck the edge of the child labor problem and glanced off into other endeavors. The children remained and their numbers increased. In 1869 the *New York Times* warned that "a great multitude of the youth of the City are . . . growing up, stunted in body, and with not even the rudiments of school training, a prey to the insatiable requirements of industry and capital."[17]

In 1874 Brace and the Children's Aid Society took advantage of a wave of anti-Tweed sentiment and obtained New York's first compulsory education law. Believing that he had achieved all that was necessary, Brace abandoned his effort to secure a factory law. "If we could train the children of the streets to habits of industry," he wrote, "and give them the rudiments of moral and mental education, we need not trouble ourselves with anything more. A child in any degree educated and disciplined can easily make an honest living in this country."[18]

The reformers were going to have to "trouble themselves more." At the time the Compulsory Education Law of 1874 was passed, New York was in the midst of a tremendous expansion of her men's clothing industry, the leading enterprise in the state between 1880 and 1909 with an annual output worth over $81,000,000.[19] The largest part of this thriving industry, which employed German, Jewish, and Italian immigrants, was carried on in New York City tenements, which by the late 1860's numbered over 18,000 and housed half a million persons.[20] A large number of children worked in the clothing industry. About 25 per cent of the ready-made clothing was manufactured by tenement family homeworkers.[21] It was common for an entire family to be engaged in the operation with the younger children sewing, pulling bastings, or carrying clothing in and out of the building. The children faded in and out of the tenement working force like guerrilla troops. One minute they were working and the next, when an inspector arrived, they were at play or "just there." As late as 1911, Florence Kelley of the National Consumers' League said that the only way to find the number of children in industrial homework was to have two inspectors to check each tenement in the city, one by day and one by night.[22]

The tenement grapevine was remarkably efficient and often fooled investigators. In 1897 W. J. Neely, a factory inspector, complained that the tenement workers "place in charge a janitor paid to lie and deceive by the sweaters, so as to fool the inspectors both of the health board and the factory department, giving warning from front house to back, and floor to floor, to clear out the children." A factory inspector, he added, "must have the abilities of the fabled French detectives in the popular novels."[23] The warning system was good enough to deceive a trained university investigator who observed the city at about the same time as Inspector Neely. Jesse E. Pope reported that he had "visited during the last six years, scores of [clothing] shops of all classes in all parts of New York City." He had not "recorded one instance of flagrant abuse of children." Pope said that he had seen only a few cases of child labor in all that time, yet he commented that while "many children were employed in carrying garments to and from the warehouse . . . clothing is bulky rather than heavy, and the bundles . . . therefore, would not in general weigh enough to overtax the strength of the child."

While Pope was asserting that "the number of children employed has been greatly overestimated by sympathetic visitors, who [have] . . . seen a few children engaged in pulling bastings,"[24] New York City granted 9,644 licenses for tenement house manufacturing, the "vast majority" for the garment trade. Investigating tenement homework in 1910, federal agents concluded that "all children of a household where home work is done are drafted into this work with more or less regularity, after school, at night, and on Sunday."[25] The New York Bureau of Labor Statistics warned in 1902 that in estimating the number of child tenement workers it was "advisable to ascertain the total number of children, for even those who attend school regularly do more or less work at home."[26] In 1874 a ratio of *one* employed child to each of New York City's tenements would have meant about twenty thousand children. Would they be guaranteed "the rudiments of moral and mental education" by the new compulsory education law?

Concern over an uneducated working class prompted twenty-eight states to pass compulsory education laws during the post-Civil War period; New York patterned hers upon an earlier Massachusetts statute of 1852.[27] The 1874 law required children between the ages of eight and fourteen to attend school fourteen weeks a year, of which at least eight must be consecutive. No such child might work in any business without a certificate showing that he had attended school for fourteen weeks in the year preceding employment, and the employer had to keep a list of all these children as well as their school attendance certificates. This act was doomed by both its failure to require adequate proof of age and its ridiculous enforcement provisions. A child of eleven found working without a school certificate could easily claim, with parental backing, to be fifteen. Moreover, the enforcement burden was placed upon local school officials, who were expected to visit factories. Since there were no funds to pay the expenses of school authorities,[28] the alacrity and enthusiasm with which they enforced the compulsory education laws can be imagined. This attempt to use already overburdened school officials as unpaid factory inspectors reveals at best the naivete and at worst the calculated hypocrisy of the legislators.

Some educators did not believe in compulsory education and

would have agreed with B. B. Snow, the Auburn Superintendent of Schools, that "the compulsory attendance of the element attempted to be reached by the law would be detrimental to the well-being of any respectable school."[29] In 1882 while some of the reformers complained about the metropolitan area's 100,000 "little toilers," C. L. Brace found that the New York City Board of Education had issued only 688 school attendance certificates in compliance with the compulsory education law.[30] The public did not care; it agreed with Superintendent Snow that "while every community would approve the compulsory attendance, in a suitable school, of idle and vagrant boys, there would be little sympathy in the project of taking children from work when the proceeds of their labor are needed for the support of indigent and infirm parents."[31]

In 1882, Elbridge Gerry, President of the Society for the Prevention of Cruelty to Children, and Dr. Abraham Jacobi, President of the New York State Medical Association, tried a frontal assault on the problem. The two were alarmed not only by the number of children employed in the manufacture of artificial feathers, in the tobacco factories, and in the paper collar industry, but by the health hazards to which they were exposed. While tobacco presented the most immediate physical danger, both feathers and paper collars required excessive hours of work. It was not unusual for eight-year-olds to work ten hours a day cutting, steaming, curling, and packing feathers from cock tails or for a child of twelve to count and box twenty thousand paper collars in a single day.[32] Moreover, the manufacture of paper collars involved the use of dangerous aniline dyes. One of the first medical attacks on child labor occurred in 1879 when Dr. Roger S. Tracy published an article in *Buck's Hygiene* sharply criticizing the "inexorable discipline of the factory" and its effect upon the physical condition of growing children.[33]

Gerry and Dr. Jacobi now proposed a child labor bill that was much more sweeping than Brace's effort of ten years before. Many of its provisions anticipated modern statutes. It required every prospective child worker to be examined by a physician and barred all factory work for those under fourteen. The bill established a ten-hour day for children over fourteen and prohibited them from operating dangerous machinery or working in hazardous industries such as glass, mercury, lead, arsenic, iron, bricks, and matches. It also banned work in the home manufacture of cigars.

It was a tribute to the growing strength of the movement for child labor reform and to the increasing political leverage of labor that political leaders permitted this bill to pass the state Senate unanimously.[34] It was then killed by the time-honored device of placing it so late on the Assembly calendar that it could not be considered before the legislature adjourned.[35] In the same session, however, another Gerry-sponsored bill to prohibit the "hiring out" of children in houses of refuge and reformatories was passed. This system had two advantages: it enabled employers to obtain cheap labor from the poorhouses and it saved the state money because the child's earnings were used to pay his living expenses. After hearing Richard M. Hoe, manager of the house of refuge in New York City, state that the bill would add $40,000 a year to the cost of running the house, Governor Alonzo B. Cornell vetoed it. "It will hardly be questioned," he asserted, "that some regular system of industry is in the highest degree desirable, not only to make the institution as little burdensome to the public treasury as possible, but especially to accustom the children to industrious habits."[36]

The charitable organizations failed to pass their bills because they had been unable to mobilize public opinion against child labor. Most people, if they thought about it at all, believed that a comparatively small number of children were working to support needy parents. The average New Yorker in the 1880's was as opposed to state interference in the family as he was to state meddling in the market place. The state legislature was composed, for the most part, of blocs or groups whose votes were controlled by powerful economic interests. Only one force could outbid the business group: an aroused public threatening recalcitrant legislators with political extinction. The public was apathetic, but another large pressure group with the power to inflict political penalties was coming into existence: organized labor.

Drawing its strength from the hundred trade unions in New York City and from others in upstate cities, the New York labor movement included such strong craft unions as the typographers, hod-hoisters, lathers, cabinetmakers, bricklayers, and plumbers. Since 1865, New York labor had maintained a lobby, The Workingmen's Assembly, to work for favorable legislation; by 1880 labor was powerful enough to elect twenty supporters to the legislature.[37] Under the leadership of George Blair, an enthusiastic Knight of Labor from New York City, the Workingmen's Assembly had opposed child labor since 1877, at least for the record. Labor was not, however, primarily concerned with the abolition of child labor. Of much greater importance were its demands for changes in the system of contract prison labor, for establishment of a board of arbitration and mediation, and for creation of a bureau of labor statistics.[38] While legislation passed in response to pressure from labor might benefit working children, these benefits were not the main reason for labor's interest. Two examples are the Cigar Law of 1883 and the Bureau of Labor Statistics Law of 1884. Both were steps in the fight against child labor, but neither was intended primarily as a child labor bill.

For several years the Cigarmakers' International Union had been aware that a large number of children were employed in the home manufacture of cigars, a practice that was having a disastrous effect on the wage level of union cigar makers. The homeworkers could not be organized, their low wages threatened nontenement manufacturers and frustrated the attempts of the Cigarmakers' Union to control the trade. According to statistics compiled by Samuel Gompers in 1881, the manufacture of cigars in tenements accounted for almost one-half of the city's cigar production. About ten thousand persons were engaged in the trade, including several thousand young children.[39] The working conditions were appalling. A typical tenement sweat-shop jammed two hundred persons into "a space 14 x 40 feet, five stories and more, toppling skyward."[40] Knowing that they would be turned out of their homes by their tenement landlord-employers if production lagged, entire immigrant families worked fourteen to twenty hours a day. Clare de Graffenried found a five-year-old girl busily stripping out the midrib of tobacco leaves. The tobacco was everywhere. "Children delve in it," De Graffenried wrote, "roll in it, sleep beside it. The dust seasons their food and befouls the water they drink, and the hands of the mother are seldom washed when she leaves the cigar table to prepare meals or nurse her babe."[41] Under these circumstances health deteriorated. Describing the appearance of the little tobacco workers, a New York cigar maker likened it to "that which we would find in some of the pauper schools that Dickens describes in England."[42] In 1879 Dr. Roger S. Tracy declared that "sexual development is decidedly retarded in young girls who enter the factories before sexual evolution has begun." Whether it was retardation or simply frequent miscarriages, Dr. Tracy found that as a class cigar makers had far fewer children than did other tenement residents. The infant death rate in cigar tenements was about 20 per cent higher than in tenements generally.[43] "Day after day, year after year," De Graffenried reported, "children are born into this poisoned air, take it in with mother's milk, wilt and die in it, or live through puny, wailing infancy into abnormal childhood, pre-destined to nervous excitation, disease and depravity."[44]

The New York City Board of Health did not agree. In 1883 when the New York labor movement successfully sponsored a bill to prohibit cigar making in tenements, the Board of Health opposed it, claiming that no one's health was endangered by tenement manufacture. The Health Department knew better, of course, but was alarmed at the prospect of having to enforce the proposed law.[45] And what of the compulsory education law? Could not the Health Department and the Board of Education combine to eliminate child labor in the tenements during school hours? When a New York City cigar maker was asked this in 1883, he replied that

> Occasionally . . . the board of education wake up and for about ten to thirty days at a time they send out inspectors to pick up children on the streets who do not attend school, and then they lapse into this stupor again and that's the last of it; as far as having any effect on the moral condition of these children, the board of education does absolutely nothing.[46]

Piloting the cigar bill of 1883 through the legislature, its sponsors encountered the same problems that were to impede the efforts of later reformers. Attempts were made to delay the progress of the measure. On one occasion the bill was called up for consideration in the Senate at the end of a session and the clerk was unable to find the official copy; on another, Assemblyman Lucas Van Allen of New York City tried to cripple the bill with an amendment stating that it would go into effect only when the New York City Board of Health certified that the tenement trade was injurious to health.[47] Another problem stemmed from the labor union's tendency to view tenement manufacture as the concern solely of organized labor. The union made only halfhearted attempts to interest charitable organizations in the fight and thus had to work alone. Labor's main motive in proposing the law was to secure control of the cigar trade; exposure of tenement conditions and the education of the public were secondary considerations. Success finally came when the cigar bill passed in 1883 with the support of "silk stocking" representatives like Theodore Roosevelt, trade union legislators such as David Healy and Godfrey Ernst, and Tammany men led by Senator Thomas F. Grady.[48] Limited to New York City, the bill prohibited the manufacture of cigars or the preparation of tobacco in rooms used as dwellings.[49]

Not realizing that they would make more money by using large factory rooms and better machinery for cigar making, the tenement manufacturers hastily obtained signatures from their dependent workers on petitions asserting the joys of tenement living. Thus armed, they descended upon Albany in force to defend their liberty at a hearing before Governor Grover Cleveland on March 8, 1883. In presenting their case, the tenement manufacturers used two arguments that were to become standard among opponents of child labor regulation: they pleaded that the proposed statute would throw needy families out of work and predicted that its passage would drive industry out of the state.[50] Representing the Cigarmakers' Union at the hearing was a young assemblyman, Theodore Roosevelt, whom Gompers had recently shown through several tenements. Roosevelt assured Cleveland that while he usually opposed trade union proposals, the horrible conditions he had seen in the tenements made this an exceptional case. Later Roosevelt reported that although the conservative Cleveland had had reservations about the cigar bill, the facts had convinced the governor.[51] He signed the bill on March 12, 1883.

The tenement manufacturers lost no time in arranging a court test. Determined to find some constitutional flaw in the law, the New York Court of Appeals discovered that it embraced more than one subject ("tenements" and "all dwellings"), thus violating the state constitution's requirement that local or private bills deal with one subject only. The section of the law prohibiting the manufacture of cigars in all dwellings was therefore declared unconstitutional in January, 1884.[52] Ironically, the court did not pass upon the constitutionality of another section of the act, which prohibited anyone from living in a room in which cigars were manufactured. This section was left on the statute books, and conceivably might have been used to control the tenement trade although it would have presented immense problems of interpretation and enforcement.

In May, 1884, the legislature passed a second cigar bill. Prohibiting the manufacture of cigars on any floor of a tenement house if the floor was also used as a home or residence, the 1884 bill eliminated the confusion over the definitions of "tenement houses" and "dwellings" that had proved fatal to the first law, but it applied only to cities of the "first class" with more than 500,000 population (New York and Brooklyn). Mistakenly believing that the need for reform was related to the size of a community, the drafters left cigar homework in upstate cities like Troy unregulated.[53]

The second cigar law was struck down by the same court that had rejected the first on the grounds that it permitted unconstitutional interference with personal freedom and private property. The court maintained further that the act did not concern public health and hence could not be justified as a proper use of the police power. "What possible relation can cigar-making in any building have to the health of the general public?" the court asked. The judges found it difficult to see "how the cigar-maker is to be improved in his health or his morals by forcing him from his home and its hallowed associations and beneficent influences, to ply his trade elsewhere."[54] The statute was also found to impair the obligation of contracts. The courts were a perennial obstacle in the path of labor legislation. As Samuel Gompers put it years later: "One of the most difficult problems which the labor movement has had to meet has been the inability of the average judge to understand that industrial justice is not an abstract matter, but must be shaped to meet working relations and the needs of workers for a better life."[55] Eventually the Cigar-makers' Union succeeded in putting an end to tenement manufacture. By 1900 its agitation and, more importantly, the development of better cigar-making machinery requiring large factories, effected a sharp reduction in the number of tenement cigar workrooms.[56]

Before 1886, the most significant legislative gain for the cause of child labor reform was the organization of a state bureau of labor statistics in 1883. In demanding such a bureau, the New York labor movement anticipated one of the fundamental principles of successful reform—the accumulation and mastery of data. Because of public apathy, those who opposed change had always been able to assert that a proposed reform was unnecessary. The reformers had to marshal overwhelming evidence. In later years the Rev. Charles H. Parkhurst would preach against Tammany with a fat envelope of affidavits at his elbow, and Florence Kelley would rise in a public hearing to answer manufacturers' objections by telling each factory owner of the specific abuses in his own plant. Labor in the 1880's needed data to support its legislative demands.[57]

Since there were no accurate labor statistics for New York, the new bureau was to "collect, assort, systematize and present" data on "all departments of labor in the State, especially in relation to the commercial, industrial, social and sanitary condition of working-men." It was high time; ten other states had already established such bureaus, beginning with Massachusetts in 1869.[58] But from the outset the bureau was severely hampered by lack of personnel, funds, and power. The legislature regarded the new organization as an offhand concession to labor and did not intend, at least initially, to take it seriously. The staff of the new bureau consisted of Charles F. Peck, the Commissioner of Statistics of Labor and a personal friend of Lieutenant Governor David B. Hill; and David Healy, the Chief Clerk. These two men were to examine the entire state. Attempting to buttress his staff by using trade union members as investigators,

Peck dispatched a union cigar maker to check on one of the tenement cigar companies. Upon entering the premises, the cigar maker was thrown out. His assailant was arrested and brought to trial, but the case was dismissed by a police justice who said the investigator had no right to be in the factory without the owner's permission. In 1884 the state attorney general warned Peck that his bureau could not "safely undertake to compel owners . . . of manufacturing establishments to open them to . . . examination and visitation." He reminded the new commissioner that the right of citizens to be secure in their property "against unnecessary searches and inquisitorial examinations is sacredly regarded."[59]

Perhaps this climate of opinion was responsible for the rather meager statistical results of the bureau's child labor survey—the first official inquiry into New York's child labor problem. Conducted in 1883-84 at the request of the Workingmen's Assembly, the study revealed that of the 15,928 persons employed in the 151 factories visited by Peck's investigators, only 261 were under the age of fourteen. This was a lower percentage of child employment than that reported for New York by the conservative Federal Census of 1880. In 1886 the New York factory inspector was to discover that the Harmony Cotton Mills in Cohoes alone employed two hundred children under thirteen.[60]

There are several reasons why this first official study was worthless as a statistical measure of New York's child labor problem. In the first place, Peck was justifiably doubtful about the legality of his surveying activities, and in many cases his investigators accepted the word of the employer as proof of the ages of his child workers. Furthermore, the commissioner was no Florence Kelley; he lacked the fire, determination, and analytical power of that remarkable woman. Miss Kelley, soon to be appointed Chief Factory Inspector of Illinois, always assumed that employers were guilty until proven innocent; Peck was less suspicious. While the commissioner did develop (and express) some social convictions as he saw how work affected children, his studies, largely conducted by trade unionists, inevitably reflected the rather pedestrian attitude of organized labor toward the problem of working children. Labor was against child labor because children depressed wages and could not be unionized, but the unions had so many irons in the fire that they could not attack the problem with the single-minded crusading zeal of the philanthropic and social-work reform groups. And it was not only that labor had many other interests. Some trade unionists believed that child labor regulation was an interference with family rights; indeed, some of their own children worked. In an age when some union men opposed the minimum wage because it violated the right of employer and employee to free negotiation, one could not expect to find effective opposition to child labor.

However paltry the statistics produced by his study, Commissioner Peck became aware that the state did have a child labor problem and was the first official to suggest a concrete solution. An investigation of the Harmony Cotton Mills in Cohoes, a few miles from Albany, was his introduction to child labor. Standing in the street one cold day in 1883 he saw "hundreds of thin and scantily clad girls and boys ranging from eight to fifteen years of age, hurrying home with dinner pail in hand." Peck observed that "their sallow, parchment-like complexion, dwarfed bodies, pinched and care-worn faces spoke more eloquently than words," and he expressed doubts about the stability of American institutions under such a system of labor.

This investigation had started with one of the worst offenders. In 1886, the Harmony Mills were found to employ 3,200 workers, 1,200 of them under sixteen and 200 under thirteen. According to the Cohoes Police Sergeant, Matthew Smith, a majority of the children supported shiftless parents "in idleness and beer." Peck found some of the children ignorant beyond belief, unable to name the state in which they lived, the county, the state capital, or the president of the United States. The Compulsory Education Law of 1874 was on the statute books, but the mayor of Cohoes told Peck that he was still deciding whether or not to enforce it. After all, parents were out of work and starving. Why compound their misery by taking away their children's jobs? Some felt that the education of mill children was a waste of time. In a moment of public dedication the Cohoes fire chief started a night school, but found to his amazement that the children were restive after a day in the mills. Nine out of ten of them went to the school "out of pure deviltry; we have been compelled to call officers to restrain them," he complained.

The argument that children's earnings were necessary for parental survival was reiterated through the years as an answer to demands for reform. Many parents joined eagerly in the destruction of their own standard of living; by allowing their children to work, these people were keeping their own wages down. An overseer at the Harmony Mills reported that he had found it necessary to tell some parents who "bring their little children here, that if we took them in they would have to bring their cradles with them." While it was true that in some cases the earnings of children were essential to the home, in many other instances the parents were deliberately avoiding work or the children were taking home only a small fraction of their pay. The police chief of Little Falls believed that most of the children's money was spent on cigarettes and crap games. In any case, the times clearly demanded that some question be raised about the validity of a system under which honest and well-intentioned adults were forced to rely upon the wages of their children.

The prevailing ethic shied away from such questioning. Business executives like Stephen Sanford of the Sanford & Sons carpet firm in Amsterdam were concerned lest enforcement of the compulsory education law lead to "prying" and "interfering with family rights." He need not have worried. In 1880 the school attendance figures for Albany showed that of the 35,500 children of school age only 13,914 were attending school, and the Albany superintendent believed that "compared with other localities in this state, this is a favorable exhibit." Some of the missing children were, of course, in parochial and private schools but State Superintendent Ruggles simply did not know where "many" of them were. Besides, work never hurt anyone. "There are worse calamities that may befall the children of the poor than being put at regular employment," Calvin Patterson, the Brooklyn Superintendent of Schools, asserted. The only alternative to child labor was the "reconstruction of the whole social fabric, upon a new basis." That was unthinkable. "The most we can do," said Patterson, "is to temper the conditions of child labor with humanity."

Commissioner Peck believed that more could be done. His investigation of child labor had convinced him of two things: that New York had a serious child labor problem and that the compulsory education law was "to all intent and purpose, a dead letter." In his 1884 report, he strongly urged that New York pass a factory act and provide a force of factory inspectors.[61] Even this modest proposal is sufficient to mark Peck as one of the most perceptive and radical state officials of his day. Because of the political climate of the mideighties his plan was destined to succeed.

Their bleeding, mangled arms, legs and bodies are terrible witnesses of the cruel system which makes their play-time the time of toil and danger. "Carelessness," say the manufacturers. Carelessness, not of the children, but of the law-makers to permit the helpless little ones to be dragged or driven into these grinding mills of destruction.

—JAMES CONNOLLY, *Chief Factory Inspector, State of New York, 1891*

II. *Legislation without Enforcement (1886-1902)*

During the 1880's New York continued her tremendous industrial growth. The number of manufacturing and mechanical establishments in the state increased from 42,739 in 1880 to 65,840 in 1890, and a similar increase took place in the labor force, which now numbered almost two and a half million persons.[1] While reliable statistics for the exact number of child laborers under sixteen in the state are unavailable, one can infer that at least 200,000 such children— over 8 per cent of the labor force and about 17 per cent of the state's children—were at work. About 300,000 New York children, ages five through fourteen, were out of school.[2] Not all of them worked, of course; some simply roamed the streets. It is also inaccurate to assume that children who were attending school were not child laborers, for some of them worked in the street trades or in tenements after school until past midnight. Perusing the registers of New York City night schools in the early 1890's, noting the occupations listed, and compiling data from "many other sources," Helen Campbell, an early investigator of child labor, concluded that there were over 100,000 "little workers" in that metropolitan area alone.[3] But the conservative Federal Census of 1880 found only 60,000 children between the ages of ten and fifteen employed in the entire state.[4] Considering the unreported child labor in the metropolitan area's 35,000 tenements, the employers who lied about the ages of workers in the state's 50,000 manufacturing establishments, the absence of any systematic data on newsboys, bootblacks, peddlers, messengers, or farm laborers, a figure of 200,000 child laborers for New York State during the mid-eighties seems conservative.

They worked making artificial flowers, driving teams, laying bricks, packing fish, tanning leather, and butchering cattle. Some were machinists, buttonmakers, confectioners, painters, plumbers, or glassworkers. Others worked in the fields and canning factories, or in the cotton, hosiery, silk, woolen, hemp, and jute mills. There were livery stable keepers, bartenders, seamstresses, janitors, sailors, and even auctioneers under sixteen.[5] The state did nothing to ameliorate their conditions of work, to enforce their attendance at school, or to safeguard their health. Political expediency finally forced an awareness of their existence; in 1886 a Democratic governor found it necessary to take the first steps toward a child labor code for New York.

Lieutenant Governor David Bennett Hill became governor in January, 1885, upon Cleveland's election to the presidency, and the following November was elected in his own right by the narrow margin of eleven thousand votes. A shrewd politician from Elmira, Hill knew that he must cultivate labor's support. When the Workingmen's Assembly sent him a questionnaire during the 1885 campaign, he supported labor's position on all the issues. He favored a law facilitating the organization of labor unions, the use of arbitration, and the abolition of child labor.[6] Although labor proved an important factor in Hill's close victory over Ira Davenport in 1885, the workers had not been united, and there had been some labor opposition to his candidacy. One of the most prominent labor journalists in the country, John Swinton, had written that New York labor had little to hope for from either Hill or Davenport. Alarmed by indications that labor was forming an independent party—a threat that was to be realized in the meteoric Henry George mayoralty campaign of 1886,[7] the governor knew that, in this case, he must make good on his platform promises.

New York labor was moving in the direction of unity. In 1887 the Workingmen's Assembly, which had hitherto been hampered by contention between the Knights of Labor and the craft unions, came firmly under the control of the latter group.[8] Then a steady accretion of power began, which eventually transformed the Workingmen's Assembly into the State Federation of Labor, New York's strongest lobby. With the developing labor situation in mind, Hill paid close attention to bills backed by the Workingmen's Assembly and mentioned child labor in his message to the 1886 legislature, conceding "the necessity for some legislation in reference to it."[9]

In 1884 the Workingmen's Assembly had supported Elbridge Gerry, the Chairman of the Society for the Prevention of Cruelty to Children, in his attempt to obtain a factory law. Long interested in child welfare, Gerry was the grandson of Elbridge Gerry of Revolutionary War fame. In 1874 he and Henry Bergh, both active in the Society for the Prevention of Cruelty to Animals, decided to do something about the more pressing problem of the city's children. Aroused by the spectacle of a woman begging in Fourteenth Street "with three children, all drugged and placed in the most agonizing positions,"[10] the two men organized the SPCC. Like Brace's Children's Aid Society, the SPCC was interested primarily in the correction of idleness and vagrancy and only secondarily in the abolition of child labor. While Gerry strongly advocated factory legislation, he did not want the state to control children who worked in the streets. They were his responsibility; when his society reported idle and vagrant children to the authorities, the law required that any fines collected should go to the SPCC.[11] While this philosophy was later to bring him into conflict with child labor reformers and to subject him to considerable public criticism in his declining years, Gerry's role in publicizing the need for a factory law is important.

Gerry's proposed factory bill was relatively advanced for 1884. The measure barred children under fourteen from factory employment, required a physical examination for every working child under eighteen, prohibited the employment of children under sixteen in certain hazardous occupations, and established a ten-hour day and sixty-hour week for all minors under twenty-one. The SPCC was authorized to inspect factories, sharing its authority with a state factory inspector.

Fearing that a ten-hour day for minors was the first step in a campaign to make it the standard day for adult workers, many legislators denounced the bill as too radical. It passed the Senate, but the Assembly introduced a substitute bill that eliminated the ten-hour day and the inspection rights of the SPCC. It also dropped the working age to thirteen and weakened the sixty-hour-week provision by exempting from the total hours worked the time spent in making "necessary repairs." Stung by the elimination of the SPCC from factory inspection (Gerry probably feared that politically appointed state inspectors would lack zeal), Gerry denounced the Assembly measure as "utterly worthless" and broke with the Workingmen's Assembly, which wanted to take what it could get. The Senate immediately killed the bill.[12]

During 1885 a number of similar bills were introduced in the legislature; all of them failed, even one that would have established a twelve-year minimum age for factory work. In each case the manufacturing interests threatened to leave the state, and urged the legislators to have pity on the hosts of widowed mothers who needed their children's earnings. By the start of the 1886 session, however, pressure for some kind of factory legislation was too strong. The support of labor, the activities of the SPCC and the state medical society, the evidence presented in the 1884 report of the bureau of labor statistics combined with the political sagacity of Governor Hill made some kind of legislation inevitable.

Urging its enactment in his 1886 legislative message, Hill threw the full weight of his office behind the effort. The manufacturers saw what was coming and, seeking a law with as many loopholes as possible, agreed to support the bill introduced by Senator Henry Coggeshall.[13] Passing both the Senate and Assembly by unanimous votes, the measure was signed by Governor Hill on May 18, 1886.[14]

The Factory Act of 1886 prohibited children under thirteen from working in manufacturing establishments (factories engaged in the actual manufacture of goods). It did not apply to department stores or to any other form of business. To prove that he was at least thirteen years old, each child had to have his parents sign a notarized affidavit. The employer was required to have a certificate for each of his working children under sixteen, showing the young employee's name, age, date, and place of birth. Minors under eighteen and women under twenty-one were forbidden to work more than sixty hours a week, except for time spent in making "necessary repairs." Any person who "knowingly" violated the law could be fined up to $100.[15]

To enforce the act, a chief factory inspector and his assistant were appointed by the governor at annual salaries of $2,000 and $1,500. The men selected, James Connolly and John Franey, were prominent members of the New York labor movement.[16] In what must rank as one of the most unrealistic job descriptions ever set forth by a legislative body, Connolly and Franey were told to "visit and inspect at all reasonable hours, and as often as practicable, the factories, work-shops and other establishments in the state where the manufacture of goods is carried on." To insure the effective inspection of the 42,739 manufacturing establishments in the state with their 629,869 workers, an annual departmental budget of $2,500 was established. Since the legislature had not provided office space, Connolly and Franey were forced to operate from their homes in New York and Buffalo and to handle their own correspondence and paper work.[17]

It is as difficult to evaluate the New York Factory Act of 1886 as it is to judge the merits of the Interstate Commerce Commission or the Sherman Anti-Trust Act. On the one hand, the Factory Act was the first step in the development of New York's labor law—the cornerstone or, more accurately, the first square in a patchwork quilt. On the other hand, it was a weak law; the manufacturers would not have supported it had it been strong, and neither would the public, which was still unaware of the problem. It passed because something had to be enacted, and because the articulate and substantial factory owners of the state were not prepared to wage a public fight for the right to use child labor. They would maneuver and evade instead, and the new statute allowed them many opportunities.

The two factory inspectors now tried to enforce a law that was virtually unenforceable. They encountered many kinds of violation, and many more varieties of evasion, and they even had to fight to establish their right to do the job. But they went on inspecting factories, and in four months of energetic work, Connolly and Franey had visited 857 factories in twenty-one counties. This was a very small percentage of New York's 42,739 manufacturing establishments and the inspectors were quick to point out that New Jersey, with only 8,000 factories, had four inspectors and Massachusetts, with about 17,000 plants, had a force of twenty-seven inspectors.[18] In 1887 the New York legislature permitted Connolly to hire eight additional inspectors, but each man still faced an impossible enforcement task within his district. Deputy Inspector James P. Hooley, for example, was responsible for the counties of Albany, Rensselaer, Schenectady, Saratoga, Washington, Warren, Hamilton, Fulton, Essex, Montgomery, and Schoharie; one of his colleagues, George A. McKay, was supposed to inspect all the manufacturing establishments in New York County.[19]

With such an inadequate working force, the Bureau of Factory Inspection not only found it impossible to visit all the factories but was seriously hampered in the important task of reinspecting establishments that had been caught violating the law. The legislature steadily increased the number of factory inspectors, but in 1896 there were still only twenty-nine. Even in 1907 with fifty inspectors at work, and armed with much stronger legislation, the enforcement problem was by no means solved. That New York took twenty years after the passage of its Factory Act to appoint a minimally decent force of inspectors is clear evidence that the act was not taken seriously. Certainly, there would have been no difficulty in finding inspectors, for more than four hundred men filed applications for the eight positions open in 1887.[20]

Although he was overworked, Chief Inspector Connolly objected strenuously to the hiring of women factory inspectors. Alice Woodbridge, who organized the Working Women's Society in 1888, proposed the idea. The plan was to have women inspectors investigate the working conditions of women and girls and organize the nonunion women. To Connolly, the whole scheme seemed impractical, for he felt women would be incompetent to inspect industrial machinery. When it was suggested that the ladies confine their duties to checking on women, children, and their hours of labor, he said that would be inefficient and would lead to "repeated partial overhaulings" of factories. Finally the Working Women's Society, which by 1890 had embodied its ideas in a legislative bill, amended the bill so as to take the women inspectors completely out of Connolly's department and put them under a separate authority. The Chief Inspector gave in and accepted a compromise enactment whereby seven women inspectors were placed under his Bureau of Factory Inspection.[21] Connolly never really accepted the idea. Noting that one reason for appointing the women had been to encourage working girls to tell the female inspectors about the "gross evils and indignities" they suffered from their male supervisors, the chief inspector reported that no such disclosures had taken place. "The manufacturers of this State," he declared, "are almost to a man very careful of the character of their hands, and are prompt in weeding out both men and women who show any disposition toward moral degradation."[22]

Fully aware of the small number of inspectors, manufacturers unlucky enough to be inspected and found violating the law, simply bided their time. In Valley Falls, for example, the owner of a flax mill fired all his child workers under thirteen, waited a few weeks, and then put them to work again. The provision in the factory act restricting its application to manufacturers who "knowingly" employed underage children offered the factory owners a broad avenue of escape. It meant that the mere discovery of a child under thirteen was insufficient to convict the employer, who could set up two kinds of defense. First, he could deny ever having employed the child, a particularly effective argument when the child did not happen to be working but just standing around at the time the inspector arrived. Secondly, he could produce the required parental affidavit of age sworn before a notary; this affidavit protected the factory owner even if it was presented by a six-year-old. Theoretically, the child's parents or the notary might be prosecuted for false swearing, but in practice the courts simply would not find them guilty. Each factory inspector argued his own court cases since no funds were available to hire lawyers. When in 1886 Silas Owen, a notary public in Cohoes, was charged with notarizing false affidavits for child workers at the Harmony Mills, a grand jury failed to indict him.[23] Owen and other notaries placed the entire blame upon the parents, claiming correctly that the law did not require the notaries to cross-examine parents on the truth of their statements. Parents are "almost willing to swear to anything; they do not know the nature of an oath," Deputy Inspector George L. Guetig complained.[24]

It was almost impossible to convict a parent for perjury, not only because of the widespread feeling that it was praiseworthy for a child to help support his parents, but also because of the difficulty of obtaining documentary proof of age. While compulsory birth registration had existed in New York since 1853, the law was not well enforced. In 1900 Helen Sumner and Ethel Hanks estimated that about 22 per cent of the state's births were unrecorded; in 1911 the *New York Times* gave a figure of 16 per cent.[25] It was particularly difficult for recent immigrants to get birth certificates, and other parents were honestly ignorant of their children's ages. The parental affidavit was legally unassailable. In 1893, the Bureau of Factory Inspection managed to obtain only five convictions of manufacturers who were allowing underage children to work without *any* certificates.

Being conservative, the courts were inclined to favor the employer, but part of the factory inspectors' difficulty in conducting prosecutions resulted from the reluctance of employees to testify. In 1887 the bureau swore out warrants for the arrest of five New York City clothing manufacturers whose young workers had complained of working ninety hours a week. At first the employees agreed to testify, but on the witness stand their courage failed. As the factory inspector reported bitterly, "the girls and boys showed every symptom of dread of their beetle-browed task-masters and nothing could be more evident than that they were perjuring themselves solely through fear" of losing their jobs. And what kinds of jobs? These were sweatshop children, working in buildings "ill-smelling from cellar to garret" with "noxious gases emanat[ing] from all corners" and common toilets standing in the middle of the workrooms. Exhibiting a typical reaction to tenement conditions, the factory inspector marveled "that there exists a human being that could stand it for a month and live."[26]

In 1886 the bureau had found another serious child labor situation at the Harmony Cotton Mills of Cohoes, a notorious employer of children whose activities had been previously investigated by Commissioner Peck's bureau of labor statistics. Estimating that about twelve hundred children under sixteen were employed in the mills, the factory inspector forced Harmony to fire about two hundred youngsters under thirteen, in spite of complaints by the manager that their release would stop a large part of the machinery and idle "hundreds" of older employees. Over the years, Harmony Mills showed gradual improvement, although in 1888 an inspector complained about the use of false affidavits of age, and in 1893 the factory bureau undertook a second unsuccessful prosecution against Silas Owen, the cooperative Cohoes notary public. Owen was an obvious case; less so were political hacks such as the district leader in a New York City tenement section whom Jacob Riis discovered issuing false certificates without charging a fee because the "parents swore in a good cause." This astute politician was an undertaker by profession.[27]

It should have been clear that child labor could not be controlled so long as the crucial matter of proof of age was left in the hands of the parents, the employer, and the notaries public. In 1896, the state took a potentially important step by requiring that working children between the ages of fourteen and sixteen obtain an employment certificate from their local board of health. This plan had the merit of bringing the state into the picture at the beginning of the child's employment, but was ineffective because the boards of health continued to accept parental affidavits as proof of age. The new law also failed to set up any physical standards for working children, since the local health boards were simply to certify that they were "satisfied" that the child could do the work he intended to do and that his age was correctly stated on the certificate.[28] The idea of using local boards of health as enforcement agencies originated with the department stores. In their fight against the regulatory laws proposed by the 1895 Reinhard Committee (which investigated working conditions of women in New York City), the stores succeeded in having enforcement entrusted to local boards of health, rather than to the Bureau of Factory Inspection.[29] The Working Women's Society and the New York City Consumers' League vigorously opposed this step, knowing that it would cripple the new labor law by fragmenting and decentralizing its enforcement and by creating opportunities for local "pull" to be used. The unfortunate precedent of enforcement by local boards of health was followed in the employment certificate law. In both cases financial expediency influenced the legislators: the numerous local health boards could carry out the laws' provisions with their existing personnel, while the chief factory inspector would be sure to ask for more inspectors.

The enforcement record of the health boards justified the fears of those who had opposed this feature of the employment certificate law. While in 1896 the Bureau of Factory Inspection spoke optimistically of "the entire harmony which prevails between the . . . health and factory departments relative to the enforcement of this most important provision," just a year later it reported that "in a number of instances . . . local influence was potent in [the child's] securing a certificate." The factory inspectors noted that "considerable difficulty was experienced in getting some of the boards, especially in the smaller towns, to effectually take hold of their new duties." The resident health officers, usually physicians with practices, were displeased at the extra work involved in certifying child workers, concerned whether their local communities would pay them, or annoyed at not being supplied with the necessary forms.[30] The entire process of issuing employment certificates—the foundation of any successful system of child labor regulation—floundered.

Although the enforcement of New York's labor law was lax, the legal framework continued to grow. In 1889, the minimum age for factory employment was raised from thirteen to fourteen,[31] where it remained until 1935. Although this change had the support of some charitable organizations, most of the newspapers, and a few employers, the main impetus came from the factory inspector. Connolly had scarcely begun work when he discovered a serious gap, if not an actual conflict, between the 1886 Factory Act and the Compulsory Education Law of 1874. While the education law required children under fourteen to attend school at least fourteen weeks a year, the factory act merely prohibited the employment of children under thirteen in manufacturing. A large group of children was thus barred from factory work, but after going to school for fourteen weeks was free to "roam the streets . . . for a greater part of the year . . . form[ing] corrupting associations and habits."[32] According to the state superintendent of public instruction, about 644,000 or approximately one-third of New York's school-age children were receiving no education at all.[33] The factory and education laws conflicted in still another way. Because the factory law permitted a child to work at thirteen while the education law required him to put in fourteen weeks of schooling that year, theoretically he had to interrupt his employment.

The law raising the minimum age for factory work to fourteen did eliminate the education problem of the thirteen-year-olds, but a new conflict resulted when the compulsory education law was finally revised during 1894-96.[34] The education law was changed to require full-time school attendance for children ages eight to twelve. Those twelve to fourteen were required to attend at least eighty days a year, and full-time when "not regularly engaged in some useful employment." Thus the education authorities assumed that many in the twelve- to fourteen-year group would be employed, if not in factories, then in department stores, street trades, agriculture, or tenement work. The two laws still worked at cross purposes, and there was no effective coordination between the factory bureau and the education department. Indeed, there was no incentive for the education authorities to chase down working children; they had more than enough pupils already. In 1891, Florence Kelley reported that the average New York City primary-school teacher taught seventy children. It was not surprising, therefore, that "when a zealous Sunday-school teacher finds that one of her little charges has gone to work under age . . . she hunts up a truant officer, who takes the child before a magistrate, who, in view of the want of school accommodations, promptly discharges the truant."[35]

The point was, of course, that the factory law was not supposed to be seriously enforced and Inspector Connolly's attempts to do so were destined to be frustrated. Theoretically, the inspector was to deliver every oppressed, illegally employed child into the waiting arms of its parent-surrogate, the school. Somehow the child's real parents were to be shown the error of their ways and all would be well. But if the typical "interested citizen" of New York gave any thought to child labor at all, he desired simply to *know* that child labor laws were on the statute books; he was not prepared to advocate the social planning necessary for the improvement of the entire environment of New York's children that would be essential if the elimination of child labor were to produce beneficial results. As Alfred Hodder, a philosopher and one of the more neglected turn-of-the-century muckrakers, put it: "Public opinion demands the passage of . . . laws; and the laws once passed, public opinion demands their violation; and it enforces both at the polls." Officials "must choose between a violation of their oath of office on the one side and on the other an enforcement of these laws. The one is perjury and the other is political suicide."[36] Hodder was referring to the vice laws, but the same dichotomy of intention can be found with respect to the child labor laws. No one, certainly not the school officials, would rise and call for allowing ten-year-olds to work twelve-hour days. So the labor groups and the social "uplifters" would be given their law. But that would be the end of it. Besides, most people did not know or care. William Travers Jerome, a reform district attorney during Seth Low's term as mayor of New York (1902-03) saw this clearly. Castigating Tammany Hall, Jerome observed that when labor went to Albany, it got its way because "there are few laws the laboring man can ask for that Tammany is not willing to put upon the statute book; but the habit of enforcing the laws . . . has long since been lost by Tammany, and anyone may disregard those laws who chooses to put down the stuff."[37]

In 1889, Inspector Connolly bypassed the school officials and obtained authority for the inspectors to require any factory employee under sixteen to demonstrate his ability to read and write simple English sentences.[38] While the chief inspector was undoubtedly motivated by a sincere desire to solve the child labor problem and at the same time compel the education authorities to do their job, this literacy test was used principally against immigrant children. Reflecting the general anti-immigration position of organized labor, Connolly reported that the new law had been "strictly enforced" against the "non-English speaking immigrants who have come among us in such vast numbers of late years." He rejoiced in the discharge of ninety illiterate (non-English speaking) Italian children from a single factory in September, 1892, and urged that immigration officials exclude children under sixteen from New York unless they could read and write English or their parents were able to support them.[39]

The literacy test was evaded as successfully as were the other child labor laws. When a suit was brought against a clothing contractor in New York City for employing a fifteen-year-old Russian girl who could not read or write in any language, the contractor arranged for the girl to have a cram course in English during the six weeks before the trial. The judge then dictated a sentence to her: "This house is built of bricks," and the girl wrote "this hous is bilt of briks."[40] The case was dismissed, the employer escaped a fine, and the girl was ready to return to work. The standard of literacy that would be upheld in future suits was reduced to a nullity.

Even though the chief factory inspector had secured more men and had obtained changes in the factory law establishing the employment certificate, raising the minimum age for factory work to fourteen, and lessening the conflict between the education and factory laws, there were still other problems. A child might be legally employed and working illegal hours. Violations of the hours provision of the factory law were widespread, not only because of defects in the act itself, but because hours were such a sensitive area in labor-management relations. While some manufacturers argued that shorter hours for children would upset their production schedule, others believed that such legislation would be an entering wedge for the general reduction of working hours. The hours clause in the original factory act had been quite general, limiting women under twenty-one and men under eighteen to a sixty-hour week with the exception of time consumed in making "necessary repairs." This provision invited violation; in fact, the factory inspector estimated that 75,000 minors were regularly working more than sixty hours a week. Almost any work in excess of the weekly maximum could be called a "necessary repair." Moreover, the inspector could check only on the total number of hours worked in a week, as the act said nothing about a daily maximum. Some manufacturers began releasing their employees at noon on Saturday so that an eleven-hour day could be maintained during the rest of the week. Other employers, such as mail-order houses, were free to work their girl clerks twenty-four hours a day on two or three days a week so long as the sixty-hour weekly limit was not exceeded.[41]

Night work was completely unregulated. Children as young as ten were often employed in Hudson River brickyards, getting up at 3:00 A.M. to row across the river from their homes to their jobs.[42] In 1886 two Buffalo bakers were indicted by a grand jury for working children all night long, then having them deliver bread the next morning: a total of more than seventy-six hours a week.[43] In 1897, a woman factory inspector, Katie L. Kane, visited one of the most fashionable dress-making shops in New York City and found twenty-eight girls working in one room which had air space for only eighteen, twenty-seven jammed in another room with air space for thirteen. The girls, some of whom were under sixteen, were working from 8:00 A.M. to 10:30 P.M. on a wedding trousseau belonging to "one of the multi-millionaires of the 400." The factory inspector found about twenty such shops violating the law "in the same manner as Eastside sweatshop operators."[44]

In 1889, a significant hours amendment to the factory act was passed. It set a daily limit of ten hours for women under twenty-one and men under eighteen and prohibited them from working at night (9:00 P.M. to 6:00 A.M.). Overtime was permitted on one day a week, but only if another day was shortened by the amount of the overtime. Ten years later, in 1899, these provisions were extended to *all* women.[45] The new hours law was frequently violated, and presented the same enforcement difficulties as did the amendments on age, employment certification, and education, but one good result of this Topsy-like expansion of the labor law was that it was *potentially* enforceable. At the same time, it performed the double function of showing later reformers what to avoid and giving them a structure upon which to build.

The greatest immediate danger of child labor was the risk of physical injury. There was no such thing as a modern safety program in factories, and such statutes as did exist were weakened by court interpretation. The "fellow servant" doctrine, under which an injured employee had to prove that his employer had been negligent, that this negligence had been the immediate cause of his injury, and that neither he nor any fellow employee had been negligent, was generally accepted by the courts. There was no court-upheld workmen's compensation law in New York until 1913. While child labor reformers were later to establish that certain occupations should be legally identified as hazardous, and that an injured child worker who had been unlawfully employed ought to receive double or triple compensation, before the turn of the century children, like adults, received no legal compensation.[46]

The child workers were exposed to three general kinds of occupational risks: inhalation of harmful dusts or fumes, injury from constant standing or working in a cramped position, and injury from machinery.[47] It was comparatively easy to establish a cause-and-effect relationship in the case of machine injury. However harmful it might be for a child to inhale tobacco dust or stand long hours in a cracker factory, his injury might not be apparent. Children operating industrial machinery faced two inherent dangers in addition to those presented by the machine itself: they had a shorter attention span than adults and tired more easily. Injury could be instantaneous and spectacular. In the box-making industry, for example, the operation of a corner-staying machine required that the operator's hands "approach or reach a spot at which a few seconds later a crushing blow is to be delivered by a metal stamp or die." While the risk of fingers slipping between the anvil and the press was great, many of the operators themselves objected to the installation of guards because it slowed down work, and they were paid by the piece rather than by the hour.[48] In a New York City twine factory, Helen Campbell found two hundred children under fifteen employed in spinning, winding, and twisting flax. A youngster from the twisting room, where flax was fed to a machine, explained how she and her sister had lost fingers: "You mustn't talk or look off a minute. My sister was just like me. She forgot and talked, and just that minute her finger was off, and she didn't even cry till she picked it up."[49]

The factory law was amended in 1887 to prohibit women under twenty-one and men under eighteen from cleaning *moving* machinery, but this was a mere gesture toward reducing accidents. Children continued to operate power saws, tin and sheet-iron stamping machines, and other complicated industrial apparatus. If a child escaped injury from a machine, he ran the risk of being caught in exposed belting and shafting or falling down an unguarded elevator shaft or hoistway; forty-three such elevator and hoistway injuries were discovered by the inspectors in 1891 alone.[50] When Connolly and Franey began their rounds in 1886, they remarked on the number of working children with fingers or a hand missing. On two occasions during their first six months, they were in the factory when a child was injured. The small force of inspectors was merely scratching the surface of the accident problem; as inspection became more efficient, more and more injuries to children under sixteen were recorded: 25 in 1887, 89 in 1888, 92 in 1890, 106 in 1891, 126 in 1902.[51] Other changes in the law came in 1892 and 1899. Children under fifteen were forbidden to operate elevators, and those sixteen to eighteen years old were limited to the operation of elevators that ran at speeds of less than two hundred feet per minute. Youths under eighteen and all women were barred from operating emery, polishing, or buffing wheels, and from assisting in the operation of "dangerous machinery."[52] Unfortunately, "dangerous machinery" was a definition open to conflicting interpretations, as "necessary repairs" had been. What was needed was a specific statutory listing of dangerous occupations, but this was not to be achieved until 1909.

At the same time factory inspectors were having enforcement difficulties, the bureau itself was experiencing internal troubles. Politics had begun to affect the bureau, particularly after Daniel O'Leary of Glens Falls replaced James Connolly as chief factory inspector in 1896. After the initial shock of the 1886 labor uprising had worn off, jobs in the bureau descended more and more to the regular level of political patronage. When Theodore Roosevelt became governor in 1899, a storm of criticism broke upon the bureau. Organized labor charged O'Leary with being more interested in maintaining Thomas Platt's Republican machine than in factory inspection. Benjamin B. Odell, a lieutenant of Platt who would succeed Roosevelt in the governorship, wrote T. R. that "care should be exercised in any action taken with O'Leary . . . as he has been a pretty good friend of ours." Nevertheless, Roosevelt removed O'Leary from office in April, 1899, and replaced him with John Williams, an official of the Carpenter's Union. In 1900, at Roosevelt's request, Jacob Riis investigated the Bureau of Factory Inspection and in his report criticized Williams for holding no conferences to insure that his men understood the factory law. Careful not to antagonize Platt, Roosevelt followed the "Easy Boss'" suggestion, naming John McMackin, a man who ultimately was driven out of his job by the child labor reform groups, head of the newly organized labor department. Charges of inefficiency mingled with cries from employers that the factory law was "class legislation" put forward by "secret" labor groups and enforced by a chief factory inspector with "vast discretionary powers."[53]

Had New York really done anything by 1900 to solve its child labor problem? Theoretically, the state's labor law was now relatively impressive; New York was one of twenty-eight states that had some legal protection for children and one of nine states that had a minimum age of fourteen for factory work.[54] In 1875 there had been no child labor laws, with the exception of a few pre-Civil War enactments on paupers and the unenforced Compulsory Education Law of 1874. By 1900 children under fourteen were forbidden to work in factories. Those between the ages of fourteen and sixteen were required to obtain an employment certificate and to meet minimum standards of health and education. Minors under eighteen were limited to a ten-hour day and a sixty-hour week. Other legislation restricted night work and hazardous employment, and one major enactment extended the bulk of the factory law to department stores.[55]

In practice, however, the new laws had not accomplished any significant reduction in child labor. They were not only difficult to enforce, but probably were not intended to be enforced. There is at least a possibility that some of the factory laws were used to "milk" businesses— that is, to threaten them with real factory legislation if they didn't pay the legislators for passing either no legislation or, depending upon the aggressiveness of the factory inspector and organized labor, watered-down legislation. It is difficult to imagine that a legislature seriously interested in regulating child labor would have sponsored the kind of legislation passed up to 1900, with its use of unenforceable phrases like "knowingly," "necessary repairs," and "dangerous machinery," with its glacial increase in the number of inspectors, and with its reliance for much enforcement upon the local boards of health. The record speaks for itself. During the period 1887-1901, the average annual total of fines levied for violations of the *entire* factory law (including child labor violations) was $969. This figure itself is misleading, as will be apparent from Table 1.

TABLE 1 [56]

FINES LEVIED FOR VIOLATIONS OF THE FACTORY LAW, 1887-1901

Year Ending November 30	Fines Imposed	Prosecutions	Number Fined	Acquitted, Suspended Sentence, or Complaint Withdrawn
1887	$ 615	62	17	45
1888	225	15	9	6
1889	60	12	3	9
1890	510	42	19	23
1891	390	20	15	5
1892	980	51	44	7
1893	2,305	118	89	29
1894	2,430	141	115	26
1895	2,525	149	116	33
1896	640	47	26	21
1897	40	2	2	0
1898	185	17	12	5
1899	675	53	33	20
1900	2,503	209	119	90
1901 (10 mos.)	2,010	107	70	37

The increase in fines during 1893-95 was due principally to the enforcement of a law passed in 1892 requiring tenement shops to obtain licenses, a measure not primarily concerned with child labor.[57] The increase in 1900-01 can be explained by the creation of a labor department and the stimulus of increasing public criticism. It is significant that 1897, when the total fines plummeted to $40, was the first full year of the much-criticized O'Leary regime. When O'Leary left office in 1899, the fines began to rise again. Granting the conservatism of the courts, it is still difficult to arrive at an honest explanation for twenty-nine inspectors finding only 2 cases to prosecute in 1897, when in 1893, twenty-four inspectors had found 118 cases. Moreover, only part of these prosecutions dealt directly with child labor violations.

This record was not entirely the fault of the inspectors. Not all of them were political hacks; most of them were well-intentioned men and women with considerable faith in the good will of the manufacturers. By 1891, the bureau was supervising the expanding labor law and, in addition to child labor enforcement, was involved in sanitation inspections, installations of safeguards on industrial machinery, enforcement of the weekly wage payment law, investigation of accidents, and supervision of fire escapes.[58] Their efforts were diffused, but some inspectors remained alert. In June, 1890, Deputy Factory Inspector George Schaubert was walking past the New York City Button Works at Canal and Center Streets about 7:30 P.M., when he observed all the lights on and the employees at work. He decided to go in and see if the ten-hour provision of the factory law was being violated. The doors were all locked, but Schaubert succeeded in getting inside the plant "after some parley." Several employees then told him that they had been overworked at night for some time, whereupon Schaubert made a tour of all the floors in the building. Finding the supervisor, he threatened the plant with prosecution, an action which sent the supervisor scurrying through the building ordering all the employees to go home at once. All 450, including 380 women and girls, left. Within an hour a fire broke out, and the building burned down. Had the employees been working, according to the New York *Herald,* "there would have been a panic and many would doubtless have lost their lives as the doors were all locked."[59] It is interesting, if grisly, to speculate on what effect a Triangle fire would have had in 1890, but perhaps events need their time; in 1888, forty had died in a fire at the Steam Gauge and Lantern Works in Rochester, including at least one child worker "who stood at one of the windows and exhibited such a pitiful face. His cries for help were heart-rending."[60]

Opinions differed on the effectiveness of New York's factory law. Writing in 1890, Florence Kelley complained that "wherever the capitalistic method of production prevails there is child slavery, and wherever there is child slavery we find . . . some pretence of restrictive legislation embodying one or more of the conventional prohibitions of labor." Advocating prohibition of all labor for children under eighteen, Miss

Kelley warned that "half measures will slumber forgotten."[61] Just four years later, Factory Inspector James Connolly announced that "the child labor evil has almost passed away from the State of New York."[62] Then in January, 1896, the Reinhard Committee made its report to the New York State Assembly, concluding "that large numbers of children were employed in manufacturing places contrary to law" and that "the employment of child labor under the statutory age . . . [is] one of the most extensive evils now existing in the City of New York."[63] In 1905 Fred R. Fairchild, a professional economist, published his study on *The Factory Legislation of the State of New York.* In it he concluded that "the factory law has been effective to a remarkable degree in bringing about the results for which it was designed" and that "the number of children employed in factories has been greatly reduced . . . in spite of the growth in the population and industries of the state."[64]

Perhaps Table 2 will resolve some of these conflicting reports. As in so many matters of historical judgment, it is partly a question of which set of statistics one is using.

TABLE 2 [65]

NUMBER OF EMPLOYED CHILDREN UNDER SIXTEEN REPORTED BY THE
N.Y. FACTORY INSPECTOR AND THE FEDERAL CENSUS, 1887-1900

Year	Number of Separate Bakeries and Plants Checked	Number of Employees in Inspected Plants	Percentage of Inspected Plant Population Who Were Children under 16 Acc. to Factory Inspector	Percentage under 16 of Population in Mfg. and Mechanical Pursuits Acc. to Census
				(1880) 4.0
1887	2,098	169,011	8.4	
1888	4,749	276,402	6.7	
1889	5,083	277,207	5.5	
1890	6,197	327,878	4.5	2.0
1895	21,148	567,994	2.4	
1900	24,039	732,389	2.2	4.0

The 1890 census counted child laborers in the ten to fourteen age group (inclusive), while the censuses of 1880 and 1900 counted them in the ten to fifteen group (inclusive). Moreover, in 1890 the census takers were told to ask children their age as of their nearest birthday instead of their age on their last birthday. The result is that the 1890 census includes children up to the age of fourteen and one-half; the other two include children up to the age of sixteen. The 1890 census, therefore, excluded a whole year and one-half from the child labor count.

While it might seem from Table 2 that the number of census-reported child laborers was about the same in 1900 as in 1880, there was actually an increase over the twenty-year period. In 1900 for the first time the enumerators were told not to list a child as "working" unless his period of employment was longer than his period of school attendance for the year.[66] A child who worked in a factory for five and a half months a year, twelve hours a day, might not be counted by the 1900 census as a child laborer. Neither would a full-time child worker whose parents lied to the census taker. How, then, can one account for economist Fred R. Fairchild's position that the factory laws brought about a reduction in child labor? First, although Fairchild had some qualms about the sharp reduction in the number of child workers in the 1890 census (he admitted that "some of the decrease may be only apparent" and that "different methods of handling the figures . . . may have had something to do with the result"), he came to the conclusion that these factors were not "of sufficient importance to very seriously affect the reliability of the figures."[67] Doubtless he was confirmed in this belief by certain census figures on child labor in manufacturing and mechanical establishments for 1900 which showed the same percentage of employed children in the factory force as in 1890: 1.6 per cent. How can a figure of 1.6 per cent be reconciled with one of 4.0 per cent in Table 2? Fairchild's figure of 1.6 per cent and his evidence for a decrease in the number of child factory laborers in New York rests upon Volume VIII of the *Twelfth Census,* a report on manufacturing in the United States. The statistics for New York in this 1902 volume are at such variance with those contained in the 1904 special report on occupations issued by the Census Bureau as to explain the error in Fairchild's conclusion. The 1900 "manufactures" report, upon which Fairchild relied, lists the average number of employees or "hands," a figure which probably was based on reports submitted to the Census Bureau by the manufacturers themselves. The 1904 "occupations" report was definitely compiled by census enumerators in the field. For example, according to the "manufactures" report, the average number of children, ages ten to fifteen inclusive, employed in New York's manufacturing and mechanical trades in 1900 was 13,189. According to the "occupations" report the total number of children, that is, those who were at work when the 53,000 census enumerators began asking questions in June, 1900, was 37,599. Even if one reduces this last figure by 25 per cent (the number of all wage earners in New York's industries who were unemployed at any time during the year), the two figures are hardly compatible. According to the "manufactures" report, the paper and wood pulp industry in New York employed an average number of six children under sixteen, but the "occupations" report lists 258 such children actually at work in that industry during the summer of 1900.[68]

The most conservative conclusion possible, then, is that the percentage of children under sixteen employed in New York's factories remained constant between 1886 and 1900 at about 4 per cent of the total number of factory workers. It is true (see Table 2) that the factory inspector's figures show a steady decrease. The bureau's figures, however, are simply not reliable for the purpose of making generalizations, for the factory bureau checked less than one-third of New York's manufacturing establishments; in 1890, for example, they inspected only 6,197 of the state's 65,840 factories. Furthermore, the factory inspector began his investigations in the worst factories and discovered a very high percentage of working children during the early years; during the later years his figures on child labor were distorted because the bureau's preoccupation with enforcing other parts of the labor law inclined them to overlook child laborers.[69] Assuming for a moment that the factory inspector's 1900 figure of 2.2 per cent for employed children under sixteen (Table 2) is accurate, then the number of children he found in New York's factories must have been about 16,112 (2.2 per cent of 732,389 employees). In that same year, the inspector noted that 16,840 employment certificates had been issued to child workers under sixteen. If every one of the 16,112 factory children had a certificate, a most unlikely situation, there could only be 728 additional certificates issued to those working in all the department stores of the state. The "occupations" report revealed that, on the contrary, 4,180 children under sixteen were employed as salespeople in mercantile establishments and 37,599 worked in manufacturing and mechanical industries.[70] The inspector's figures, therefore, may show a decrease in the number of children *he found* in New York's factories, but they show little else.

If the number of factory children remained fairly constant during the first fourteen years of the factory act, the inspectors are entitled to some credit for holding the line. Not the least of the bureau's defects were its lack of personnel and small budget. The inspectors constantly reiterated the need for extension of the labor law to cover children working in the streets and to list more occupations as hazardous. They demanded regulation of the sweatshop. When the Bureau of Factory Inspection, the Bureau of Labor Statistics, and the Bureau of Mediation and Arbitration were placed under the new Department of Labor in 1901, the commissioner of labor complained vigorously about the inadequate enforcement of the department store laws and recommended that this work be taken away from the local boards of health and given to the bureau of factory inspection.[71]

It is also true that the percentage of illiterate children in the ten- to fourteen-year age group dropped from 1.4 in 1890 to 0.7 in 1900, a substantial decrease at that low level, with much of the credit going to the chief factory inspector. A number of night schools opened in various parts of the state, and several factory inspectors reported that those in their districts were overcrowded.[72] Moreover, the amount of paper work the bureau required of manufacturers complying with the factory law—keeping a record book on the children, collecting the parental affidavits, etc.—undoubtedly caused some employers to stop hiring children under sixteen.

But in the last analysis there was no significant reduction in factory child labor; according to the most conservative statistics, roughly the same percentage of the labor force was at work in 1885 before the factory act as in 1900. The underlying difficulty was not the act, the inspectors, or even the legislature. Public opinion was largely indifferent, and no real attempt had been made to mobilize it. Even among those most interested in social problems, there was indecision about goals and a tendency to rush from one creaking spot in the industrial structure to another. While there were cases of child labor that were really not abusive (some thirteen-year-olds actually might have been happier working than in school), the habit of judging each case on its merits was fatal. Only a concerted drive on the child labor problem in its largest sense—careful attention to the entire environment of the child—would be of lasting benefit. But the belief in untrammeled Spencerian competition was too strong. The general attitude remained unchanged in spite of occasional insights, such as the one voiced by a factory inspector in 1888: "Herbert Spencer had not an opportunity of going into our stores, workshops, and factories to find the cause of so many debilitated and broken down men in America."[73] In the 1890's, Jacob Riis found better conditions in the factories; the children had "a good enough time to make me feel that they are better off there learning habits of industry than running about the streets," he declared.[74] And the chief statistician for the state labor department predicted in 1904 that it would take relatively little work to stop the employment of all children under sixteen "save those who must support dependent families."[75]

As the century closed, perhaps 400,000 children between the ages of five and eighteen worked in the Empire State. Fifteen years had passed since the enactment of the factory act, and a small segment of public opinion was concluding that an organized and sustained effort must be made to strengthen and enforce it. The factory inspectors had started their work in Cohoes in 1886. In October, 1901, a letter from some of the city's mill girls reached Albany. "Dear Sir," it began, "will you pleas come to Cohoes and stop our superintec from working us ore time. We work from 630 am to 9 oclock at night in all we work from 77 hours to 84 a week we pray to god you will help us." And a postscript: "Come at once."[76] A new kind of help was on the way.

The purpose of the bill is to save the children of the state, and, gentlemen, I appeal to you to get it out of the Judiciary Committee. For God's sake, get it out of the Committee and let the kids have a fair chance. We have our hearts in this thing. We have worked night and day on this thing to put it through.

—Robert Hunter, Hearing before the Judiciary Committee of the New York Senate, 1903

III. The New Committee and the Breakthrough of 1903

While it has been conventional and convenient to raise the curtain on the progressive era in 1900, no such arbitrary line marked its beginning. Although child labor became with apparent suddenness a topic of public interest at the turn of the century, change had been in the air for some time. As early as the 1870's a few New Yorkers had decried the flagrant misuse of children in industry. People long had been accustomed to the work of charitable societies with their hot meals and warm beds for starving ragamuffins—the poor ye had always with you, and charity not far behind. There had been concern: earlier factory legislation, although unenforceable, gave recognition to the problem. What was new was a growing feeling that public attention must be directed to the particular issue of child labor and to the pressing need for enforceable laws. In the twentieth century child labor reformers tried a new approach: they formed pressure groups to lobby for effective legislation.

There is no single explanation for their success. The invention of machines to do the jobs formerly performed by children "automated" some youngsters out of the factories. As Robert Bremner has demonstrated, many people in 1900 no longer regarded poverty either as inevitable or as a blessing.[1] If society could ameliorate the extreme conditions of poverty, child labor should be unnecessary. If children could be barred from working and made to stay in school, they might eventually contribute something to society. A rash of new magazines and newspapers popularized the ideas of the environmentalists and reform Darwinists who were reacting against the Calvinist heritage, with the latter's emphasis on man as a creature innately predestined to rise above all earthly obstacles or to sink into the morass of damnation. Perhaps the best explanation for New York's rapid strides in child labor reform following 1900 was the appearance of an exceptional group of men and women in a time ready for them. In 1901 about 379,000 children in New York, ages five to eighteen, were not in school. The factory inspector said 50,000 worked in industry; the census officials reported that another 54,000 were employed in agriculture, personal and domestic work, and trade and transportation; leaving 275,000 unaccounted for by either the school officials, the factory inspector, or the census bureau.[2] Most of the remainder worked in two unregulated areas of employment: tenement homework and street trades.

At the time, almost nothing was known about tenement or street work—so difficult was it to investigate them—except the huge number of children involved and the dreadful working conditions. In 1891 Dr. Annie S. Daniel, a visiting tenement physician for the New York Dispensary for Women and Children, deplored the lack of reliable statistics on the immense tenement problem:

> Whenever children are members of families manufacturing, they invariably assist either directly or indirectly . . . thus a child of nine years does all the housework for a family of five persons, including the washing and ironing, that the mother may devote her entire time to sewing. Another girl of six years carries three or four dozen vests at one time up five flights of stairs, and the mother cannot understand why the child is not well.[3]

"We are suffering from stygian darkness on this whole subject of the work of children in tenements," Florence Kelley asserted as late as 1911.[4] A typical tenement of the 1890's housed twenty families, about eighty-five persons. Each family had the use of a kitchen 13 by 10 feet and two sleeping rooms, one 7 by 10½ feet and one 6 by 7 feet, with ceilings eight feet high. Cooking, eating, working, and sleeping were all done in the same living area. The surroundings were normally foul: in 1903, for example, the newly created Tenement House Department found it necessary to clean 13,617 toilets and to remove 11,611 "accumulations of filth" from New York City tenements.[5]

Although tenement workers assisted in the production of hundreds of different items, the principle of the sweating system was basically the same. In the clothing industry, for example, the manufacturer cut the material in his own factory and then distributed it to a contractor-middleman. This individual farmed out the cloth to the tenement workers, sometimes directly and sometimes through a subcontractor. Then the work began under a system described by a factory inspector as "nearly akin to slavery as it is possible to get."[6] At the turn of the century, nearly three-quarters of the workers in Manhattan sweatshops were Jews, the remainder Italians. In one of the largest "sweating" districts—that bounded by Eighth Street, the Bowery, Catherine Street and the East River—some 450,000 persons worked and lived. Brooklyn had its tenement problem, too, with Germans, Jews, and Lithuanians concentrated in "Dutchtown," an area bounded by Ten Eyck Street, Leonard Street, Flushing Avenue, and Hamburg Avenue. Jews populated Brownsville, while Italians and Lithuanians jammed the north side of Williamsburg in the Fourteenth Ward.[7] Tapping an almost unlimited supply of immigrant workers whose language handicap, social unacceptability, and clannishness inclined them to work in small groups of their own people, the manufacturers lowered wages to starvation level. In 1907 the going rate for making, counting, and bunching 1,440 artificial flowers was eighty cents, and as late as 1910, federal inspectors found a fifteen-year-old girl sleeve-maker who had worked 241 days for $127. A clothing cutter who worked by the piece, as did most tenement workers, had to cut two hundred children's jackets to earn one dollar.[8] "The exposure of infants in the highways of China is not more obvious to the people of China," thundered Florence Kelley, "than the preventable mortality of infants in New York City has for years been obvious to the people of the United States."[9] And it *was* obvious. In 1906 the Memphis, Tennessee, *News Scimitar* printed an article denouncing the shocking infant mortality rate in New York City tenements. One hundred babies, it reported, had died in a single hot summer day. And the cause? Like so many reformers of the time, the *News Scimitar* sought a particular, rather than a general, explanation. "The greedy ice trust," it complained, "having succeeded in doubling the price by cutting down by one-half the size of a '10-cent piece' has its responsibility for the wholesale murder of the innocents." Hundreds of sick babies were put out on the fire escapes to escape the heat; sometimes they fell off.[10] Dr. Antonio Stella found in his study of "The Effects of Congestion on Italian Women and Children" that while the death rate per thousand for all ages in New York City during 1905-06 was 18.35, it rose to 24.4 in one of the congested areas he examined. For children under five living in tenements, the death rate was nearly double: 92.2 per thousand as against 51.5 for the entire city.[11]

Addressing the New York City Consumers' League in 1904, Dr. Annie S. Daniel specified the four greatest evils of the tenement sweating system. The first was employment of youngsters ages three to twelve, who added only a dollar a week to the family income. Hours were a second problem with children and adults working "as long as . . . strength endures or work remains." Wages, the third evil, were abysmally low. Dr. Daniel found that during December, 1904, the average *monthly* income of forty-nine new tenement families was $13.24, while the average monthly rent was $8.57. This left $4.67 for food, fuel, and clothing. Meager wages led directly to the fourth evil—dangerous overcrowding of tenements.[12] Hours, wages, and over-crowding were themselves direct causes of child labor, and child labor, in turn, depressed wages.

Accurate figures on the number of youngsters who escaped the tenements to work in the streets were also impossible to obtain. A 1901 estimate placed the number of New York City newsboys at four thousand.[13] Thousands more worked peddling, bootblacking, running errands, making deliveries, and carrying messages.[14] "The life of the street," observed Frederick A. King of the University Settlement, "is at best a rough school of experience and at worst a free field in which the most evil and corrupting influences may work against the morals of the community."[15] A coworker of King, Ernest Poole, pointed to street work's failure "to train for any permanent trade, its irregular periods for work and meals and sleep, its tense nervous life, sustained and poisoned by double a man's portion of coffee, cigars, and cigarettes."[16] One might suppose general agreement that ten-year-olds should not be thrown on their own resources in the streets of a great city. This was not the case. The most formidable obstacle to street trade regulation was public insistence upon drawing a distinction between street traders employed by others for wages and those who were self-employed for profit. The independent street trader, particularly the newsboy, was regarded as a kind of romantic Galahad, braving adversity to win economic success. He seemed a delightful combination of Horatio Alger's heroes and Huck Finn—a diamond-in-the-rough, the stock from which future great men would spring. The newsboy was believed to be waiting for the kind of opportunity described by Elizabeth Oakes Smith in a conversation between her fictional hero-newsboy and his benefactor:

> MR. DINSMOOR: You shall have learning, Bob. I will be a friend to you in the best way. You shall be taught everything to render you an accomplished merchant; and let me tell you, Bob, you have a capital in your own honest, manly integrity, worth millions in a city like this. . . .

BOB: When you speak of the learnin', Sir, you comes very near to me. Rack-o-bones has been a teachin' of me, and I'm bound to say I learns fast, seein' I wants the learnin' as I wants bread.

MR. DINSMOOR: You shall have it, Bob, and I will learn of you also; learn the uses of life and the uses of wealth through your great heart, Bob. . . .

BOB: I thinks, Sir, God designed you for something handsome, he did.[17]

Not all street traders met Mr. Dinsmoor. In 1902, a boy who had worked as a helper in a delivery wagon from early in the day until three o'clock the following morning went to sleep in the rear of the wagon. The driver covered him and left, returning after daybreak to find him frozen to death.[18] The idea of the newsboy as a "little merchant" or "junior independent merchant" has survived to the present day.

By 1902 the time was ripe for a campaign directly focused upon new child labor legislation. For years there had been active concern about the problem, as one group after another confronted it in the course of other activities. The Association for Improving the Condition of the Poor (1843), the Children's Aid Society (1853), the Society for the Prevention of Cruelty to Children (1874), and the Charities Organization Society (1882) saw the effects of child labor because they worked in the environment of the poor. The New York City Consumers' League, organized in 1891, faced the problem in its crusade to abolish tenement-made goods and to improve conditions in department stores. At the turn of the century, the New York settlement house movement had grown under the leadership of Dr. Stanton Coit, the founder of the Neighborhood Guild (1886), to include thirty-one settlement houses. The settlement movement was an early attempt at treating the entire culture of poverty. Volunteer workers (often wealthy) would live together in the city's worst sections in an effort to improve living conditions and to bring some conception of a "better life" to local residents. The idea that members of the upper class were simply descending from the heights to hold out hopeless ideals to the poor was repugnant to the settlement workers. Writing of the University Settlement on Eldridge Street, Howard Brubaker insisted that

The group [Wiles Robert] Hunter gathered together carried on the more democratic tradition of Jane Addams and . . . Lillian D. Wald. . . . We residents were of all shades of opinion and various lines of interest, but we all agreed that we had much to learn from our East Side neighbors and precious little to teach. Our

favorite jest was the phrase invariably used by visitors from up-
town, "You are doing a noble work." The word uplifter was an
affectionate insult to be spoken with a smile.[19]

Modeled on England's Toynbee Hall, the Neighborhood Guild established kindergartens, a gym and other recreational facilities, and a
penny-provident bank; it also organized the Tenth Ward Social Reform Club, which sponsored public baths, laundries, parks, and cooperative stores.[20] Lillian Wald's Henry Street Settlement (1893)
offered what would become a world-famous visiting nurse service;
while Greenwich House, under Mary Simkhovitch, worked to improve
health and housing.

In May, 1899, Florence Kelley, the "Joan of Arc"[21] of the social
workers, arrived in New York from Chicago to organize the National
Consumers' League. It was an epochal date for the cause of child
labor reform in New York State. The daughter of a well-known pro-
tectionist congressman, William D. "Pig-iron" Kelley, she was graduated from Cornell in 1882, presenting as her thesis a study of the
common and statute law concerning children. Traveling in Europe,
Miss Kelley toured the industry-ravaged English countryside and
studied at the University of Zurich. There, converted to socialism, she
translated Engel's *The Condition of the Working Classes in England
in 1844* into English, and married a young Polish-Russian physician,
Lazare Wishnieweski.[22] The marriage failed miserably, and after the
couple's return to the United States, they were divorced. Florence
Kelley then went to work at Chicago's Hull House, and in 1893 Governor John P. Altgeld appointed her chief factory inspector for Illinois,
the only woman to hold such a post until Alfred E. Smith named
Frances Perkins to a similar position in New York in the 1920's. As
chief factory inspector, Miss Kelley vied with Governor Altgeld for the
hostility of business. To battle the Illinois courts over their constitutional hairsplitting she took her law degree from Northwestern University in 1894. She conducted the first careful sociological study of
Chicago's sweating system, and personally prevented the sale of
smallpox-infected garments. Always the pioneer, Florence Kelley gave
the manufacturers a memorable four years; her administration's principal accomplishment was the compilation of information for future
reformers. Miss Kelley was a big woman, with dark braided hair and
indescribable energy. "No other man or woman whom I have ever
heard," wrote Josephine Goldmark, "so blended knowledge of facts,
wit, satire, burning indignation, prophetic denunciation—all poured
out at white heat in a voice varying from flute-like tones to deep organ

tones."[23] She was, however, in the opinion of a later child labor reformer who knew her well, "a tormented soul."[24]

In New York Florence Kelley took up residence with Lillian Wald on Henry Street. It was a significant conjunction of personalities, because both women were intensely interested in stopping child labor; for Miss Kelley it was "her first concern."[25] By 1902 the Association of Neighborhood Workers, a group composed of representatives of New York City's thirty-one settlement houses, responded to pressure from the two women and formed a temporary organization known simply as the "Child Labor Committee."[26] The group included, in addition to Miss Kelley and Miss Wald, Mary K. Simkhovitch of Greenwich House, Pauline Goldmark of the National Consumers' League, and Wiles Robert Hunter of the University Settlement. Its original purpose was to investigate "accounts from various quarters of the shocking exploitation of children" and to recommend necessary legislation. "The problem of child labor is one which curiously enough has escaped attention in the general movement for improvement in industrial conditions of this city," the committee observed in its first appeal for money. We "therefore propose to discover the extent of this evil."[27]

The fund-raising letter and personal contacts of Robert Hunter brought in about a thousand dollars, enough for the committee to hire a full-time investigator, Helen Marot, who later became secretary of the Women's Trade Union League. Assisted by settlement residents, schoolteachers, and labor union members, Miss Marot began an investigation of factory work and street trades in August, 1902. Her preliminary survey immediately turned up 212 underage and 92 illiterate children working in factories, and revealed that the earnings of many street traders were not necessary for the support of their families.[28] The complete Marot study convinced Robert Hunter that sufficient public support could be found for a permanent child labor committee.

Hunter was much more than an interested and "well meaning" amateur. A graduate of Indiana University, he had been chairman of the Chicago Tenement Inquiry Committee and a resident of Hull House before coming in 1901 to the University Settlement in New York. A director of the Fouts and Hunter Manufacturing Company, he was one of the so-called "millionaire socialists," joining the Socialist Party in 1905 and running unsuccessfully on the party ticket for the New York Assembly (1905) and for governor of Connecticut (1910), before leaving the party on the war issue in 1914.[29] Like Florence Kelley, Mary Simkhovitch, Jane Addams, Lawrence Veiller, Robert W. De-

Forest, and Julia Lathrop, Hunter was one of the first professional sociologists, a member of the "factual generation."[30] In 1904 he published *Poverty*, the most searching study of the subject written in the United States up to that time.[31]

There was almost no precedent in the United States for the organization of child labor committees. The Alabama Child Labor Committee, organized by Edgar Gardner Murphy in 1901, was the only state committee in existence; the National Child Labor Committee did not organize until 1904. Seeking information, Hunter wrote to the English Committee on Wage-Earning Children, but received in reply only a sheaf of current English child labor publications with no practical advice on formation of a permanent committee. One thing, however, was obvious to Hunter and his associates: a permanent child labor committee would require a permanent source of funds. Socially prominent persons must, therefore, be invited to join. Years later the New York Child Labor Committee claimed that it originated in

> a fireside conversation among five prominent New Yorkers . . . in 1902. One told about the tiny cash boy whom she had found standing with his head against the counter—sound asleep—too tired to bring back her change, and too little to be noticed. Other flagrant abuses of childhood were then recalled. *That Night* the New York Child Labor Committee was born.[32]

Whatever the details, a permanent committee studded with important names from the metropolitan area and upstate New York was quickly organized. In part, this was due to the connections of Hunter and his highly placed brother-in-law, J. G. Phelps Stokes, president of the Phelps Stokes Corporation, founder of Hartley House, and later head of the Intercollegiate Socialist Society. But the committee's rapid initial success was also indicative of the response that could be obtained from the heads of society by an appeal based upon "expert" surveys and statistics. If the committee said that child labor was a serious problem, it must be so. Since the small group of upper-class businessmen supporting the committee did not depend upon cheap child labor, its regulation was something they could sponsor. Indeed, the abolition of child labor could be viewed as a means of driving out marginal manufacturers and tenement operators, hence increasing the consolidation and efficiency of business. Their motives ranged from honest humanitarianism to the feeling that this was just another "good cause." When an appeal for the use of his name was made to John H. Rhoades, president of the Greenwich Savings Bank, he readily gave permission, asserting that while "of my own knowledge I cannot say that the conditions [of child labor] are as represented, I have perfect faith in the statement as coming from the Committee."[33]

Joining the committee as treasurer was Valentine Everit Macy of the Title Guarantee and Trust Company, while the German-born banker, Paul M. Warburg, brought to the group his experience as a firm member of Kuhn Loeb Investment Banking Company. Other founding members included William H. Baldwin, the president of the Long Island Railroad; John H. Hammond, a former deputy attorney general of New York and a member of the Republican county committee; and Jacob A. Schiff of Kuhn Loeb. From the academic field came Charles Sprague Smith, who had organized Columbia's modern languages department; and Felix Adler, a newly appointed professor of social and political ethics at Columbia and founder of the Society for Ethical Culture.[34] William H. Maxwell, the New York City Superintendent of Schools, became an active member; as did George W. Alger, a young attorney from Vermont who was counsel to the State Federation of Labor. Another attorney, Mornay Williams, an active Baptist layman with a very high standing in the New York Bar, would succeed Hunter as chairman of the committee.[35] The professional social workers were, of course, already represented by Kelley, Wald, Goldmark, and Simkhovitch; completing the triumvirate of "millionaire socialists" was William English Walling of the University Settlement, who joined Hunter and Stokes on the committee. Among others who gave support to the committee in its early days were Abram S. Hewitt, the steelmaker; Dr. Lyman Abbott, social gospeler and editor of the *Outlook;* Jacob Riis; Dr. Abraham Jacobi, professor of pediatrics at Columbia; and Bishop H. C. Potter of the Protestant Episcopal Church.

While the interests of the committee naturally were centered in New York City, it did seek upstate support from the beginning, and gradually widened its activities to include the entire state. The upstate founders included Joseph T. Alling, Rev. Thomas A. Hendrick, Dr. Max Lansberg, and George A. Carnahan of Rochester; Frederick Almy, William H. Gratwick, Ansley Wilcox, and T. Guilford Smith of Buffalo; Theodore F. Hancock and Bishop F. D. Huntington of Syracuse; William J. Milne of Albany; and Jacob Gould Schurman, president of Cornell University.[36]

While organized labor was represented on the committee by Samuel B. Donnelly, of the Central Federated Union of New York City, labor was by no means a dominant factor within the committee. Nor was the new group in any sense an extension of the state federation of labor (known at that time as the Workingmen's Federation of the State of New York). Labor did at times provide valuable assistance to the committee, and as the state federation grew more powerful, its support for child labor bills was of great importance to the committee in Albany. But labor almost always had to be asked; it was the committee or some other private group such as the Consumers' League that took the initiative. In the summer of 1902, for example, when Hunter and his colleagues at the University Settlement were organizing the Marot investigation, they requested and received help from the Central Federated Union. The union even appointed its own child labor committee and lent Helen Marot about twenty-five workers for her study. But, as the labor officials pointed out in their report, they had been "greatly agitated over certain other grave industrial problems," and although they had done what they could when the settlement workers asked for help, the union's child labor committee could not be permanent.[37]

As finally constituted, the Child Labor Committee was eminently "respectable." Composed predominantly of upper-class people with money, its letterhead alone seemed to promise financial support. The trustees and other active members all worked without compensation; only the secretary, Fred S. Hall, and an occasional assistant were salaried. By the end of 1902 the committee had taken office space in the Sohmer Building at Fifth Avenue and Twenty-second Street, just a block away from the Charities Building where Florence Kelley had her office.[38] They immediately sent out form letters to inaugurate a highly successful financial campaign, and within two years, 420 persons had contributed $12,566.56 to the Child Labor Committee.[39]

Upon receipt of his letter, Jacob Riis urged the committee to open a legislative campaign at once; public opinion, he thought, was "now sufficiently awake and robust to warrant the effort."[40] Hunter and his associates agreed. Marshaling their arguments in a 1902 memorial to the legislature, they recited the defects of the existing factory law. According to the Marot investigation, a large number of underage children were still working in factories. The system of issuing employment certificates for factory and mercantile work was inefficient, with many children securing certificates to which they were not entitled. The local boards of health had no enforceable check on the child's age and usually accepted without question the age he gave in school.[41] A manufacturer could evade the law by hiring a child under fourteen and paying his wage to an older brother or sister, so that the name of the illegally employed child would not appear on the payroll. The ten-hour law for children over fourteen was ineffective because any weekday could be lengthened if the working hours on Saturday were shortened. Children twelve years old were permitted to work in factories and stores during summer vacations, and it was difficult to return them to school in the fall.[42] This was especially so when the education authorities saw no reason for adding to the already overcrowded classrooms.

The perennial conflict between the factory and education laws was creating loopholes that made any enforcement of either almost impossible. The factory law prohibited all factory work for youngsters under fourteen, but the education law required working twelve- and thirteen-year-olds to attend school *only* eighty days of the year. The boards of health, which issued the employment certificates, were required to *accept* the certification of the school as the sole evidence that the child had complied with the education law, but were not required to *ask* for such evidence. An 1897 enactment told school principals to certify *upon demand* that the child had been in school for a period "equal to one school year" and had received instruction in prescribed studies. At best, this guaranteed only that the youngster had been physically present; it said nothing about his education—in fact, he might be illiterate.[43] The very terminology of these measures was self-defeating. The Child Labor Committee contended that New York could not afford to congratulate itself upon being one of a select group of states (Massachusetts, Connecticut, Ohio, Indiana, Illinois, Michigan, Minnesota, and Wisconsin were the others) prohibiting the employment of children in factories and department stores. Not only did the law fail to stop such employment, but whole areas such as street trades were still unregulated. The committee believed that all children working for wages should be protected by law.[44]

An intensive campaign for new regulatory legislation now began. The committee strenuously pressured newspapers, clergymen, physicians, educators, labor unions, and legislators. To rally public opinion the committee hired a press agent and instructed him to supply upstate and metropolitan newspapers with semiweekly news stories about child labor conditions, the raw data to be furnished by the committee. Pathetic case histories such as the following were soon improving the breakfasts of countless New Yorkers.

> David——was a newsboy at nine. He was an unusually bright, attractive little chap, and made usually $4 a week, though a large part of this was made with the dice. . . . With him, as with scores of other little waifs, the common process began working. In gambling he lost heavily one night, and the next time he lost it was very natural to stay out all night. So the process went on. At

13 he spent most of his nights on the streets . . . and during the coldest three months he slept in basements or in halls of tenements. . . . He had been "put wise" to all the streets could teach. At 12 he contracted a loathsome venereal disease. Unnatural vice was common among his companions.

The committee investigator wrote of a fifteen-year-old messenger boy:

I had a glimpse of him through the sweet sickening smoke of a tiny opium stall, in a dive in Chinatown. He was seeking an opium pill for a *white* woman who was a slave to Chinamen and the opium habit. It was his business to run errands for a dozen women of her type.

And the case of Angeline Perati, who

according to her employment certificate . . . was 15 years old, but her actual age was 12. She worked in an artificial flower factory from 7:30 in the morning until 6 in the evening. In the evening she helped her mother and younger sister make artificial flowers at home. She was in a pitiful physical condition, being subject to epileptic fits and being troubled with a weak heart. In all her life she has attended school just one month.[45]

Such stories made news; when prominent citizens representing the Child Labor Committee followed up with visits to editors, the newspapers responded. "Great interest has been taken all over the country recently in the efforts to reform the evils of child labor in the cotton mills of the South," said the New York *Tribune*. "It now appears that we need to turn our attention homeward." "Selfish interests will be arrayed against the child-labor bills," the Albany *Express* observed, "but the committee which is nobly striving to save boys and girls . . . undoubtedly has the sympathy and support of every person who wishes to save future generations from the evils of degeneracy." The New York *World* expressed alarm at the state's "army of child toilers" and urged the legislature to "lighten the heavy burdens which rest upon shoulders too young to bear them." Joining in support of the Child Labor Committee were metropolitan papers like the *Journal, Commercial Advertiser, Mail and Express*, and *Evening Post*, as well as upstate journals like the Buffalo *Express*, Syracuse *Post-Standard*, Elmira *Advertiser*, Schenectady *Star*, and Newburg *News*. Reprints of their editorials were sent "by the thousand" throughout the state.[46]

More than thirty religious leaders were persuaded to speak on the necessity for child labor regulation, and several church and ethical organizations such as the St. Vincent de Paul Society, the Religious Society of Friends, the United Hebrew Charities, and the Ethical Culture Society endorsed the committee's program.[47] Committee members visited philanthropic organizations and women's clubs to enlist support. Several physicians expressed their delight at having a channel of protest opened to them by the committee. One doctor said: "If my work among the poor and my studies of the causes of the fearful prevalence of tuberculosis among the masses has taught me anything it has taught me the banefulness of child labor."[48]

The Child Labor Committee clearly had tapped a wellspring of public support. The favorable reaction to the publicity given the Marot investigation seems amazing considering the modest scope of the study and that most of Helen Marot's findings could have been inferred from the state labor department's reports. But the official reports were not intended for the casual reader; they were badly written and their tables were statistical monstrosities. The newspapers and the steadily proliferating popular journals were different. Tragedy sells papers, and accounts of child labor abuses, particularly when accompanied by photographs, were good copy for the journalists. To some ministers, physicians, union workers, middle- and upper-class businessmen, the committee was an alarm bell. Hunter's group had stated forcefully and publicly that New York's child labor problem was real—this in itself was a major contribution. Many people, including some who supported the committee, believed that it was perfectly all right for children to work at fourteen, but not at eight or nine and not under the conditions described by Hunter. It became difficult to oppose child labor regulation publicly. The Southern crusade was getting national attention and a dozen muckraking news outlets were just waiting to pounce on employers who defended the rights of little children to work twelve hours a day in jute mills or twine factories.

Before drafting his legislative programs, Robert Hunter consulted as many of the people who would be involved as possible. He scheduled conferences with the New York City Health Department; Factory Inspector John Williams; State Labor Commissioner John McMackin, who was still on friendly terms with the Child Labor Committee; and School Superintendent Maxwell, already a member of the committee.[49] Of the five major child labor laws passed by the 1903 legislature, three were drafted by McMackin and the committee, one by William H. Maxwell and other state school superintendents, and the other entirely by the committee.

Focusing its attention directly upon the legislature, the committee saw that each lawmaker received child labor literature and that his constituents followed up with supporting letters. The two legislative committees to which the bills would be referred were bombarded with requests for favorable action; the chairman of the Assembly Committee on Labor and Industries later announced that he had personally received eighty letters.[50] The Central Federated Union of New York City sent letters to upstate unions, which in turn pressed their legislators for action. Labor's support, Fred Hall asserted, "made a marked impression upon the legislature."[51] To sponsor its bills in the Assembly, the committee relied upon Edward R. Finch, who had represented the fifth district of New York County for less than a year. A young Republican attorney and Yale Phi Beta Kappa, Finch came from an old New York family. Selected to introduce most of Mayor Seth Low's home rule bills in the 1903 session, he had been recommended to the committee as "the very best man to introduce, push, and defend" its measures. The committee's choice in the Senate was Henry W. Hill of Buffalo, a lawyer and scholar with a strong progressive background in educational administration and reform.[52]

The first encouraging sign from Albany came when Governor Benjamin B. Odell urged the lawmakers in his opening message to the 1903 legislature to amend the law "so as to make effective the statutes regarding the employment of children."[53] Although Governor Odell was no reformer, he felt that he needed support from the reform element in New York politics. He had risen to power as a lieutenant of Thomas C. Platt, but upon being elected governor in 1900, had tried to take over the Republican state machinery himself. With President Theodore Roosevelt personally handling New York's federal patronage and Odell apparently controlling the state jobs, Boss Platt's influence began to decline. Odell, however, was not equal to the job. He had to spend the first two weeks of January, 1903, in a desperate effort to prevent a three-man Republican revolt in the legislature from going any further. State Senators Elsberg, Brackett, and Brown, all close associates of Theodore Roosevelt, made a short-lived attempt to prevent the renomination of Senator Platt by the Republican caucus. Caught between his desire for independent power and his doubts about the chances for success, Odell finally came out for Platt's reelection as senator. Realizing that he would need their support for his tax legislation, Odell did not punish the three rebellious state senators. Instead, he gave all of them good committee posts, with the result that Edgar T. Brackett, a powerful Saratoga lawyer, was named chairman of the Judiciary Committee to which the new child labor bills would be referred. The senatorial revolt certainly did not hurt the chances of the Child Labor Committee's bills.[54] Sponsoring mild labor reform measures was something Odell could do for his erstwhile enemies, particularly since the measures seemed to have some public support and since Roosevelt's approval would help him with the reform group.

Assemblyman Finch's first bill for the Child Labor Committee concerning factories met with almost no opposition. Introduced on February 11, 1903, it sailed through the legislature with comparative ease, passing both houses unanimously, and was signed by Governor Odell on April 15. Perhaps the most important change effected by the Finch-Hill Factory Act was to make the employer directly responsible for any illegally employed child found in his factory. Under the old factory law, employers had often avoided prosecution by claiming that the underage child worker must have "wandered in," for they personally had never hired the youngster. The Finch-Hill Act made the mere finding of a child under fourteen *at work* in a manufacturing establishment evidence of illegal employment by providing that no child under fourteen could be "employed, permitted, or suffered to work" in a factory.[55] The child who was found "standing around" was another matter: for some years the courts refused to admit that "presence" meant "employment." The bill did prohibit the employment of children under fourteen in, *or in connection with,* a factory, and this brought office boys and some delivery boys within the scope of the factory law. Previously manufacturers had been able to hire such youngsters under fourteen on the grounds that they did not work "in" the plant itself but in an office or outside the building. The new law also forbade children under sixteen from working more than nine hours a day, thus achieving a fifty-four-hour week for fourteen- and fifteen-year-olds in factories.

While the Finch-Hill bill was being discussed in the legislature, the New York Court of Appeals handed down a decision awarding damages to an illegally employed thirteen-year-old boy who had been injured operating a printing press. Although in the eyes of the state the employer was guilty only of a misdemeanor (employing an underage child), he was also, the court said, liable to the child for making a contract with a person legally incompetent to do so.[56] The decision increased the manufacturers' risk in using illegal child labor, and probably speeded the passage of the Finch-Hill bill.

In addition to closing these loopholes, the new measure strengthened the proof of age requirement. The parental affidavit had been a complete failure, and although not entirely effective, the new procedures were an improvement. Every child seeking an employment certificate was now required to submit "a passport or duly attested transcript of the certificate of birth or baptism or other religious record." Any proof of age other than a birth certificate had to be accompanied by a parental affidavit, but this document would be sworn before the health officer issuing the certificate, not before a notary. To encourage compliance with the intent of the law, Assemblyman Finch persuaded the New York City Board of Health to issue birth certificates free (it had been charging fifty cents).[57] But because many children had no record of their birth, false swearing and record-faking were still possible. Under the new law, a child who wished to work in a factory must have his school record sent to his local board of health. (Previously the school record was sent only if the health officer had asked for it.) In it the school principal would certify that the child had regularly attended school for at least 130 days of the preceding year, that he had "received" instruction in reading, spelling, writing, English grammar, and geography, and that he was familiar with the fundamental operations of arithmetic, up to and including fractions. The health officer would then attest that in his opinion the child was fourteen years old, was "normally" developed for his age, and could do the work he intended to do. In practice the health officers, some of whom were not physicians, regularly swore to these things without ordering a physical examination. Thus a child with a weak heart, defective vision, or poor hearing might easily obtain working papers.[58]

Although an undoubted improvement over the existing factory law, the Finch-Hill Act lacked precision. Under the new act, for example, the child controlled his working papers. He might get a certificate and then idle on the street, not working and not going to school. Once the child had received his working papers, all official record of him was lost as he went from employer to employer, for there was no check between employers and health boards until 1921. The measure also unwisely divided responsibility for sending children into the labor market between the schools and the boards of health. Educational standards were practically nonexistent. What child, assuming his presence in the classroom, had not "received" instructions as prescribed by law? And what was "normal" physical development? Notwithstanding its defects, the new factory law did make it difficult for employers to avoid legal responsibility for hiring underage children, and it tended to call attention to itself because of the extra paper work. Factory owners were now subject to more inspections by a larger force of factory inspectors; 24,000 factories were inspected in 1900 as compared with 13,000 in 1894.[59]

The department stores were another matter; here there was a real need for young workers, particularly to deliver packages and relay cash. Before the invention of the change-carrying pneumatic tube, children ran about the stores with change for customers. Even though the 1896 mercantile legislation supposedly regulated their employment, serious violations existed because of the laxity of local health boards. The only reform group directly concerned with department store conditions had been the New York City Consumers' League. Active since 1891, the league sought to improve the working conditions of women and children by promoting a "white list" of department stores that met league standards and urging the public to patronize only these stores. By 1900 thirty-nine stores, including some of the largest, had complied with the "standard of a fair house," which meant, in part, that the concern did not employ children under fourteen.[60] But the Consumers' League had barely scratched the surface, for hundreds of stores continued to use underage children. The league had difficulty in persuading some newspapers to carry its white list advertisements for "fear of antagonizing . . . regular advertisers . . . not on the white list."[61] Dissatisfied with the New York City Board of Health's enforcement of the mercantile labor laws, league members tried to enlist the aid of the police. This proved futile. Finding a store on Avenue A that was violating the hours law for children by making them work from 8:00 A.M. until 11:00 P.M. on Saturdays, one league member stayed in front of the store while the other went to the nearest police station. Suddenly all the customers hurried out of the store, the shutters were put up, and the building closed. When a policeman arrived, he inquired with some annoyance of his league escort: "Why didn't you tell us you had left a friend to watch the store?" Obviously the police had telephoned the store to warn them.[62]

In the Finch-Hill Commercial Establishments Bill, the Child Labor Committee sought more effective regulation of the department stores. In an important change, the measure brought business offices, telegraph offices, restaurants, hotels, and apartment houses—none of which previously had been regulated—within the scope of the mercantile child labor law. Delivery and messenger boys of all kinds were specifically included. Any person under sixteen who sought employment in any of the occupations covered by the bill must get an employment certificate. The procedure was identical with that prescribed for factory work, and the same documentation was necessary.[63]

While the existing mercantile law had prohibited the employment of children under fourteen in department stores during the regular school term, it had permitted twelve- and thirteen-year-olds to work during school vacations. New York's three-class city system forced the drafters of the new bill to take an illogical but politically necessary course. While barring children under fourteen from vacation work in first- and second-class cities, they permitted such work in third-class cities (those with less than 50,000 population) and in villages of more than 3,000 inhabitants. In order to work in a commercial establishment during his vacation, the child had to obtain a vacation employment certificate; the documentation and procedure were the same as for a regular certificate except that the applicant need not furnish a school record. There was no provision for the surrender of the vacation certificate at the end of the summer, thus making it possible for a child to get a vacation certificate and remain at work past the opening of school in the fall. In the smaller villages and towns, there were no restrictions whatsoever, and it was this fact that helped the bill to pass. New York's rural-dominated legislature did not mind passing bills so long as the urban areas demanding them were the only ones regulated. The hours provision of the commercial establishments bill was the only one to provoke open opposition. The old mercantile law permitted a ten-hour day for children under sixteen, and the department stores made a concerted effort to remove the clause in the new bill establishing a nine-hour day and fifty-four–hour week. According to Fred S. Hall of the Child Labor Committee, it was all a matter of fifteen minutes. The department stores were open from 8:00 A.M. to 6:00 P.M. with a forty-five-minute lunch period. With their employees working a nine-hour-and-fifteen-minute day, the stores would have had to release their child employees fifteen minutes earlier than the rest to comply with the proposed law. This they were unwilling to do.[64] When the bill was announced for a third reading in the Senate, the committee discovered that the Judiciary Committee had inserted the old ten-hour-day and sixty-hour-week clause. Fortunately for the Child Labor Committee, Senator Charles P. McClelland, a Westchester reform Democrat, successfully moved to return the bill to committee with instructions to restore the original nine-hour-day and fifty-four–hour-week provision. On April 14, 1903, the Finch-Hill Commercial Establishments Act passed the Senate unanimously; the Assembly followed suit on April 17; and Governor Odell signed it on April 24. The law was an advance over the existing mercantile legislation, but unfortunately it still perpetuated old problems. The ultimate failure of the new bill was assured when local health boards were once again charged with the entire inspection task.[65]

The third Finch-Hill bill proposed to tighten the loophole of parental perjury, which had thwarted enforcement of the factory law for years. Designed as an amendment to the section of the Penal Code that dealt with violations of the child labor laws, the bill provided fines and imprisonment for any person making a false statement in connection with the documentation required for an employment certificate.[66] Passing the Assembly on April 10, the Penal Code amendment was emasculated when the Senate changed it to apply only to those who "knowingly" made false statements. Although this word had been one of the most notorious weaknesses in past labor legislation, Assemblyman Finch moved that the lower house accept the Senate's change. By this time (April 22), Finch had already obtained passage of his factory and mercantile bills, both of which attacked the old contention that an employer must commit his illegal acts "knowingly," so he undoubtedly felt that the new doctrine was sufficiently established. In 1904, a New York court agreed, holding that an employer who hired an underage child could not rely upon a false parental affidavit as his defense. The Penal Code amendment became law on May 6, 1903.[67]

On February 24, 1903, Senator Merton E. Lewis of Rochester introduced a bill amending the compulsory education law. Drafted by the state school superintendents, the measure tried to reconcile the child labor provisions of the factory law and the school attendance requirements of the education law. While the factory law forbade the employment of children under fourteen, the education law required full-time school attendance only up to the age of twelve. The Lewis Bill proposed the simplest solution: that children stay in school up to the age of fourteen. To insure that every child had at least an eighth-grade education, the superintendents asked that working children between the ages of fourteen and sixteen who had not been graduated from the eighth grade be required to attend night schools. To bypass the rural legislative barrier, this night school provision was made applicable to first- and second-class cities only.[68]

Although the Lewis Bill passed the Senate unanimously, it was voted down in the Assembly 66 to 46. Assemblyman Finch immediately made a successful motion for a reconsideration of the vote. When the lower house adjourned, he telephoned the Child Labor Committee in New York and told them to get in touch with the governor immediately, alerting them that the session would end in two days. Several committee members went to Albany and persuaded Odell to send an emergency message to both houses urging passage of the Lewis Bill. Picking up the cue, the Assembly sent the bill back to the Committee on Public Education with instructions to make a few minor changes. Emerging from committee on the last day of the session accompanied by the governor's message, the bill was passed by both houses and became law on May 7, 1903. The education bill's difficulty in the Assembly resulted from rural opposition to the increased school attendance requirements for twelve- and thirteen-year-olds. Rural children of that age were more likely to work on farms (which was legal) than to seek illegal factory employment, and the new law would simultaneously deprive farmers of labor and raise school expenses. Final passage came because of increased pressure from the school superintendents and the governor.[69]

Four child labor bills—the revisions of the factory and mercantile laws, the Penal Code change, and the education amendment—passed the 1903 legislature without significant opposition, but reformers' attempts to regulate street work ran into severe resistance. Drafted entirely by the Child Labor Committee, the Hill Street Trades Bill applied only to first-class cities, and was clearly intended as an attack upon the New York City street trades problem. Although Buffalo would be affected, its street difficulties were not so severe as those in the metropolitan area. The controls set up by the bill were simple: all children under the age of twelve would be prohibited from working as newsboys, bootblacks, peddlers, or street vendors. Between the ages of twelve and fourteen, street traders were to obtain a permit and badge from the school authorities with documentation and procedure similar to those required for an employment certificate. All street work for those under sixteen was banned after 9:00 P.M., after which child violators would be arrested. Parents who did not prevent their children from engaging in illegal street work were subject to fine.[70]

Much of the opposition to street trades regulation came from Elbridge Gerry of the Society for the Prevention of Cruelty to Children, who regarded the new proposal as a threat to his organization. Gerry's proprietary attitude toward street children did not endear him to a delegation of Child Labor Committee members present at a hearing before the Senate Committee on the Judiciary on March 4, 1903. Robert Hunter, Felix Adler, Samuel B. Donnelly, J. G. Phelps Stokes, Ernest Poole, and John Elliot saw Gerry jump to his feet within seconds after Senator Edgar T. Brackett had opened the hearing. The proposed legislation was unnecessary, Gerry said: Section 292 of the Penal Code already prohibited children under sixteen from peddling. Admitting that violations of the Penal Code were occurring, Gerry, addressing the committee, generously offered to solve the whole problem himself.

> If the distinguished gentlemen . . . here . . . for whom I have
> the greatest respect and who are competent to do admirable work

in their own line of occupation will simply turn these children [who violate the Penal Code] over to the police, the Society which I represent will take care of them.[71]

Perhaps some of the Child Labor Committee recalled what their investigator, Francis H. Nichols, had reported about the Gerry Society when he conducted a study of New York City bootblacks in February, 1903. Nichols found that

> the one great enemy of the Italian child bootblack is the Gerry Society. [So were the Greeks, whose shoeshine stands were driving the itinerant shine boys out of business.] Every once in a while an agent of the . . . Society appears among a group of little boys playing cards or tossing pennies. . . . He deftly seizes one of the group and carries him away. . . . In a few hours the bootblack is committed to some reform institution on the charge of gambling or vagrancy. Here he associates for several months with criminals older . . . than himself, and then returns to take up the old life again, equipped with a more comprehensive knowledge of vice than he ever possessed before. This is done in conformity to the Gerry Society's system of "making an example."[72]

Regulation of street traders was particularly offensive to Gerry because it included newsboys. Charging that the bill would place the newsboy "under a system of espionage," and would make him a "suspicious person" and a "presumptive criminal in advance by being badged and marked," Gerry truthfully claimed that not all newsboys were neglected or vicious. He believed that each case should be decided individually, and that his society was best equipped to perform the task.[73]

Although many of the child labor reformers themselves used the case approach in drafting their patchwork quilt of legislation—often because of political imperatives, they favored state control through legislation. Gerry had sponsored other regulatory measures in the past, but he would have none of them where his own interests were concerned. To him the street trades were comparatively healthful occupations. He lamented the fact that children were "to be shut up by this badge system. I wish you could see them in their hot tenements. They cannot go out into the fresh air of heaven." The New York *Evening Post* commented that the Gerry Society, "although a noble institution . . . has been under such eccentricities of management as to be at cross purposes with almost every institution in the state . . . and at loggerheads with public opinion as well."[74]

Eccentric or not, Gerry's testimony hurt the street trades bill. An even heavier gun was being wheeled into position. Hardly had Gerry finished his indictment when the President of the SPCC, John D. Lindsay, began reading a letter from three judges of the New York City Court of Special Sessions in which the Hill Street Trades Bill was unreservedly damned. They complained that the Children's Court (a branch of Special Sessions created in 1902) could dispose of only 75 per cent of its case load in an eight-hour day, and if the Hill Bill were to pass, the court would experience a 50 per cent increase in its work. According to Judge Julius M. Mayer the bill would create incredible complexities of procedure. Under the proposed statute, parents could be held liable and since the Children's Court had no jurisdiction to try persons over sixteen, the child guilty of violating the law would be tried in his chambers while the parents' case was being heard in the Court of Special Sessions. Judge Mayer's comment that he could only "imagine the . . . inconvenience of many of the families involved" led Mornay Williams to remark acidly that this was "not a bill for the relief of the Court of Special Sessions." Mayer, who interestingly enough had been one of the signers of the Child Labor Committee's 1902 Memorial, had other objections. One section of the Hill Bill stated that once a parent had been officially warned of his child's illegal street trades work, the mere finding of the child at work would be presumptive evidence of the parent's guilt; in other words, the courts could not judge each case on its merits but must infer parental guilt from the fact of the child's employment. To Mayer and his colleagues this provision was "exceedingly dangerous and vicious." Thus the first attempt to get away from the case method and improve enforcement by providing a readily ascertainable test of parental complicity was branded as "a dangerous legislative expedient to be resorted [to] only on rare occasions." Judge Mayer justifiably labelled other provisions of the bill ambiguous. One section, for example, empowered the courts to deal with illegally employed street children "to the same extent as now or hereafter may be authorized in the case of truant or pauper children." To Mayer "the provision 'or hereafter' [was] . . . of course absurd as a piece of legislation." He also inveighed against loose references which "constantly embarrass the Courts in their construction of statutes," yet when the reformers created a precise test as in the presumption of parental guilt, Judge Mayer condemned their action. The clinching argument was the judges' claim that the bill would cost New York City more money.[75]

The proponents knew that now their problem was not to save the Hill Bill but to obtain some form of street trades regulation. When

Felix Adler rose to answer Elbridge Gerry, the Senate Judiciary Committee had already reduced the minimum age for street trades work from twelve to ten. Adler, therefore, directed his rebuttal against Gerry's contention that no legislation was necessary. If Gerry could lament the plight of little children barred from street work and shut up in hot tenements, Adler could ask the senators to

> think of those children under ten being allowed to be out at four o'clock in the morning, in a cold winter's morning, waiting for the newspapers to be delivered, and remaining in the streets until midnight. . . . Is that the kind of business we want to encourage little children in? I cannot help expressing my surprise that the Commodore [Gerry] who is so noted and so distinguished for his accuracy, should not be as accurate in his description of the newsboy's life. I am quite sure if his social information was as accurate as his legal information evidently is he would not have represented the life of the newsboy as the stepping stone to a subsequent honorable career.

In reply to Gerry's hoary argument that some of New York's most successful men had once been newsboys, Adler produced statistics showing that a large proportion of the inmates of the state's prisons and reform schools had also sold papers.[76]

The judges' objections received short shrift from the Child Labor Committee. To Mornay Williams the proposed law was "an act for the protection of children . . . and even if it does throw more labor upon the Court, it is not a matter with which I concern myself very much." Rising to support the Child Labor Committee, Samuel Gompers recalled from long experience that "there has never yet been a bill introduced to save the children from . . . exploitation . . . but what the legal technical objections have been urged. . . . We are not straining at a gnat; we are not fighting for the shadow, we want the substance." Robert Hunter ended the hearing with an impassioned appeal to the legislators to get the bill "out of the committee and let the kids have a fair chance. We have our hearts in this thing. We have worked night and day on this thing to put it through. We took the little children in our arms and slept with them and Mr. Gerry makes the greatest mistake in his grand career when he opposes a thing as humane as this."[77]

The Child Labor Committee continued its attack on the Gerry Society in the press. While agreeing with the SPCC that there was nothing intrinsically wrong with selling newspapers, the reformers pointed out "that the temptations inseparable from such work are so great that no child under ten should be permitted to engage in it." The committee assured readers of the *New York Times* that about 75 per cent of the newsboys who worked at night "have the most loathsome of all diseases by the time they are fifteen years of age." In the hearing Gerry suggested that the existing Penal Code was sufficient to regulate street trading; in answer the committee produced a statement from within the Commodore's own ranks. According to the superintendent of the Brooklyn SPCC, his branch

> had tried to put a stop to the evil [of street trading] here in Brooklyn in many ways in the past, but we have encountered obstacles in the shape of Magistrates. . . . English cities, and in this country Boston, have attempted to regulate street trades by the general provisions of the Penal Code; but have within the last ten years abandoned this attempt and have adopted the License [or badge] System.[78]

When the smoke had cleared, the Child Labor Committee had an emasculated street trades bill. Applying to first-class cities only, it prohibited boys under ten and girls under sixteen from selling newspapers in the streets. Newsboys between the ages of ten and fourteen were required to obtain a badge and permit, but no formal documentation of age was required; in fact, a school official could issue the badge on receipt of "satisfactory" proof of age. Other amendments eliminated the original provision of parental responsibility, authorized badged newsboys to sell until 10:00 P.M. instead of 9:00 P.M., and put enforcement in the hands of the police. All other forms of street trading were left unregulated. It was a weak bill; perhaps Hunter was thinking of it when he wrote that the country was going through "a transitional period in which the old individualistic ideas are still strong and the social ones . . . vague and groping."[79]

Actually, the passage of any street trades law was a triumph for the Child Labor Committee; it was the first such law in the nation.[80] Hunter's fledgling committee had conducted a difficult legislative campaign and emerged with the passage of all five bills in which his group was interested. In less than a year the Child Labor Committee had helped bring about more significant changes in New York's child labor laws than had occurred in the preceding century. It was a good record. "At the outset," wrote Assemblyman Finch to Hunter, "I found it to be the almost universal opinion held by members of the legislature that the legislation was too advanced, and would never be enacted into law. That the fortunate contrary result was obtained was due solely to the magnificent campaign waged by you." Hunter thought the new labor laws would protect at least 93,000 of the state's children and that 231,000 would benefit from the Lewis Act on compulsory education. This was a substantial achievement for an inexperienced pressure group, and had been accomplished at a cost of $5,500.[81] Even President Roosevelt was impressed; he wrote Fred S. Hall:

> I heartily congratulate you upon the fact that we now have, in New York State, child labor laws, which I believe can be enforced. It is of the utmost importance that these laws shall not be left idle on the statute books. Your committee has been instrumental in securing their passage, and I wish you God-speed in your efforts to complete the great service you have thereby rendered the community.[82]

At least one member of the Child Labor Committee knew how little the new laws might actually mean. "The child labor question in New York," William English Walling observed, "is . . . not to be solved in one year or at one session of the legislature."[83] With astute political insight, Roosevelt had put his finger on the unanswered question: could public outrage be sustained long enough to insure adequate enforcement?

I have met dreamers before. Young men who are going to change everything by impracticable means . . . I was a dreamer myself, when I was a young man, but I am a practical man now.

—JOHN McMACKIN, *Commissioner of Labor, State of New York*, Speech before the Central Federated Union of New York City, December 25, 1903.

The experimental development of legislation to remedy social adversity in Wisconsin was of great value and was quoted in support of the New York legislation, even though in Wisconsin it was of lesser scope. But New York! If it could be done there, it could be done anywhere.

—FRANCES PERKINS, *The Roosevelt I Knew*

IV. Success in the Factories

Since the reformers were attempting to enforce their new laws within the nation's largest industrial state, the sheer number of factories should have been sufficient to give them a feeling of hopelessness: in 1900 the State of New York had 79,000 factories employing over a million persons. Of these workers, the Chief Factory Inspector claimed that 50,000 were children under eighteen. His was a conservative estimate, for he based it on a figure of 35,000 such children actually discovered by factory inspectors and then he added an extra 50 per cent for uninspected factories. Considering that the inspectors checked less than one-third of the state's industrial establishments in 1900,[1] the figure could have been as high as 75,000 children, or, allowing for the rare visits of inspectors to the factories they did inspect and the superior techniques developed by some employers for befuddling them when they came, even higher. The factory inspector's findings showed that it was routine to use children under sixteen in industries throughout the state; youngsters were found working in a Gloversville stove polish factory, a Schenectady boiler plant, a Buffalo blast furnace factory, a Victory Mills woolen mill, a Nyack hosiery mill, a Binghamton cheese factory, a Lowville cannery, a Troy laundry, a Penn Yann printing plant, a Rochester shoe factory, and a Canandaigua sheet metal company. Conditions in many of the factories where children worked were abominable. The factories were dirty, inadequately ventilated against poisonous fumes and dust, and without fire protection. The child workers often performed in cramped or stooped positions for hours at a time at monotonous and repetitive tasks or on particularly dangerous machinery.[2]

For the administration and enforcement of the new child labor legislation, New York relied upon four principal agencies. One was the Department of Labor, which through its Bureau of Factory Inspection was charged with investigation of factories and tenement manufacture. Another was the Department of Education whose truant officers were to enforce the Compulsory Education Law. The various boards of health issued all employment certificates and were to enforce the child labor laws in department stores, while the police departments were to check on violations of the street trades law.

Even the most effective of these four agencies, the Bureau of Factory Inspection, was an extremely weak reed. Difficulty in enforcing the Finch-Hill Factory Act stemmed from the bureau's lack of power and competent personnel. State Labor Commissioner John McMackin was entirely correct when he complained that he could not inspect all the factories from Manhattan to Niagara Falls with just thirty-seven inspectors. Florence Kelley thought that five hundred inspectors, two hundred in New York City and the rest upstate, might be able to do the job *if* tenement manufacturing were abolished.[3] Other problems resulted from evasions and violations of the law by the manufacturers. Factory inspectors found employers who falsified the registers listing their child workers. Some of the ever-cooperative notaries public were still attesting to parental affidavits falsely swearing that the child was sixteen years old, thus beyond the reach of the child labor laws. These affidavits, a logical means of evasion for a fourteen- or fifteen-year-old with inadequate schooling, were illegal, but as McMackin continually pointed out, with only thirty-seven factory inspectors there was no time "to hunt up the evidence that would disprove such false affidavits." Commissioner McMackin's dilemma was clear: he first claimed that child labor had been reduced in the fourteen- to sixteen-year group because only 13,385 such children were found in 1904 as compared to 18,160 in 1903, but he then had to admit that these figures were unreliable because of the widespread use of false sixteen-year affidavits by fourteen- and fifteen-year-olds.[4] Still other employers accepted the certificate of attendance issued by principals of night schools as if it were a legal employment certificate. Vacation working papers for fourteen-year-olds in factories had been declared illegal in 1903, but many employers continued to accept them. The new nine-hour law for children under sixteen was ineffective: a large majority of the factories continued to work the youngsters ten hours. During

1904 the Bureau of Factory Inspection issued 1,586 orders lowering the working hours to nine, better than four orders a day.[5] As late as 1912 there was no law requiring the builder of a new factory to notify the Bureau of Factory Inspection. As a result, some factories ran for years without being inspected.[6]

The general procedure for inspecting factories made it almost certain that the inspectors would find only the obvious violations and practically impossible for them to obtain convictions. When an inspector arrived at a factory his instructions were to report to the owner's office, and while the inspector passed the time of day in the office, the switchboard could easily alert the shop. Sometimes the child workers were rushed into a freight elevator and lowered between floors until the inspector had gone.[7] When a factory inspector did discover an offense, he was required to report it and then *return later* to the factory with a second inspector who must also witness the violation. Assuming that the illegally employed child had not vanished by the time the two inspectors returned, they would then appear before the police magistrate's court or the Court of Special Sessions with evidence of a violation. Instead of fining the employer immediately, the court normally granted him time to correct the trouble. Upon expiration of the time limit another inspection was made, and if the employer had complied with the law, the charges were dropped. An employer risked little by ignoring the child labor laws. During 1903, 119 prosecutions were started for violations of the entire factory law (including child labor), but only 46 convictions resulted. In 1904, only 49 prosecutions were begun, 25 convictions obtained, and $630 levied in fines. "The law," said McMackin, "is an excellent one, but this Department cannot expect to thoroughly enforce it unless it is furnished with the necessary tools."[8] As the Child Labor Committee watched its potentially powerful enactments flounder, members decided that the major obstacle to enforcement was not the courts, the shortage of factory inspectors, or public apathy, but the Commissioner of Labor himself. If measures would not work, a man must be responsible.

In 1904 the New York Child Labor Committee launched a determined campaign against the reappointment of John McMackin whose term as Commissioner of Labor would expire in May, 1905. Joining the committee in the fight was much of organized labor, which had long resented McMackin's rise to a position of authority. In 1899 when Theodore Roosevelt appointed McMackin to the post of Commissioner of Labor Statistics, labor leaders branded the choice an "insult to organized labor." A former house painter who had not worked at his trade for fifteen years and did not belong to any trade union, McMackin was charged with being nothing more than a party hack for Platt's Republican machine. Roosevelt defended McMackin's original appointment on the grounds that having served as Deputy Commissioner of Labor Statistics, he had more experience than the other candidates. Actually Roosevelt made the appointment at Platt's dictation, a fact that probably moved the Governor to follow labor's wishes in his next major state appointment—that of John Williams of the Carpenters' Union as Chief Factory Inspector. Williams turned out to be an excellent choice, but McMackin remained *persona non grata* to labor, particularly after Governor Odell named him to head the new Department of Labor in 1901.[9]

The Child Labor Committee scored McMackin in the press charging that his motive for not enforcing the child labor laws was graft, "the same which enabled saloons and gambling houses to remain open in violation of the law."[10] On December 18, 1904, in a speech before the Central Federated Union of New York City, Robert Hunter denounced the Labor Commissioner as a "time-server and seat warmer."[11] More specific charges followed in a thirty-page indictment of McMackin's administration sent by the Child Labor Committee to Frank W. Higgins shortly after he became governor in 1905. The authors, V. Everit Macy, J. W. Sullivan, and Hunter, charged the Labor Commissioner with deliberately refusing to perform his duties. In 1902 when the Child Labor Committee had shown McMackin the results of the Marot investigation, they claimed that he had blamed loopholes in the child labor laws, but when the laws were changed in 1903, the commissioner found a new "excuse" for his failure to enforce them: too few men and no attorney to help prosecute employers. The committee then tried to get more factory inspectors appointed. Failing, it minimized the need, saying that "it has never been our belief that Mr. McMackin could not, if he wished to do so, enforce the law." (Its determination to have McMackin fired carried the committee far from the facts; Hunter knew perfectly well what thirty-seven inspectors could accomplish in a state the size of New York.) To meet McMackin's request for an attorney, the committee persuaded the District Attorney of New York County, William Travers Jerome, to appoint Keyran J. O'Connor legal assistant to the Labor Department. After this appointment, the committee indictment continued, "seven months passed, and inquiry brought out the fact that there had been only one case, involving two children, brought to the attention of the District Attorney during this time."[12] In an attempt to prove his case against the child labor reformers, McMackin dispatched his own open letter to the governor. Although the letter was well organized and superficially convincing, McMackin's argument that conditions were good could not be sustained. "The small proportion of child labor in New York State," said the commissioner, "demonstrates clearly that our people . . . have no desire to put their children at work until . . . the age of 16." Thousands of tenement workrooms gave the lie to this assertion. The reformers could see no reason for celebration when even the conservative Twelfth Census reported over 55,000 boys and 36,000 girls under fifteen at work in the Empire State.[13]

The Child Labor Committee accused McMackin of permitting child labor in upstate canneries, but the commissioner contended that at the time the committee had found the children working there, his entire force was centered in New York City checking on violations of the eight-hour and alien-labor laws. According to the committee McMackin should bear full responsibility for a disastrous fire at the Brooklyn Chair Company in February, 1904, but in reply he cited a legal opinion that his department did not have jurisdiction over fire inspections. His adversaries then insinuated that he had obtained the opinion after the fire and dated it earlier. Stung by Robert Hunter's charge that the only prosecutions for dangerous machinery conducted by the Labor Department in 1904 were against "six poor Jews on the East Side," McMackin expressed amazement that "the Chairman [of the Child Labor Committee] should so far forget himself as to make an appeal to race prejudice."[14] In answer to the committee's contention that he had failed to use the attorney whom he himself had requested, McMackin offered a series of letters written to Keyran J. O'Connor by Assistant First Deputy Commissioner of Labor Thomas A. Keith. On three occasions Keith had attempted to see O'Connor, but "Mr. O'Connor not only did not provide for the conference requested, but did not even deign to acknowledge receipt of the letters." The Child Labor Committee, however, chose to rely upon William T. Jerome's statement that O'Connor had been consulted only once by the Labor Department.[15]

McMackin's chief grievance was that the Child Labor Committee had gone off on its own and had not given his department a fair chance to show what it could do. If violations of the law had been reported "the Department would have dealt with them instantly, and there would not have been any cause for complaint." Yet it was precisely because of McMackin, the committee replied, that the child labor reformers were forced to turn elsewhere. His department was not efficient. Moreover, how could the labor commissioner deal "instantly" with complaints when he had so often described the state courts as inclined "to dismiss complaints against manufacturers charged with violating the child labor law without scarcely giving the deputies a hearing"? McMackin was indeed reluctant to bring cases into court. In December, 1904, he told the *New York Times* that his department's policy was simply to order illegally employed children discharged rather than prosecute manufacturers who were "generally . . . unfamiliar with the provisions of the new law." (McMackin had previously distributed thirty thousand poster-sized copies of the revised factory laws to employers.)[16] To the Child Labor Committee one case, that of the Chelsea Jute Mills of Brooklyn, symbolized McMackin's inadequate approach to the problem of child labor and branded him an unfit Commissioner of Labor.

In 1903 a relief society had drawn the committee's attention to child labor in the Chelsea Jute Mills. The company, it was alleged, employed Irish, Italian, and German children as young as ten. When it requested the Labor Department to make an investigation, the Child Labor Committee met with what it regarded as an administrative runaround. McMackin refused to act; his defense was the hopelessness of proving a case against "sixteen" year-old immigrant children armed with false parental affidavits whose birth certificates could not be found. The state attorney general had ruled that in order to convict an employer McMackin must prove that the affidavits were false. Even though in 1900 the Bureau of Factory Inspection had discovered twenty-two violations of the labor law in the Chelsea Mills, McMackin now declared that "the Chelsea Jute people are doing all that can possibly be expected of them to comply with the provisions of the law."[17] Rebuffed by the Labor Department, the committee got the New York City Board of Education to send truant officers to the mill. They found

> hundreds of little boys and girls, so childish in appearance, in the expression of their faces, that it was possible only by the strongest self-control to conceal the evidence of emotion their presence under such conditions aroused. . . . In one room dozens of them were in their bare feet, running through water on the floor to the depth of about half an inch. The material at this point of manufacture had to be kept moist. Such tiny looking things, with bodies that looked as if they might be crushed between one's hands.[18]

Working in close cooperation, the Child Labor Committee and the truant officers managed to find one child with a legitimate birth certificate. Annie Ventre had gone to work in the Chelsea Mills on April 7, 1903, with a parental affidavit stating she was sixteen years old. By checking the register of her last school and by turning up her birth certificate the reformers proved that she was only eleven years old—a fact finally admitted by her parents. With this evidence the Board of Education sued the mill for violating the Compulsory Education Law. During the trial the prosecution revealed that in addition to having been illegally employed at the age of eleven, Annie had been working more than ten and a half hours a day.[19] By allowing her to work the Chelsea Mills had violated three regulations: the Compulsory Education Law prohibiting the employment of children under fourteen during the school term, the provision of the Factory Law against the employment of such children in factories, and the provision against work in excess of nine hours a day for children under sixteen.

The company's defense maintained that the Compulsory Education Law was "an unwarranted, illegal and unconstitutional deprivation of their liberties," that the provision on illegal employment was outside the normal scope of a school law, and that the company was absolved from responsibility because it had accepted in good faith the statement of Annie Ventre's parents regarding her age.[20] Justice Roesch rejected the defendant's claims. In the first place, the judge said, the applicable section of the Compulsory Education Law was clearly constitutional under the police power of the state, and the illegal employment provision was within the scope of an education law; the prohibition of child labor and the enforcement of compulsory education were complementary rather than opposing forces. Most significantly, the court dismissed the employer's contention that he had acted in good faith, thereby upholding the new feature of the 1903 legislation which made illegal employment prima facie evidence of the employer's guilt. "Good faith," said Roesch, "could easily be alleged and seldom disproved." When Annie Ventre appeared in court, Roesch described her as "a living picture of the results of child labor in a factory at a delicate age" whose "very appearance . . . refuted her statement" that she was sixteen. Summing up, the judge declared that in upholding the new law he was "impelled solely by principles conservative of the supreme welfare," and anxious to make it "impossible to enfeeble and deteriorate the future citizenship of the state."[21]

The Chelsea Jute Mills paid a fine of fifty dollars and did not appeal. Even though the company had bitterly contested the case, it offered to cooperate with the education authorities in dismissing other illegally employed children. A few months later, however, Felix Adler of the Child Labor Committee reported that there were still eighty-five children under fourteen at work in the Chelsea Jute Mills,[22] but notwithstanding Judge Roesch's sentiments, the child labor reformers were still required to find birth certificates to prove that all of them who claimed to be sixteen had been illegally employed. Even more infuriating to the frustrated Child Labor Committee was the knowledge that they had won their case under the education law, not the labor law, and with the help of truant officers rather than factory inspectors. Under McMackin's procedure a factory would be visited and the employer told to get rid of his underage children. The next day they would return to work because the owner knew that in all probability the inspector would not return for a year. When manufacturers were faced with a rush season, they did not hesitate to hire large numbers of children secure in the knowledge that even if their presence were discovered, the employers would only be ordered to discharge them. The Labor Commissioner's answer that he had to enforce fifty-four sections of the labor law besides the one on child labor did not satisfy the committee. At this point nothing would have. Citing statistical arguments, the child labor group blamed McMackin's poor administration of the department for the increase in the total number of reported factory and mine injuries from 2,373 in 1900 to 5,660 in 1903. The commissioner's plea that that statistic merely represented more efficient reporting of accidents fell on deaf ears.[23] To trump McMackin's final card, the reformers pointed to his total of reported labor law violations for 1903—50,572—and then to his total convictions—39—and rested their case. By this time they had persuaded thirty-five other organizations including the Brooklyn Central Labor Union, the Rochester Machinists Union, the Yonkers Building Trades Council, the Buffalo Consumers' League, and the State Congress of the Knights of Labor to join them in petitioning for McMackin's removal.[24]

The Child Labor Committee was finally successful. On May 4, 1905, Governor Higgins nominated P. Tecumseh Sherman, son of the Civil War general, as Commissioner of Labor; the committee stated that although it had not suggested his name it was most pleased with the appointment.[25] P. T. Sherman served as Commissioner of Labor only from May 8, 1905, to October 3, 1907, but during his short administration he succeeded in raising the number of factory inspectors from thirty-seven to fifty and in obtaining some sorely needed salary increases for his men. He also doubled the Bureau of Factory Inspection's office force and revised its obsolete system of files and records. In the spring of 1906, Sherman with the help of the Child Labor Committee prevented the legislature from cutting his Labor Department budget of $157,000 back to $124,940, a figure $8,000 less than the 1905 budget.[26] In contrast to McMackin's last full year in office (1904) during which 49 prosecutions had been started and 25 convictions obtained with fines totaling $630, Sherman in his last year (1907) prosecuted 443 employers and secured 294 convictions with fines of $3,835. Sherman, however, had been the first to recognize that the defects in the Labor Department were not entirely the fault of John McMackin. "That it has failed at many points is . . . true," he declared, "but . . . with its present field force it is absolutely impossible for it to enforce the provisions of the law . . . even to a reasonable extent." He told the Consumers' League that between five and ten thousand New York City manufacturers regularly violated the sixty-hour-week law. While in 1904 McMackin's inspectors had found 13,385 children between the ages of fourteen and sixteen at work, in 1907 Sherman's men discovered 14,817.[27] Sherman's progress in bringing more child labor to light elicited praise from the reformers: "He has in ten months made [such] a record in inspections and prosecutions that . . . if he is given the funds he will give to these . . . laws an enforcement unknown hitherto," the Child Labor Committee announced enthusiastically.[28]

During the course of the McMackin fight the NYCLC realized that a long and vigilant campaign of public education would be necessary if the new laws were to be effective. The committee had been set up as a temporary group, a subsidiary of the Association of Neighborhood Workers, and still resembled a group organized to accomplish one aim: the enactment of the 1903 legislation. In 1905 the resignation of the committee's only salaried member, Secretary Fred S. Hall, forced it to decide whether it would continue. When the committee hired George Albert Hall (Fred Hall's twenty-six-year-old brother) as secretary on June 8, 1905, it had, in effect, chosen permanence.[29] On November 15, 1907, the Committee confirmed its new status by drawing up a constitution, adopting by-laws and officially incorporating as the New York Child Labor Committee.[30] The 1907 Constitution created a policy-making board of twenty directors elected at the annual membership meeting. The directors elected the chairman, the vice-chairman, and the treasurer from among themselves and appointed the paid secretary on a yearly basis. Three standing committees were authorized: an executive committee charged with policy making, the presentation of a yearly legislative program, and the supervision of staff work; a finance committee to supervise the collection and investment of funds; and a law committee to draft bills for presentation to the legislature. For the first time since 1902 the NYCLC stated its aims:

To promote the welfare of society with respect to the employment of children in gainful occupations; to investigate and report the facts concerning child labor; to raise the standard of parental responsibility with respect to the employment of children; to assist in protecting children, by suitable legislation, against premature or otherwise injurious employment, and to aid in securing for them an opportunity for elementary education and physical development sufficient for the demands of citizenship and the requirements of industrial efficiency; and to aid in promoting the enforcement of laws relating to child labor.[31]

As a temporary organization the NYCLC's work had been centered on its immediate surroundings—metropolitan New York, but when it became a permanent committee it extended its activities throughout the state. In 1910 the committee hired a field secretary, Zenas L. Potter, who helped organize subsidiary child labor associations in Rochester and Buffalo. By 1912 he had enlisted active workers in Syracuse and Elmira. The policy decisions of these groups were subject to the approval of the NYCLC; their charters stated that no action could be taken to secure new laws or to obtain legal interpretations of old ones without permission from the "home office." The upstate members were at a certain disadvantage since all of the NYCLC meetings were held in New York City, but they did receive all the minutes and written reports and maintained contact with metropolitan members when they met at legislative hearings in Albany.[32]

Permanence also made possible a more systematic appeal for money. The overall financial picture indicated that the public was willing to sustain the NYCLC; in 1905 contributions totaled $5,710; in 1909, $7,025; in 1912, $12,776; and in 1920, $14,571. Until 1929 the committee's receipts averaged about $3,000 a year less than its expenses and the difference was made up by drawing on an occasional legacy or foundation grant.[33] Occasionally, even in predepression days, the group had to meet a financial crisis. In 1914, for example, George Alger, Lillian Wald, and Manfred Ehrich held an emergency session and decided to ask every member for an extra hundred dollars. In addition to its cash contributions, prominent New York City attorneys such as George Alger, Mornay Williams, Manfred Ehrich, and Frederick A. O. Schwarz donated their legal advice and bill-drafting services.

This growing financial support enabled the committee to start a scholarship program for potential child laborers in New York City in October, 1905. One of the oldest arguments against child labor legislation had been that the earnings of many children were necessary to the welfare of their families. Commissioner of Labor Sherman estimated that the financial loss to families of children ordered discharged from factories under the child labor laws was about three dollars a week. He offered to have his inspectors report any hardship cases directly to the NYCLC. The committee began making weekly payments of one to three dollars to these families; this money would make it possible for a child to stay in school until he could meet the educational requirements for an employment certificate. If a family appeared to need more money than the NYCLC could provide, the case was referred to a regular relief society. The scholarships went "almost entirely to widows or deserted women, or families in which the father was permanently disabled through sickness or accident."[34] Even before the depression there was "Mrs. S." who,

> eager to make a home for Thomas, her orphan grandson . . . goes out every day with her little basket of matches, candles and tooth picks to peddle. Her small earnings are supplemented by his two older sisters who are factory workers, but the old grandmother has been finding it increasingly difficult to get money to buy shoes and clothing for the boy. . . . After the death of his parents, Thomas had spent six years away from his home, so he is retarded in school and unable to obtain working papers for eight months. To cover that period a scholarship has been arranged and the boy, who has a good mind, is attending school regularly.

And there was Sadie, whose parents died in Russia. When she was nine an aunt brought her to this country.

> For a few years the aunt's grown sons willingly supported their mother and the little cousin, but as Sadie grew bigger and living costs increased, they rebelled. . . . [Sadie] was blamed for the shortage in income and her life was made miserable. [She] . . . often came breakfastless to school. . . . Since a scholarship has been given to this girl the sullen discontent has disappeared. Her . . . school work is steadily improving and in a few months she will be able to . . . go to work lawfully.

Names were submitted by school officials and charitable organizations; the NYCLC turned down 75 per cent of the recommendations because either there was no real need for the child's earnings, or the child was under fourteen, or the family was already receiving charity. To receive his weekly payment, the scholarship child visited the NYCLC office and presented a signed school attendance card. During the first seven years of the program 494 families received weekly payments extending over periods of three to twenty months; before the

First World War the NYCLC was spending about $3,000 a year on such work. While the number of scholarships granted was quite small in comparison to the need, the NYCLC did allocate a generous portion of its budget to the program. The depression of the 1930's brought the scholarship program to an end. The rapid rise in unemployment forced families "where the need formerly would have been covered by a small sum . . . to apply to relief societies for . . . larger sums." Contributions to the NYCLC dropped from $15,884.75 in 1929 to $7,093.25 in 1935; nevertheless, the scholarship program struggled on with help from the Havens Relief Fund Society, the Rotary Club of New York, the *Herald Tribune* Fresh Air Fund, the Jewish Big Sisters, and the Children's Aid Society,[35] until 1933 when the Board of Directors of the NYCLC voted to stop the scholarship work. In 1935 Secretary Hall was forced to take the unique position of turning down money for child labor scholarships. "The great decrease in the number of children leaving school to go to work . . . due to lack of jobs," he explained to the Havens Relief Fund Society, "augmented by the requirements of the N.R.A. which . . . [prohibited] in most instances, child employment under sixteen . . . [has] reduced to a negligible number the calls . . . for scholarships."[36]

The activities of the Child Labor Committee in the state of New York reminded Americans that child labor was a problem outside the South. After the NYCLC's legislative triumph of 1903, Edgar Gardner Murphy, a leading Southern child labor reformer, came to New York to enlist the committee's aid in forming a national organization. Discussions between Murphy and Dr. Felix Adler of the New York group led to the appointment of an organizational committee composed of William H. Baldwin, Florence Kelley, and Adler, which sent out letters proposing the creation of a National Child Labor Committee. Receiving a favorable response, on April 15, 1904, Murphy and the New Yorkers proclaimed the National Child Labor Committee with headquarters in New York City and Felix Adler as the first Chairman.[37] In spite of its help in forming the national group, the New York Committee never became a subsidiary division of the National Child Labor Committee, for the latter spent most of its time in states that had not achieved the relatively high legislative standards of New York. Indeed, the two committees clashed bitterly on occasion over appeals for funds made by the National Child Labor Committee to supporters of the New York Committee. The New Yorkers regarded such appeals as completely unjustified since their committee stood the expense for all child labor work carried on in New York. There were policy differences as well. By no means did all of the New York group favor a federal child labor law, nor did they stand united on the later proposal for a constitutional amendment regulating child labor. In 1934 it even became necessary for the two groups to hold a formal conference to iron out differences. However, the National Child Labor Committee did cooperate with the New Yorkers by assisting in investigation and promotion in return for access to the New York sources of information about the state.[38]

One of the first actions taken by the National Child Labor Committee was to take advantage of a growing concern over child labor among churchmen.[39] On May 13, 1906, the National Child Labor Committee organized a "conference of representative clergymen of many denominations" which adopted a series of resolutions. One resolution urged that the national governing bodies of the churches sponsor discussion groups on child labor to give the memberships enough information to deal with the problem "practically in their homes and . . . neighborhoods." The clergymen, including representatives of the Manhattan-Brooklyn Conference of Congregational Churches and the Committee on Applied Christianity of the Congregational Association of New York, also recommended the enactment of a model child labor law by the District of Columbia, the creation of a Federal Children's Bureau, and the establishment of a National Child Labor Sunday when appropriate sermons could be delivered. The federal government, they felt, should do as much for the American child as it did to investigate soils and propagate fish.[40]

The next year the New York committee utilized favorable church sentiment when it joined forces with the Church Association for the Advancement of the Interests of Labor (an Episcopal society whose chapter at St. Michael's Church in New York was particularly active in tenement reform and labor controversies) to obtain passage of a bill establishing an eight-hour day and forty-eight–hour week for factory children under sixteen. By limiting the legal working hours to the period from 8:00 A.M. to 5:00 P.M. (with an hour for lunch), the measure made it possible for the inspectors to assume that any child found working in a factory after 5:00 P.M. was illegally employed. Several manufacturers who opposed the bill succeeded in having the Assembly Committee on Labor and Industries change the legitimate period of work to 7:00 A.M to 7:00 P.M. Taking a middle ground, Labor Commissioner Sherman favored a 7:00 A.M. to 6:00 P.M. period, but as Secretary Hall explained to the New York City Assembly delegation "an eight hour day between limits 12 hours apart would allow so much margin that the temptation to manufacturers to employ their children *more* than eight hours would be very great." The open support of Governor Charles Evans Hughes was decisive in seeing the bill through in its original form.[41]

In spite of the NYCLC's success in obtaining laws regulating child labor, the opposition never ceased trying to weaken existing legislation. In 1905 Robert Hunter succeeded in halting action on the Fitzgerald Bill, a measure that would have allowed any public-school teacher to dismiss pupils and permit them to go to work if she thought they were "backward" in their studies. Hunter maintained that this definition would fit about 200,000 New York school children.[42] Not all opposition to the factory legislation came from employers who wished to hire young children. Indeed, some of the most effective opponents were manufacturers whose opposition resulted not from their desire to hire child workers, but from their conviction that their constitutional rights were being infringed. In 1906 Hunter received a long letter from Joseph L. Gitterman, a New York City manufacturer of tin foil, bottle caps, and collapsible tubes, who did not use illegal child labor. The child labor reformers, he said, were actually injuring the very class they were attempting to help. He wrote:

> I have yet to hear that the average poor man . . . loves his child less than their richer brother or richer sister. The average family in our City could not exist by means of the support of a single worker. Until the worker gets a larger return for his labor . . . child labor will exist. Until the laws of taxation have been changed . . . the poor man will have to send his children to work. Do you really believe that the really worthy poor take charity? . . . This class prefers to have their children go to work rather than receive alms. Yes, the average child wants it because the work is interesting. . . . Every human being longs for independence and it is no wonder that a child should long to help to support rather than be a burden.

Gitterman said that as a "law abiding citizen" he had "cheerfully" complied with the labor laws and "received compensation in the slight cost of . . . accident insurance," but he felt that the removal of children from factories only served to drive them into worse conditions in dressmaking establishments—the factory was better.

> During the hot summer of 1903, on one hot day we had decided to close down certain departments where young girls were employed and [I] . . . had told the foreman. . . . He argued strenuously against this and said—"Why send them home to stuffy

tenements? Here you have high ceilings and air on all sides of the factory. . . . [The girls] . . . will have to go to their stuffy rooms and then will no doubt have to help at cooking or washing. My [own] little ones who are too young to work have it much harder than the girls who are working here."

He contended that rather than propose new laws, the child labor reformers should persuade other states to pass laws similar to those of New York. Until that time manufacturers such as he would have "to meet on one hand the ruinous competition of the European manufacturer and on the other hand the keen competition of those . . . in States where there are no [child labor] laws."[43] J. K. Paulding of the NYCLC assured Gitterman that "with the substance of most of your criticisms . . . there would be no great disagreement on the part of most of the members of our Committee." Of course, there were many honest and humanitarian manufacturers, Paulding argued, but new laws must be obtained simultaneously with the enforcement of old ones. The National Child Labor Committee was working to improve national standards but New York could not afford to wait for other states to catch up.[44] Gitterman's argument that varying state standards gave some manufacturers an unfair competitive edge was true and indicated the need for federal legislation, but there was hesitation on the part of some reformers to raise the specter of federal intervention in state affairs. The South was historically sensitive on this point. Felix Adler, Edgar Gardner Murphy, and others in the National Child Labor Committee were concerned lest Senator Albert J. Beveridge's proposed law to prohibit the use of child labor in the manufacture of goods shipped between states would hurt the chances of achieving a Federal Children's Bureau and cripple the activities of Southern child labor reformers within their states.

Strong opposition to federal legislation had already been aroused. The National Civic Federation, a business-oriented reform group organized at the turn of the century to promote better labor-management relations, whose membership included August Belmont (New York financier), Nicholas Murray Butler (President of Columbia University), Samuel Gompers (President of AFL), Nahum J. Bachelder (Master of the National Grange), and Ellison A. Smyth (President of the South Carolina Cotton Manufacturers Association), was denying the existence of a serious national child labor problem. The NCF contended that in relation to the whole economic life of the country, child labor was "comparatively insignificant" and occurred principally on home farms. The agrarian myth died hard. Long hours of farm work without schooling were somehow considered as more ennobling for a child than the same working conditions in tenements, but as Florence Kelley pointed out, the "children on the southern farms are not school children. They are the 500,000 illiterate children (white and Negro) who disgrace our country."[45] In an attempt to forestall federal regulation of child labor, the NCF advocated uniform child labor laws in all the states and supported higher state compulsory education standards, claiming that children are "in danger of moral degradation when they will not go to school and are not allowed to work."[46] In a further attempt to draw support away from federal regulation, the NCF formed its own Commission on Child Labor to attack the problems of child labor, truancy, industrial training, and compulsory education. Both the National Child Labor Committee and the National Conference of Charities and Correction refused to appoint members to this commission, for, as Felix Adler told August Belmont, the study contemplated by the NCF could "only be done satisfactorily by the Federal Government." Indeed, by this time a governmental investigation of child labor which would culminate in a nineteen-volume report had already been authorized by President Theodore Roosevelt; nevertheless, the NCF Commission on Child Labor was supported by the National Association of Manufacturers, the American Federation of Labor, and the General Federation of Women's Clubs. Ralph Easley of the NCF assured Daniel A. Tompkins, a leading Southern cotton mill owner, that the commission would not include "such radicals as Miss Jane Addams, Miss Florence Kelley, and Mrs. Frederick Nathan [of the Consumers' League]." Alluding to the general purpose of the NCF investigation, Easley noted that "the Beveridge people were very much disturbed about this Commission. . . . They fear that the conservative character of this investigation will nullify the radicalism which they were trying to develop, and I think you will agree with me that *their fears are not groundless* [italics mine]."[47] The activities of the NCF annoyed the National Child Labor Committee, and their spokesman, Samuel McCune Lindsay, contended that although the cotton mills of Ellison A. Smyth, President of the NCF Investigating Commission was reputed to be a model operation, it was "unfortunate when a good mill owner is put forward as a representative of a class and thereby becomes the defender and apologist of conditions which he would not tolerate in his own establishment." Attacking the inconsistency of those who opposed child labor laws, Lindsay noted that "at one point . . . it is said that the enactment of such laws will ruin the cotton mill business on account of the large number of children employed, while at another point the statement is made that the mill owners do not want to employ children, that their labor is unprofitable, and that they really need protection from the parents." Opposition to national regulation of child labor delayed the enactment of a federal child labor law until 1916, but during this time state child labor groups continued their efforts.[48]

In the New York factories accidents were continuing to take their dreary toll. Considering the great variety of perils to which industrial workers were exposed (the factory inspectors' grisly "particulars" of fatal accidents list everything from fireworks explosions to flying boards thrown out by saws, from sulfur dust explosions to bursting boilers), it is not surprising that over fourteen thousand persons of all ages were injured in factories during a typical year, 1908.[49] Of that number 731 were children under eighteen. Most of their injuries came from operating machinery. Some of the injured youngsters were described by plant owners as "not employees," and while this was probably true of a four-year-old boy who fell down an unguarded elevator shaft to his death in a metals factory, one might wonder about the thirteen-year-old who while "playing" under a sawmill was caught in the belt of the main shaft and "hurled to instant death." One sixteen-year-old rack boy in a tin plate factory "fell into a vat of boiling oil; entire body scalded; death ensued following day." An eighteen-year-old baker who was cleaning a moving dough mixer became caught and was "literally ground to pieces." Young children could not be expected to use proper judgment in industrial situations. A fifteen-year-old errand boy attempting to carry a bicycle off a moving elevator fell down the shaft, another fifteen-year-old opening a door to an elevator shaft stepped into thin air, and a fourteen-year-old coil cleaner in an appliance factory was set on fire when the rags he was using to clean the coils ignited from gas flames. He died twenty-two days later. Another eight-year-old was waiting for his parents outside a cannery shed when he crawled under the side of the shed into a sprocket wheel, breaking his skull, arms, and ribs.[50]

Alarmed by these tragedies, the NYCLC pushed for remedial legislation and was largely responsible for the Voss Dangerous Trades Act of 1909. It flatly prohibited employment of children under sixteen in more than thirty occupations specified as dangerous, including the operation of circular saws, planers, picker machines, paper lace machines, burnishing machines, stamping machines and rolling mill machinery. Children were also forbidden to adjust belts on machinery, oil machinery, operate elevators, or work in the manufacture of matches, dynamite, paint, beer, or liquor.[51] One major weakness of the

Voss Act was that it did not include all dangerous occupations. When a child was found working at an *unlisted* hazardous occupation, nothing could be done, and children continued to be hurt on a variety of unlisted machinery such as heeling machines in shoe factories, baling presses, and automatic cutting machines.[52] Reporting to the Factory Investigating Commission, Dr. Charles T. Graham-Rogers, Medical Inspector for the State Labor Department, described his visit to an incandescent mantel factory where

> children were sitting in a frame probably 20 × 30 feet long, lighted with gas flames. The frame is probably 6 or 7 feet wide and these children were sitting right in the midst of the escaping illuminating gas which contains large quantities of carbon monoxide gas, a most dangerous poison because it destroys blood cells. The children were legally employed because they had working certificates, yet it is an occupation I would very much hesitate to put a robust man in to work at.

Secondly, the act forbade children from working only in certain *stages* of the manufacture of some particularly dangerous products; this provision was impossible to enforce. Dr. Graham-Rogers said that there were children under sixteen who, although not working in the actual manufacture of matches, were still packing the finished matches in boxes.

> Q. In the boxes? A. In the boxes, at times—they are exposed to just as much danger as the men who work on the phosphorus machine; they are exposed to just as much danger as the female adults, . . . who sort the matches and put them in the box. Q. They do that with their hands? . . . naked hands? A. Yes. Q. What is the danger? A. The danger is the absorption of this phosphorus. They get phosphorus necrosis. Q. What does that mean in plain English? A. That means, practically, decay of the bone . . . especially of the jaw.[53]

By 1913 two laws had been passed that made possible more effective control of hazardous child employment. One was the Workmen's Compensation Law of 1913 (an earlier such law—the first in the nation—had been enacted in 1910 but was declared unconstitutional by the New York Court of Appeals; the state constitution was then amended to clear the way for a successful law). The other was a 1913 measure allowing the Commissioner of Labor to extend the list of dangerous occupations without separate legislation and to "tag" unguarded machinery so that it could not be used. The availability of workmen's compensation quickly produced more accurate accident figures. While in 1908 the Bureau of Factory Inspection had reported 14,000 injuries to workers of all ages, in 1918 it listed 280,000 industrial accidents and claims for compensation were filed on 51,500 of them at a cost of about $15,500,000.[54]

After the First World War, the NYCLC responded to the urging of one of its younger lawyers, Manfred W. Ehrich, and began a drive to obtain triple compensation for minors under eighteen who were injured while illegally employed. In 1922, the committee submitted a draft of a bill for triple compensation modeled on a similar Wisconsin law to Commissioner of Labor Bernard L. Shientag. Foreseeing legislative difficulties, Shientag advised that the committee seek *double* rather than triple compensation. With the NYCLC's approval he redrafted the measure and sent it to the legislature through the New York State Commission to Examine Laws Relating to Child Welfare, a state body of which George Hall was currently Executive Secretary. As an official recommendation of that quasi-legislative body, it would have a better chance of passage. Introduced in the legislature on March 22, 1923, by Senator Salvatore Cotillo, Chairman of the New York State Commission to Examine Laws Relating to Child Welfare, the Double Compensation Bill nevertheless provoked opposition. Objections were raised by both Raymond V. Ingersoll, Secretary of the City Club of New York and also a member of the NYCLC and Mark A. Daly, lobbyist for the Associated Industries of New York State (a group organized in 1914 representing fifteen hundred of the state's largest employers) who pointed out that employers accepting in good faith the word of a minor that he was *over* eighteen might unjustifiably be held liable under the proposed law.[55] George Alger of the committee argued that the bill was necessary, because the New York Court of Appeals had decided that an illegally employed injured child had to rely on workmen's compensation for redress and thus could not sue separately for damages for negligence. There was a difference, he felt, between employers who conducted their business in compliance with the labor law and those who did not. There was also

a difference between the rights of little children unlawfully employed and the rights of adults in cases of industrial accidents. The infant has far more to surrender of common law right when he comes under the Workmen's Compensation. . . . To take away all the common law rights of these children and give them simply the scanty compensation which their low wages would entitle them to under the Workmen's Compensation . . . would . . . work a distinct injustice.[56]

To meet the objection that there was no protection for employers, the NYCLC agreed to an amendment permitting minors over sixteen to obtain certificates of age from the officer who issued employment certificates. For the under-sixteen group, of course, an employment certificate would provide the necessary proof. With the help of Charles D. Hilles, a friend of the NYCLC who was a power in the Republican Party, the way was cleared and the bill passed the legislature with little difficulty. Signed by Governor Smith on May 21, 1923, the new law stated that compensation and death benefits normally payable under workmen's compensation were to be doubled in the case of an injured minor under eighteen years of age employed in violation of any provision of the labor law. The employer was held personally liable for the amount of the increased compensation and he could not relieve himself from this liability by taking out insurance.[57]

The new law had been in effect only a few months when a sharp attack on its provisions appeared in the *Brooklyn Citizen*. Claiming that the measure was preventing sixteen- to eighteen-year-old boys from learning a trade, the newspaper called for the speedy repeal of "this asinine law." Just five years before, the same newspaper had complained when a New York court permitted a fourteen-year-old girl to sue the Fulton Bag and Cotton Mill for damages because she had been injured while illegally employed. Under the 1913 Workmen's Compensation Law, Mary Wolff would have received about $1,500 for the loss of her right arm, while a suit at law would have produced perhaps $20,000; the *Brooklyn Citizen* felt that the latter award was much too high. Although double compensation actually would produce a lower amount than that likely to be awarded by a jury, the newspaper still opposed it. Other complaints reached Industrial Commissioner Bernard Shientag who went personally to the NYCLC office with reports that many firms were refusing to employ minors under eighteen because of the Double Compensation Law. Actually only three occupations were illegal for sixteen- to eighteen-year-old youngsters and all of them involved the operation of elevators and the cleaning of moving machinery. Yet, in response to pressure from Shientag, the NYCLC began drafting an amendment lowering the age limit for double compensation from eighteen to sixteen until some of the committee members traced Shientag's complaints and discovered that they came from just a few factories, whereupon the amendment plan was dropped.[58]

The Double Compensation Law was successful in accomplishing its main purpose: to reduce *illegal* factory child labor. In 1933 George Hall noted that "employers are beginning to discover that it does not pay to hire children who are forbidden to work by the labor law"; indeed, during the period 1923-31 New York employers had paid a total of $317,052.35 in double compensation awards. The number of such awards to illegally employed youngsters decreased steadily from 43 in 1923 to 4 in 1937, although prior to the depression the yearly figure had stabilized at about 25. The number of compensated accidents to *legally* employed minors under eighteen averaged around 2,000 a year through the 1920's and then dropped sharply in the depression to 473 in 1935. Studying the figures through 1931, Hall noted that 75 per cent of the children had been working less than three months before receiving double compensation for an injury. One girl under sixteen who was hired by a tin can manufacturer to operate a metal stamping press (in violation of the law) "had been working only ten minutes when both her hands caught in the machine, with the result that she had to have both index fingers amputated." The employer paid $2,835.84 for ten minutes work.[59]

While its aim was praiseworthy, the Double Compensation Law actually gave small recompense to injured children. During the mid-thirties, for example, an eleven-year-old boy who lost partial use of each foot in one of the frequent elevator accidents recovered only $394 in double compensation. While some awards were higher, the human cost was difficult to measure as in the case of Joe, who

> managed a real grin in the hospital; but as the Doctor cut through his right arm just above the elbow, in order to free the boy from the roller press in which his arm had been crushed, tears stood in his eyes and his remaining hand was clenched. It took ten minutes for the amputation, but for the twenty minutes before the boy had been suffering untold agony. . . . Joe was employed at a Press down on Hudson Street. He took the job when he was only fifteen, and was working from 8 p.m. to 5 a.m. On the third night in his new job, Joe caught his arm while working at an electric power press and lost his right arm. This accident cost $10,982.40 paid in compensation; but the cost to Joe was his right arm for which he can never find an adequate substitute. Can anyone say that $11,000 was too much to give this boy of fifteen who was put on a power press at which only older persons can legally work, and at night hours which are forbidden by the labor law?[60]

In his study of Workmen's Compensation Laws, Harry Weiss estimated that the average benefits provided to *all* workers in New York State in 1930 amounted to less than 30 per cent of the worker's projected lifetime earnings. Meager as these benefits were, the compensation referees sometimes failed to award them. In August, 1937, the NYCLC challenged twelve single compensation awards to minors under fourteen made during 1936 and succeeded in having nine of them changed to double compensation.[61] The enforcement of the law required constant supervision. In the early 1930's the NYCLC found that the Double Compensation Law applied only to children injured while doing work that violated a provision of the labor law. The rulings and regulations of the Industrial Board, which had the force of law but which were not technically part of the labor law, were thus excluded, a deficiency not remedied until 1935. The two most important developments for the protection of children against accidents in the modern period were the passage of the New York State Sixteen Year School-leaving Age Law in 1935 and the federal Fair Labor Standards Act of 1938. Under the former law, most children under sixteen were kept out of dangerous manufacturing occupations, and under the latter, children under eighteen who were employed by firms engaged in interstate commerce were subject to the hazardous employment rulings of the Federal Children's Bureau as well as to state regulation.

Double compensation was important in cutting down the number of illegally employed factory children, although by the time the law was passed in 1923 the reformers had already achieved a significant reduction. During 1908, 50,396 inspections revealed only 1,633 cases of illegally employed minors. By 1914, 40,996 inspections disclosed only 633 cases, and while it rose again to 1,944 cases in 1920, 62,731 inspections were conducted in that year. Many of these children were over fourteen but had no employment certificates or they were working illegal hours. The number of *recorded* legally employed factory children under sixteen was reduced gradually from 18,169 in 1903, to 13,158 in 1906, 12,330 in 1910, and 11,828 in 1920.[62] As early as 1905 Commissioner of Labor Sherman had reported that the employment of children under fourteen in the larger factories was rare and that most of the problems occurred in tenement shops and smaller manufacturing establishments. The tenements, which will be discussed in another chapter, received some of the illegal child labor being driven out of the factories through relatively more efficient inspection. Manufacturers were becoming less enthusiastic about hiring children. In 1916 an agent of the NYCLC conducted a survey of seventy-one industrial firms in the New York City area to determine their views on child labor. Twenty-seven said they did not hire children because the eight-hour day required by law for children under sixteen made it difficult to fit the young workers into a normal manufacturing schedule; twenty-six others reported that their use of expensive and easily spoiled materials and their contracts with labor unions prevented their use of child labor, and seventeen companies declared that they were against child labor on principle.[63] In a survey of forty-three employers conducted for the Associated Industries of New York State by Joseph P. Murphy, Chief Probation Officer of Erie County, twenty-three said there were no advantages in using child labor because

> the demand for specialization in the modern industrial world, and the almost complete absence of any system of apprenticeship or adequate training methods, [make] the opportunities for advancement open to children who leave school with insufficient education . . . comparatively few.

Nevertheless, twenty of the polled manufacturers disagreed, claiming that youngsters were quick to learn, had greater dexterity, more respect for their superiors and that by beginning at the bottom, children could work up to become valuable employees. Abner M. Seeley, President of the Empire Paper Box and Tube Company of New York City, undoubtedly spoke for many employers when he told the NYCLC that his only reason for not hiring children was the labor law. He believed that the employment of children at the age of thirteen would be "beneficial both for the family as well as for the child." The earnings would help in the home, the child could learn a trade thoroughly. Besides, children over sixteen were difficult to manage. "If the foreman does not please [them] . . . they become discourteous, remain only for a short while in any particular factory, never learn a trade and become what we know as the 'floating labor supply.'" Furthermore, Seeley claimed, it was dangerous to allow poor children to remain in school until fifteen or sixteen. They might associate with "children of . . . better economic situation" and might acquire "certain high notions of life." Then factory work would appear dull. Anyway, the education gained between the ages of thirteen and fourteen taught the youngsters nothing useful for their future jobs.[64]

One explanation for the successful extension of the Voss Dangerous Trades Act and the Double Compensation Law (with the resulting reduction in both legal and illegal factory child labor) was that because of the Triangle Fire, the year 1911 became a watershed for labor reform in New York. As the year opened the NYCLC, the New York Consumers' League, and other groups were continuing their slow efforts to build up the labor law. On January 16 the National Child Labor Committee and the NYCLC sent a joint report on the enforcement of New York's child labor statutes to Governor John A. Dix. The laws, they conceded, were good, but their enforcement still left much to be desired. It was the old story: not enough inspectors. Although the statutes authorized sixty factory inspectors and ten mercantile inspectors, the legislature had appropriated only enough money for fifty-three men in the factories and eight in the department stores. Somehow the inspectors were managing to average one visit a year to each factory (some had to be checked and rechecked); the reformers contended that a visit every three months was essential. The inspectors were overworked or, more accurately, their job descriptions were very broad. They were to enforce the labor law not only in factories and commercial establishments but in public works and brickyards, and on street, steam, surface, and elevated railroads. Furthermore, they were responsible for working conditions in mines, quarries, tunnels, and tenement houses, and the enforcement of the weekly wage payment law. While the reformers praised the Labor Department for its much-improved record system, its annual reports, which were "well in advance of what [might] . . . be found in other states," and its zeal in prosecuting factory owners (see Table 3), they had harsh words for the courts. To the NYCLC the failure of the lower courts to cooperate with the Labor Department in prosecuting employers was a "serious obstacle" against which Labor Commissioners P. T. Sherman and John Williams had been repeatedly and publicly contending.

TABLE 3

PROSECUTIONS FOR EMPLOYING CHILDREN ILLEGALLY IN FACTORIES, 1904-10
(Year Ending September 30)

	1904	1905	1906	1907	1908	1909	1910
Cases	22	158	193	325	586	400	492
Convictions	10	104	107	205	327	288	364
Fines	$135	1,100	810	2,700	3,905	3,125	3,655

The child labor groups were particularly indignant at a Brooklyn official, Magistrate Kempner, who on January 5, 1911, dismissed a child labor prosecution brought for a violation of the hours law by telling the factory inspector that he should *wink* at such violations during the holiday season.[65]

"Winking" ceased with the first puff of smoke from the eighth-floor window of the Asch Building at Washington Place and Greene Street in lower Manhattan. The disastrous fire on March 25, 1911, in the Triangle Shirtwaist Company cost the lives of 146 employees, most of them women and girls as young as fourteen who jumped to their death from windows like flaming torches or fell from the heat-twisted fire escape in a "flaming human load to the yard below." An enormous sense of public outrage boiled up as a result of the fire. A fire prevention expert, H. F. J. Porter, gave this statement to the *New York Times:*

> There are only two or three factories in the city where fire drills are in use. In some of them where I have installed the system myself, the owners have discontinued it. One man whom I advised to install a fire drill replied to me: "Let 'em burn. They're a lot of cattle anyway!"

For the moment the public appeared ready to believe that all employers took the "cattle" view of their workers. Just nine days before the Triangle Fire New York's Socialist party organ, *Call,* had published the report of the New York Joint Board of Sanitary Control which had investigated working conditions in 1,243 coat and suit shops in New York City.

> Ninety-nine per cent of the shops were found to be defective in respect to safety: 14 had no fire escapes; 101 had defective drop ladders; 491 had only one exit; 23 had locked doors during the day; 58 had dark hallways; 78 had obstructed approaches to fire escapes; and 1,172 or 94 per cent had doors opening in instead of out.

The owners of the Triangle Shirtwaist Company, Isaac Harris and Max Blanck, were indicted on charges of first and second degree manslaughter. The prosecution presented evidence that the Triangle plant had been overcrowded, that some of the doors had been locked or blocked, that the stair exit was inadequate, that the vertical fire escape ladder ended six feet over a glass skylight and that accumulations of rags (where the fire had apparently started) had been allowed to pile up, but after a brilliant defense by Max D. Steuer, the defendants were acquitted by a jury. During 1914 the Triangle Company settled twenty-three individual suits out of court at an average figure of seventy-five dollars a dead employee. That the Triangle Company was haled into court on several occasions *after* the trial—once for having a door locked with 150 girls at work, once for using a counterfeit label of the National Consumers' League, and for other labor law violations—attests to one of the greatest problems of factory inspection: the uncaring attitude of many employers toward the basic welfare of their workers.[66]

Although most of the public outrage died within a few months after the fire, a group of prominent citizens known as the Committee on Safety, headed by Henry L. Stimson and including Frances Perkins, Mary Dreier, Amos Pinchot, and Rabbi Stephen Wise led other reform organizations in a demand for the creation of a Factory Investigating Commission. Authorized by the legislature on June 30, 1911, the nine-member commission continued for four years under the direction of Senate Democratic leader Robert F. Wagner and Assembly Speaker Alfred E. Smith. During the life of the commission the labor law was completely recodified, the Labor Department reorganized, and thirty-three new labor laws were passed.[67] The presence of the two most important legislators on the commission led to the passage of most of its recommendations with relative ease; among these, children under fourteen were barred from working in cannery sheds (previously sheds had not been considered factories) and in tenement manufacture, the educational standards for working children were raised, the procedure for issuing working papers was tightened, and medical inspectors of the Department of Labor were authorized to make on-the-spot physical examinations of factory children ages fourteen to sixteen.[68]

The Triangle Fire, however, by no means eliminated all opposition to labor reform. The Jackson Bill establishing a nine-hour day and fifty-four-hour week in manufacturing for all women over sixteen and boys sixteen to eighteen was one of the most bitterly contested measures of the 1911 and 1912 sessions. The ashes of the fire had scarcely cooled when Assemblyman Bridenbecker of Herkimer tried to have the fifty-four-hour bill amended to give the Commissioner of Labor the power to suspend the hours provisions upon request. Claiming that Labor Commissioner John Williams "does not wish to be given such discretionary authority, for it would subject him to such pressure in support of appeals for exemption, as to interfere seriously with the administration of the law . . . ," Frances Perkins and Mary T. Bissell of the New York Consumers' League joined George Hall in sending out seven thousand telegrams and fliers denouncing the amendment. The amendment was defeated, although the groups urging passage of the bill (the Women's Trade Union League, the New York City Consumers' League, the State Federation of Labor, the Socialist Party, the United Textile Workers of America, and the NYCLC) had to wait until 1912 for success and then took a bill exempting canneries, which gave Bridenbecker what he wanted. According to Frances Perkins the opponents had been hoping that this exemption would compel the reformers to reject the entire bill.[69]

After hearing a host of witnesses, including Florence Kelley, Seth Low, Frederick L. Hoffmann, President of the American Statistical

Association, Maud Nathan of the New York Consumers' League, George Hall, Frances Perkins, and others condemn the State Labor Department's lack of "power, funds, personnel, equipment and authority," the Factory Investigating Commission sponsored the Reorganization Act of 1913 which created a State Industrial Board as a special legislative agency to "enact rules and regulations to carry into effect the provisions of the labor law"; the Industrial Code thus formulated would have the force of law. The force of factory inspectors was doubled to 125.[70] Unfortunately, the reorganization and expansion of the Labor Department collided head on with the dead weight of political patronage in the state. "It looked as if New York was to have the best kit of tools in the country to regulate the human side of industrial operations," lamented *The Survey*, but "today it looks as if this kit of tools had been purloined bag and baggage by the spoils politicians." Legislation passed in 1911 had divided New York into eight factory inspection districts, each of which would be run by a supervising factory inspector, presumably a man who could "meet engineers and superintendents on a footing of equal equipment and competency." According to charges made by the reformers, the State Civil Service Commission held an unannounced meeting and decided to exempt the eight new "expert" positions from Civil Service. When the news leaked out, there was such an uproar from the social workers that two hearings were held at which the reform group argued for competitive examinations, but the State Federation of Labor urged that the first qualification of an applicant be his membership in a labor union. In a logically faulty, but politically understandable, decision—derided by *The Survey* as "unparalleled in the history of wise men since the days of Solomon"—the Civil Service Commission decided to make four of the new positions subject to examination and four exempt. In listing the qualifications for the nonexempt positions, the commission specified that the applicant must have had at least ten years practical experience in a mechanical occupation and that "scholarship and technical training" would be considered only when combined with such practical experience—a clear attempt to favor the labor unions. These requirements, noted *The Survey*, "debar a late graduate of an engineering school no matter how large his ability or how high his standing . . . [or] any engineer . . . no matter . . . what his experience, if he shall have had nine years . . . instead of ten." The four political (exempt) appointments brought down the wrath of a large number of civic organizations. Two of the choices, Edward Bates of Utica, a former secretary of the State Federation of Labor, and James Murphy of New York City, a former president of the Typographical Union, were perhaps justifiable. But there seemed to be no good reason for making labor "experts" out of Edward J. Pierce, a janitor on Front Street, appointed "for Al Smith . . . [who] was present at the hearings . . . and showed a great interest in this matter" or of Jeremiah J. Flood, a plumber and former Superintendent of Sewers, who had become notorious in 1909 with the publication of the "Tom and Jerry" letters between Flood and political boss Tom Frawley concerning Jerry's attempt to find "a snug place" in the dock department. Pressed by public opinion, three of the exempt appointees voluntarily took the examinations and passed them. Flood refused.[71]

Presiding over this uproar was Commissioner of Labor John Williams, a relatively able man who after serving as a deputy factory inspector and chief factory inspector had succeeded P. T. Sherman in 1907. The social workers charged that Williams' zeal had flagged after the Democratic administration of John A. Dix had taken over the state in 1911; as a Republican anxious to keep his job, Williams was embracing the spoils system. "There never was a time," expostulated *The Survey*, "when Commissioner Williams could not have rallied to his support the decent people of all parties in this state . . . if he had appealed to them and let them know the plight that he was in. But he kept silent."[72] Commissioner Williams justified these fears when on April 19, 1913, he asked the Civil Service Commission to place twenty-eight new positions authorized by the 1913 Triangle Fire legislation in the exempt category. For a time the reform group took heart as Democratic Governor William Sulzer replaced Williams with John Mitchell on May 16, 1913, an appointment which had the support of the NYCLC. Within the same year, however, the legislature impeached the progressive Sulzer himself "because he refused to obey [Tammany Boss Charles E.] Murphy's orders," and shortly thereafter Governor Martin Glynn appointed James M. Lynch to replace Mitchell as commissioner of a now badly demoralized Labor Department.[73] A large number of reform-minded civic leaders pressured Lynch to withdraw the application to exempt the new factory positions, but Lynch refused and the Civil Service Commission then designated twenty-one of the new positions exempt. One of Lynch's first appointments was that of Jeremiah Flood as Chief Factory Inspector for the city of New York. In an effort to "provide a remunerative position" for former Labor Commissioner John Williams, Lynch forced the removal of John R. Shillady, a friend of the reform groups, as secretary of the Industrial Board, and then appointed Williams to replace him. When a member of the board, Pauline Goldmark, demanded to know the charges against Shillady, none were forthcoming. In anger, twenty-four leading citizens signed a public protest; among them were Mornay Williams and George W. Alger of the NYCLC; Homer Folks of the State Charities Aid Association; John M. Glenn, Director of the Russell Sage Foundation; Maud Nathan of the Consumers' League; Lillian Wald; Edward T. Devine, the housing reformer; Rev. John Haynes Holmes; Frederic Hazard, President of the Solvay-Process Company of Syracuse; Ansley Wilcox of Buffalo; Thomas V. O'Connor, President of the International Longshoremen's Association; and Adelbert Moot, a former President of the State Bar Association.[74]

More difficulties were ahead. Despite protests from various reform groups, in 1915 the Factory Investigating Commission decided to consolidate the Department of Labor and the Industrial Board by placing the former under a five-member Industrial Commission and abolishing the Industrial Board. Convinced that such a bipartisan commission (not more than three of the commissioners were to come from any one political party) would open "the door to patronage and political jobbery of the most objectionable sort," the NYCLC joined the National Child Labor Committee in petitioning Governor Whitman to veto the proposal.[75] Others felt that it would be difficult to fix responsibility under the new system and that the Commissioner of Labor should "bear the responsibility and either make good or get out,"[76] but because the idea had the support of some of the labor groups, it carried. With John Mitchell as chairman, the new Industrial Commission took over the Labor Department on June 1, 1915, and James M. Lynch, former Commissioner of Labor, was one of the new commissioners. In August when Secretary Hall talked with James L. Gernon, the newly appointed Chief Factory Inspector, Gernon said he had found the Labor Department "much disorganized" and loaded with seat-warming, buck-passing inspectors. He had immediately sent seven of them "who had been having a soft snap in the office" out on field work. It was also apparent to Gernon that as a result of the Triangle Fire "the Department had gone crazy over fire protection matters at the expense of other important subjects."[77]

In 1921 during the administration of Republican Governor Nathan L. Miller, the Labor Department was again reorganized. The Industrial Commission was abolished and replaced by the old Department of Labor under a single Industrial Commissioner. The Industrial Board was resurrected to act as a quasi-judicial body hearing appeals from employees, enforcing compliance with Labor Department orders, and interpreting the labor law. While in the past some of the reform groups had favored just this type of organization, Governor Miller was now denounced by the American Association for Labor Legislation which warned that "the attempt to put into the hands of one man [the Commissioner of Labor] a lump sum appropriation with power to abolish bureaus and create new divisions and hire and fire at his personal or political whim, are aspects of a determined effort to put through a scheme—as crude as it is shortsighted—to destroy joint representation at the head of the labor department—the best known device to protect the administration of the labor laws." The NYCLC, of course, favored the new system, having objected earlier to the commission form because it encouraged buck-passing. This final reorganization of the Labor Department was beneficial in the long run. The department enjoyed a series of exceptionally able industrial commissioners such as Bernard L. Shientag, Frances Perkins, and Elmer Andrews, who were materially assisted by the increased power of the office.[78]

The national emergency created by the First World War gave opponents of labor reform an excuse for suspending child labor laws. Their most drastic attempt, the Klingmann Bill, stated:

All provisions, prohibitions, rules, regulations and requirements, in relation to the employment of children under the age of fourteen years, or the hours of labor thereof either during the school term or the vacation period, in factories, mercantile establishments, street trades or other employment of any kind . . . are hereby suspended during the period that the war continues.

Fortunately, it failed to pass, but in 1917 the NYCLC was forced to accept the Brown Act, which exempted boys over fifteen in cities and over fourteen in rural areas from compulsory school attendance. They could then engage in military, agricultural, or industrial work at the discretion of the State Department of Education. The New York City Bar Association branded the act "clearly unconstitutional" but not until after the Armistice did the NYCLC persuade the Commissioner of Education to suspend the measure.[79] Because the war brought an influx of children into all types of employment, the committee's work was increased. With the New York City Consumers' League it investigated and halted the use of tenement labor to produce U.S. Army uniforms and it complained vigorously about the use of children as solicitors for the Red Cross. When the war ended, the NYCLC cooperated with the federal government in a Back-to-School Drive that was moderately successful because of the pressure on the job market from returning veterans. Firms made room for the soldiers by firing employees many of whom were under eighteen. The juvenile wage scale for factory work fell drastically after the war from a high of $40 to $50 a week to its prewar rate of $10 to $14 a week.[80]

By the 1920's child labor in the factories had diminished. Although the Child Labor Committee should receive much of the credit for this decrease, the NYCLC was quick to give recognition to other forces such as

> compensation laws, safety first campaigns, scientific personnel management, the need to meet sharp competition by reduction of overhead cost, in which labor turnover is an important item, the late realization that efficient work means the health and general welfare of the workers, the imperative need for the training of more highly skilled artisans . . . [which were] powerful aids in bettering working conditions for working children.

The NYCLC field secretary pointed out that although a child might legally go to work at fourteen, "his 44 hr. working week [achieved for the fourteen to sixteen group in factories and mercantile establishments in 1925], his 4 hours weekly attendance at continuation school, his inability to enter apprenticeship training until he is 16—these and other protective measures . . . tend to restrict the industrial child to unimportant jobs of little educational value in minor industries."[81] The increasing political activity of the State Federation of Labor after 1921 was also significant; while labor did not take the initiative in child labor legislation, it was the most powerful lobby to which the NYCLC could appeal for legislative help.

Although child labor in factories was no longer a major problem, some youngsters continued to work, and evasions and violations still persisted if on a greatly reduced scale. In 1930, for example, the factory inspectors found a fourteen-year-old girl illegally operating a paper-cutting machine. She had no working papers, but the employer hopefully produced a letter from her school principal saying that it was all right for her to work, and begging a job for the child on the age-old grounds that she was the oldest of six children of a "poor widow." And some factory inspectors would never be zealous. When a complaint reached the Labor Department in 1930 that the K & J Hat Works in New York City was employing children under sixteen *before* 8:00 A.M. and *after* 5:00 P.M., the inspector visited the plant at 9:00 A.M. on one day and twelve noon the next. He then reported: "Complaint not sustained as posted hours and statement of superintendent agree that minors under 16 do not work during prohibited hours." Nor were the health requirements observed. A boy under sixteen was found working at 6:00 P.M. (illegally) on a punch press (also illegal). Pale, thin, and hollow-chested, he "coughed intermittently raising each time considerable sputum." Then there was the undefined area of work. A complaint came in that two boys, ages twelve and thirteen, were working seven days a week during the summer from 10:00 A.M. to 10:00 P.M. at a miniature golf course, but the factory inspector could do nothing since a golf course was neither a factory nor a mercantile establishment. As always, there was public apathy and the desire not to become involved. One of the continuation school principals telephoned the Labor Department about a sixteen-year-old boy who was running an elevator (illegally) in a large Manhattan department store. The principal said he knew it was illegal, but since jobs were hard to find in 1930, he did not want his school blamed for causing the boy to be fired.[82]

The Great Depression caused even more reduction in factory child labor; the Labor Department found in 1933 that "the general tendency is for employers to hire older people and to pay them the wage the child formerly received." When jobs were available for youngsters under seventeen, they paid only $5 to $10 a week as compared with $12 to $14 a week in 1929. The resurgence of labor unions under the New Deal and the existence of the NRA Codes during 1933-35 continued the trend. On the other hand the depression brought back some of the sweatshops, and Frances Perkins claimed that it was still possible to find New York City youngsters earning only thirty-five cents a day for factory work. Although there were unquestionably fewer children in the factories, the NYCLC could not believe that the total number was as low as the factory inspection reports indicated. The committee insisted that the upstate reports "present[ed] almost unbelievable conditions"; it was impossible for them to accept that there was not one worker under eighteen illegally employed in any of the Albany and Syracuse factories during 1939. And certainly there should be more than one or two such cases found in the other large cities of Yonkers, Rochester, Troy, and Utica.[83]

The Second World War occasioned another relaxation of the labor laws, which allowed children to work in factories. In 1943 the state legislature authorized the State War Council to grant exemptions to individual manufacturers allowing them to employ sixteen- and seventeen-year-olds during normally forbidden hours. Four thousand sixteen- and seventeen-year-old boys were working for Curtiss-Wright Aviation until 12:30 A.M. The canneries were permitted to return to their old practices and employ girls for ten hours a day and sixty hours a week (one day of twelve hours was also authorized). Reports from

Rochester indicated that 50 to 60 per cent of the high-school students were working, some as long as seventy and eighty hours a week, as well as going to school—a backbreaking schedule. At the height of the war half a million youngsters had joined the labor force. Despite the national war effort the reformers objected strongly to the Exemption Bill, reminding Governor Thomas E. Dewey that an earlier governor, Charles S. Whitman, had vetoed similar legislation during the First World War. Mayor Fiorello H. LaGuardia was also concerned. "I have a list here . . . ," he said, "of youngsters who are making $28, $30, $35, $40 a week. Yes, and what will they be doing later on? They will not have a good skilled trade, they will not have the educational background . . . they'll have no profession. They will go backward."[84] Fortunately the war did not establish a trend. After 1945 the Labor Department gave a steadily increasing percentage of its time to child labor inspections in an effort to return the youngsters to school. By 1955, only 410 children were discovered working illegally in factories; 340 of these were over the legal age of sixteen but had not secured working papers. Even though some factory child labor escaped the notice of the inspectors, and allowing for discrepancies in the statistics, the problem of illegal labor by young people in factories was still negligible. However, the ominous dropout situation of the 1960's was already apparent in 1950 when 150,000 children (20 per cent of the children fourteen through seventeen) were either employed or seeking legal employment.[85]

   If the NYCLC had been successful in its campaign to end child labor in factories it was because of the committee's early recognition that the reduction of child labor depended on what could be done about two critical matters: the age at which the state authorized children to work and the manner in which it processed them for the labor market. The drive to make the employment certificate effective and to raise the school-leaving age was therefore of paramount importance.

All persons acquainted with the child labor problem agree that the school authorities are able to do more through their ability to hold children back from work than a whole army of inspectors in driving children out from the factories and stores where they may have been at work illegally.

—New York Child Labor Committee, 1905

We are turning out each year in New York City some 40,000 untrained workers, children, with employment certificates, and the very large majority of them are totally unfit for any trade or any occupation whatever. They go into the very large majority of those jobs which have no possibility of training them, and within a very few years they have reached adult life and are still earning a child's wage. They are not worth any more in the industrial market.

—Dr. S. Josephine Baker, Testimony before the United States Commission on Industrial Relations, 1914

V. Employment Certificates and the School-leaving Age

An employment certificate system gives the state a chance to determine a child's eligibility for work *before* he is employed. The moment working papers are issued the youngster enters the ranks of labor and thereafter is much more difficult to control. One of the best tests of the state's commitment to its youth is the scope and quality of its procedure for issuing certificates. Technically, New York may be said to have had an employment certificate as early as 1874, for under the Compulsory Education Law of that year school officials were to issue attendance certificates for working children between the ages of eight and fourteen. The Factory Act passed in 1886 required manufacturers to keep a file of certificates showing the name, age, and date and place of birth for each employed child under sixteen, a law widely evaded through the use of false parental affidavits as proof of age. Then, in 1896, local boards of health were brought into the picture by an act making them at least theoretically responsible for certifying that a child was physically able to do the work he intended to perform and that his age was correctly stated on the employment certificate. Unfortunately, because the boards of health were subjected to pressure from local employers, they continued to accept worthless parental affidavits.[1]

The 1903 Employment Certificate Law was the real beginning of New York's employment certificate system, for it was the first serious attempt to get proof of a potential child worker's schooling and age. While Massachusetts had set up age and schooling requirements as early as 1878, and had largely avoided the pitfall of the parental affidavit by requiring that these be checked against the school census, it was in New York that imaginative efforts were devised to meet the problem of finding accurate proof of age when a birth certificate was not available. The Hill-Finch Act of 1903 required that the child's school record be sent to the health officer in every case and not, as in the past, only when that official requested it.[2] This part of the law was opposed by some school officials who knew that it would make it more difficult for them to get rid of "undesirable" or "uneducable" children—including recent immigrants with language difficulties—by sending them to work. The Child Labor Committee realized that it could not simply require the substitution of a birth certificate for a parental affidavit and expect the law to work by itself, as Jacob Riis had urged. "The objection will be raised that the child in New York *has no* birth certificate half the time," he asserted, "but it is no real objection. If born abroad, the child is registered there, and the certificate can be obtained in a few weeks."[3] Riis was much too optimistic; in spite of the rather flexible documentary requirements of the Hill-Finch Act (passports, baptismal, and other religious records were acceptable in lieu of a birth certificate when accompanied by a parental affidavit) many children simply could not obtain such evidence from far-off Central and Eastern Europe. In 1904 about eight thousand fewer New York City children applied for working papers than did in 1903. These children under sixteen who could not obtain evidence of age were now presenting parental affidavits swearing that they were sixteen directly to the employers, a procedure that effectively placed the youngsters beyond the reach of the NYCLC and the Labor Department. The large number of rejected applications in 1904 represented children who had tried the legal procedure but who had been turned away because of their inability to produce the necessary documents. Even George Hall, Secretary of the NYCLC, conceded that "the right of the State to demand evidence of age which . . . is out of the power of the child . . . to obtain—which, in point of fact, *nowhere exists*— seems fairly open to question."[4]

Unable to obtain proof of age from their parents, some children turned to their teachers for assistance and soon the schools were complaining that the law was unfair. Lillian Wald noted that the zeal of Seth Low's municipal administration in catching truants had brought on a great increase in school attendance. To some educators there was no reason why a fourteen-year-old should not be allowed to relieve classroom pressure by going to work. Julia Richman of the New York City Board of Education told Paul M. Warburg of the NYCLC that she knew of "possibly scores" of children over fourteen who were working without employment certificates, and she deplored any law under which "children morally entitled to work . . . are forced by the arbitrariness of the law into being lawbreakers." The teachers could not understand why the age the child gave in school could not be accepted by the health officers even though the New York City Consumers' League claimed that of every hundred children, thirty would overstate their age. Lack of age documentation was not the only reason for the rejection of applications for working papers. Some of the responsibility fell on the schools themselves, for of the 2,859 refusals during the first part of 1904, almost half (1,176) were children who had not spent 130 days or more in school since their thirteenth birthday, and 160 were youngsters who failed to show that they could read and write in English and perform simple operations with numbers.[5]

Harassed by the Women Principals Association, the NYCLC attempted to solve the documentation problem by sponsoring a successful bill making it possible for a health officer to accept proof of age other than a birth certificate, a baptismal certificate, or a passport. A child might now submit proof of having been graduated from the eighth grade of a New York public school, or since the provision for "other" documentary evidence was broadly interpreted, he might use a Bar Mitzvah certificate, a life insurance policy, a family Bible, a vaccination certificate, records of the family physician, the transcript of a relief society's records, or even an affidavit sworn by two disinterested persons having personal knowledge of the birth of the child. During the first year this amendment was in effect (1905-06), 565 certificates were issued by the New York City Board of Health which would have been refused under the 1903 provisions of the Hill-Finch Act.[6]

Yet this change did not go far enough, for many children could provide no documentation whatever. Their inability to obtain working papers—to which many of them were actually entitled—was making enemies for the cause of child labor reform among school principals, charity workers, and police magistrates. The assistant superintendent of schools in New York City stated flatly that the city's police magistrates invariably refused to fine parents for allowing their children to remain out of school if their children were over fourteen and had been unable to obtain working papers for lack of documentary age proof. Angered by what they regarded as too rigid a law, many school superintendents simply ignored it. Although the Compulsory Education Law required children who could not qualify for working papers to remain in school until they were sixteen, a child who left school for work but failed to receive an employment certificate was not likely to appear in the classroom again, nor was anyone likely to care. Upon investigating 161 such children, George Hall discovered that only 62 of them had attended school at all after their certificate applications were rejected and that only three had eventually received the amount of schooling required by the Education Law. Those principals who did try to keep their children in school found that youngsters unable to secure employment certificates could get out of school at fourteen by stating that they wished to take a job where formal evidence of age was not required—domestic work or newspaper selling, for example. According to the Compulsory Education Law, a principal must release a child for full-time work in a noncertificate occupation if the child's school record showed him to be fourteen.[7] It made no difference whether the youngster was illiterate or physically handicapped, if he wanted to enter a noncertificate occupation he had to be allowed to do so. Even if his school record age rested on a false statement by his parents, there was no alternative. It is not surprising that this attractive loophole was used, nor that the factory inspectors began finding over one hundred children every month who had left school ostensibly to work in noncertificate occupations and then had secured illegal employment in a factory or department store. To close the gap, the NYCLC sponsored the Agnew Act of 1907 which provided that any fourteen- to sixteen-year-old child in a first- or second-class city must obtain an employment certificate *before* he would be permitted to leave school.[8] New York City School Superintendent William H. Maxwell, a member of the NYCLC, promptly cracked down on principals who had been eager to release children. Asserting that "many hundreds" of children between the ages of fourteen and sixteen had been giving their employers school record certificates instead of working papers, Maxwell ordered his principals to withhold the school record from any child who could not give documentary proof of age until the Board of Health notified the school that such evidence had been received.[9] Maxwell's action proved insufficient. When in 1909 Secretary Hall learned that 320 children over fourteen had been refused working papers because they could not write the simple English sentences given them by the health officers (an increase of 127 over the 1907-08 figure) he asked Maxwell for additional aid. The superintendent immediately directed all metropolitan school principals to hold special examinations for applicants for working papers. This effort to stop principals from sending semi-illiterate children to the Board of Health enjoyed some success, although progress was slow. In 1912 the New York City Board of Health rejected 239 children as unable to write; "This box is green" became "This lox is bring"; "I have a black and white suit" was rendered as "I have a block shout"; "There are lots of girls here" as "There are loind girl," etc. All of these candidates had supposedly met the requirements of New York's Compulsory Education Law. By 1914, however, Maxwell's policy had reduced the number of applicants rejected for insufficient schooling to sixteen.[10]

Maxwell's attempts to make his principals stop hurrying children into the labor market were praiseworthy, but the NYCLC knew that it must broaden the acceptable proof of age still further or see the law reduced to a farce. Perhaps the child who could find no documents could submit his own body as proof of age. Superintendent Maxwell suggested that a physician's certificate be used, but some of the NYCLC members did not believe that a doctor could tell whether an applicant was fourteen years old. Secretary Hall put the question to several prominent physicians in New York, Boston, and Philadelphia. While none of them believed that the actual age of a child could be determined by a physical examination, a majority agreed that a physician *could* tell whether a child had reached the normal physical development for a fourteen-year-old. With this assurance the NYCLC secured a 1907 amendment to the labor law specifying that in first-class cities only a child unable to produce any documentary evidence of age might apply for a physician's certificate. After a ninety-day waiting period (this was included to encourage the children to find documentary evidence), the child would be examined by two board of health physicians and should they disagree as to whether he was fourteen, the decision of a third doctor would be final.[11] All of these changes, of course, weakened the law and increased the time necessary for its administration. Ideally, every child should have had a birth certificate although even that evidence was sometimes unreliable. In 1909 Secretary Hall was sent to a Stanton Street drug store where he saw a large sign in the window advertising "Birth Certificates, 25 Cents." The druggist, Abraham Deutsch, was using a regular notary public affidavit form writing "Birth Certificate" across the top, and selling them to immigrant children. Deutsch was arrested, but released when he promised not to sell any more certificates.[12]

If operators such as Deutsch represented the only way some children could get birth certificates, perhaps the NYCLC could help them secure genuine ones. In 1907 the committee got permission to place an agent in the Manhattan office of the New York City Board of Health and hired a young graduate of the New York University Law School to do the job. This was a significant step, for Jeanie V. Minor was to remain as the paid representative of the NYCLC at the Board of Health until 1915, and then to serve the Child Labor Committee itself as field secretary until 1932 taking over as secretary during 1921-25 when George Hall was on leave. Jeanie Minor's zeal, energy, and organizational ability made it possible for the NYCLC to continue the thrust of child labor reform through the 1920's and to bridge the so-called gap between the Progressive Era and the New Deal. George Hall with his rather drab air of middle-class respectability could make a good impression on the state legislature and he could run a "tight ship" in the New York office, but Jeanie Minor was the activist, covering the entire state, checking up and inspecting, writing lucid reports that crackled with good humor and were filled with sardonic observations. On one occasion she reported from Rochester: "There is a conference of the Children's Court judges—grubby old gents—taking place . . . and I am elected to go up and listen attentively to their words of wisdom and forestall any iniquitous moves on their part."[13] If her energy resembled that of Florence Kelley, her politics did not. In 1932 she was outraged at those who described Herbert Hoover's program to provide school lunches as "meager charity," and announced that she would campaign for him because "like St. Christopher, President Hoover has waded through the perils of these days with the childhood of the nation on his shoulder."[14]

One of Jeanie Minor's first tasks at the Board of Health was to clarify the procedure for finding the birth certificates of foreign-born children. In the past many such children had simply been told to write their native country, but no address had been suggested and no information on fees had been provided. Agent Minor wrote abroad, and after ascertaining the procedure for obtaining birth certificates in several European countries, gave this information to foreign-born applicants. By 1913 Jeanie Minor was reporting an excellent response to requests for birth certificates from Austria, Rumania, Italy, and England, but very poor results from Russia. She attributed the difficulty east of the Elbe to pogroms which had destroyed many Jewish records, a significant fact, for in 1911 almost two thousand of the five thousand foreign-born applicants in Manhattan were of Russian birth. Nevertheless, by 1913 an estimated 64 per cent of the foreign-born children seeking employment certificates at the Manhattan office of the Board of Health presented birth certificates.[15] With the outbreak of the First World War in 1914 the program of obtaining foreign birth certificates was curtailed, but this did not increase the number of rejected applicants, for if all else failed, the physician's certificate could be used.

Children born in the United States sometimes faced similar difficulties in finding their birth certificates; in New York State it was estimated that in 1900 only about 78 per cent of the births were recorded. Sometimes registrars failed to put the newborn's given name on his birth certificate; the practice was common enough for the NYCLC to sponsor and secure a 1904 amendment to the public health law positively requiring the insertion of the given name on a birth certificate.[16] When a birth had not been recorded, other evidence was used, but in some instances the clerks in the Bureau of Vital Statistics had simply failed to make a thorough search for the child's name. In most instances it was a matter of Agent Minor demanding a thorough check, then the error would be discovered and some child would receive working papers without having to wait ninety days for a physician's certificate. Foreign names were often spelled in a variety of ways, and Minor finally secured the use of a duplicate set of index books for New York City births. When she conducted her own searches for births reported as "not found" by the official bureau, she discovered certificates for over two hundred children who had been told that their births were not recorded.[17] There were inevitably some people who tried to profit from the situation. Occasionally Jeanie Minor would send a child to the Lying-In Hospital on Eighteenth Street to see if his birth was recorded there. When complaints came in that the hospital clerk was demanding a fee of from fifty cents to two dollars for making a search, Miss Minor saw to it that the clerk was fired.

In August, 1908, the New York City Board of Health organized a Division of Child Hygiene as a part of its Sanitary Bureau, and Jeanie Minor began to work closely with its chief, Dr. S. Josephine Baker. By 1915 the two women had brought a semblance of order to the chaotic process of issuing working papers in New York City. As a result of their improved procedure, there was a sharp increase in the number of successful applications for employment certificates. In the year prior to Agent Minor's arrival at the Board of Health (1906) there had been 21,220 certificates granted in New York City, and 4,797 refused; during her last year (1915) there were 37,131 certificates issued and 2,364 refusals. The number of certificates issued in 1915 would have been even higher had it not been for a 1913 law promoted by the NYCLC requiring that each employment certificate applicant complete his school work through grade 6B; otherwise the youngster must wait for working papers until he was sixteen. The Compulsory Education Law had been very loose on this point, for while it did specify certain subjects as required, a child was only to have "received" instruction in them, and in practice the local superintendents were setting varying grade levels which working paper applicants must reach. In New York City this had been grade 5A, in Yonkers, 6B, and so on. While the 1913 law was praiseworthy as an attempt to standardize the procedure throughout the state, it still required only the physical presence of the child in the classroom until he reached the sixth grade—a level most children attained by the age of twelve. From Columbia University came criticism. John Dewey told the press that the new law had increased the demand for special schools and courses adapted to the needs of boys and girls about to enter industry and that these ought to be provided. Child labor laws, he contended, had been based too long on the negative idea of simply keeping children out of work until they reached a certain chronological age or until they had been passed up to a particular grade.[18] There was much evidence to support Dewey's charge of negativism; yet if the child labor reformers must bear some of the responsibility for not developing more imaginative approaches to legislation, they had learned from their battles in Albany that they were often lucky to get "negative" prohibitions. Perhaps the schools should have interested themselves more in their potential child laborers, but these children usually came from the poorest and least articulate groups in the school districts, and the general weight of public inertia took its toll. To George Hall the situation was clear. Writing in 1917 he observed that the NYCLC's "experience with school authorities . . . throughout the state" had convinced him "that not all of them 'have nothing but the interest of the child at heart.' " He spoke of "numbers of instances where school officials were only too anxious to push out of school children who are particularly in need of further education, both of the hand and of the head type" because they were "troublesome."[19]

The procedure for issuing employment certificates in New York City developed by Jeanie Minor and Dr. S. Josephine Baker between 1908 and 1915 was still in use in 1939. While somewhat cumbersome, it represented the best thought of the day and was carefully designed to close as many loopholes as possible. When a New York City child wished to obtain working papers he first requested permission from his school principal who, after testing the child's ability to read and write, would send him to the appropriate borough office of the Department of Health. If the child had been born in New York City, he would be told to visit the Bureau of Records to obtain a birth certificate, and, if one was on file, the bureau would so certify. In the event no certificate could be found, the applicant was referred to the Employment Certificate Office where Jeanie Minor would counsel him about securing evidence of age. Once the child obtained acceptable proof of age he was sent back to the school principal who then issued a record of school attendance on an approved Department of Labor form. Accompanied by one of his parents, the child now returned to the Department of Health and made a formal application, countersigned by the parent. After 1912, every applicant for working papers was next given a physical examination, a decided improvement over the old system where health officers had simply to state that in their opinion the child was "normally" developed for his age and could do the work he intended to do. The Factory Investigating Commission, one of whose recommendations resulted in the passage of the physical examination law, had found "many sickly children" in the state's factories; Robert F. Wagner thought that the new law would "save . . . many children from early graves."[20] In giving physical examinations, the doctors were supposed to take as "normal" development for a fourteen-year-old child a weight of eighty pounds and a height of four feet eight inches. According to Dr. S. Josephine Baker the examiners recognized varying "racial characteristics of children of foreign birth" (in other words children from southern Italy might have a smaller bone structure than those from Scandinavia) but any child below the minimum standards of height and weight had to be examined by two physicians. If they disagreed, Dr. Baker would decide the case. If an easily correctible defect were found, the employment certificate would be withheld until it was taken care of: these cases usually involved defective vision, hearing, or teeth, enlarged tonsils, or contagious skin diseases. The child's school nurse would follow up the case, making reports of her findings to Dr. Baker. If the child failed to appear for a re-examination within six weeks, the application was cancelled. More serious physical defects such as a defective heart, malnutrition, and tuberculosis led to permanent rejection for the applicant. While it might have been possible for a limited employment certificate to be issued restricting the child with heart trouble to specified occupations, the New York City Corporation Counsel ruled that the Health Department could not issue such papers—a decision which was wise, for there was still no effective way of keeping track of a child's employment once he walked out the door of the Health Department. In later years limited certificates were brought into use. Once the child had passed the physical examination, the Board of Health examiner was to determine whether the youngster could read and write, to have the child sign the employment certificate, and to stamp all of the documents to insure that they would not be used again.[21]

Table 4 summarizes the work of the New York City Board of Health through 1917. The number of rejections may appear small, but there were enough to annoy some metropolitan school officials. In 1914 Assistant Superintendent of Schools John H. Walsh testified before the United States Commission on Industrial Relations that the educational requirements for working papers were too rigid. To George Hall and Dr. Baker who felt that they were just scratching the surface of the metropolitan child labor problem, Walsh's statement was outrageous.

TABLE 4 [23]

EMPLOYMENT CERTIFICATES ISSUED TO CHILDREN FOURTEEN TO SIXTEEN BY THE NEW YORK CITY BOARD OF HEALTH, 1901-17

Year	Granted	Refused: (Temporary and Permanent)
1901	23,492	2,203
1902	14,482	3,024
1903	23,591	7,175
1904	15,191	8,277
1905	18,389	5,266
1906	21,220	4,797
1907	23,013	2,669
1908	23,932	2,427
1909	29,843	1,635
1910	36,351	1,767
1911	40,530	1,325
1912	41,548	1,181
1913	41,507	1,617
1914*	33,192	1,390
1915	37,131	2,364
1916	47,033	4,033
1917*	39,290	3,518

* The drop in certificates issued in 1914 resulted from the new requirement that all applicants complete the sixth grade; the drop in 1917 shows the effect of the Wellington Law requiring elementary-school graduation certificates before working papers could be issued.

Dr. Baker testified that fourteen was too young for any child to work, and Hall said that 43,000 New York City children were using their working papers to escape both school and work; 61,400 certificates had been issued over the last two years, he told the commission, but only 17,700 boys and girls were at work. There was an obvious explanation, and a week later Hall admitted that most of the missing 43,000 children were actually at work in small stores, restaurants, telegraph offices, hotels, and bowling alleys, which could not be checked by the twenty-one overworked inspectors of the Labor Department's Mercantile Division.[22]

In August, 1915, Jeanie Minor was eased out of her post in the Division of Employment Certificates of the Department of Health. Although offered the position of head worker at the Riis Settlement House, Miss Minor decided to remain with the NYCLC as its field secretary. Her work was more varied now, but she managed to keep her hand in at the Division of Employment Certificates, telling George Hall that the work of that office was subject to her "thorough supervision" and that she "to a large extent . . . directed and controlled" its policy.[24] Minor's supervision was important, for it was very largely due to the work of Dr. S. Josephine Baker and herself that the metropolitan area was conducting a minimally decent program of employment certification.

In the rest of the state, the process of issuing working papers lay under a fog of public apathy and active evasion broken only occasionally by the work of some dedicated official. The extent of the problem is suggested by the figures in Table 5.

TABLE 5 [25]

EMPLOYMENT CERTIFICATES GRANTED TO CHILDREN AGES FOURTEEN AND FIFTEEN IN NEW YORK STATE CITIES, 1918-19

City	1918	1919
New York	50,300	50,700
Buffalo	3,152	3,211
Rochester	2,412	2,460
Syracuse	none reported	1,013
Albany	360	520
Yonkers	509	597
Troy	239	385
Utica	none reported	547
Schenectady	none reported	636
Binghamton	none reported	303

Visiting Mount Vernon in 1915, George Hall interviewed the clerk of the Board of Health who had been issuing about one hundred certificates a year but had rejected only one child for physical incapacity in two years: a case of tuberculosis. He accepted school records without personally verifying the child's ability to read and write and admitted taking parental affidavits of age "as a last resort."[26] In Amsterdam, Health Officer Dr. H. M. Hicks charged that it required "a constant system of supervision and espionage on the part of the [local Health] Department to approximate the requirements of the law." Dr. Hicks found half the children he examined were "below normal physical development," but nevertheless they found their way into the Amsterdam mills.[27] The situation in Buffalo in 1914 was not much better. The committee found that many school children there obtained their school records as if they were going to apply for working papers but then stayed out of school for a year or more doing nothing. The assistant secretary of the Buffalo Chamber of Commerce told the NYCLC field secretary that local businessmen were forming an organization to have the Triangle Fire legislation amended; they believed the new factory regulations would cost New York employers thirty million dollars in one year. The businessmen opposed workmen's compensation and other such laws drawn up "irresponsibly" by "that bunch of mutts" who call themselves reformers.[28] In October, 1917, Jeanie Minor descended upon Utica where she addressed an audience of two people, the president of the local Consumers' League and a reporter for the Utica *Observer*. The league head told her that Utica "was a corrupt town, machine ridden, [with the] Health Officer totally indifferent, [and the] Superintendent of Schools new and untried." The health officer was, moreover, "generally in a state of intoxication and frequently absent from duty for weeks at a time." In Syracuse Miss Minor found a very haphazard method of issuing employment certificates; as in Buffalo, there was no check to make sure that the child who obtained his school record actually applied for working papers. No one seemed to care, least of all the superintendent of schools whose main concern was his difficulties with backward fifteen-year-old boys. "He would unquestionably break the law and permit these children to work," observed Miss Minor.[29] The widely varying standards of enforcement strongly suggested the desirability of a centralized state agency capable of giving constant supervision to the issuing of working papers. Scarcely had the committee realized the need when the First World War opened, bringing problems of its own.

The NYCLC was fortunate to obtain the passage of the Wellington Law in 1916 before the wartime atmosphere produced a demand for relaxation of child labor standards. Drafted by the committee, the measure prohibited children from going to work until they were fifteen unless they had been graduated from the eighth grade.[30] If the Wellington Law represented progress, the Vacation Permit Statute passed in 1918 did not. Proposed by many school superintendents as a war emergency measure, the law permitted children between the ages of fourteen and sixteen to work in mercantile establishments and business offices during July and August of each year. The child was not required to have completed any particular school grade, but only to show that he had attended school for 130 days prior to the summer application. Saddled with this additional task, the local boards of health were left to handle the rush of vacation permit applicants with methods of their own choosing. Considering the fact that the health offices were already crowded with end-of-the-school-year applicants for *regular* working papers, it is not surprising that most health officers bungled the job of issuing vacation permits. The law did contain two potentially important provisions: one required the child to have a written promise of employment before a permit could be granted, and the other compelled employers to return the vacation certificate to the appropriate board of health by September 3 of each year. In contrast to the Labor Department and the NYCLC, the school superintendents were quite enthusiastic about the new law; indeed, a number of them urged that the vacation working age be lowered to twelve years and that factory labor be permitted. As one superintendent said, vacation work was "a great blessing to the poor."[31]

Although the vacation work permit became a permanent feature of New York's child labor law, it created more problems than it solved. Since it was very difficult to secure accurate proof of a child's age on such short notice, the tendency was to use short cuts. Factory work on a vacation certificate was prohibited, but to the consternation of the Labor Department some children began to appear in industrial plants armed with vacation working papers. Some employers failed to return the certificates in September and an appreciable number of children took out vacation certificates as a means of avoiding school in the fall. They had a good chance of success because the average school superintendent was not going to send truant officers searching high and low for some fourteen-year-old boy who had not been graduated from the eighth grade, or for a "backward" fifteen-year-old who had not completed the sixth grade. There was no incentive for school administrators to return such "assets" to their classrooms and consequently the problem of idle and truant children increased. The chief probation officer of the New York City Children's Court asserted that the Vacation Permit Law had "practically doubled" his work during 1918-19.[32]

As the 1920's began, it seemed to the NYCLC that more school-age children than ever were working; 74,686 employment certificates were issued in 1920 as opposed to 45,272 in 1910. To the Child Labor Committee this was a portent of disaster. They asked:

What does it mean to our Commonwealth to have seventy-five thousand children finish full-time schoolwork with barely a grammar-school preparation for citizenship? What does it mean to the community to allow this army of boys and girls to shoulder the burdens of adult life with bodies and minds in a formative period when they are especially susceptible to accidents, industrial strain, occupational disease and the moral dangers incident to certain employment? What does it mean to families to take a chance of mortgaging their children's future health and happiness for a few dollars a week?[33]

The increase was more apparent than real, for the NYCLC failed to take into account, at least publicly, the beneficial effects of the changes it had sponsored in the employment certification procedure. Children obtained working papers in 1920 who would have worked without them in 1910. As is apparent from Table 6, more certificates were issued to fourteen- and fifteen-year-olds in 1920 than in any year

TABLE 6 [35]

INITIAL EMPLOYMENT CERTIFICATES GRANTED TO FOURTEEN- AND FIFTEEN-YEAR-OLD CHILDREN FOR WORK IN FACTORIES AND COMMERCIAL ESTABLISHMENTS IN NEW YORK STATE, 1920-35*

Year	Number Granted	No. of 14 and 15 yr. Olds in State
1920	74,686	325,678
1921	58,003	
1922	37,984	
1923	54,351	
1924	48,831	
1925	48,669	
1926	53,644	
1927	53,348	
1928	52,174	
1929	54,570	
1930	47,350	421,279
1931	36,399	
1932	29,278	
1933	25,335	
1934	9,020	
1935	5,473	

* These figures show only the number of certificates issued for work in factories and commercial establishments and do not reflect children employed in the street trades, in agriculture, or in illegal employment; nor do they show vacation certificates or those granted in villages or rural areas. The school-leaving age was raised to sixteen in 1935.

through the depression of the 1930's. If the unexpired certificates from each preceding year are included, there was an average of at least sixty thousand New York youngsters legally employed in factories and commercial establishments during each year of the 1920's; roughly two-thirds of these were employed in New York City.[34]

What concerned the NYCLC even more than the number of children seeking employment certificates was a proposed change in the method of issuing them. In September, 1921, in response to pressure from the state school superintendents, the legislature transferred authority to issue working papers from the local boards of health to the school officials. An employment certificating officer appointed by each local superintendent of schools would now exercise supervisory authority over employment certification, but the physical examination of applicants and the evaluation of evidence of age remained in the hands of the local boards of health. The State Council of School Superintendents had been pushing for this since 1917, and at first the NYCLC had succeeded in sidetracking the proposal. Privately, the Child Labor Committee was afraid that school authorities would use their direct control over the certificate system to get rid of "undesirable" children. Publicly, the NYCLC praised the growing efficiency of the health officers and complained that the transfer to the schools "would result in as many standards as there are heads of the different school systems."[36]

The problems arising from the employment certificate system were not caused by the change in the issuing authority but by lack of progress in resolving the old fundamental difficulties. Since the child still controlled his employment certificate, it was easy for him to obtain working papers and then not report to his job. While a 1921 enactment finally required that each applicant present a written promise of a job from a specific employer, there was still no guarantee that the child would not remain idle. George Alger believed that "thousands of children . . . [were] annually evading the intent of . . . [the] law by leaving school, nominally to work, but actually to remain idle." To correct this situation the NYCLC in 1922 proposed an amendment to the Compulsory Education Law that required employers to notify the employment certificating officer within three days whether the child had reported for work. Shortly after this measure was passed, the NYCLC made a survey of 106 girls who had been granted employment certificates to do housework at home and found 64 of them still idle.[37] Employers were also supposed to return to the education authorities the employment certificate of any child who quit his job. This provision was designed to end the practice of children being released from a job and then roaming the streets using their employment certificates to forestall truant officers, but it proved very difficult to enforce. Some employers released children, kept their certificates, and used them for other children whom they were employing in violation of the law. In fact, once a child left school with working papers and his employer reported that he had been put to work, there were few opportunities for further checking. If the child was discharged and his employer kept the working papers, the chances were quite good that the youngster could remain out of work and out of school indefinitely, for the Labor Department inspectors might or might not discover a discrepancy in the employer's certificate file. The argument of the educators and child labor reformers that it was economically more profitable for children to stay in school might have logic on its side, but the fact remains that many youngsters sought working papers for no other purpose than to avoid school.

After the First World War the NYCLC conducted a "Back-to-School-or-Stay-in-School" drive, beginning a theme that has been reiterated to the present, and marking the formal recognition of New York's dropout problem. In spite of the campaign, a large number of New York's working children whose families did not need their earnings oscillated from one low-paying job to another, from work to idleness and back again. By 1931 money was much more important. Clare Lewis, Director of the New York State Division of Junior Placement, maintained that "when boys and girls arrive at an employment office minus breakfast and carfare and when they faint with hunger while they wait . . . [talk about] further education is simply worse than a farce."[38] One reason for New York's failure to do something about its dropouts was the continuation of the ancient conflict between the labor law and the education law. The discrepancies opened the way for a game of hide and seek in the forest of legal ambiguities. The education law, for example, unequivocally prohibited employment of children under fourteen during school hours "in any business or service whatever," while the labor law simply listed specific prohibited occupations.[39] The requirement that after September 1, 1925, sixteen-year-olds must obtain working papers was added to the education law but not to the labor law. A similar situation existed with respect to the provision requiring employers to report the start of a child's employment, and the provision regulating employment of girl messengers. All of these sections were of importance to employers and should therefore have appeared in *both* the education law and the labor law, or in the labor law alone, since that was the code most likely to be read by employers. To make matters worse, the education law was in conflict with itself on several significant points such as the scope of vacation employment certificates and the procedure for issuing working papers to minors over sixteen. Section 626B, 1-6, for example, authorized vacation employment on *days* when attendance upon instruction was not required, while Section 631 permitted it "when attendance upon instruction is not required," thus leaving the status of after-school work undefined.[40]

By 1928 the NYCLC had been able to secure amendments to both the education and labor laws, which resolved some of the conflict. Instead of reciting a list of illegal occupations, the labor law now flatly prohibited the employment of any child under fourteen in any "trade, business or occupation carried on for pecuniary gain." Unfortunately, this provision was now considerably stronger than the education law's prohibition against employment in a "business or service" —the question being what a "business or service" was and was not. In 1930 Industrial Commissioner Frances Perkins issued an order definitely classifying scallop sheds as workshops and the need for this kind of interpretation was to continue. Nevertheless, the strengthening of the labor law was significant. The original Factory Act had been passed in 1886, and it had taken forty-two years for a provision to appear on the statute books barring all child labor under the age of fourteen in occupations inspected by the Labor Department. Work such as street trading and agriculture, of course, were not under Labor Department jurisdiction. New York's tapestry of overlapping and sometimes conflicting legislation, divided in its enforcement authority and restricted in its operation by geography and population, made centralized and intelligent control of the education and labor of her youth extremely difficult.[41]

After the legislature placed the employment certificate system under the direction of the schools in 1921, the NYCLC decided that its best course would be closer supervision of the physical examinations to insure that youngsters were at least healthy before they entered the labor market. The law specified that each child be given a thorough medical examination: the standard form requested information on the applicant's posture, vision, hearing, teeth, throat, glands, lungs, heart, nervous system, kidneys, and skin. Any applicant with an organic cardiac disease, syphilis, irremediably defective vision, tuberculosis, diseases of the bones, joints, or glands, or a serious orthopedic defect was to be refused a certificate, and children with other defects such as poor teeth were to have these remedied. Yet, in city after city these standards were simply ignored. While it was as difficult to inspire health officers to give adequate examinations as it was to persuade school superintendents to initiate dramatic efforts to corral their potential dropouts, the NYCLC did make some progress. Its representatives dropped in on unsuspecting health officers, wrote letters to the Education and Labor Departments, and occasionally exerted very tangible pressure. Journeying to Lockport in 1921, the NYCLC field agent, Ethel H. VanBuskirk (Jeanie Minor was temporarily serving as secretary in George Hall's absence) found the health officer claiming that the school authorities were not requiring documentary proof of age; *his* department "made them get other papers." In Cortland, where a number of Russian, Polish, and Italian children were employed in rolling mills and skirt, corset, typewriter, and wallpaper factories, the health officer admitted that in eight years of giving physical examinations he had never turned down a child. He blamed the official forms; they were "damned rotten," said the doctor, solving the difficulty by ignoring the detailed information requested on the applicant's physical condition and simply writing across the top of the form "physically fit to go to work." He showed the NYCLC agent a copy of his latest "sarcastic" letter to the State Education Department ridiculing their forms and procedures.[42] When the school medical inspector in Cohoes began to refuse working papers to applicants with physical defects, parents complained to politicians who in turn pressured the school board. The school board ordered the physician to issue the papers or resign. Hearing of the difficulty, Jeanie Minor persuaded C. L. Mosher, Director of the State Division of Attendance, to threaten the Cohoes School Board with suspension of their state aid if they did not cease ordering their medical inspector to violate the law. This modified the board's position, but they nevertheless announced that they would appoint another physician to the post at the end of the year. In another upstate city Minor watched the city burial permit clerk issue working papers. This individual tested the applicant's vision by asking whether he could see an ordinary desk blotter at a distance of twenty feet, and marked all those who succeeded as having passed the *entire* physical examination.[43] In New Rochelle the doctor did use a stethoscope but placed it over the applicant's shirt instead of bare skin and in Troy the medical examiner left everything to his nurse, seeing applicants only on her recommendation. In her 1927 tour of upstate cities, Jeanie Minor found that not one child had been refused working papers in Albany, Beacon, Dunkirk, Newburgh, New Rochelle, Niagara Falls, Port Chester, Rome, Schenectady, Troy, or Utica.

Yet the picture was not entirely discouraging. In Buffalo, although the main employment certificate office was used for other purposes and was often a scene of "intolerable" confusion, the health officer did give good examinations, carefully filled out the forms, and rejected about 25 per cent of the applicants for poor vision or teeth.[44] There was one Albany doctor who was helping children with defective vision obtain free eyeglasses "in spite of vigorous opposition on the part of commercial opticians with considerable unpleasant newspaper publicity." In Syracuse, where employment certification in the past had been indifferent, Mrs. Horace Eaton of the local Consumers' League led a drive to improve conditions and secured the appointment of a highly effective physician to direct the examinations.[45] Notwithstanding the committee's efforts to oversee physical examinations, the legislature in 1928 completed the transfer of control over employment certificates by authorizing the schools to give the physical examinations. The NYCLC did succeed in having New York, Buffalo, and Rochester (the first-class cities) exempted from the law and thus kept physical examinations there in the hands of health officers. Jeanie Minor was most concerned about this change and said that she knew of "several superintendents whose attitude toward their . . . school health problem is one of general indifference."[46]

Although standards for medical examinations were higher in New York City than upstate, Jeanie Minor was convinced that even in the metropolis they had deteriorated since the First World War. When Dr. S. Josephine Baker resigned as director of the Bureau of Child Hygiene in the metropolitan Department of Health in 1923, the NYCLC decided that they wanted Dr. J. L. Blumenthal to be her successor. George Alger, Jeanie Minor, and Dr. Baker sought the help of another committee member, George S. Gillespie, a lawyer with political connections through the New York City Water Board who was successful in having Dr. Blumenthal named to head the Bureau of Child Hygiene.[47] Within a few years, however, the committee found Blumenthal inadequate and bombarded Commissioner of Health Shirley Wynne with requests for his removal. By 1931 Jeanie Minor was lamenting Wynne's failure to obtain Blumenthal's voluntary resignation and asserting that "the situation cried aloud for a man of organizing ability, integrity, and the courage to face the results of several years of inactivity which has badly punctured the morale of the Bureau."[48] Perhaps it was too much work for one man. During 1928, for example, 61,637 physical examinations were given in New York City and although the rate of rejection was the highest in the state, George Hall was convinced that most of the physical examinations were inadequate. Children with obvious physical defects kept turning up at the large West Side Continuation School and complaints reached the NYCLC from concerns such as R. H. Macy and the Metropolitan

Life Insurance Company that they were "constantly and increasingly" rejecting youngsters with working papers because of their poor physical condition.[49] Observing the physical examination process in New York City at the beginning of the 1930 summer rush, Miss Minor noted that some of the doctors arrived late at the schools and that

> despite precautions taken . . . congestion and confusion reigned —mildly in some places and wildly in others. To make adequate examinations was . . . most difficult and to examine hearts or hearing with any degree of accuracy simply impossible.

Since doctors were ordered to check at least seventy-five children between 9:00 A.M. and 12:00 noon, they could give only perfunctory examinations. Minor reported that "crowds of interested youngsters filling corridors and doorways watched the examinations, heard the questions and answers, studied the eye-charts and enjoyed it all hugely." The examination itself was

> for the most part . . . limited to a vision test—at varying distances in the various offices—a swift . . . examination of teeth and tonsils and a heart examination which usually consisted in a momentary placing of the stethoscope at the apex of the heart either on the bared skin or over the clothing. . . . Except in a few instances there was no examination of lungs, ears, skin or spine. The paucity of supervisors and the lack of any previous instruction on the nature of the work . . . resulted in turning loose on this job a group of men and women few of whom realized its vital importance to the child's industrial future.

On another occasion Minor watched a New York City doctor examine sixty-six hearts in twenty minutes—pronouncing all perfect.[50] In an effort to meet the NYCLC objections, Health Commissioner Wynne brought in "experts" (among them Jeanie Minor; Courtenay Dinwiddie, formerly of the American Child Health Association; and a young man from the New York Tuberculosis and Health Association named Harry Hopkins) to advise the Bureau of Child Hygiene,[51] but the employment certificate system failed to show much improvement. While the metropolitan rejection rate for working paper applicants during the 1930's remained constant at about 25 per cent, examinations given by vocational high schools in 1939 to 42,000 New York City students planning to go to work showed that *all* but 5,700 were in need of corrective treatment. The high-school examinations had been thorough, lasting fifteen to thirty minutes; working paper examinations normally lasted only three minutes.

Medical examinations in the rest of the state were as inadequate as ever. Journeying upstate in the late 1930's George Hall found that physical examinations for working papers had been abandoned entirely in Rochester and Albany. In Syracuse and Buffalo it had become the practice to grant regular working papers to children with correctible physical defects for temporary periods. Employment certification officers reasoned that the families were too poor to pay for having teeth or vision corrected and the child must therefore begin working to earn the money. While admitting that there was no really effective way to follow up these "temporary" certificates, some doctors justified their action under the limited physical fitness section of the labor law. Hall contended that "rejections accomplished far more speedy correction of physical defects." During 1937-38 three-fourths of the cities failed to reject a single applicant for physical reasons.[52] The main defect of the employment certificate system was probably beyond the control of the officials or the NYCLC, for any attempt to demand high physical and educational standards would run against the tide of public opinion. For this reason the system was doomed to remain largely a symbolic operation.

TABLE 7 [53]
FULL-TIME INITIAL CERTIFICATES ISSUED TO CHILDREN IN
NEW YORK STATE, 1927-60*

Year (Ending Aug. 31)	Number Issued	Ages (Incl.)	No. of 14-16 Year-Olds in State (Incl.)
1927-28	72,551	14-16	
1932-33	44,178	14-16	629,347 (1930)
			No. of 16-17 Year-Olds in State (Incl.)
1937-38	37,939	16-17	
1940	59,323	16-17	443,104 (1940)
1945	121,937	16-17	
1950	81,385	16-17	353,367 (1950)
1955	57,146	16-17	
1960	60,077	16-17	

* These figures do not include farm work permits, newspaper carrier-boy certificates, or street trade badges.

Realizing that many children would go to work before graduating from high school, the NYCLC had long sought a method whereby these youngsters might continue their education. In 1913 the committee was pleased about the passage of its law establishing voluntary

Six-Year-Old Boy Taking Home Work, 1923

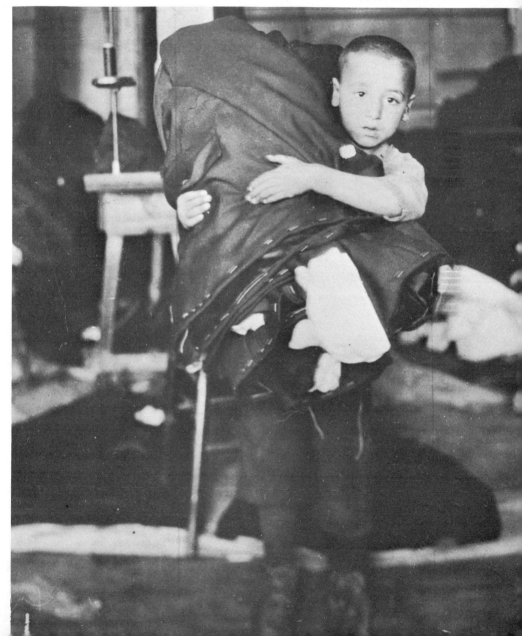

Factory Child Labor

Culver Pictures, Inc.

Bean Pickers, New York, 1939

National Child Labor Committ

Tenement Homework on Feathers, Early 1900's

Messenger Boys in City Hall Park, 1903

National Child Labor Committee

Potato Pickers on Long Island

New York Newsboys about 1900

Young Bean Picker, 1954

Bootblack, 1920's

Eisenstaedt-Pix for the
National Child Labor Committee

Gum Vendors, Manhattan, Early 1900's

evening "continuation" schools for working children between the ages of fourteen and sixteen. In 1919 the committee cooperated with the National Society for the Promotion of Industrial Education in sponsoring the Lockwood Act, New York's first compulsory continuation school law. In order to gain the rural legislative support necessary

TABLE 8 [54]

PART-TIME (AFTER SCHOOL) AND VACATION WORK PERMITS ISSUED IN NEW YORK STATE TO CHILDREN FOURTEEN AND FIFTEEN YEARS OLD, 1927-58*

Year	Number Issued	No. of 14 and 15 Year-Olds in State
1927-28	17,971	
1932-33	6,544	421,279 (1930)
1937-38	18,143	
1940	10,482	430,413 (1940)
1941	17,770	
1942	35,521	
1943	91,962	
1944	107,695	
1945	97,322	
1946	53,259	
1947	39,002	
1948	35,758	
1949	27,984	
1950	27,824	346,025 (1950)
1951	40,282	
1952	47,360	
1953	46,712	
1954	41,067	
1955	43,808	
1956	50,209	
1957	51,595	
1958	42,549	

* These figures do not include farm work permits, newspaper carrier-boy certificates, or street trade badges.

for its passage, the committee inserted a provision stating that school districts in which there were less than two hundred employed minors need not set up continuation schools. As finally amended in 1924, the law required all fourteen- to eighteen-year-old working children who were not high-school graduates and who were not attending full-time day instruction to attend continuation school at least four hours a week between the hours of 8:00 A.M. and 5:00 P.M.[55] The State Education Department was enthusiastic about the program announcing that in addition to vocational training in woodworking, electrical

wiring, printing, auto mechanics, salesmanship, bookkeeping, type-
writing, homemaking, and costume design, the continuation schools
would also give courses in "the essentials" of English, mathematics,
history, civics, and hygiene. Moreover, they would encourage thrift,
further social activities and "bridge . . . the gap between the child and
young man or young woman."[56] According to the Education Department, the state's employers gave "excellent cooperation" because they
realized "that besides contributing their share to education and up-
building of the youth of the community, the training that such pupils
receive in continuation schools makes them more reliable and efficient
workers." Instruction was to be "entirely individual and correlated with
the pupil's employment."[57]

A large number of students attended the schools. From an initial
30,234 pupils for the state in 1920-21, the continuation school enrollment rose to a peak of 168,377 in 1927-28. Some of the schools were
well run; when George Hall visited a Rochester continuation school in
1931 he was impressed by the variety of courses offered, the unusually
good attendance, and the excellent spirit of the students.[58] Supporters
of the continuation system claimed that the great majority of employers
were hiring continuation school pupils without prejudice and did not
resent the four hours "lost" from the work week. The Education Department surveyed 18,300 male continuation school students and
found that 60.7 per cent of their employers were paying them for
the hours they spent in school. Some employers organized their own
schools, a practice permitted by law if the company school met Education Department standards. The Onondaga Pottery Company of
Syracuse informed prospective employees that "there is a good job,
a prize of at least $46.00 and a diploma from the Onondaga Pottery
Company waiting for you if you have the stuff in you which makes
successful men." Not all employers were so progressive. Each year
there were about a dozen bills to change the Continuation School
Law initiated in the legislature, for many employers felt that the
best hours of the working day should belong to them and youngsters
wishing to continue their education should do so at night.[59]

As the program continued it become obvious that a large number
of youngsters were attending the continuation schools four hours
a week and then loafing in the streets the rest of the time. Occasionally
an active school official would crack down, such as the Jamestown
superintendent who imposed the twenty-hour weekly attendance
requirement for "temporarily unemployed" minors. Within a month
60 per cent of Jamestown's young loafers had found jobs. In larger cities
the problem was more severe. A study conducted by the NYCLC in

1925-26 revealed that of the 51,081 New York City continuation school students, only 13 per cent were actually seen at work in factories and stores by the state inspectors. The factory and mercantile inspectors found only 4 per cent of the continuation school students actually at work in Albany, 17 per cent in Buffalo, 20 per cent in Rochester, 14 per cent in Syracuse and 17 per cent in Troy.[60] Some continuation students, of course, were working at home or in occupations not regularly inspected, but the low percentage of students who could actually be seen at work indicates the grave difficulties in coordinating education and employment and justifies the conclusion that for a large number of New York's youngsters the continuation schools were a passport to Pleasure Island: four hours of school and no work.

The continuation schools became a center of controversy. A New York City teacher wrote George Hall that "the money expended on . . . [continuation schools] has been largely thrown away. Among the teaching fraternity they are a joke." In 1929 a twenty-year-old former continuation school student, E. Ehrlich, replied to a letter in the New York *Sun* written by George Hall praising the experiment. Ehrlich recalled his difficulties in finding a job which would permit him to attend continuation school and then described the institution itself as

> situated in the slums of the lower east side. On arriving there, I found myself among a rough crew, assigned to a man, who being considered incompetent as a teacher in a regular school, had obtained this position . . . through some kind of political pull. He gave me a French grammar and although he knew nothing of the language himself, told me that I would learn it by reading this book one day a week. . . . I . . . . found that he knew little of mathematics, science, or as far as I could ascertain, any subject. In the meantime the rest of the surley crew were dozing off or reading newspapers.

Ehrlich urged that employed youngsters be permitted to attend night schools which he thought employed much more competent teachers.[61] There was always the lunatic fringe. About 1925 Hall received a copy of a circular put out by the "City Division of the Anti-Red Society of America, Anti-Continuation School Bureau" which addressed the city's pupils as follows:

> Imagine yourself losing from $1. to $3. week after week, or losing a good job because of the [continuation] school. As any intelligent person knows, very little can be taught in the short space of four hours weekly yet this has been going on for a long time with

none or very little effort used to fight these conditions! Why? Because you are not organized![62]

The death blow to the continuation schools was not to come from the courts—which upheld their constitutionality in 1928—nor from the Anti-Red Society, but from the depression of the 1930's. The collapse forced thousands of children out of permanent jobs and hence out of continuation schools. Moreover, the school-leaving age was raised to sixteen in 1935, a measure that removed a large group of fourteen- and fifteen-year-olds from the continuation schools. The institutions consequently began to organize as full-time vocational schools, and by 1938-39 only 32,024 of the state's youngsters were attending continuation classes.[63]

For some time the Child Labor Committee had realized that their best chance of controlling child labor was to keep children in school rather than attempt to regulate them once they had gone to work. As early as 1915 Dr. S. Josephine Baker had urged the committee to campaign to raise the school-leaving age from fourteen to sixteen. The Wellington Law of 1916 did, in effect, establish a fifteen-year school-leaving age because it barred all fourteen-year-olds who were not graduates of an eighth-grade elementary school from work. (Fifteen-year-olds might work if they had completed the sixth grade.)[64] The difficulty with these laws and with subsequent proposals based upon them was that they permitted the brighter children to leave school earlier for work and kept in school just those "backward" children whom much of society felt *ought* to be employed. In 1920 George Hall tried to persuade the Commissioner of Education to back a bill requiring all children to attend school until their sixteenth birthday. A provision exempting fourteen- and fifteen-year-old elementary school graduates reduced the NYCLC proposal to nothing more than an attempt to keep backward fourteen- and fifteen-year-olds in the classroom for one or two additional years. This plan met with a justifiably cool reception from the Education Department whose officials were concerned lest the appearance of this "sixteen year" bill in the legislature provide the lawmakers with a ready excuse for scrapping the 1919 Continuation School Law and passing the less restrictive sixteen-year bill. Outcries against the Continuation Law were already coming from the "financial authorities who make up the state budget." Even Hall agreed that it would be foolish to trade the sixteen-year bill for the Continuation Law. Lewis Wilson, chief of the Division of Industrial Education, stated bluntly that he questioned the value of "keeping more than

50,000 children in school who are clearly slow-minded as evidenced by the fact that they were unable to graduate [from the eighth grade] by their fourteenth birthday." James D. Sullivan, head of the Division of Attendance, was alarmed by the enforcement problem a new minimum age could present; the state, he pointed out, "had not provided sufficient machinery" to enforce the current standards. In the end the education officials politely shelved the proposal.[65] The NYCLC, however, would not give it up. In 1923 they polled 338 school superintendents, and of the 196 who replied only 84 were in favor of the sixteen-year proposal without reservations. Those who opposed the age limit change were "practically unanimous" in decrying the folly of keeping overage boys and girls hanging around classrooms in view of the "utter lack" of manual training facilities in most parts of the state.[66] One stumbling block was the powerful New York City Board of Education which throughout the 1920's opposed any change in the school-leaving age because it would result in severely overcrowded schools. No further steps were taken until 1930 when at Florence Kelley's insistence the NYCLC decided to support a fifteen-year-age bill in the 1930 legislative session. She felt that such a move would give jobs to the depression-unemployed and would also produce a more intelligent working class in the future.[67] Although realizing that the bill was in for tough sledding, the committee was hopeful because it now had the support of the State Education Department and of the New York City, Rochester, and Buffalo school superintendents. The measure passed the Senate but died in the Assembly Rules Committee. Instrumental in its defeat was the NYCLC's failure to persuade the State Federation of Labor to support the bill even though the federation had been on record for several years as favoring a school-leaving age of sixteen. Secretary John M. O'Hanlon told Jeanie Minor that the unemployment of many union members made the earnings of fourteen-year-olds essential for the support of their families. Since the continuation schools were largely staffed by trade union personnel (whose salaries, at least in New York City, equalled the regular high-school salaries) the jobs of many teachers would be eliminated if the fifteen-year bill passed, for 9,000 fourteen-year-olds would be taken out of the metropolitan continuation schools. As George Hall put it, "There [were] . . . wheels within wheels."[68]

The fifteen-year bill was presented again in the 1931 legislative session. Strongly committed to raising the school-leaving age, Lieutenant Governor Herbert H. Lehman (a member of the NYCLC Board of Directors from 1913 to 1925) made a radio address and wrote articles in support of the measure. To Lehman the case was clear. With an estimated 125,000 New York children under seventeen holding jobs during 1930, he could not help wondering what it would "mean this winter to many discouraged and thinly-clad breadliners, sometimes only a few years beyond school age, if these [employed] boys and girls had remained in school and left the jobs for their elders to fill?"[69] Unfortunately, this argument cut two ways, for to some parents the earnings of their children were a bird in the hand while their own chances for jobs appeared problematical even if the children were made to stay in school. After the bill failed to pass in the 1931 session, Frances Perkins had some realistic words for the NYCLC. In a stinging memorandum she charged the committee with lack of vision. "Is it not true," she asked, "that throughout the state a great many intelligent people questioned . . . the bill, because they could see no gain to the child from the extra year of schooling?" The NYCLC, she believed, had

> done very little toward presenting for popular consideration a program of what might be done with these early adolescent years that would in the end give to society and to the children themselves a much greater return than if those same years had been spent at low wages repetitive jobs which very likely serve as training to prepare the young person for a lifetime of low wage repetitive job holding.

It was the committee's obligation to show not only what harm befell child laborers but "what tremendous social gains we stand to make through carrying out a program of proper training for life during those very impressionable early adolescent years."[70]

In preparation for the 1932 campaign, Jeanie Minor traveled the state drumming up support for the fifteen-year bill addressing such groups as the Scarsdale Women's Club, the Westchester County League of Women Voters, and the annual State Conference of the League of Women Voters. She found that "many League chairmen are making this bill their chief objective this winter and will help it along not only by good publicity but by personal contact with legislators"; nevertheless, the bill failed to pass in the 1932 session. George Hall believed that the most potent influence against the bill had been the State Council of Catholic School Superintendents whose "representatives have been talking against it to members of the legislature."[71]

By 1933 the situation was somewhat different. The New Deal was about to begin, and the country had passed through still another year of depression. With fewer children employed, the NYCLC felt that it had little to lose by trying for a sixteen-year school-leaving age, because those who opposed a sixteen-year bill would also oppose one set at fifteen years. Consequently, a sixteen-year measure was introduced with the backing of the State Federation of Labor, Governor Herbert H. Lehman, and U.S. Senator Robert F. Wagner.[72] Yet in spite of this powerful support, the 1933 sixteen-year bill became stalled in committee almost immediately, and when Hall conferred with the governor, Lehman told him that there appeared to be no chance of moving it. The chairman of the Assembly Committee on Education reported that it was "hopeless" to try for the bill because it was going to cost the state money. Senator T. C. Desmond, one of the bill's sponsors, was under strong pressure from the State Department of Mental Hygiene and the Attendance Division of the State Department of Education to amend the measure so as to permit fourteen- and fifteen-year-olds who were "mentally backward" to leave school. Hall was also convinced that "under cover" Catholic opposition was being exerted. To break the stalemate, he told Senator Desmond to offer the old fifteen-year bill as a substitute.[73] This was foolish, for the opposition continued unabated. The Roman Catholic Church strongly opposed the measure. As expressed by the Reverend William R. Kelley, representing the State Council of Catholic School Superintendents; by the Reverend Joseph V. S. McClancy, Superintendent of Catholic Schools in the Brooklyn Diocese; and by the Catholic Church's attorney and Albany lobbyist, Charles J. Tobin; the Catholic opposition charged that the bill was an invasion of parental rights, that it would create poverty by reducing family earnings, and that it would overcrowd parochial classrooms. Not all Catholic leaders agreed with the parental rights argument—in 1931 Jeanie Minor had met with Patrick Cardinal Hayes in New York and reported that His Eminence "was emphatic in his declaration that the Roman Catholic Church does not endorse or oppose school legislation. Its only concern [was] . . . with the dogma taught in its own schools." One of the Cardinal's aides "derided the argument advanced . . . by . . . parochial school officials that such legislation was an unwarranted interference with parental rights, adding that that argument would lie also against the . . . compulsory school law."[74] Nevertheless, the NYCLC could not persuade the State Council of Catholic School Superintendents to drop its opposition. Father William R. Kelley appeared convinced that the proposed age increase would adversely affect some family earnings and he was also concerned about the lack of classroom space. So were the public school officials. Manfred Ehrich, now Chairman of the NYCLC, reported marked opposition from the rural areas of the state whose "financial plight made hopeless the securing of funds for transportation of older pupils to consolidated high schools, much less any appropriations for new buildings and equipment."[75] But the NYCLC kept up the fight. George Hall met with Catholic leaders, some of whom were not above needling him about certain inconsistencies in the NYCLC position. Father Joseph V. S. McClancy, the Brooklyn Diocesan Superintendent wrote his Albany counterpart that "Our friend, Mr. George Hall, was at the office . . . to see if our Council [of Catholic School Superintendents] would join forces with his group in the furtherance of the increase in the legal school-leaving age. I told him that I would present his petition at our next meeting but gave him no hope unless his group would labor in the open to give us state aid for our secular education products. He was a beaten man." McClancy found Hall "shallow" and judged that he "works best in the dark."[76]

As the Desmond Fifteen Year Bill moved toward a vote in 1933, Father Kelley wired Senator Hyman G. Schackno, a Bronx Democrat, that the measure was sponsored by "small private and unrepresentative organizations," and asked him on behalf of 400,000 Catholic-school children to defeat the measure and thereby preserve the liberty of parents to shape the careers of their children. Father Kelley denied that any appreciable number of fourteen-year-olds would be affected by the bill; the NYCLC admitted that only five or six thousand such children had received working papers in 1932-33 but insisted that the legislation pass "before the rush of children begins when jobs are plentiful again."[77] While the Catholic-school superintendents were not simply inventing the poverty and parental rights arguments, it is much more probable that their stand against the school-leaving bill was taken as school superintendents rather than as Catholics. The proposed law would limit the ability of superintendents to get rid of "backward" fourteen-year-olds, and while this restriction would not operate as strongly on the parochial schools (which could always send their fourteen-year-olds to the public schools), it would create problems and tensions. New school buildings would also be required. To a lesser degree the fight then being waged in New York to secure ratification of the federal Child Labor Amendment—a proposal to which many of the New York clergy were unalterably opposed—conditioned their opposition to the school-leaving bill.

Secretary Hall was in the Senate Chamber on April 5, 1933, when the Desmond Fifteen Year Bill came up for a third reading. As Senator Desmond was speaking in defense of his bill, he was interrupted, according to Hall, by Senator Schackno waving a telegram. He described the message (which was actually from Father Kelley) as a "mandate from the Cardinal" (presumably Hayes) to defeat the bill.

After Desmond regained the floor, he pointed out that his bill was supported by Governor Lehman, Secretary of Labor Perkins, the State Federation of Labor, the NYCLC, and other reform organizations. Senator O'Brien of Brooklyn then read a letter from Father McClancy and was followed by other senators who read similar communications from Catholic clergymen in Buffalo and Rochester. Then, wrote Hall

> Schackno moved to recommit the bill and ayes and noes were called for. A roar of ayes with not more than 2 or 3 noes were heard and so the bill was beheaded without a roll call vote by order of the Church. Dunnigan [John J. Dunnigan of the Bronx, Democratic leader in the Senate] never raised a finger to stand by the Governor [Hall claimed that Dunnigan had been given a direct order by Lehman's counsel to pass the bill] or keep his party in line. The Church first and Party second seems to be the rule here. It was an irony to have the opposition led by a Jew and a Democrat.

Hall was understandably bitter. He blamed Albany attorney Charles J. Tobin for "instigating" the letters and telegrams, a charge that was probably true, for in 1935 Father McClancy wrote Irwin Steingut, then Speaker of the Assembly, that "Mr. Charles J. Tobin received his instructions from our State Council of Catholic School Superintendents on this measure [the 1935 sixteen year bill]."[78]

During 1934 the NYCLC continued its work for the bill, holding conferences with the Catholics, the State Labor and Education Departments, the State Federation of Labor, and a host of other groups including the League of Women Voters, the New York Federation of Women's Clubs, the Women's Christian Temperance Union, the Women's Committee of the Republican and Democratic Parties, and the Y.W.C.A. By 1934 the National Recovery Administration codes had virtually established a sixteen-year minimum age for New York industries engaged in interstate commerce, and when the sixteen-year bill again failed to pass the 1934 legislature, Fred S. Hall blamed the NRA for giving the lawmakers an easy way out.[79] While there is some truth in this charge, it does not follow, as Hall contended, that the jettisoning of NRA by the United States Supreme Court made possible the passage of the sixteen-year bill. It seems more likely that the sixteen-year federal minimum age of 1934 conditioned many people to the idea that some kind of sixteen-year school-leaving age was inevitable. If so, it might better be administered by the states. By the opening of the 1935 legislature the opponents of the sixteen-year proposal were on the defensive. The poverty argument now appeared unrealistic as only 9,020 employment certificates had been granted to fourteen- and fifteen-year-olds in 1934, and the absence of any sizable number of working children forced the poverty argument to give way to the more symbolic view that children should not take jobs from their elders. But Father McClancy wrote that they were ready for a compromise, and Fred Hall reported that the only open opposition at the 1935 bill's legislative hearing was that of the Associated Industries of New York State.[80] The NRA experience had also forced many school districts to face the problem of finding room for fourteen- and fifteen-year-olds who had to stay in school under federal law. According to an NYCLC survey, the classroom shortage long predicted by opponents of raising the school-leaving age never materialized under NRA, because in most cities the extra pupils were simply housed in the buildings used by the declining continuation schools. Those proposing the 1935 sixteen-year bill also pointed out that it was only a slight enlargement of an existing federal requirement (that is, the state enactment would bring businesses wholly in intrastate commerce up to the standards required of those in interstate commerce). Introduced by Senator A. S. Feld of Manhattan, the bill passed the Senate without difficulty, but on March 25 it was defeated by ten votes in the Assembly. There was a successful motion for reconsideration, however, and George Hall began working frantically to line up ten votes. In close cooperation with Governor Lehman's counsel, Charles Poletti, Hall sent urgent telegrams to absent legislators in Buffalo, Rochester, Elmira, and Binghamton. On April 12 the measure was reconsidered. It now contained a compromise amendment permitting children to leave school at the age of fifteen if they had been certified by the Education Department as incapable of profiting from further instruction. This change was supported by the Catholic-school superintendents who had also tried unsuccessfully to allow dismissals at fifteen for children whose earnings were needed at home.[81] The ten votes obtained by pressure from the governor's office and the NYCLC provided the margin of victory for the Feld-Breitbart Bill. Governor Lehman signed it on April 24, 1935, presenting one of the pens to the NYCLC and praising the committee for "the splendid work which you did in the enactment of this bill, as well as many others affecting the children of our state." In its final form, the Sixteen Year School-leaving Law permitted a number of exceptions to the general rule that minors must remain in school until the age of sixteen. They were: fourteen- and fifteen-year-olds lawfully employed at the time of the bill's passage; fourteen- and fifteen-year-olds who wished to work during vacations and after school; fourteen- and fifteen-year-olds who were high-school graduates; and fifteen-year-olds who had been certified as incapable of profiting from further instruction. The latter exemption for "backward" children was used with great caution. During the period September 1, 1937, to December 31, 1937, only fifteen were issued throughout the state. The sixteen-year-old school-leaving age was established although there have been suggestions to the present day that it be lowered to fifteen and that the requirements for releasing "ineducable" youngsters be relaxed. Hailed by the NYCLC as "the greatest single gain in this field for the last thirty years" the law went into effect on September 1, 1936. When George Hall polled ninety-five school superintendents in 1937 about the operation of the statute, their replies indicated an almost unanimous sentiment in favor of the measure now that it had been passed.[82] The NYCLC knew the full significance of this law, for the committee's efforts to end child labor in commercial establishments, tenements, and the street trades had been long and arduous. The record of that struggle was clear evidence that the best way to prevent the abuse of children in the labor market was to keep them in school.

And these little children . . . are running . . . as
cash girls and stock girls . . . at the bid of everybody. Everybody has a say to the child. She has got
to go for everybody, and she only gets $3 a week.
They are very little girls and they work hard. . . .
And we hear that they work shorter hours, but they
certainly do not. They work to the last minute.

—SYLVIA SCHULMAN, *Clerk*, Testimony before the United States Commission on Industrial Relations, 1914

VI. Commercial Establishments, Tenement Homework, and Street Trades

A commercial, or mercantile, establishment is a place where
goods are offered for sale. Although at the turn of the century the
term "mercantile establishment" usually referred to a department
store, the meaning was broadened over the years until it included
work in, or in connection with, business offices, telegraph offices,
restaurants, hotels, apartment houses, theatres, places of amusement,
bowling alleys, gas stations, barber shops, and shoe shine parlors.
Eventually all delivery work for stores, the distribution of handbills,
the selling of vegetables from trucks and ice cream in the street,
and caddying on golf courses came within the scope of the mercantile
law and were regulated as occupations in commercial establishments.[1]
It is impossible to state with any accuracy the precise number of
children engaged in commercial occupations at any given period.
Again the federal census is of little help; probably the best indications
are the employment certificate figures in Tables 6, 7, and 8 (Chapter
V), which show the combined totals for factory and commercial
work.[2] The difficulty was the sheer quantity of small stores and commercial enterprises of all kinds in a state the size of New York and
the impossibility of checking on each one with the small number of
inspectors available. Although New York's factories tended to be
broken into comparatively small units under the control of many
different owners, it was much easier to find and inspect them than
to check on the thousands of commercial establishments ranging
from giant department stores to "hole-in-the-wall" East Side shops
and upstate poolrooms.

128

Before the passage of the 1903 child labor legislation, exploitation of very young children in New York's commercial establishments was common. Florence Kelley told of finding twelve little girls, ages ten to fourteen, sitting on the curb at Broadway and Grand Street in December, 1902.

> They had reported for work [in the stores] at 7:30 in the morning. . . . They had had scant time for luncheon, and worked again until suppertime. Then, in one store, they were given ten cents each and in another . . . a meal ticket. Several meal tickets proved worthless because there was nothing left to eat at the late hour at which the children were allowed to stop working. After supper they had all worked again until ten o'clock when they had been sent home. After waiting half an hour for a car, it was proposed to walk home together; but one little girl sat down on the curbstone crying and saying that she could not walk, if she never reached home. The others stayed with her in the cold of December with midnight approaching, little victims of the cruelty that, year after year, travesties the Christmas season.[3]

A ten-hour day and sixty-hour week for boys under sixteen and girls under twenty-one working in stores had been established in 1896, but the enforcement of the statute by local health boards was a farce. Children fourteen or older might legally be kept at work until 10:00 P.M. and under the "Christmas exception" (December 15-January 1) until any hour. Twelve- and thirteen-year-olds were permitted to work during Christmas and school vacations. In 1903 the Hill-Finch Commercial Act broadened the existing coverage of the mercantile law to include business offices, telegraph offices, restaurants, hotels, apartment houses, and delivery and messenger boys. It also barred twelve- and thirteen-year-olds from vacation work in stores in first- and second-class cities, established a nine-hour working day for children under sixteen, and repealed the "Christmas exception," but the 1903 legislation was of little immediate effect, for local health boards retained the enforcing power. Agents of the New York Consumers' League investigated Manhattan's major shopping centers during the 1905 Christmas season and found many "little pale-faced sleepy children"—some younger than twelve—coming off shift in the department stores at 10:30 P.M. Most of them had been working since 8:00 A.M. The League reported that the Health Department had verified these conditions but was unwilling to do anything about them.[4] In 1906 the NYCLC conducted an investigation of the New York City Department of Health, which revealed shocking inadequacies in the Department's inspection procedure, filing system, and record of prosecutions. The NYCLC found that the Health Department records were so snarled that "information absolutely essential for proper supervision . . . is so buried by the system of recording it, and is so mixed in with records of sanitary inspections, as to make it almost useless to the officials." While the Health Department had fifty-three inspectors, they devoted only a part of their time to mercantile inspections. The department insisted that each man checked at least twenty stores a week, but the NYCLC was convinced that the actual number was much lower. How else could the poor prosecution record be explained? During the entire year 1904 only *one* department store owner was prosecuted for employing children illegally and even he was not convicted. The usual policy of the Health Department was to order illegally employed children discharged, but this procedure was ineffective, for although the department claimed to be making 1,060 mercantile inspections a week, it discharged a weekly average of only six child laborers. This record made John McMackin's administration of the Labor Department appear extraordinarily efficient: the factory inspectors were discharging about twenty-five children a week.[5] Florence Kelley accused the New York City Retail Dealers Association of controlling the Health Department. The Association Secretary, she charged, had told an incoming Commissioner of Health that the merchants did not "consider it desirable that the [labor] law should be enforced in stores with the same rigor with which it . . . [was] enforced in factories." The prosecution record of the Health Department showed that it understood the warning. If factory owners were daring in their use of illegal child labor, store owners were even bolder. In 1909 *51.4 per cent* of the children found employed in department stores in New York City, Buffalo and Rochester were working illegally; the rate for factories was 7.9 per cent. Manufacturers often moved their child packers into rented department store space during rush seasons to work them unlimited hours with less risk of detection. Miss Kelley was furious at the lack of enforcement. Observing about 150 children working illegally in a big department store at 10:20 P.M. she noted that

> If one of those children had stolen any small article [from the store] . . . the heavy hand of the law would have carried that child promptly into juvenile court. But one hundred and fifty children were robbed of sleep in violation of the law and . . . their employer who robbed them has never been prosecuted . . . and will never be.[6]

The reformers were upset by what they regarded as the callous indifference of the merchants to human needs. Robert Hunter told of hearing an owner of a dry goods store complain that the nine-hour law was unjust to children under sixteen and must be repealed— otherwise the stores would have to hire children over sixteen who could fit into the normal operating schedule of the stores. Hunter asked him if there were not enough workers over sixteen available. "Oh, yes," was the merchant's reply, "there are enough children over sixteen but the smaller ones would be unemployed."[7] Store work was oppressive, not only for children but for older workers as well. As late as 1914 Gertrude Beeks, Secretary of the Welfare Department of the conservative National Civic Federation, maintained that "among . . . wrongs to be righted" in the stores were

> the long workday, including Christmas and general overtime work; slow promotions; inefficient pay of a large class after the apprenticeship period; the fining and docking system; no dismissal notice to rank and file; inadequate fire protection; makeshift or unattractive lunch, hospital, and rest rooms; lack of attention to physical needs of mature workers, such as separate lunchrooms and special quiet rooms for relaxation of women; instruction talks and conferences "after hours"; [and] no general plan for summer vacations with pay.[8]

Long hours of work with surprise overtime and Sunday tasks were the rule. Surveying 216 stores throughout the state, the Factory Investigating Commission found that over half of the 38,383 women employees worked more than 54 hours a week and only 35 of the stores closed regularly at 6:00 P.M., with the others staying open much later. In some stores the employees were subjected to tyrannical control. Merchants would lock out workers who arrived more than five minutes late for work and levy fines out of all proportion to offenses. Girls and children were on their feet constantly while working and as a result "almost without exception they complain[ed] of extreme discomfort and fatigue . . . swollen and aching feet and broken arches . . . pain [that] reached up to the thighs." Such standing could have serious effects on the female reproductive organs.[9] The mercantile law required that the store furnish one seat for every three girls, but when a floorwalker saw a girl sitting down he would move her to a busier location. Other stores had no seats at all. Benjamin Gitlow, President of the Retail Clerks' Union, recalled working in Bloomingdale Brothers store where chairs were brought in only when the store thought an inspector was coming, but any girl who had the temerity to sit down in one of them was rebuked. As soon as the alarm was over the chairs would be returned to a warehouse.[10] Many department stores were inadequately ventilated—even the customers complained. Almost 10 per cent of the 61,717 employees surveyed by the Factory Commission were working in basements and subbasements where the only ventilation was dust-laden air pumped in directly from street level.

Job security in the stores was practically nonexistent. Employees could be fired without a moment's notice at the whim of any superior. The New York City Consumers' League persuaded one of its "White List" stores to keep a job open for an old employee so that she might take a vacation without pay to recuperate from an illness. A solemn promise that her job would be held was made to the league, her clergyman, and her physician, but when she returned from vacation the job was gone. "Old houses that pride themselves on their honorable business records," the League raged, "should be just as keen to keep their agreements . . . with their employees as they are to keep those made or implied with their customers or manufacturers." The large stores blamed the continuation of many bad practices on the pressure from their smaller competitors. If the little operators cut costs to the bone, so must the big ones. If the small stores on the East Side stayed open late, the big ones must follow suit. In one respect the large stores were better than the little East Side shops— they were heated in winter. In store after store on the lower East Side the Consumers' League found the clerks shivering in the cold with "hands . . . so red and numb that they could scarcely do up parcels." To the league the customer bore some of the responsibility and it urged the public to patronize only stores that met league standards and not to accept late deliveries of goods carried by young children. "Some New York merchants actually treat their horses better than . . . their human employees," the League commented, citing the case of a delivery man who had regularly to go all the way to Tarrytown from New York City and back, reaching home after 3:00 A.M. —his horse was changed enroute.[11]

There was still a more serious problem. An ugly undertone about the fate of underpaid shopgirls runs through much of the testimony on store conditions before the Industrial Commission. In 1913, 61.9 per cent of the department store saleswomen in major New York cities and 91 per cent of the five-and-ten-cent store girls earned less than eight dollars a week. Since nine dollars was the "amount generally conceded to be the minimum on which a girl can live decently in New York City," some of the girls turned to prostitution, a profession that enabled them to earn enough money to buy the finery with which they were surrounded during their working day. Benjamin Gitlow was particularly concerned about the fifteen- and sixteen-year-old girls who were "thrown into an atmosphere in department stores that is not good." A fifteen-year-old girl was sent to work alone in a stock room with ten stock men "all burly fellows who were not a bit particular about what they said or did. . . . Girls have been seduced in the storerooms," reported Gitlow. "There is evidently no chance for ignorance on sex matters for anyone employed in a department store," echoed an investigator for the National Civic Federation. A study of New York City prostitutes committed to the state reformatory at Bedford Hills revealed that many of them had once been engaged in department store work.[12]

The child labor reformers attacked the mercantile problem on several fronts. Recognizing that a nine-hour day for minors afforded them little protection because the children might legally be in a store until 10:00 P.M., the NYCLC strove to stop those under sixteen from working in stores past 7:00 P.M. In 1906 members of the Consumers' League, the NYCLC and other groups boarded trains for Albany and in spite of heavy opposition from the department stores, they succeeded in pushing through the legislature a 7:00 P.M. closing-hour bill for first-class cities only. "The impossible seems to have been achieved in the redemption of Christmas," the New York *Evening Post* rejoiced, "this year there are to be no weary cash-girls and boys, no sleepy messengers dragging leaden feet as they carry tokens of cheer and good will." By 1910 a 7:00 P.M. closing hour was established for stores throughout the state and in 1914, as a result of the Factory Investigating Commission, the existing eight-hour factory law for minors under sixteen was extended to almost all commercial establishments. By 1925 a forty-four-hour week (an eight-hour day with a half-holiday on Saturday) had been achieved for children under sixteen in both factories and stores.[13]

To secure more effective enforcement of the mercantile law, the child labor groups wanted to transfer the inspection of stores from local boards of health to the State Labor Department. This would centralize enforcement and place it in an agency less subject to pressure from individual stores than were the local health boards. Although the factory inspectors were hardly crusaders, the transfer idea met with constant bitter opposition from the mercantile interests. In 1908 the NYCLC drafted a bill transferring the inspection authority in first-class cities only. Commissioner of Labor John Williams agreed to have the bill introduced as a Labor Department measure, which meant that he would regard its passage as a vote of confidence. The bill passed the Assembly easily but the mercantile group succeeded in having it stalled in the Senate committee. On the last day of the session efforts were made to suspend the rules and force a vote, but the legislature adjourned without taking action on the bill although appropriations to carry it out *were* included in the budget. Fortunately for the NYCLC, however, 1908 was the year of Governor Charles Evans Hughes' cataclysmic fight with the legislature over race track gambling. When the death of a senator gave Hughes the chance to pick up more support for the repeal of the "race track" provision of the New York Constitution, he called the legislature into special session and won his victory. In the meantime the reformers had persuaded Hughes to make the mercantile transfer bill one of his recommendations to the special session. On May 20 the bill was discussed at a joint legislative hearing at which a dozen representatives of department stores in New York City and Buffalo were present to denounce the measure. While their opposition might appear strange in view of the rather lax standards of the Labor Department, there is no question that the latter's inspections were far more efficient than those of the health boards. Moreover, P. T. Sherman, one of the best labor commissioners appointed up to that time, had just retired and the department stores feared a continuing crack-down if their businesses were placed under Labor Department supervision. Some newspaper opposition to the bill appeared after the measure again passed the Assembly and the reformers charged that the stores were using their position as advertisers to compel such attacks. Concerned, George Hall urged Thomas D. Fitzgerald, Chairman of the State Federation of Labor's Legislative Committee, to get out more letters to legislators; the NYCLC, he reported, was sending letters to one hundred unions in metropolitan New York asking that they urge their senators and assemblymen to vote for the transfer. The bill finally passed the Senate and was signed by Governor Hughes in June, 1908.[14] Applying only to New York City, Rochester, and Buffalo (it was extended to second-class cities in 1913 and to third-class cities in 1919), the law empowered the Commissioner of Labor to appoint a Chief Mercantile Inspector and ten deputies thus making New York, together with Illinois, Massachusetts, and Oregon, one of four states to establish a centralized system of mercantile inspection. The main benefit of the 1908 transfer was not that it quickly eliminated child labor in stores but that it subjected commercial establishments to real inspection. To all intents and purposes the stores had gone scot free until 1908 and this was one reason why their opposition to an apparently mild law had been so severe. The law was responsible for some reduction in mercantile child labor, as shown in Table 9.

TABLE 9 [15]
CHILDREN UNDER SIXTEEN FOUND AT WORK IN
NEW YORK STATE MERCANTILE ESTABLISHMENTS, 1909-15

| | | | Children Employed Illegally | |
Year	Number of Inspections	Total Children**	Over 14 No Papers	Under 14
1909	12,803	6,070	2,365	756
1910	9,687	4,832	1,660	711
1911	8,997	3,828	1,154	421
1912	8,395	4,925	1,346	756
1913	12,860*	6,794	1,820	940
1914	27,216	7,494	1,761	846
1915	29,011	4,713	1,418	726

* Second-class cities began to be inspected in this year (Yonkers, Albany, Troy, Utica, Syracuse, Schenectady).

** These figures are approximate, as the Labor Department reports are often in disagreement with each other. The 1915 and 1909 reports, for example, show 6,070 children under sixteen found employed in mercantile establishments throughout the state during 1909, while the 1920 report lists 5,314 for the same year.

Generalizations about the extent of child labor in commercial establishments after 1908 are difficult to make. The inspector's reports did not give an accurate picture of the number of working children. In 1920, for example, when the Labor Department reported a total of 20,412 children under sixteen as employed in factories and stores, the state had issued 74,686 full-time employment certificates to fourteen- and fifteen-year-olds for work in factories and stores. The relatively small number of inspectors could not possibly cover the very large number of businesses. When the mercantile inspectors concentrated on checking stores, the number of inspections made in offices, hotels, bowling alleys, barber shops, and shoeshine stands declined.[16] Perhaps there was no child labor in the uninspected establishments, but probably there was. In the large New York department stores such as Gimbels or Wanamaker's there was a marked improvement after 1908. By 1914 James L. Gernon, Chief Mercantile Inspector, reported that "In the larger stores the labor law . . . is strictly complied with. . . . I don't think any of the larger stores will take any chance in not complying." This was true. Because there were only about forty of them, the great stores stood out like beacon lights; they were easy to inspect and were visited regularly by members of the Consumers'

League. Although Gernon was pleased that the smaller stores had recently dropped their percentage of illegally employed children from 51 per cent to 41 per cent in 1914, he warned that it would take more than five years to cover all the mercantile establishments under his jurisdiction. The number of illegal child workers in the state's mercantile establishments was likely to depend more on supply and demand than on inspection and regulation.[17]

One type of commercial enterprise outside the jurisdiction of the Labor Department was public entertainment. Not very many children were employed in stage and screen work, but some of those who were ran risks that equalled or exceeded those taken by factory children. When the Child Labor Committee became aware of this problem in 1915, it conducted an investigation and found:

> Edith R—— fourteen years old had been engaged in this [movie] work for two years and acted in six films. In one of these . . . she had to run out of a burning tenement house. The smoke was so blinding that she ran into a board, blocking the entrance and fell back stunned. She was not rescued until her hair had almost been burned off. During the making of another picture, she had to wade, waist deep, in thick snow with only a thin dress on and caught a severe cold.

and

> Ethel M. O—— eight years old has been working for one year and has acted in three films. When acting in the last one, she was obliged to walk barefooted along a thorny path and five large thorns had to be subsequently cut out of her foot. . . . [On location] mosquitoes were so bad that the child's legs and eyes were badly swollen for several days. The staging . . . took place near a refuse heap and the smell of decaying fish was almost unbearable.[18]

Jeanie Minor saw the movies as a real threat to young children. Speaking before a child labor group in Dutchess County, she deplored children acting in what she regarded as objectionable films, viz. "The Unborn Child," "The Soul of a Woman," "The Vampire," etc., and the danger of physical injury to children who were thrown out of buildings and caught in nets, and the high movie salaries that tempted unscrupulous parents to live off the earnings of their children. On one occasion a representative of the Children's Aid Society saw an eight-year-old girl make a forty-foot dive in a Madison Square Garden diving exhibition promoted by Tex Rickard. Rickard was arrested but was discharged because he was not paying the child a salary.[19]

In 1916 when sixteen movie companies were filming in New York studios, the NYCLC and the Society for the Prevention of Cruelty to Children obtained a law prohibiting the employment of children under sixteen in movies without a permit from the mayor. The local Society for the Prevention of Cruelty to Children was to make a preliminary investigation of the child's part in the movie before a permit could be granted. The most serious weakness of this law was the lack of any state-wide enforcing agency. Many small communities had no SPCC (less than a dozen had one as late as 1941) and most mayors were "unaware that any duty rests on [them] . . . to issue permits." The Movie Statute had been grafted onto the state's penal code provisions covering public performances and the result, according to Jeanie Minor, was "a relic of antiquity pieced with a few modern patches, so loosely sewed together . . . as to make its interpretation difficult at best, ridiculous at worst." The provisions on stage performances, for example, permitted five-year-old children to sing or play musical instruments, but not to speak lines. Each case was judged upon what appeared to be its merits. In 1924 New York City Mayor John F. Hylan refused a permit to some Negro children, ages ten to thirteen, who were supposed to read the prologue to Eugene O'Neill's play "All God's Chillun Got Wings." Hylan denied charges that his action was taken in response to protests about the racial issue raised by the play, but the *New York Times* pointed out that children of six and seven were appearing in other metropolitan plays at the same time.[20]

Effective regulation of theatrical children required careful investigation of each application. With sporadic enforcement the rule, the NYCLC could only remain vigilant and watch for the most obvious cases. In 1932 George Hall spotted an advertisement for girls ages six and seven to appear in the Earl Carroll "Vanities." The NYCLC sent a strong protest to New York City Mayor Joseph McKee: "No argument is necessary," Chairman Manfred W. Ehrich wrote, "to show the undesirability of permitting young children to appear in a musical revue." Permits for the youngsters were denied. For a while the NYCLC was interested in securing a minimum age law for theatrical children but eventually dropped the plan. As Frank Gillmore, President of the Actor's Equity, pointed out to Jeanie Minor, if a twelve-year age minimum were adopted it would be impossible to present plays like "The Pied Piper."[21] During the Second World War the duty of licensing children to appear in public entertainment was taken away from the mayors and given to the local school authorities; in cities where a Society for the Prevention of Cruelty to Children existed, it had to be notified of the application at least forty-eight hours before the permit was issued. The sole exception to the law was New York City where because of the volume of such applications, the Mayor's office continued to exercise control.

During the 1920's and 1930's the NYCLC continued its campaign for higher standards of child employment in mercantile and commercial establishments. Most of the reforms it obtained were in the field of working hours: in 1921 women over sixteen years of age in department stores won an eight-hour day and a forty-eight-hour week; in 1924 sixteen- to eighteen-year-old boys were limited to a nine-hour day and fifty-four-hour week, and in 1925 all children under sixteen were barred from working in mercantile and commercial establishments for more than eight hours a day or forty-four hours a week. The employment of such children between the hours of 6:00 P.M. and 8:00 A.M. was also forbidden.[22] These measures were not passed without opposition, because some employers regarded hours limitations for minors as an entering wedge for similar limitations for all employees. The "idle children" argument also remained strong; during the fight for passage of the forty-four-hour week for children in factories and commercial establishments, a number of Children's Court judges protested that such a law would encourage juvenile delinquency. After the forty-four-hour bill became law, these judges attempted to retaliate by supporting the Truman-Miller Bill in the 1926 and 1927 legislatures. This measure would have authorized the "occasional" employment of thirteen-year-old boys in department stores and business offices between 8:00 A.M. and 6:00 P.M. and would have permitted fourteen- to sixteen-year-old boys to work at these occupations outside of school hours without an employment certificate. Believing that this bill was "vicious" in that it reduced the minimum age for work and destroyed the employment certificate, the NYCLC rallied the State Federation of Labor and the State Society for the Prevention of Cruelty to Children to oppose it. With the help of Charles D. Hilles, a member of the NYCLC and the Republican National Committee, and Luella R. North, a Children's Court judge from Plattsburgh, the bill was killed in committee both years.[23]

Although by 1919 the mercantile inspectors had the right to inspect commercial establishments in any of New York's cities, the villages and towns (some containing thousands of people) remained under the jurisdiction of local boards of health. Admitting that the enforcement of the mercantile law was nonexistent in the villages and towns, the State Commissioner of Health, Mathias Nicoll, strongly supported a bill proposed by the NYCLC in 1929 transferring such inspection to the Labor Department. Writing to Industrial Commissioner James A. Hamilton, Nicoll asserted that

> It is almost impossible for the part-time health officers of towns and villages to perform more duties than at present, and the duty prescribed by Section 391 [mercantile inspection] . . . has never been carried out and never will be. . . . I am not in a position to enforce compliance with the present law regarding the inspection of mercantile establishments.

Hamilton agreed, replying that it was foolish to inspect the factories in villages and towns and not mercantile establishments where some twelve thousand children under sixteen were employed. "Experience has demonstrated," said Hamilton, "that enforcement entrusted to local officials is ineffective."[24] In spite of the combined support from the Departments of Labor and Health, the NYCLC bill was not successful until 1935. Although Charles D. Hilles did all he could, the strong opposition from small-town merchants and the reluctance of the legislators to appropriate the additional $27,000 yearly expenditure necessary to administer the change delayed its passage. As finally passed in 1935, the law placed all mercantile and commercial establishments throughout the state under the supervision of the Labor Department.[25]

As far as is known the problem of child labor in commercial establishments has diminished during the modern period. The most obvious abuses such as the little cash girls subjected to the insults of leering floorwalkers and the strain of long hours are gone. Nevertheless, as late as 1935 the NYCLC found an eleven-year-old Syracuse boy delivering bread as a helper on a truck, working from 7:00 A.M. to 5:00 P.M. for $1.00 a week and a White Plains boy of twelve working in a grocery store all day for ten weeks at a wage of $1.75 for a seven-day week. In Peekskill a nine-year-old was found helping deliver milk from a truck, working all day in return for a bottle of milk. In New Rochelle a fourteen-year-old clerked in a grocery store for eleven hours a day and eighteen hours on Saturday for $4.00 weekly. While the number of violations was small, they continued to exist.[26] Since the Second World War the Labor Department has been inspecting only about 25 per cent of the establishments subject to its jurisdiction (including factories and commercial establishments), and most of the child labor violations found have been in retail stores and amusement parks. The reformers had made progress, but their record in commercial work was not as good as it had been in factories, for during the 1950's the Labor Department was still finding about 3,500 children a year illegally employed in commercial establishments. The immense number of small stores and enterprises in which a child could go to work made total enforcement of the labor law almost impossible.[27]

> A walk through the tenement district is a page from Hugo. Galley slaves never marched more gloomily than the boys and girls who trudge up and down, either lugging home huge bundles or else returning the finished product to the factory. Yet these weary journeyings . . . are joyous diversions to most of the children, for they permit a brief escape from the darkness and drudgery of the "home." In these "homes" where cooking, eating, and sleeping merge into one great blob of squalor, there are not idle moments for idle people, save for the baby that still sucks at the mother's breast.
>
> —EDWIN MARKHAM, BENJAMIN B. LINDSAY, and
> GEORGE CREEL, *Children in Bondage* (1914)

To the reformers child labor in the tenements was the most heart-breaking of all.[28] No other form of labor sapped the strength and spirits of children in quite so pervasive a fashion, for tenement work combined the evils of long hours in a filthy, badly ventilated, over-crowded room with those of neglected education and shattered health. The factory child, at least, went home to a different environment at night—the young tenement worker was already home.

A tenement was defined as a structure housing three or more families residing independently of one another, cooking separately but sharing toilets, stairways, and yards. These tenement buildings in which homework was done were often filthy, with inadequate plumbing spilling sewage into the halls and vermin infesting the cramped, overcrowded rooms. Shortly after the passage of New York City's Tenement House Law of 1901, the newly created Tenement House Department ordered structural alterations in about half of the city's 82,000 tenements (housing a population of 2,327,070 persons), plumbing repairs in 21,584, and toilets cleaned in 13,617. Although considerable progress was made in cleaning up the tenements between 1900 and the First World War under the leadership of Lawrence Veiller and Robert W. DeForest, the problem persisted, and the Tenement House Department continued to issue hundreds of thousands of violation notices every year.[29] Homework was carried on by immigrant families in tenement districts throughout Greater New York; although it was concentrated on Manhattan's East Side, particularly on Madison and Monroe Streets, between 4th and 33rd Streets, in the fifties, and between 90th and 119th Streets, it was also carried on in Greenwich Village, near the Brooklyn Bridge, and was moving out into Brownsville, Canarsie, Queens, and even Coney Island. Before 1900 Jews had dominated the homework trade and as late as 1911 comprised 33 per cent of the metropolitan homeworking force, but they were gradually being displaced by Italians as strong unions developed in the two trades where most Jews worked (clothing and cigars).[30] A typical tenement apartment was in a building containing anywhere from three to forty families. The apartments normally had only three or four rooms measuring ten by twelve feet each, to house perhaps a dozen people. One room was often used to store the homework materials, intensifying already severe overcrowding (in 1894 New York City's population density of 143.2 persons per acre below the Harlem River was the world's highest). This overcrowding often necessitated sleeping in shifts. Heat was supplied from the family's coal cook stove, since steam heat and hot water were luxuries as late as 1914.[31]

Almost any commodity small enough to be carried and not requiring the use of elaborate machinery or highly skilled labor could be manufactured or finished in a home. Employers sought homeworkers because they saved the cost of additional factory space and would work more cheaply than "inside" help. This saving in labor cost was not passed on to the consumer; in most cases the manufacturer calculated his labor cost for homeworkers as if they were regular factory hands, thus increasing his own profit. As late as 1924-25 the wages of homeworkers in the men's clothing industry averaged only one-third of the earnings of regular factory workers. While eager to use homeworkers, most manufacturers chose to remain ignorant of the conditions under which the work was carried on, believing that their responsibility ended when the homeworker picked up his material at the factory. While accurate statistics are almost impossible to find, want ads in newspapers indicated that before the First World War most New York City homeworkers were engaged in hand embroidery; hand crocheting; attaching passementerie (trimming), buttons, or ornaments to clothing; or in some other form of needle finishing work on coats, vests, trousers, knee pants, shirts, blouses, dresses, underwear, sheets, pillow cases, napkins, infants' wear, dolls' clothing, or hats. Work was also done on toys, gloves, artificial flowers, paper boxes, calendars, pincushions, fly swatters, umbrellas, ice cream, spaghetti, candy, and cigarettes.[32]

The tenement child's chances for a decent education were almost hopeless. Because much of the homework could be done by unskilled labor, parents kept their children out of school to assist in the work. Although the Compulsory Education Law was on the books, school officials were not anxious to exert themselves to bring these non-English-speaking immigrant children into the schools. Between 1897 and 1906 when a record-breaking number of immigrants was pouring into New York City, the local education authorities did not see fit to take even one school census. Children simply disappeared into the tenements to do homework and because they never came out to play, even other children in the neighborhood were not aware of their presence. A fourteen-year-old Italian girl, one of many such cases, who had come to this country at the age of seven, had never attended school one day although she lived across the street from the building. Because certain of the homework tasks could be performed by very young children, some parents never allowed them even to start school. Since the law did not require children to attend school until they were seven and since they were not paid wages, the reformers' only recourse was to charge the parents with cruelty. This they hesitated to do, reasoning that if the court threw out the charge it would encourage more child labor and if the parents were convicted, the children would be sent to an institution. So nothing was done and children as young as three continued to work making such things as the dance programs that dangled from the wrists of debutantes, and artificial flowers, a women's hat decoration fad of the day that had started when birds and wings went out of fashion. (While rejoicing that more birds were being allowed to live, the National Consumers' League urged women to "extend their intelligent interests beyond the birds to the children in the tenements.")[33]

Often a child who did start school would work at home afterwards; then, finding it impossible to keep up in his studies, he would drop out of school and be unable to obtain an employment certificate because of insufficient schooling. In a study of one hundred New York City child homeworkers, the Factory Investigating Commission found that they averaged twenty-nine and a half days absent out of an eighty-nine-day school term. School children were assigned to classes for "defectives" only to have the teachers discover that they were simply too exhausted or undernourished to study. It was common for children old enough to get working papers to combine labor in a factory or store with work at home; delinquency was often the result. Maud E. Miner, Secretary of the New York City Probation Association, told the Factory Investigating Commission how the fatigue of overwork tempted young girls into lives of prostitution. They "have told me that they have become tired of work . . . long before it was time for them to go out into the factory, simply because they had to work in the home day after day, night after night, and on Sunday."[34]

Intense family labor in the tenements not only robbed children of their health and education but also presented serious risks to the consumer of home-manufactured articles. A piece of cloth soon to be sold in a fashionable men's shop to a member of the "400" might recently have been used to cover up a hacking tubercular grandfather as he snoozed in an East Side tenement. Nuts, candy, macaroni, and other food being prepared for the market were often stored on the floor where pets investigated them, or on filthy tables where little girls suffering from impetigo worked on them. Members of families who had been quarantined for typhoid or diphtheria continued their homework on clothing. In 1912 Dr. Annie S. Daniel found that of the 182 homeworking families she had investigated, as many as 79 of them had contagious diseases ranging from scarlet fever to polio, the latter described by Dr. Daniel as "a very horrible disease"; remembering a family where it had struck, she claimed that "the woman hardly stopped her work while the child was dying."[35]

The overwhelming majority of homework licenses were issued for metropolitan New York (11,691 as against 520 for upstate in a typical year such as 1912), but the proportion of homework going on upstate was much greater than the figures indicated, since much of it was carried on in one- and two-family houses where licenses were not required until 1935. Although pressed by its many-sided investigation, the Factory Commission managed to send agents into fifteen upstate communities during the summer of 1912.[36] Gloversville with its ninety glove factories was practically supported by homework and even taught glovemaking in the public schools. Rochester had the second largest number of homeworkers and also the greatest variety of homework. Buffalo had less homework because the Italian families got better pay in local canneries and vineyards. "The cannery season and the clothing season come about the same time and the canneries can utilize all the little children in the sheds snipping beans, husking corn, etc., while in the clothing trade they can only be utilized in pulling bastings," commented a Factory Commission investigator. In the Tonawanda-Lockport area near Buffalo, however, about a thousand homeworkers were engaged in sewing hooks and eyes on cards. The highest wage any of them earned averaged seventeen cents a day. To earn sixty cents, one had to card a gross of hooks and eyes—a process involving 10,368 separate operations. One Tonawanda family with a disabled bread-winner worked from 7:00 A.M. to 10:00 P.M. and managed to earn six dollars a week. Unlike Rochester, which contained mostly one- and two-family homes, Little Falls was a "tenement city." Located in a narrow valley on the Mohawk River where land was at a premium, this community of about twelve thousand persons had a congestion problem resembling that of New York City. Shoe, glove, and slipper factories jammed the riverbank, while workers crowded four and five families into frame houses meant for half that number. In one such tenement, investigators found a twenty-eight-year-old Italian immi-grant woman finishing felt slippers. By sewing twelve to sixteen hours a day with the assistance of a six-year-old child, she averaged eighty-five cents a day. She "proudly showed the enlarged joints, the cuts and calloused places on the little six year old child's hand as evidence of the child's work." Another former child laborer was now

> A woman 35 years old [who] has been making gloves ever since she was 11 years old. She is prematurely old, has lost all her upper teeth, and complains of nervous indigestion and looks like a skeleton. This woman's husband is a day laborer receiving $1.65 per day but his work is so irregular that she must work in order to pay their rent. . . . Working at the machine all day long from 7 in the morning until 8 and 9 o'clock at night this woman can make 10 dozen pairs of gloves a week, for which she receives 18 to 45 cents per dozen pairs.

Upstate employers did not keep accurate records on their homeworkers and did not care about their working conditions. "In Utica no one ever bothers the factories about these things," a shoe factory manager told investigators, "Why are we bothered in this way? No, we do not keep the names and addresses of our homeworkers. Women wanting such work come in and get it and that's all there is about it." A man in this same factory was brushing homework slippers carefully; "they come in with all sorts of dirt and things in them," he said, "too dirty to handle otherwise." The upstate survey revealed conditions similar to those in New York City: "Child labor was found in every trade where it could be utilized, and in the few trades [such as turning collars] where more skill was necessary than could be furnished by children, they were used to carry the material to and from the factory."[37]

    Against these conditions stood a feeble barrier of legislation. The Cigar Laws of 1883 and 1884 had been declared unconstitutional in

1885; the Jacobs decision cast a long shadow and prompted the drafters of future legislation to move cautiously. In 1892 the activities of the Anti-Tenement House League and the agitation of the factory inspectors induced the legislature to pass a law requiring individuals to obtain permits for the homework manufacture of certain specified articles in tenements or dwellings. Then, as if to prove it was not serious, the legislature *exempted* the immediate members of a family from the provisions of the act. In short, families were still permitted to do homework without regulation, but if they hired anyone outside the family to work on any of the listed prohibited articles, they must get a permit from the factory inspector. In 1899 the statute was amended to require a license for each family workroom producing articles on the prohibited list regardless of whether outsiders were employed. Neither of these enactments had any effect upon child labor. In the first place, only licensed tenement workrooms were subject to inspection; and secondly, only homeworkers who were not members of the family were under the factory inspector's jurisdiction. If an inspector happened to appear in a workroom before a warning could be given, every child in the room would be identified as belonging to the family. Who could dispute it? While the inspectors *could* require that each licensed workroom manufacturing listed articles be in "sanitary" condition, free from any contagious disease and with at least 500 cubic feet of air per person, they could not halt child labor on homework. "The Department of Factory Inspection can . . . force the child under fourteen . . . and the illiterate child out of the workshop or factory, but is powerless to molest them when they are found employed in their own home circle."[38]

No one knew how many children were working: writers as early as 1910 and as late as 1939 admitted that accurate figures simply did not exist. It is significant, however, that within the first three months after the 1899 licensing law went into effect the factory inspector received over 10,000 applications for family workroom licenses. By September 30, 1901, there were 28,787 licensed tenement workrooms in the state, 20,000 of these in New York City. The factory inspector thought that with luck he and his men might be able to visit each one twice a year, but in between their trips much could happen. As Mary VanKleeck pointed out, "There is nothing to prevent members of a family from catching TB *after* they get a homework license."[39] Besides, the 20,000 licenses were only for *rooms.* How many unlicensed workrooms remained in the city's 80,000 tenement *buildings?* There work on such unlisted items as bed quilts, babies' socks, garters, kimonos, and kid gloves could be done by disease-ridden workers of any age who never need fear the arrival of a factory inspector. Assuming that an inspector actually did burst into a licensed workroom during school hours and found five or six school-age children visibly employed on homework, he might be able to return them to school if the school and the inspector followed up aggressively. But most of the schools were overcrowded and the number of tenements each inspector must visit precluded efficient rechecks. When an inspector did find a violation, the tenement workers were resourceful. On one occasion an investigator from the Child Welfare Association succeeded in taking a picture of a homeworker and his four young children sitting around a sewing machine used for buttonhole work. When an attempt was made to use the picture as evidence that the children were being kept out of school, the father protested indignantly that the photographer had told him to group the children around the machine because it would make a better picture.[40] Since there was usually time for a warning, the children were hidden or, if visible, "playing" by the time the inspector arrived.

In 1904 the Labor Department abandoned the practice of licensing individual workrooms, requiring instead that each tenement house in which homework was done be licensed. The main purpose of the new law was to cut down the volume of licensing made necessary by the frequent moves of workers from one tenement house to another, but its effect on the regulation of child labor was to remove a substantial number of "dwelling" homeworking families from Labor Department jurisdiction. In 1892 and 1899 statutes had applied to tenements *and* dwellings, but the 1904 law applied *only* to tenement buildings; two-family dwellings, in which much upstate homework was done, were not covered. Jurisdiction over tenements was shared by the State Departments of Labor and Health and the Tenement House Department of New York City, but regardless of their efforts, homework continued unchecked. Adequate enforcement of the homework law, the Factory Investigating Commission said, would require "several thousand inspectors, and the work of inspection would have to be continuous throughout the day and night . . . because the work is continuous." Licenses could be revoked but unless an inspector spent the rest of his life in the tenement, the work would be done anyway. If the homeworkers wished to be lawful, all they had to do was begin making some article for which a license was not required. Forty-one articles were on the licensing list—sixty were not. By 1911 there were 13,268 licensed tenement buildings in New York City. How many of the city's 80,000 unlicensed tenements were doing homework is a matter for speculation. No one really knew, although the Factory

Commission finally decided that their estimate of 125,000 home-workers of all kinds in New York City was conservative.[41]

As a result of its tenement homework investigation, the Factory Commission suggested several new laws. Such was the influence of this remarkable body that the legislature responded. In 1913 the tenement manufacture of food, dolls, dolls' clothing, and children's wearing apparel was forbidden. Employers who gave out homework were required to put a tag bearing their name and address on each bundle of work sent out, and homework in cellars or basements was prohibited. Most important to the Child Labor Committee was the provision barring children under fourteen from tenement homework. This statute proved even more difficult to enforce than the other labor legislation of the day. Its constitutionality was upheld by a lower New York Court in 1915, and because the plaintiff ran out of money the decision was not appealed. Actually there was little reason for employers to do battle in the courts.[42] Since the statute failed to include "dwellings" in its homework prohibition, employers had only to send their materials into one- or two-family homes or into New Jersey or Connecticut. If they still wished to give out homework to families living in New York City tenements, they were not likely to be caught. The child labor reformers were unable to make much headway against homework, but the labor unions did succeed in ending some of it. During 1909 and 1910 two bitter strikes by 80,000 New York City shirtwaist makers and cloak-makers against the bad sanitary conditions, homework, long hours, and low wages in the trade resulted in the signing of a number of "protocols" between local unions of the International Ladies Garment Workers Union and the Cloak, Suit, and Skirt Manufacturers Protective Association. Between 1910 and 1913 several such agreements prohibited homework in the production of various articles of clothing. Opinions differ on the effectiveness of the protocols in eliminating homework. They undoubtedly succeeded in preventing some of it, but the practice continued on a sufficiently large scale to worry the unions. The historians of both the International Ladies Garment Workers and the Amalgamated Clothing Workers, one writing in 1924 and the other in 1934, viewed the continuation of homework as a definite threat to organized labor.[43]

During the First World War there was a brief flurry of public interest in homework when it became known that U.S. Army uniforms were being manufactured by tenement homeworkers. It was nothing new; in 1901 John R. Commons had stated that during the Spanish-American War "the contagion of measles and other diseases in the army was owing directly to tenement-house manufacture [of uniforms]." In 1917 Sidney Hillman of the Amalgamated Clothing Workers, Florence Kelley, and Secretary of War Newton D. Baker (who also happened to be president of the National Consumers' League) established an investigating committee that substantiated Sidney Hillman's charges of homework. As a result Army contracting procedures were tightened, preference on government contracts was given to manufacturers with union shops, and government inspectors were hired to see that no homework was given out. By Armistice Day, 1918, Florence Kelley could report that homework on army uniforms had ceased.[44]

Not all the battles were fought in Europe. Early in 1918 Tenement Inspector G. E. Reynolds and a woman colleague named Seymour went to Harlem to investigate the activities of one Sylvia DeToris who they were convinced was doing illegal homework on children's dresses. Knocking at the door of her tenement apartment, Reynolds and Seymour announced themselves as tenement inspectors from the Labor Department. After a long wait during which Mrs. DeToris hid a large pile of children's dresses (one of the inspectors saw them through a keyhole), they were let in, but when they demanded to know who was supplying her with the dresses, Mrs. DeToris ordered them out. Then, Inspector Reynolds reported:

> She . . . began to push me, trying to get me out of the apartment . . . she struck and kicked me repeatedly. In spite of this, Inspector Seymour and I began to search for the goods, looking under the beds and in the closets. . . . Finally . . . I found a bundle of several dozen baby dresses . . . [but] before I could seize them, Mrs. DeToris began screaming terribly and jumped on my back. Just then Mrs. D'Iorio [the landlady] rushed in and began also to kick and strike me.

At this point Reynolds tried to talk to Mrs. D'Iorio, but she, too, ordered him to leave. When Reynolds again refused

> both women attacked Inspector Seymour and myself with the most violent fury. Mrs. Seymour was kicked with great force in the stomach . . . and her eyeglasses were broken. Mrs. D'Iorio then pushed her out of the room and tried to throw her down the stairs and nearly succeeded in doing so.

Mrs. Seymour departed to look for a policeman and came back with one after two hours. In the meantime Reynolds strove manfully.

> After Inspector Seymour had left, both women continually assaulted me and I defended myself as best I could without hurting them as I did not want to injure them in any way. They threw a

milk bottle at me . . . and a plate. . . . Mrs. D'Iorio bit me severely
on the right hand and afterwards hit me over the head with a
heavy cut-glass vase about two feet high.

The women finally succeeded in getting the baby dresses away from
Reynolds and although he was able to have each fined five dollars
(presumably for disorderly conduct), he could not bring an action for
violation of the labor law because there was no evidence. The courts
were still far from cooperative. A few weeks later Reynolds followed a
man carrying a bundle of baby coats out of a factory and home to his
apartment in an unlicensed tenement house, where the inspector
found his wife working on them. The woman refused to give the name
of the factory owner and dared Reynolds to take her to court. A judge
found her not guilty, saying that he could not see that she had committed any crime (although she was working in an unlicensed tenement
on forbidden items).[45]

After the 1913 legislation, manufacturers began to send even more
homework into the suburbs. In 1919 when reports reached the
NYCLC that children were being used on homework in an Italian
tenement colony in White Plains, the committee requested the Labor
Department's Homework Division to send an inspector. Inspector
Alexander Bell found a number of Italian families supplementing their
incomes by having their children string beads. He was able to locate
the woman who acted as local bead distributor for the New York City
manufacturer, and found that she regarded herself as a community
benefactor. Was she not helping the children to support their families
and keeping them out of the streets where they would only wear out
shoe leather and get into trouble? Actually the bead-stringing children
were not contributing very much money: for making 144 chains of
beads (each twenty-eight inches long and composed of fourteen beads
to the inch) the child was paid two dollars. To earn this sum he would
have to pick up one thousand beads an hour and work a fifty-six-hour
week. When Inspector Bell entered one home, he found a nine-year-old
girl crying; her mother said it was because she wanted to stop stringing
beads and go out to play. Several of the children were suffering from
eyestrain—one seven-year-old, Bell said, was definitely crosseyed. The
school principal reported considerable absenteeism; the children, she
said, were "in mortal terror of not being able to do a certain quantity
of beads." The Labor Department secured a promise from the New
York City bead supplier that he would stop sending out such homework to unlicensed houses.[46]

Child labor on homework remained almost impossible to prove.

The 1913 legislation amounted to little more than official recognition that children under fourteen should not do the work. The inspectors were powerless to do anything about the most obvious violations. During 1919-20 only six of the 653 children under fourteen found engaged in tenement homework were actually used in prosecutions against the manufacturers.

> The employment of the child in the home differs very much from the employment of the child in a factory [said the inspector]. The attitude, speech and acts of the tenement inspector is made up of bluff pure and simple. He is in the home of the child, not in the factory of the employer.

Parents could not be prosecuted, for they were not legally the "employer" of the child. The employer was the owner of the goods, but to convict him the inspectors must prove conclusively that he knew illegal child labor would be used on his homework. "The only course left to the inspector is to fuss and bluster . . . after which [the child's mother] will gladly promise not to offend again." And so the seventeen inspectors of the Labor Department's Homework Division carried on their job of inspecting New York State's 20,000 licensed tenements meeting all kinds of parental righteous indignation. A mother in Troy complained that Americans knew little of child-rearing—*her* child was not going out to run the streets. When an Amsterdam parent was told that child labor on homework was forbidden she inquired: "What will the children do on winter nights?"[47]

In 1924 at the insistence of the Child Labor Committee and the New York Consumers' League, the legislature appointed a subcommittee on tenement manufacturing to serve as part of its Commission to Examine the Laws Relating to Child Welfare (a group created in 1922); George Hall was named executive secretary of the subcommittee. Assisted by the Labor Department, the New York City Health Department, the Consumers' League, the Women's City Club, NYCLC and various charitable organizations, Hall undertook an investigation of homework. The results were depressing.

> In the 10 years that have intervened since the factory commission's report [the tenement subcommittee stated] practically nothing has been done toward the solution of the problem. If the advice of the factory commission [to abolish all homework] had been followed, manufacturing in tenements would either have been completely eliminated or the problem would have dwindled to one of much smaller proportions. Instead this system has become so deeply

entrenched in our industrial life that its very involvement is the only reason that can be given for not now recommending the immediate complete prohibition of homework in tenements.

The subcommittee recommended that the list of prohibited articles be extended and that the Division of Homework be transferred within the Labor Department to the newly created Bureau of Women in Industry (a step that was eventually taken) which the subcommittee felt would infuse more vigor into the inspection process. Bills to extend the prohibited list failed in the legislatures of 1924, 1925, and 1928.[48]

Under the NIRA of 1933 tenement homework in industries engaged in interstate commerce was prohibited for the first time and the new requirements were to be enforced by New York's homework inspectors. The effect of the NRA codes on New York's homework is difficult to assess. In a study of the men's clothing code in a four-state area (New Jersey, Pennsylvania, New York, and Rhode Island) the Federal Children's Bureau found that of 2,301 homeworkers employed by 48 clothing firms before NRA, 2,153 were still employed during NRA.[49] Ruth Shallcross, who worked as an inspector during 1931-36 reported that the NRA experience was marked by a great deal of confusion, and that when the NRA was declared unconstitutional in May, 1935, the homework inspectors viewed its demise with "great relief." One difficulty with the NRA homework codes was the injustice their flat prohibitions worked on people who were trying to eke out a living during the depression. In May, 1934, a White House executive order exempted homeworkers who could not work in factories because they were disabled, too old, or had to take care of a disabled person. The fact that the exemptions came midway in the NRA period contributed to the confusion, with inspectors going back and forth telling people that they could and could not do homework. According to Ruth Shallcross, sudden changes in code provisions "made without thought of what result they would have on homeworkers were extremely difficult for inspectors to understand or interpret to others in a manner which would be helpful to the Federal Government."[50]

Concurrently with NRA, New York began her own program of homework control. Under the Neustein-O'Brien Law which went into effect on July 1, 1934, the state ceased licensing *buildings* and returned to the nineteenth-century principle of licensing *individuals*. Every individual homeworker now had to have a state certificate (whether she lived in a tenement or a "dwelling"), and every employer had to have a permit costing twenty-five dollars to give out homework. In spite of vigorous opposition from Labor Commissioner Elmer F. Andrews, certain of the homeworking industries succeeded in exempting from the act homeworkers in one- and two-family houses in communities with less than 200,000 population. In Commissioner Andrew's opinion it was

> conservative to say that the bulk of industrial homework in the State is carried on in 1-2 family dwellings . . . on articles forbidden to be made in tenements, especially on infant's and children's knit-wear, crocheted garments and hand made dresses. This is true both in outlying sections of big cities and in small towns, hamlets and rural areas. The exploitation of these workers so far as rates of pay are concerned is unbelievably worse than among factory workers.[51]

In 1935 the exemption was removed and the homework provisions of the law now applied throughout the state. Most importantly, the 1935 statute empowered the industrial commissioner to issue administrative orders banning homework in a particular industry. Since 1935 the trend in New York had been toward the "strict control and gradual elimination" of homework. During 1936-38 Commissioner Andrews ordered homework stopped in the men's and boys' outer clothing industry, in the men's and boys' neckwear industry, and in the artificial flower and feather industry. All of these orders, as well as the 1934-35 legislation, survived court tests. More recently orders have been issued barring homework in the glove industry and the direct-mail industry. While the orders all recognized certain NRA-type exemptions (i.e., for employers who held homework permits prior to the promulgation of the orders and for workers who were unable to hold factory jobs because of age, physical disability, or the need for their presence at home to care for an invalid), the Labor Department was committed to the eventual elimination of homework. The preamble to Article 13 of the labor law now states that the employment of women and minors at low wages and under conditions injurious to their health and welfare is a matter of public concern and defines homework "as fostering such conditions and, therefore, destructive of the purposes already accepted as sound public policy." After 1936, of course, the sixteen-year age minimum for working children applied to homework. Moreover, the revised definition of an "employer" established by the 1934 Homework Statute made it easier to prosecute factory owners. Once homeworkers were held to be the employees of a manufacturer who gave out homework, it was possible to hold him responsible for any child labor used in work on his products. Still another factor in reducing homework (and hence child labor) was the minimum wage standard established by the Fair Labor Standards Act of 1938 and its amendments. Normally, the minimum wage in any industry covered by the act applied to work done in homes as well as in factories and this destroyed one of the major advantages of homework to the employer. By 1955 New York was issuing only 5,616 licenses to homeworkers as compared with 52,026 certificates issued in 1937;[52] in spite of this reduction, there is undoubtedly still some child labor being used by the licensed homeworkers and some unlicensed homework being done.

Efforts to eliminate child labor in homework were unsuccessful until the depression. The resulting New Deal on both state and national levels and the leadership of Herbert H. Lehman provided the stimulus for a move toward total prohibition of homework—a course that had been favored by the NYCLC since 1920. The historical evidence on tenement homework indicated the futility of regulatory measures and demonstrated that complete prohibition was the only answer. Attempts to regulate homework because poor people needed the money had failed and were nothing less than an admission of society's failure in the face of poverty and an incentive for the use of child labor.

> Surely the boy who learns business fundamentals, who meets human nature, who learns the value of business policies on dependability, honesty, courtesy and promptness is better equipped to make his way in the world than is the youngster who secures his education wholly within the four walls of a schoolroom.
> —H. W. Stodghill, National Chairman of the Newspaper Boy Welfare Committee, Remarks Before the NRA Newspaper Code Hearing, September 22, 1933

To most people the words "street trader" meant newsboys—individual enterpreneurs beginning their drive toward success. Tenement or factory children conjured up different images, but for the newsboy "laissez-faire!" was the watchword. He was the pristine symbol of the Horatio Alger ethic and to hamper him by regulation would be wrong, especially when his work was carried on in the healthful atmosphere of the open air. Probably some of the progressives themselves saw the newsboy as the last symbol of independence in an ever more organized world. In any event the durability of this myth blinded many people to the presence of other street traders (delivery children, peddlers, messengers and bootblacks) and to the evils inherent in street selling itself.[53] Delivery children had an advantage over peddlers and messengers in that they traveled a fixed route to a usually respectable location and were covered by mercantile legislation. Newsboys, peddlers, and boot-

blacks were more difficult to regulate because they were "self-employed"; delivery children and messenger boys were clearly working
for an employer who might be held responsible. "Independent" street
sellers also fell easy prey to the bad influences of a great metropolis.[54]
Edward N. Clopper of the National Child Labor Committee divided
the effects of street work into three categories: material deterioration
in which children came to hate regular employment and formed the
habit of drifting; physical deterioration due to night work, exposure
to bad weather, the use of stimulants, and the contraction of venereal
disease; and moral deterioration with its incitement to lives of vice and
crime.[55]

The provisions of the 1903 mercantile legislation applied to children
working as messengers, but here the enforcement work of the local
boards of health was even more ineffective than it had been in department stores. The NYCLC discovered that between December 1, 1903,
and May 13, 1904, the New York City Board of Health had inspected
only *thirteen* telegraph offices in the entire metropolitan area (the
Borough of Manhattan alone contained 390 such offices). The managers
of both the American District Telegraph Company (a subsidiary of the
Western Union Telegraph Company) and the Postal Telegraph Company freely admitted to a member of the Child Labor Committee that
their *minimum* working day for all boys was ten hours.[56] Even this
might have been acceptable had the messengers confined their work
to delivery of telegrams and messages during normal business hours,
but the telegraph offices stayed open very late, and during the night
the telegraph companies provided "errand" services. In the course of
providing these services many messengers became gatekeepers for
New York vice. While prostitution was nothing new in New York, it
had undergone "rapid and extraordinary" expansion following 1896
when the state legislature took away New York City's control over its
own liquor licenses and began to issue them directly from Albany. This
ended the control New York City reform groups had been able to exert
over the local saloon-licensing (excise) authorities; the State Excise
Commissioner became "a mere peddler of licenses [whose] . . . business
was to sell as many . . . as possible and to secure as much revenue for
the state as possible." In addition, the law of 1896, sponsored by State
Senator John Raines, stated that only hotels could sell liquor on Sunday.
A hotel was defined as a building with at least ten bedrooms of specified
dimensions, a kitchen, and a dining room, but in practice a hotel liquor
license was issued to any person who wished to buy one if he said that
it was for a hotel. No one inspected the "hotels." In no time at all saloon
keepers throughout the city rushed a few beds into their premises and

declared themselves hotel keepers in order to remain open on Sunday. Having the beds, they were put to use and "Raines Law hotel" quickly became a euphemism for "house of prostitution with a barroom attached." By 1904, 1,205 of the 1,405 licensed hotels in Manhattan and the Bronx were Raines Law hotels.[57]

The uniformed messenger boys became indispensable to the prostitutes, pimps, bartenders, and gamblers of New York. They carried notes back and forth, brought in food, and obtained liquor or narcotics for the prostitutes and their customers. The boys sought such work because prostitutes, pimps, and drunks were notoriously big tippers. Best of all, the boys could walk in and out of the bawdy houses without fear because should anyone question them they had only to claim that they were delivering telegrams. One of the more ludicrous sections of the New York Penal Code attempted to regulate messenger boys but actually sanctioned their activities (note the italicized phrases):

> A corporation or person employing messenger boys who *knowingly* sends or permits any person to send any messenger boy to any disorderly house, unlicensed saloon, inn, tavern or other unlicensed place where malt or spiritous liquors or wines are sold, on any errand or business whatsoever, *except to deliver telegrams at the door of such house* is guilty of a misdemeanor.[58]

Technically, a messenger boy under sixteen was not supposed to work after 10:00 P.M., but neither this provision of the Hill-Finch Commercial Establishments Law nor the Penal Code section just cited was enforced. An antivice group known as the Committee of Fourteen checked through the annual reports of the New York District Attorney's Office for 1906, 1907, and 1908 without finding a single case of prosecution under either law. The Committee commented:

> The chief difficulty seems to be that the companies do not comply with the law and are unaware or indifferent to what may happen to their employees at these houses [of prostitution]. The obtaining of evidence requires that some person or society interested in children must not only ascertain that boys go to these houses but that these places are in reality disorderly. The testimony of the boys in many instances might be sufficient if they would give it.[59]

In 1909 and 1910 the NYCLC got direct evidence from an agent of the National Child Labor Committee, Edward F. Brown, who reported a conversation between a seventeen-year-old messenger boy and himself (by 1910 some of the telegraphy companies *were* trying to hire boys who were at least sixteen and therefore not subject to the 10:00

p.m. mercantile closing hour). In response to Brown's telephone call at
10:10 p.m. (this was done to prove that the boys were going out after
the hour reformers wished to establish as a closing hour for all boys
under twenty-one), the Western Union Company dispatched a boy who
met Brown at the Union Square Hotel at Fifteenth Street and Fourth
Avenue. Soon Edward M. Barrows, another agent, joined them to act
as a witness. Brown suggested that the boy needed an overcoat and the
following conversation occurred:

> Boy: All winter I go about this way throughout the night, and
> never feel cold.
> Brown: All night? You surely don't work all night.
> Boy: Don't hey! Well I'm kept pretty busy around here every
> minute. We have lots of hospitals around this way, and when any-
> body is hurt and taken there I go out with messages to their home.
> And then the [police] station houses . . . keep me on the jump. Lots
> of whores get locked up around here and we are called to the cells
> to take messages from the whores to the pimps to bail 'em out. I
> get my biggest tips from this stunt, because after a while you get
> to know all the pimps and you know just where to find 'em.

Another common source of extra income for the night messengers came
from showing "visiting firemen" the sights of New York. On request
Brown and Barrows were taken to the Bowery where "the boy pointed
out to us, and in many instances named the Raines Law hotels."

> Brown: How do you know they are whore houses?
> Boy: Don't I get called to them with messages?
> Brown: How can they call?
> Boy: Well, they all have call boxes. We go in all of 'em. We see
> some great sights there. Last week I got a call in the —— Hotel
> on 13th Street, and when I answered the woman let me in her room
> where she was all naked, except for a little shirt she had on, and
> that could cover very little of her. . . . She sent me to get her some-
> thing to eat and when I came back she was laying flat on the bed.
> Brown: Did you trip over her?
> Boy: I could hardly get next to her, but I get mine alright.
> Brown: What do you mean?
> Boy: Well, a lot of girls like to stay with us messengers. We have
> whores come to our office too. We have a table there and do the
> trick on it. We get a lot of coats and lay them over the table and
> in that way make a soft spot.
> Barrows: I wish I could get a look in on that. . . . I would like

to just walk in to send a telegram when that trick happens again.

Boy: You wouldn't see a thing if you did, because we do it all down the cellar.

Brown: Does your manager know what goes on?

Boy: I should say he does. He sends us out after the whores, and then he takes his whack first. But now its hard because the inspector may drop in at any time. A short time ago the manager of the 56th Street office was caught in the back of the place with five girls and he was fired quick. They even found cards and chips in there.[60]

In the same year that Brown and Barrows made their investigation of night messenger work, the New York *Evening Post* reprinted an editorial from *Telegraph and Telephone Age* that contended that "the messenger boy is constantly thrown in contact with business affairs and with methods of great leaders of industry, and can always be learning new things." The NYCLC lost no time in presenting the results of the investigation to the legislature and Governor Hughes. Two public hearings were then held with the NYCLC represented by Mornay Williams, V. Everit Macy, George Alger, Felix Adler, Paul M. Warburg, Florence Kelley, Lillian Wald, and Maud Nathan, but "no representatives of any telegraph or messenger company appeared to enlighten the Legislators." Some months later the telegraph companies did make a belated protest in which they defended *all* messenger work by citing the advantages of *daytime* work, and the companies contended that *every* boy employed by New York City tradesmen (not just messenger boys) saw the "evil side of city life." The NYCLC retorted, "Who are the tradesmen, and what [is] the occupation employing boys after 10 o'clock at night in work regularly bringing them in contact with the evil side of city life?" The reformers, the companies argued, should "recognize the impossibility in city life as at present organized of keeping unemployed boys from acquiring knowledge of evils which are deplorable"; the NYCLC contended that night messenger work forced youngsters into evil "as a part of the performance of . . . [their] regular duties." Inevitably, the companies lamented the fate of the hosts of widowed mothers whom messenger boys were supporting, but the committee pointed out that its legislative demands prohibited work during only seven hours out of every twenty-four. Accusing the NYCLC of straining at a gnat, the companies maintained that "only a small percentage of the business comes from the so-called Red Light Districts"; the committee countered by citing investigations conducted by the National Child Labor Committee in some forty-five cities that showed the contrary. Besides, said the NYCLC, "even the smallest percentage is too much." The telegraph companies were attempting the impossible in defending the right of young boys to visit whorehouses in the course of their employment and their arguments became more and more ridiculous. When they claimed that "it would be difficult to find an occupation which is as conducive to a sturdy physical development as is the messenger service," the NYCLC pounced on them, asserting that "in our files there is letter after letter from physicians who have treated night messengers, from judges and probation officers . . . and from social workers . . . all agreeing absolutely that such employment results in many cases in . . . physical and moral ruin."[61] The committee might also have argued that it was only a step from night messenger work to crime. In 1910 the number of convicted juvenile criminals (under eighteen) in New York State exceeded that of any other state by over one thousand. Boys began by working money out of drunks or overcharging foreigners, then moved on to become pimps, opium pushers, pickpockets, or burglars. One young messenger boy approached the head of a New York settlement house to ask her assistance in getting the telegraph company to transfer him back to his old territory on the lower East Side where it was easy to overcharge immigrants for delivering messages. On Broadway, he complained, everyone knew what the correct charges should be. By the time the companies were making their public protests, the reformers had obtained remedial legislation. Passed unanimously by the legislature in 1910, the Murray Night Messenger Law barred all minors under twenty-one from engaging in night messenger work between the hours of 10:00 P.M. and 5:00 A.M. The law applied only to first- and second-class cities, however, and it was not until 1934 that the committee succeeded in extending the Murray Law to all cities in the state.[62]

The NYCLC had been able to make progress in controlling the messenger boys since they were clearly employees of the telegraph companies and the companies could be held responsible for what happened to them. Newsboys were more difficult to regulate because they were "self-employed," and the newspapers were not legally their employers. In 1903, after long, acrimonious debate, the New York legislature passed the nation's first Street Trades Law. Applying only to newsboys in first-class cities, the law prohibited boys under ten and girls under sixteen from selling newspapers and required newsboys under fourteen to obtain a badge and permit (the standards for a badge were the same as for an employment certificate except that no literacy test was given). A badged newsboy might sell papers until 10:00 P.M. By the end of October, 1903, an impatient NYCLC realized that the law was having no effect; the police will "not arrest boys violating the law . . . there have been no arrests . . . although there is a large number of boys, plainly under fourteen years of age, selling papers without badges," Fred Hall told the committee members.[63] Because New York City's public schools were so overcrowded, the NYCLC's efforts to compel truant newsboys to attend school received no official cooperation. The force of truant officers was too small (it never exceeded seventy-five) to handle the estimated sixteen hundred truant children who were on the streets of New York at any given moment.[64] The Child Labor Committee persuaded the New York City Police Department to establish a special newsboy squad, but this proved so ineffective that the police commissioner abolished the special squad, claiming that his men were needed elsewhere. He promised to order his precinct captains to enforce the Newsboy Law, but after checking the Children's Court records a few weeks later, the NYCLC found that no newsboy had been arrested. In desperation the committee decided that it would have to rely upon the truant officers. To make certain that the attendance officers did their job, the NYCLC sponsored a bill passed in 1907, specifically requiring them to check the badge of any newsboy found working outside of school hours. Some of the truant officers were still reluctant to do night work and the associate superintendent of schools in New York City was insisting that his officers not be required to work after 6:00 P.M. Once again the NYCLC appealed to Superintendent William H. Maxwell who promptly placed fifty of the seventy-five truant officers on newsboy duty and ordered day and night shifts to drive the unlicensed boys from the streets. The campaign lasted for only two weeks in September, 1909, but a month after it ended the committee reported that at least 90 per cent of the metropolitan newsboys were wearing badges.[65]

Sporadic enforcement drives of this kind were all that were possible, for the New York City Board of Education simply did not have the money to provide a satisfactory inspection force. When it did request funds, the city's Board of Estimate would turn down the appropriation. After the 1909 drive was over, the unlicensed newsboys returned. This was inevitable, for the selling of papers in New York, as in most large cities, was highly organized and much depended on its orderly continuance. The newspaper publishers did not merely hand out bundles of papers indiscriminately to any boy who showed up at the plant. Busy streetcorner locations sold for considerable sums of money, and changes of ownership were often supervised and supported by newspaper circulation managers. "Corner boys" sometimes hired other boys to sell papers for them on commission or salary, or at times an adult would control the location and hire the youngsters.

There were "free-lance" newsboys but they usually earned less money (between fifteen and sixty-five cents a day) than the "corner boys" and had to be careful to stay out of "controlled" territory. While an occasional newsboy was able to make as much as five or six dollars a day, most newsboys earned far less. Nevertheless, the newspapers, like like other employers of children, continually used the poverty argument in defending the rights of ten-year-olds to sell papers. The courts were even less inclined to punish youngsters who violated the Newsboy Law than they were to fine adults who broke the factory or mercantile regulations. An employer of child labor in a factory could be made to pay a fine, but a "self-employed" newsboy stood before the judge alone—the publisher of the newspapers he sold could not be prosecuted. Since the natural sympathy of the public was with the newsboy who was "hustling" his way to success, it is not surprising that most of the newsboys who appeared before the New York Children's Court were let off with a warning.[66]

The Newsboy Law was essentially unjust. It assumed that a boy of ten who could not work in a factory or store until the age of fourteen would come to no harm selling papers on the streets until 10:00 P.M. Moreover, before the passage of the Agnew Act in 1907 the newsboy trade was deemed worthy of so little regulation that fourteen- and fifteen-year-old boys could get out of school without obtaining an employment certificate by saying that they wished to sell papers. The public heard about newsboy lodging houses and newspaper-sponsored clubs and concluded that the youngsters would be better off in the streets than in orphanages. Yet when federal investigators studied the background of juvenile delinquents in 1910, they found that the percentage of orphans in non-street trade occupations was nearly double that found in street work. Although some of them may never have gone home, street workers were more likely to have a parent living than any other group among the delinquents studied. It was not a lack of home life but the street itself that produced the alarming crime and delinquency figures. About 1910 Elizabeth Watson reported that a high percentage of the inmates in the various metropolitan correctional institutions had been street traders. A 1916 study by Mabel Ellis revealed that street traders accounted for over 70 per cent of all the Manhattan juvenile delinquents.[67] Children who were tied down in a factory or store were less likely to get into trouble with the law. The evidence is conclusive that for every metropolitan newsboy who used his work experience as a springboard to economic success, a dozen others embarked on lives of crime, became addicted to vice, or ended up as panhandlers. A life characterized by shaking down customers by pretending to be out of change, making small pay-offs to the patrolman, and learning the "ropes" about prostitution, drinking, and gambling was hardly the kind of training Horatio Alger would have approved for future captains of industry. One of the cases reported by the NYCLC indicates what could happen in newspaper selling. The boy's mother is speaking:

> My Danny was a little over 14 years old when he began to sell the papers. I was scrubbing in the Jefferson Market Court, and the [school] Principal said "Now Mrs. G——, you're a widow, working hard to take care of your children. Why don't you let Danny take the papers to sell? He won't be needing any badge to do that because he is 14 years old, and old enough to be working, but can't get his working papers until he has made up 50 days more in school." So Danny began to sell on the corner of 18th Street and 4th Avenue. There must have been a bad lot of boys there . . . for soon after Danny started there he began to stay out late nights; never came home until half past eleven, sometimes twelve o'clock. . . . He never played the truant from school until after he began to sell papers . . . it was as though he had been born again.

From this point Danny quickly deteriorated. Soon he was a jackroller.

> In the night he used to be around waiting for drunken men and women. His name became known in police courts. He made his money—and spent it—like a man. He contracted venereal disease before he was fifteen.[68]

As might be expected, enforcement of the Newsboy Law upstate was even more uncertain than in New York City (the original law of 1903 had applied only to first-class cities; in 1905 the law was extended to second-class cities and in 1913 to third-class cities). In Buffalo when the law first went into effect the city was enthusiastic; 1,500 newsboys received badges and over 300 underage boys were driven from the streets.[69] Ten years later the NYCLC field secretary, Glenn Edwards, visited Buffalo and found the Newsboy Law largely ignored; "the police department had made some effort to enforce the law . . . [but] their methods were harsh in the extreme and the efforts intermittent." By 1926 the Buffalo Children's Aid Society reported that the number of street traders had increased 161 per cent since 1919.[70] Although Syracuse had been covered by the Newsboy Law since 1905, Secretary Edwards found that the city had done nothing to enforce the law until 1912 "when a great round-up of boys" took place. With an inadequate truant force and no newsboy policeman on duty after 7:00 P.M., the street sellers soon returned. During 1914 one Syracuse policeman was assigned to newsboy duty but he spent "most of his time . . . in a limited area of the city . . . keeping the boys from rough horseplay and from defacing property . . . incidentally ordering a boy now and then to get a badge."[71] In Utica the head of the Associated Charities found a newsboy who although too young for a badge sold papers anyway because "the police man was good to him. When asked what police man, he said 'Why, all the police men.'" Similar conditions existed in Albany where city authorities ignored the Newsboy Law until 1916. Finally the Albany Women's Club created such a stir that Police Chief Hyatt announced: "There has been so much complaint lately about boys between the ages of seven and twelve running around the street late at night selling papers that we have got to put a stop to it," but three years later nothing had been done. In 1919 a questionnaire sent by the NYCLC to the fifty-nine cities of the state revealed that half of them were making no effort to enforce the Newsboy Law.[72]

Even though it was unable to secure any real enforcement of its minimum 1903 standards, the NYCLC continued its efforts to secure more restrictive legislation. The persistent opposition of the New York City Society for the Prevention of Cruelty to Children and the newspapers prevented any increase in the minimum age for newspaper selling until 1913, when it was finally raised to twelve years. Badged newsboys were also forbidden to sell papers after 8:00 P.M. and before 6:00 A.M. (in 1928 a 7:00 P.M. evening limit was established) and a 1914 enactment required newsboys up to the age of sixteen to obtain badges.[73] This upgrading of the legislative standards for newsboys resulted in a weakening of the laws governing newspaper carrier boys. In 1910 the State Attorney-General had ruled that because carrier boys were actually employees of the publishers and dealers, they were covered by the mercantile law, and were therefore unable to become carrier boys until they were fourteen years old or to deliver papers before 8:00 A.M. The NYCLC was unwilling to agree to requests from circulation managers for an amendment to the labor law permitting deliveries before 8:00 A.M.; the committee hoped that the inconsistency of street selling (a far more dangerous occupation) being permitted two years earlier than delivery work would help them raise the selling age to fourteen. Instead, in 1914 the newspapers succeeded in *reducing* the carrier age to twelve, where it remains at present. In 1921 carriers were formally brought under the Street Trades Law and required to get badges, although they were permitted to begin delivering at 6:00 A.M.

Other forms of street trading were either unregulated or controlled under different laws. Jeanie Minor summarized the situation in 1924:

> Our present law, putting newsboys under the school law, peddlers under the penal law, bootblacks over 14 working at stands under the labor law, and itinerant bootblacks under 14 under no law at all, is unreasonable in its varying provisions and chaotic in its results.[74]

In 1903 an NYCLC investigation had disclosed that most of the child bootblacks were Italians working in the poorest sections of New York City—"they black the boots of the inhabitants of Bowery lodging houses and groggeries." Francis H. Nichols, the committee investigator, believed that the Roman Catholic Church bore some responsibility for forcing young Italians into shoeshine work. "The parents of nearly all these bootblack boys are devoted Catholics who believe the priest's assertion that in sending their children to the public school they would jeopardize their souls," he declared. Since parochial schools cost money, Nichols said, the children went to no school at all. In 1928 the roving bootblacks were brought under the Street Trades Law but were supervised no better than the newsboys. Over the years the Italians were gradually driven out by Greek-operated shoeshine stands. The "Greek-padrone" system caused shoeshine stand youngsters to work long hours, but this was the concern of the mercantile inspectors.[75]

Occasionally the committee had to attack some short-term exploitation of children in street selling. During the First World War, for example, Jeanie Minor discovered that some of the New York City schools were sending entire classes out to sell thrift stamps in connection with the Liberty Loans. James Lee, a District Superintendent of Schools who was attempting to stop the practice, reported that "many children are selling thrift stamps during school hours in the streets and . . . girls are approaching, for the purpose of making sales, men and women who are strangers to them." By September, 1918, the NYCLC secured a public repudiation of such stamp selling from the associate superintendent of the New York City Schools. What concerned Jeanie Minor more than the street selling was the atmosphere of the thrift stamp rallies that preceded selling campaigns. Attending one in July, 1918, she noted that the children would give speeches "evidently written by adults . . . and . . . for the most part being mainly extravagant expressions of vindictive hate." One of the children

> declared that he would rather spend his future in ten thousand hells than one day in heaven with the Kaiser. It was not made clear as to just why he expected the Kaiser to inhabit heaven. These

speeches were almost entirely emotional rantings and many of the children worked themselves up into a frenzy. . . . There was little or no emphasis placed upon the duty of self-sacrifice . . . . [and] the chief incentive for the buying of thrift stamps as portrayed by these child speakers was the good interest which Uncle Sam would pay the investors, or in other words, that patriotism was a profitable business.[76]

From time to time the committee would receive reports of children being used to solicit funds for various charitable societies; the children would stand on street corners rattling cans for contributions. The committee would then bring the matter to the attention of the organization involved and the children would usually be dismissed.

Throughout the 1920's and 1930's, enforcement of the Street Trades Law remained almost as haphazard as in earlier years. A few communities cracked down; most of them either ignored the newsboys or engaged in periodic fits of enforcement. School superintendents in any city of less than 200,000 people might request the police to act as enforcers, but this opened up many opportunities for buck-passing. New York City had better luck when in 1931 it abandoned the policy of assigning a special group of truant officers to enforce the Newsboy Law and instead fixed responsibility for conditions in a particular attendance district upon the truant officer heading that district. Within just a few months 700 violations of the Newsboy Law were reported. In 1932 Harry M. Shulman, who had been chief investigator for the New York State Crime Commission, undertook a thorough investigation of the New York City newsboys. His findings indicated that the illegal night-selling of papers, particularly around theaters and subway stations in the metropolitan area was unhindered and that hundreds of violations of the Street Trades Law were occurring regularly. The Shulman study convinced George H. Chatfield, Director of the New York City Bureau of Attendance, that adequate enforcement of the law would require adding at least fifty truant officers to the metropolitan force. This would necessitate an increase of about $100,000 in the Bureau's budget, which in 1932 was not likely to be forthcoming.[77]

Upstate much still depended upon individual administrators. Rochester, Jeanie Minor decided in 1928, was doing the best job of enforcement in the state and it was all the doing of "Mr. Zorsch, the enthusiastic, likeable young attendance officer, friend alike of newsboys and newspapermen." George Hall found that even Albany, "where conditions have been notoriously bad for many years, has cleaned house

. . . thanks to the leadership of Miss Mary L. Farrell of the Catholic Charities." Binghamton was doing a creditable job, which Miss Minor attributed to the capable school superintendent who had the solid support of his school board. Syracuse was another story. "This city," she proclaimed, "despite its friendly and cooperative attitude, somewhat resembles the Augean stables. While one problem yields to broom and mop, another relapses and a third looms up." While the Salt City had "an exceptionally able and vigilant group of interested citizens . . . the best laid plans gang mysteriously agley [and] politics pollutes the very air you breathe." A series of flagrant violations of the Newsboy Law in Yonkers forced the local Society for the Prevention of Cruelty to Children to send an urgent communication to Jeanie Minor. "Knowing that the superintendent of schools in Yonkers never had and in all human probability never would enforce the Newsboy Law," Minor told him to call in the police. When Miss Minor visited the city she found that the Yonkers police commissioner did not know of the existence of the Newsboy Law, and after she explained its terms, he expressed eagerness to comply. A three-cornered enforcement plan was finally worked out: the police would notify the school superintendent when violations of the Newsboy Law were discovered, and the school would report it to the child's parents; if the child committed the offense a second time the parents would be prosecuted by the Society for the Prevention of Cruelty to Children. This plan proved so ineffective that five years later in 1934-35 the city of Yonkers (population 134,646) issued only *fifteen* street trades badges.[78] To some upstaters the Newsboy Law had a very limited purpose. Writing to the parents of an underage boy who had been refused a newsboy badge, the circulation manager of the Mount Vernon *Daily Argus* pronounced judgment:

> Newspaper people all over this State have more or less taken it for granted that the street trades law was designed to keep off the street half wits [and] deformed children. In view of the fact that your son Austin appears to be physically fit . . . I do not wonder that you kick and complain.[79]

Notwithstanding the committee's work over several decades, many upstate communities continued to ignore the law, not issuing a single street trades badge. By 1935, when 12,210 badges were issued in the state, fully 10,000 were for New York City. Since the Second World War, the mass move to the suburbs has caused a marked decline in the street sale of newspapers (see Table 10). More and more newspaper distribution is being done by route or carrier boys. In the

early 1950's New York established a special newspaper carrier boy
certificate for boys between the ages of twelve and eighteen; by 1955,
46,518 of these were being granted yearly.[80]

TABLE 10 [81]

STREET TRADES BADGES ISSUED IN NEW YORK STATE
AT VARIOUS PERIODS

Year	Number Issued
1909	4,376
1927-28 (1 year)	10,387
1930	4,500
1932	12,500
1935	12,210
1937-38	12,385
1940	5,588
1945	2,955
1950*	6,367
1955	634
1960	168

* The decline after 1950 was partly due to the raising of the street trades
age from twelve to fourteen.

The NYCLC had hoped that the National Industrial Recovery
Act would help them achieve a higher age limit for newspaper selling,
but they were disappointed. When the proposed provisions of the
Newspaper Code became known early in September, 1933, George
Alger found them thoroughly unsatisfactory, calling the code "an
open surrender to the newspaper industry." He explained in a letter
to Lindsay Rogers, Deputy Administrator of the NRA:

> The New York Child Labor Committee for years has been bring-
> ing pressure to bear on school authorities to clean up the de-
> plorable conditions which have been existing for some time.
> Temporary improvement has resulted from periodic raids but
> little permanent impression has been made upon the problem as
> the newspapers themselves have little to fear from prosecutions.
> The NYCLC . . . has been confidently looking to the Industrial
> Recovery Act to put the "fear of God" in the hearts of newspaper
> publishers and thus rid our city of the standing disgrace of little
> children—almost babies—crying their wares late at night in our
> public streets.[82]

The committee's principal objection to the code was that it permitted
children of any age to sell or deliver newspapers between the end of
the school day and 7:00 P.M.[83] During 1934 the National Child Labor

Committee lobbied steadily for changes in the code and the NRA finally held a hearing on proposed revisions in Washington, D.C., on June 22. George Hall reported that "the newspapers made a pathetically poor argument for lower standards." The publisher of the Syracuse *Post-Standard* brought a newsboy to the hearing but according to Hall the boy became so confused in his tribute to street selling that "he had to be coached." "Certain newspaper publishers," the New York *Post* announced afterwards, "greatly weaken the position of newspapers as leaders of public opinion—for the sake of a negligible commercial saving." The New York *Daily News* quoted a telegram from Sing Sing Prison Warden Lewis E. Lawes stating that 69 per cent of the prison inmates had at one time sold papers.[84] It was not the newspapers' finest hour; they were badly frightened by concurrent efforts of the reformers to have the Child Labor Amendment ratified and were striking out in all directions. The second Newspaper Code set a twelve-year minimum age for newspaper carrier boys and a fourteen-year minimum age for those selling papers in the streets in cities of over 50,000 population (this last provision raised the New York standard by two years), but shortly after it went into effect the NIRA was declared unconstitutional.

After the demise of the NIRA, the NYCLC continued its efforts to raise the minimum age to fourteen for newspaper selling and delivery work. As far as the committee was concerned, the newsboy problem was still serious; an investigation in New York City over ten nights during 1934 revealed that "23% of the boys counted . . . were under 12 years of age, some of them being as young as 8."[85] In 1937 the courts gave the committee some unexpected help by awarding double compensation to two injured thirteen-year-old newspaper carriers because they had been employed before reaching the fourteen-year minimum age provided by the labor law for commercial work. The court regarded the carriers as "employees" of the newspapers and hence covered by the labor law. This threw the newspapers into an uproar, for as far as they had known the two boys had been legally employed, since the carrier age had been lowered to twelve in 1914. Actually the situation was now back where it had been when "self-employed" street sellers had been outside the labor law and the less hazardous occupation of carrier boy had been included. Not until 1937 had anyone thought to inquire whether carrier boys were covered by Workmen's Compensation.

In 1940, shortly before the NYCLC went out of existence, it was still trying to raise the minimum age for all newspaper work to fourteen. A legislative hearing was held in February of that year at which the newspapers claimed that they could not find enough boys over fourteen to deliver papers in smaller cities. Not until after the Second World War was a compromise reached, and it came largely as a result of the newspapers' wish to have their liability under workmen's compensation clarified. Some of the publishers had stated in 1940 that they would not oppose a fourteen-year age for both delivery and selling if they could be relieved of liability under workmen's compensation. Instead the carrier boy age was kept at twelve, but the newspapers had to provide workmen's compensation insurance for them. The street-selling age was raised to fourteen, but since these boys were still regarded as "self-employed" the newspapers need not provide compensation.[86]

Today there are far fewer boys selling newspapers in the streets than formerly because there is no real need for them. The attitude of the public, the newspapers, and the enforcing agencies toward the "little merchants," however, has not undergone much change since the turn of the century; indeed, it has been transferred to the carrier boys who are now called "junior independent merchants."

Farms . . . present one more item of "unfinished
business" to those who are to complete the task of
the New York Child Labor Committee.
—FRED S. HALL, 1942

VII. Dilemma in Agriculture

The committee's attack on agricultural child labor faced
public prejudices and misconceptions exceeding those that had hampered street trades regulation. For decades the joys of farm life and
the superior morality of the rural environment had been celebrated
by so many writers and publicists as to have become "a mass creed"
by the early nineteenth century.[1] In 1948 the New York State Labor
Department stated categorically that "early child labor legislation in
New York State . . . specifically excluded agriculture because of the
prevalent belief that farm work . . . was beneficial for children."[2]
While the attachment of many people to the symbolic virtues of
farming was undoubtedly sincere, the congruence of their beliefs
with economic realities was nonetheless clear. New York was, and is,
an important agricultural state. Outsiders may imagine that metropolitan New York City represents the state, but the reality of New
York is as much the sound of a tractor on a lonely field in Steuben
County as the howl of a police siren in Harlem. In 1909 in the state
of New York, 4,356,861 cases of canned agricultural products were
packed; the state's canned pea production was the second highest in
the Union, its canned bean production third, and its canned corn production sixth. By the early 1920's the cash value of the state's crops
was about $255,000,000. Centered in Long Island, the Hudson Valley,
and central and western New York, the New York vegetable industry's
production was surpassed by only two other states; New York ranked
second nationally in the production of cabbage, green beans, onions,
apples, and grapes.[3] Efforts to end child labor in agriculture were thus
directed not only against a myth but against a powerful economic
interest whose strength was augmented by a badly proportioned
system of legislative representation.

The committee's first drive was against the fruit and vegetable
canneries themselves, which were factories in a rural setting. It was
then forced to conduct a separate campaign against the cannery
"sheds," but the closer the reformers got to the open field the more
difficult their task became. Canneries and sheds were one thing; they
were limited in size and a child was either there or not there. But

169

under the open sky and hot sun, young children were engaged in labor as back-breaking as that in any factory. Working on thousands of separate farms and protected by the agrarian myth, these children posed an almost insurmountable difficulty for the reformers. Against this kind of fragmented social problem, against local resistance and official apathy, the committee's achievements were negligible.

At the turn of the century over a hundred fruit and vegetable canning plants, which employed more than thirteen thousand persons, were operating in New York. The employees were usually country people living near the cannery and foreigners brought out from nearby cities. Such diverse groups confined in a single rural factory were unlikely to form much of a bond with one another, let alone to start a labor union or protest plant conditions. Although women were legally forbidden to work more than sixty hours a week (1899), and children under sixteen were limited to a fifty-four-hour week (1903) these statutes were ignored by the vast majority of canners.[4] The canners believed that the existing hours legislation for women and children did not take into account the special conditions prevailing in their industry. Since fruits and vegetables were perishable and seasonal, long hours of labor at certain periods of the year were essential. This was not the fault of the canners but of God: "The Lord ripens the crops," they said. Cannery work, moreover, was carried on in a healthful rural environment, not in some smoke-belching factory in the middle of a slum. Such beliefs made the task of the child labor reformers even more difficult. They had not only to *improve* the legislation on canneries, but to beat down perennial efforts by the canners to be exempted from the *existing* statutes.

When the New York Child Labor Committee's 1903 factory legislation was under discussion in the legislature, the New York State Canned Goods Packers' Association introduced the Cook Bill which would have allowed children of any age to work in canneries during their summer vacation without an employment certificate.[5] As described by the canners the bill sounded almost like a concession to the children:

> The class of work which the children would so do would be out of doors, not standing up but sitting, and under a sheltering protection from sun and rain, and being entirely piece work they would need to work only such length of time as they would like to. The work is not hard . . . and in many cases the mother would be with the child. To many it would be a recreation, and they would be much better off than were they in more objectionable

places and surrounded as they often times are by unprofitable environments.

When the Cook Bill failed to pass, it should have been clear that cannery work by children under fourteen was prohibited under the Factory Law. But was it? A typical cannery consisted of three types of buildings: the store house; the process building, where fruits and vegetables were sealed and cooked; and the "shed" where fruits and vegetables were prepared for processing, *i.e.*, where the peas were shelled and the corn husked.[6] After some thought the canners decided that perhaps sheds were not covered by the Factory Law. This was a reversal of the position they had taken at the 1903 legislative hearing when it was obvious that they *had* considered the proposed factory legislation to apply to sheds. After the defeat of the Cook Bill, moreover, the Factory Law was strengthened still further by the addition of a ban on all work by children under fourteen *in connection with* a factory. Since work in a shed involved the preparation of vegetables and fruit for processing in an adjacent factory, it would seem that such labor was "in connection with" a factory (there is no evidence, however, that the child labor reformers proposed this amendment with cannery sheds in mind). In 1905 the president of the State Canned Goods Packers' Association asked Labor Commissioner P. T. Sherman whether the Factory Child Labor Law applied to sheds. Sherman advised the canners to follow their attorney's advice and employ children under fourteen in the sheds, whereupon the Labor Department would then bring a test prosecution. But just to be certain, Sherman asked for an opinion from Julius M. Mayer, the State Attorney-General—the same man who as a judge of the New York City Court of Special Sessions had led an attack on the Child Labor Committee's 1903 Street Trades Bill. Mayer's reaction was prompt. The law permitted children of any age to work "on a farm or in the open air" during school vacations—what difference did it make if the employer was a corporation instead of an individual? Shed work was agricultural and there were no limits on agricultural work (other than the Compulsory Education Law). To Mayer the words "in connection with a factory" meant only "such connection as would bring the child under conditions . . . dangerous or unhealthy or otherwise detrimental to the child's welfare." As long as the shed was "devoid of machinery, in the open air, unconnected with a factory, and not subject to the discipline and hours governing factory employment" such employment was legal.[7]

The attorney-general's opinion might have been the basis of shed regulation if it had been strictly interpreted in the courts. The factory inspectors found, for example, that of sixty-three inspected sheds only fourteen were "devoid of machinery." Some sheds were combined with "vineries" where pea-threshing machines were operated and others contained conveyor belts, blanching and scalding devices, corncob crushers, and husking machines.[8] Attorney-General Mayer's other requirements must have been based upon the assumption that labor by eight- and nine-year-old children was somehow harmless if carried on in a building with one or two sides open to the weather and located three feet away from a "real" factory. As for Mayer's stipulation that a shed not be subject to the discipline and hours of a factory, this meant only that the shed not run on a fixed hourly schedule (none of them did) but vary the hours according to the amount of work which had to be done and pay on a piecework basis rather than by the hour. Mayer's opinion was a green light for the canneries to continue employing children under fourteen. Commissioner Sherman, whose work was admirable in other areas of factory regulation, did not even begin the test prosecutions against the sheds that contained machinery. Instead he regarded the attorney-general's opinion as flatly exempting the sheds from the Factory Law. Mounting criticism from reform groups induced John Williams, who replaced Sherman in 1908, to bring nine prosecutions against canners for employing children under fourteen in sheds. Four of the cases were tried and in each of them the defense relied solely upon Mayer's opinion. All four cases were decided in favor of the canners, even though all of the sheds had contained machinery. "Local courts," said Labor Commissioner Williams, "so far from strictly construing the . . . Attorney-General's opinion, have stretched it to the utmost in the direction of liberal interpretation." Now that the canners knew where they stood, they had no reason to conceal shed child labor. During 1908 the factory inspectors found 593 children under fourteen at work in sheds; 123 of these were under ten.[9]

Having settled the shed question to their satisfaction, the canners resumed efforts to have the regular processing factories exempted from the labor law. In 1910 they backed the Boshart Bill, which would have permitted women and children over sixteen to work unlimited hours in canneries between June 15 and October 15 so long as an average of ten hours a day were maintained *over that four-month period*. This proposal appalled the NYCLC. As they were quick to point out, a cannery that started work on July 1 and ended October 1 could run a thirteen-and-one-half-hour day and still comply with the law. Corn canneries, which normally opened September 1, could run twenty-four hours a day. "The only possible arguments for [the Boshart Bill] . . . ," Mornay Williams remarked, "are that the canners hope to save money and some of their employees hope to make money at the expense of life and decency." In March, 1910, the reform groups came out in force for the bill's legislative hearing as did a number of the leading canners. Pauline Goldmark of the Consumers' League argued forcefully that the cannery exemption was unjust because "work in the cannery is as exhausting as any form of factory work." When Miss Goldmark had made her own cannery investigation in 1908, she had found young women and children working as long as twenty hours a day during the peak season. "The work," she maintained, "is carried on at intense speed and lasts for cruelly long hours." The canners insisted that they were entitled to exemption because their employees worked a comparatively short season in a healthful bucolic atmosphere, but Miss Goldmark contended that *more*, not less, cannery legislation was needed. "The canner," she charged, "has no regard for human fatigue and exhaustion, he makes no effective effort to avoid an over-stocking of raw materials. Rather than lose any of his product he will work his employees to the limit . . . getting them to work for seven days in the week and as much as eighty or ninety hours." The bill was not even reported out of its legislative committee. George Hall attributed its defeat to the "active opposition of labor unions [and] equally active opposition of social workers throughout the state."[10] The victory was short-lived, for in 1912 the canners obtained a flat exemption from the newly passed Jackson Hours Act which established a fifty-four-hour week for factory women. It was a wide open exemption which permitted minors and women over sixteen years of age to work unlimited hours in canneries between June 15 and October 15. The NYCLC pleaded in vain that the Jackson exemption might establish a precedent for granting all kinds of seasonal industries similar privileges and that the canners would commit the same abuses with this exemption as they had with the shed exemption.[11]

At this point the Factory Investigating Commission turned its attention to canneries. Hiring Zenas L. Potter, Field Secretary of the NYCLC, as chief investigator, the commission launched a full-scale cannery probe in 1912. Potter and nine assistants inspected 121 of the state's 128 canning establishments; when necessary they even applied for jobs and worked with the employees, but there were signs that the canners were growing suspicious of new "employees." In one cannery a commission inspector saw an estimated two hundred children being rushed off the premises as he arrived; these children were not included in the commission's totals. The Factory Commission's investigation found 1,355 children under sixteen at work in canneries, and 1,259 of these were in the sheds, but the commission claimed that these figures were only an indication of the problem.[12] Child labor inside the sheds was not unlike industrial homework—indeed, some of the canners let the workers take home beans to snip. Most of the children were snipping the ends off beans or husking corn, operations which were performed with the bare hands and which were extremely fatiguing to the younger children. Children were often expected to carry bean boxes (weighing nineteen to twenty-nine pounds) and corn crates (weighing forty to sixty pounds) distances up to two hundred feet to the weighing station. "Small girls," the commission reported, "have been seen tugging at crates that they were hardly able to carry." The canners did not keep any record of the children's working hours and did not care about their comings and goings. They knew that the parents would keep their offspring at work, just as tenement parents did, in order to increase the family "piece work" pay. Commission investigators who worked inside the sheds turned up one case of parental exploitation after another. A little boy of eleven stopped snipping for a moment of horseplay whereupon "his father hit him brutally across the face and set him to work again." A girl of ten worked at snipping beans from 4:30 A.M. until 10:00 P.M. on August 26, 1912—even with her time off she put in a sixteen-and-one-half hour day. Then there was

> Little Jack, aged 12, up from 3 A.M. and snipping from 4:30 A.M. to 10 P.M., with only a few minutes for supper [who] said: "My fingers is broke." He went to bed last night at 12 and got up at 3. He said he was "awful tired," but his mother made him work. He tried to go home several times. His hands were swollen. His sister, aged 10, could hardly keep her eyes open, and her mother scolded her constantly. Jack made $1.40. He said he couldn't keep any of it. He said work like this was nothing [compared] to peas when his mother and sister would come home every night at 1 and 2 A.M. and "They were so sick they fell down and vomited."

In one factory a foreman actually attempted to put a ten-year-old boy out of the shed, but "his mother came to his rescue, throwing boxes and managed to bite the foreman viciously on the arm." If she would fight for the boy's right to work, the commission investigator wondered, what would she do to the boy if he refused? When the children started their working season "they were full of play and acted

like real children," but as the days wore on they sat "like little machines with their fingers tied up in rags."[13]

They did not make much money, but neither did the adults. While
a mother and father together might earn $2.75 for a ten-hour day
in the cannery, a child under ten could earn twenty-five cents and
one ten to fourteen could earn fifty cents for the same period of time.[14]
Canners probably would have preferred to rely upon local labor, but
this was often in short supply and the industry became increasingly
dependent upon Italian and Polish families, most of whom came out
to the fields from upstate cities and remained at the canneries for the
season. Providing living quarters for these workers increased the canner's expenses, but he often made up the difference by paying them
wages lower than those demanded by local "American" labor. The
camps themselves varied in quality, but many of them were unfit to
live in, "poorly constructed and in poor repair, not drained, unsanitary
and filthy, poorly furnished . . . badly overcrowded, and without such
partitions as would ensure even the segregation of the sexes."[15] Some
canners justified their use of child labor by claiming that the foreigners
would not come unless their children were allowed to work—a clear
admission that adults alone could not make a decent living in cannery
work. The environment in some of the cannery camps was not particularly suited to children, for many of the evils of the "padrone"
system which have become more apparent in recent years in connection with migrant laborers were present before the First World War.
Even if the children's home environment was no better than that of
the camps, their departure from home for cannery work often caused
their education to suffer. Immigrant families would sometimes leave
for the fields before the schools closed in June and would return after
they had begun in September. The cannery children rarely attended
the schools near the factory. "Local taxpayers," the commission reported in a masterpiece of understatement, "often lack the vision to
see what the failure to educate these foreigners means to the State
and nation." Besides, if children attended school during the canning
season, they would cut down the family income and deprive the canners of labor.[16]

The Factory Investigating Commission recommended that children
under fourteen be prohibited from working in cannery sheds. "The
question of importance," they asserted, ". . . is not whether a shed is
a field or a factory, but whether there have been child labor abuses
in the sheds." The commission also was convinced that the recently
developed mechanical corn-husker and other such machines would
reduce the necessity of child labor in the sheds. The legislature ac-

cepted the recommendation of the commission and in 1913 sheds were formally brought under the Factory Law and children under fourteen were barred from such work.[17] Important hours legislation limiting the work of women and minors over sixteen to ten hours a day and sixty hours a week during the canning season was also passed. Objecting vehemently to a provision forbidding the women to work a seven-day week, the canners had sent several clergymen to testify that the cannery workers needed a seven-day week to avoid poverty. Their plea elicited Al Smith's sardonic observation that "if these distinguished champions of women and children [the clergymen] were to rewrite the divine law I have no doubt they would change it to read, 'Remember the Sabbath day to keep it holy—except in canneries.' "[18]

Not accepting the 1913 legislation, the canners mounted two counterattacks in the 1915 and 1916 legislative sessions. The Bewley Cannery Bill of 1915 which would have permitted the canners to employ women and children sixteen hours a day and seventy-two hours a week passed the Assembly with the blessing of Republican Majority Leader Harold J. Hinman who described the existing Factory Commission Law as having been "a mistake from the outset." Minority Leader Al Smith retorted: "If you Republicans stay in power long enough you'll tear down the whole law that protects New York's most valuable asset—its womanhood." The Bewley Bill aroused a storm of opposition from the Factory Investigating Commission, the Consumers' League, the Women's Trade Union League, the Women's Municipal League, the League of Catholic Women, and the NYCLC. Republican Governor Charles S. Whitman eventually vetoed it, but compromise proposals kept popping up all during the 1915 session. One measure that would have permitted a seventy-two-hour week during rush seasons if the canner notified the Labor Department had the support of Governor Whitman and Labor Commissioner James M. Lynch but was defeated in the Assembly by a scant three votes. The state's newspapers lent so much support to the reform cause that George Hall was able to assemble for Governor Whitman an album of over forty newspaper editorials and cartoons denouncing the canners. The various bills, Robert F. Wagner charged in an hour-long Senate speech, were "wanted by a few canners with avarice enough to place the almighty dollar above child life and womanhood, who are willing to deify the dollar and sacrifice man on Mammon's altar." Mornay Williams of the NYCLC asserted that the canners desired exemption from the labor law not because they thought the law could be enforced, but because if a cannery worker were injured while working in violation of the law his employer could not claim contributory negligence on the part of the employee; "a more cynical . . . [and] anarchistic argument I have never heard anywhere," declared Williams.[19] The canners failed to obtain any favorable legislation in 1915. "The Republicans in the Assembly lost their nerve," the upstate Amsterdam *Sentinel* editorialized, "in the face of thousands of protests that poured in from all parts of the state against the proposed bills." The newspaper hailed the canners' defeat as a "step in the direction of the conservation of human life."[20] The next year the canners were back in Albany with a fresh proposal. After their 1915 defeat they had persuaded the new Industrial Commission (now running the Labor Department) to conduct a study of canneries. The commission had then proposed its own bill permitting the employment of women over eighteen to work twelve hours a day and seventy-two hours a week for a limited period during certain parts of the canning season. This bill, drawn up by the canners and the Labor Department, won the support of the president of the State Federation of Labor and Industrial Commissioner James Lynch but was intensely opposed by the Women's Trade Union League, the New York City Consumers' League, and much of labor's rank and file. It passed the Legislature in 1916 but Governor Whitman vetoed the bill.[21]

Despite the legislative gain of 1913, the canneries proved very difficult to regulate. Many of the canners honestly believed that their enterprises deserved special consideration even though the new legislation allowed them longer working hours than most factories. When a fruit or vegetable crop came in, it had to be processed or it would spoil. This position found support not only from upstate juries, which were understandably reluctant to convict prominent local businessmen of labor law violations, but from the Labor Department itself. In 1915 Labor Commissioner Lynch told the legislature that during the previous year he had been able to secure only two convictions out of forty-two cannery prosecutions. "Is there not something our Committee can do to make cannery prosecutions possible?" Fred Hall asked. To Hall "the one good man left in the Labor Department" was Chief Statistician Leonard W. Hatch whose reports clearly indicated "the hopelessness of prosecutions before judges and juries in canning counties."[22] The official attitude of the Labor Department toward the enforcement of the 1913 cannery legislation was therefore understandably lukewarm. The department also sympathized with the canners' inability to find a sufficient number of adult workers at the prevailing wage rates and asserted that "regardless of the wages paid, the Italian parents think their children should contribute to the family income . . . [and] even if the canners attempted to live within the law prohibiting child labor they would have considerable difficulty enforcing the necessary rules to effect their end." "The canners assume," the Labor Department reported, "that the law will not and cannot be enforced." When inspectors asked one canner to explain his use of some seventy-five illegal child laborers for picking in the fields and snipping in the sheds, he replied: "We didn't know that the Department of Labor was going to give any attention to . . . children on farms this season; and we don't admit the constitutionality of that section of the Labor Law."[23]

Throughout the 1920's and 1930's any canner who wished to use illegal child labor stood an excellent chance of getting away with it. The number of child laborers depended almost entirely upon the conscience of the individual canner or commercial farmer. When the crop was large and the workers few, even well-intentioned canners would be tempted to press children into service. A few canners successfully evaded the shed law by using tents (the shed law had not specifically included tents). Many canners continued to violate the hours provision of the 1913 legislation with the result that illegal overtime work in the factories and sheds remained the same, particularly during the rush season.[24] School officials in Dunkirk, for example, began finding children who went to sleep in class during the early fall of 1930. Upon investigation it appeared that

> A near-by cannery hired [the girls] at [$] 2.— a night, 6 P.M. to 6 A.M., half hour for lunch—a truck would pick up a load of girls at an appointed place and return them in the morning—the employers asked no questions as to ages or required papers. This sort of thing goes on all season beginning with berries and going on to peas, corn, etc.

When Frances Perkins became Industrial Commissioner, she tried a new approach to the canners. Admitting the Labor Department's failure to enforce the law, she contended that canning was "an industry long and futilely attacked by the big-stick method." Conciliation seemed to be the answer and after a series of conferences between the canners and the Labor Department, a new Industrial Board Rule was adopted in 1932 permitting all canners (heretofore only pea-packers had been covered) to work their employees up to twelve hours a day and sixty-six hours a week in emergencies. The cannery had to make application to the Labor Department and show that it had met certain minimum standards. Despite this agreement, hours violations continued, canneries still failed to file required reports with the Labor Department, and convictions of errant canners were just as difficult to obtain.[25]

In time the introduction of new machines was more successful than legislation in reducing child labor in the canneries and sheds, but the problem of children picking in the fields remained almost untouched. Here child labor was extensive, yet the Labor Department did nothing. Technically, the law required Labor Department inspectors to check on child labor in the fields as well as in the canning factories and sheds, for it specifically authorized twelve- and thirteen-year-old boys to pick for not more than six hours a day (by implication boys under twelve and girls under fourteen were prohibited from picking). In 1921 these restrictions were abandoned, but in 1928 the employment of any minor under fourteen in "any occupation carried on for pecuniary gain" was forbidden, a restriction which could have been used to end child labor in commercial agriculture and to require older agricultural workers to obtain working papers (children at work on their home farm were exempted from all these early statutes). Far from prosecuting the canners and commercial truck farmers who employed young children, the Labor Department did not even *inspect* the fields. When the NYCLC urged it to do so, the department cited an "informal" ruling made by the State Attorney-General in 1937 which said that the Labor Department had no legal authority to check farm work. Industrial Commissioner Frieda S. Miller told the committee:

> I have learned that there is a very definite doubt on the part of the Attorney-General that we have any authority, especially during vacation time, to look into that farm situation. We have never inspected any kind of farm work and . . . I do not think any of us in the Labor Department know too much about the size of that problem, certainly we do know enough about it to indicate to me that we haven't dealt with it nor thought what is involved by way of really covering the territory which any regulation would make it necessary to cover.[26]

It was obvious to the committee from the reports it had received that someone ought to be inspecting the fields. Very young children continued to be used as fruit and vegetable pickers. The manager of the Batavia *Times* wrote:

> They [the canners and growers] herd them together [in the trucks] like sheep or cattle, no seats to sit on, they all stand straight and they squeeze them in. They get them out of their

beds at five and bring them back at night. Sunday is no different from any other day. It is a shame and a crime the way they have been handling these children.[27]

The committee had become more concerned after the State Committee on Summer Farm Labor Problems (a group composed of representatives of the upstate Councils of Social Agencies) had made known the results of its 1936 investigation of agricultural child labor in the fields. "Almost without exception," Roy F. Woodbury, the director of the study, concluded ". . . children from about nine years of age and upwards . . . [are] used to assist in the picking of farm produce." Most of the workers in the twenty-four central New York farm labor camps visited by Woodbury's group came from Utica, Rome, or Syracuse. They were usually trucked out to the fields at the beginning of the season and they remained there until early autumn.[28] Wages were low: pea and bean pickers earned about twenty-five cents a bushel (twenty-eight to thirty pounds of beans); berry pickers earned two cents a quart for raspberries and blackberries and seventy-five cents a bushel for cherries. A twelve-hour day was normal with pickers arriving in the field by 7:00 A.M. and not returning to the labor camps for eleven or twelve hours. Although many of the growers denied hiring children directly, Woodbury's inspectors found that padrones tried to get parents to bring as many of their children as possible. An employer near Madison told the investigators that bean growers ought to be allowed to keep children after school had opened in the fall because ten- to twelve-year-olds were better and faster pickers than the older children. The growers *were* concerned about the double compensation laws. At a large canning farm near Homer the investigators found a nine-year-old boy whose fingers recently had been crushed when a 150-pound sack of beans was thrown on the weighing scale where his hand was. "The company," they reported, "was concerned about this as [the] boy had been out picking and they were faced with a possible double indemnity award if this was reported to the Labor Department." Another grower from Smyrna said that he was already spending too much money for workmen's compensation to "take a chance on employing children under 14."[29]

These fears were well founded. In August, 1935, ten-year-old Mary Moreno and five other children under fourteen had been injured when a Halstead Canning Company truck in which they were riding struck a culvert. After the company made a routine report to the Workmen's Compensation Bureau, the injured children received payment at the standard rate and the referee closed the cases in March, 1936. When

George Hall saw a report of the incident in the *Industrial Bulletin,* he persuaded the Labor Department to reopen the case because the children, illegally employed, should have received double compensation. After further hearings were held, all six children were awarded double compensation. Contesting the decision, the Halstead Canning Company denied that Mary Moreno had been employed, claiming that she had only been "with her mother" in the fields. In 1939 the Appellate Division of the Supreme Court, however, unanimously upheld the double compensation award and the Court of Appeals later refused to review the case. "The effect of the decision," George Hall rejoiced, "will be to proclaim to canners and farmers alike that they are liable both under the labor law and under the compensation law if they permit children under 14 . . . to pick on the farm."[30]

The decision in the Moreno case placed agricultural child labor definitely under the jurisdiction of the Labor Department. The NYCLC had been pushing for a full-scale investigation of this problem but had found state officials most reluctant to tackle it. This was understandable, for it was as difficult to prove that children in the fields had been illegally employed as it had been to show that tenement children were working on homework. During a discussion of the problems at an NYCLC board meeting, George Alger predicted that enforcing child labor legislation on farms would be almost impossible. For one thing, a vast territory was involved. "There has never been a complete investigation," said Industrial Commissioner Miller. Farm child labor is "pretty extensive. There is the Erie County situation, the black muck land around Batavia, Rochester and Buffalo, the berry picking along the Hudson, and the situation on Long Island." Truck farms, she thought, were "as industrialized as many other types of employment" and here something might be done. The family farms were another matter; it would be "impolitic and unwise" to inspect them.[31]

To prod the Labor Department the NYCLC decided to send Secretary Hall on a pilot investigation of truck farm labor during the summer of 1939. Assisted by a staff member of the National Child Labor Committee, Hall made an eighteen-day trip through the truck farming area of central New York, concentrating on farms near Highland, Hamilton, Cortland, Geneva, and Batavia, where the major crops were peas and beans. He found that at least a quarter of the seasonal workers on the twenty farms he visited were under sixteen, 225 children were under fourteen, and 101 were under eleven. Hall had no trouble getting into the farms and interviewing workers. He found the growers anxious to express their resentment against the New Deal relief programs, particularly the WPA, which they felt made it difficult for them to obtain field-pickers. Although most of the farmers insisted that children were much better off working in the fields than running wild in city streets and that their summer experience was actually a wonderful vacation, the overwhelming weight of evidence indicates that summer farm work in labor camps was not much fun for the youngsters. Since field picking involved "stoop labor," which could produce back injuries if continued for excessively long periods, it was not unusual that many of the children were suffering from backaches or heat exhaustion. Most of the children under sixteen carried their own bushel baskets weighing from twenty-eight to forty pounds to the weighing station—a distance as long as 300 feet. Several workers complained about the drinking water: "it was brown," "delivered in rusty cans," or "came from a dirty creek." The better camps paid some attention to elementary sanitation but others had outside privies just behind the workers' shacks. "The foul odor was continuous," according to Hall. Other privies were located in such a way as to make water pollution almost inevitable. Both adults and children suffered from diarrhea and vomiting. The camps themselves were usually one-story barrack-type structures which could accommodate from twenty to one hundred and twenty-five families. In one of the buildings Hall found ten persons sharing a room 7 feet by 12 feet with only three bunks. In another camp each family had a room 10 feet by 14 feet whose only furniture was a crude shelf. Cooking was often done in outdoor shacks with water available only from a common pump. In one such camp garbage was simply flung out the door and abandoned to the flies and summer heat. Many of the intrastate migrants were hired and controlled by a padrone (overseer, labor contractor, crew leader) who was in direct charge of them. Although arrangements varied, the padrone's income usually depended upon the amount of harvesting his workers did. The grower would not contract him the following year if his workers were slow; thus the stage was set for what the New York Consumers' League later called a "sweatshop in the sun." The workers' earnings were low. Hall found that an average family of four pickers would earn between two and four dollars a day and would gross between $100 and $150 for the summer. When it rained, they earned nothing. Some of this money went back to the padrone, for workers told Hall that the padrone-controlled "company store" was milking them dry. While some padrones got on very well with their workers, others exploited them ruthlessly. The following compaints about one boss, summarized by Hall, are typical:

Store run by padrone who charged very high prices. If you did not buy from him he would sit on the baskets and flatten down the peas so that you would have only half a basket. He struck small children, some around 6 years of age. He sold beer without a license and many times men would be walking around intoxicated.[32]

Truck accidents were an everyday hazard for the field workers. The padrones had to transport migrants to and from the labor camps at the beginning and end of each season, and drive day-haul workers to and from their home cities each day. Both groups had to be trucked back and forth daily from the labor camps to the fields. Most of the trucks were in poor mechanical condition. "The truck was so old it wobbled," one youngster told Hall, "when you stood inside you could see the wheels . . . because some of the boards of the floor were out." It was common to jam fifty to seventy pickers into an open truck with high slatted sides. Occasionally, a worker would actually faint from the crush. Hall discovered that not long before his visit the tail gate of one truck had opened while the driver rounded a curve and five small children were thrown out onto the pavement.[33] The State Committee on Summer Farm Labor Problems cooperated with the NYCLC in a drive for remedial truck legislation. "The State Police," Roy Woodbury told the legislature, "have seen trucks so crowded with human freight that the side racks were literally bulging." Between 1937 and 1939, Woodbury asserted, five workers had been killed in truck accidents (three of them under eighteen) and forty-four had been injured. The NYCLC listed eight additional accidents resulting in injuries to twenty minors under eighteen.[34] In 1939 the two groups sponsored the Ehrlich-Mahoney Bill which would have tightened the safety requirements for trucks, but it died in the Senate Committee on Motor Vehicles chaired by Senator Bewley. By 1940 the Ehrlich-Mahoney Bill had won the support of the Motor Vehicles Department, and in spite of strong opposition from farm areas its proponents succeeded in prying it out of Senator Bewley's committee. A dossier compiled by Roy Woodbury demonstrating the number of farm deaths and injuries directly attributable to unsafe trucks helped the bill along to final passage. Although Governor Lehman believed the bill to be loosely drawn, he signed it in April, 1940, as a start toward a safety program. The measure required operators of trucks to provide "suitable" seats for not less than two-thirds of the occupants, to have "securely" attached side racks at least three feet above the truck bed, and to provide a "securely" closed tail gate. The farm interests did win one important concession: the Ehrlich Act did not apply to trucks making hauls of less than ten miles, so that its major effect would be on the transportation of workers from cities to labor camps rather than from labor camps to fields.[35]

During 1940 the Labor Department finally began a very limited investigation of agricultural child labor on truck farms. After conferring with the NYCLC, the department dispatched—"for the first time in its history"—inspectors to Erie County. Studying just one small section of that county (100 farms) the department found 1,629 children under sixteen (none of whom had working papers), 30 working children under five and 330 under ten. Many of the labor camps were foul. Even this limited survey led to a departmental announcement that there was a "need for drastic action with respect to the employment of children in connection with commercial agriculture."[36] Yet the Second World War delayed any further enforcement until 1948.

After the New York Child Labor Committee went out of existence in 1942, the New York Consumers' League carried on the fight against the recurring problem of agricultural child labor. More and more interstate migrants, particularly southern Negroes, came into New York State after the Second World War. Crowded into camps that were often in abominable condition, exploited by the padrones, and trucked about like cattle, these out-of-state migrants brought the farm child labor problem into sharp focus for the first time. The squalor of migrant life became impossible to ignore. If the growers had been able to hire local workers to harvest the crops instead of trucking in large numbers of Negroes from the South, their use of child laborers might have gone largely unnoticed. According to official state figures, the number of New York's southern migrants rose from 7,000 in 1943 to 16,661 in 1948; by 1951 the Consumers' League estimated the number to be at least 25,000.[37] By 1942 the migrant problem had grown to such proportions that Governor Thomas E. Dewey appointed an Interdepartmental Committee on Migrant Camps (now known as the Interdepartmental Committee on Farm and Food Processing Labor) which at first consisted of representatives from the state departments of health, labor, and social welfare; more departments were added each year. This agency attempted to plan and coordinate the work of the several state departments concerned with migrant labor, but unfortunately could act only in an advisory capacity. Responsibility for the migrants continued to be shared by nine state agencies, each concerned with but a small piece of the problem. A migrant camp might be visited by the State Police, by Labor Department inspectors, by Health Department officials, by Farm Placement Representatives, by the Agricultural Extension Service, by school census takers and by the State Farm Labor Coordinator. Such a parade of officials not only made it impossible to fix final responsibility for the migrant problem but also tended to annoy the growers and destroy the effectiveness of the Interdepartmental Committee's efforts.[38]

The Consumers' League had been pressing the Labor Department for real enforcement of the agricultural child labor laws since 1944. It was in that year that the league conducted an investigation of twenty-two migrant camps in nine counties (there were about four hundred such camps in the state in 1944) and had found them to be in much the same condition as those visited by the NYCLC in the 1930's. Overcrowded quarters, a community water supply drawn from one outdoor cold-water faucet, miserable toilet facilities (in one camp the "privy provided for thirty-eight migrants got into such an unspeakable condition that the migrants . . . took to the nearby woods"), flies coming in through torn window screens, and bedding made of straw were often the rule. Child labor was common: "Most children over six are pickers," reported Helen Blanchard, the Consumers' League investigator.[39] Near the end of the Second World War, members of the State War Council toured some of the same camps covered by the Consumers' League and they, too, found them "disgracefully bad." Laws existed to remedy all these conditions, but they were not enforced. Not only had the jurisdiction of the Labor Department over farm child labor been clearly established by the courts in the 1930's, but inspectors could also require child workers to show a special farm work permit similar to an employment certificate that had been set up in 1944.

Although the state appeared extremely reluctant to crack down on child labor violations, the migrant problem as a whole was gaining more official recognition. In 1945 Governor Dewey called for extending "our progressive labor and social welfare programs . . . to migrant workers."[40] In response, the legislature passed a law the next year requiring any grower who imported more than ten migrant laborers to register with the Department of Labor. The department demanded a description of the growers' camp conditions and wage rates, which in turn would be presented to each migrant at the time of recruitment. Obviously, few growers would describe their camp conditions as inadequate and if, upon his arrival at the camp, the migrant worker found conditions to be other than those described, there was little he could do to protest; besides, many migrants were illiterate and unable to read the descriptions even when the crew leaders bothered to pass them out. In an effort to provide direct relief, during the Second World War the state of New York took over the administration of child care centers for the younger migrant children, which had been inaugurated in 1931 by two church groups, the Home Missions Council of North America and the New York State Council of Churches. Although officially sponsored by the New York State Federation of Growers and Processors, the centers were financed by federal funds during the Second World War. After the war the state contributed from 80 to 90 per cent of the operating expenses, but because the individual grower was required to contribute to the cost of any center set up on or near his farm, the number of such centers remained small. Only about five hundred children, the vast majority under nine years of age, were cared for annually in the centers. Although this was a small percentage of the total number of such migrant children, the toys, games, balanced diet, and professional program offered by the centers had a beneficial effect on these few. For the remainder the principal cultural experience continued to be the vagaries of migrant life.[41]

In 1948, annoyed by the Labor Department's seeming apathy, the New York Consumers' League took the unusual step of asking the legislature *not* to appropriate money for the Labor Department's enforcement of the farm child labor laws, charging that "funds appropriated for child labor law enforcement have been used exclusively [for] . . . an educational program in an effort to secure voluntary compliance with the law." Spurred by the Consumers' League action the Labor Department began its first serious effort to inspect the farms in 1948. Inspectors compiled data on 13,877 of the approximately 110,000 seasonal farm workers (migrant and nonmigrant), finding that fully one-fifth of the inspected group were children under sixteen and only 268 of these 2,840 youngsters were legally employed. Of these 1,145 were fourteen- and fifteen-year-olds without farm work permits and 1,427 were under thirteen. This official investigation revealed many of the same child labor conditions which the NYCLC and the Consumers' League had been decrying for over a decade. Hours were long and wages low: half the youngsters from whom data was obtained earned less than thirty-eight cents an hour. Children continued to risk physical strain by lifting boxes and crates that were too heavy for them. Despite the recently passed Ehrlich Transportation Act, the trucks were still dangerous. When the inspectors asked employers why they were using illegal child labor, the answers might have come from the 1890's. Some farmers protested their ignorance of the law, others claimed that they could not find enough adults to do the work and that the New York State Employment Service was unable to supply sufficient workers. (Upon checking this last complaint the Labor Department found that "many employers never contacted the Employment Service. And requests, when made, frequently were in terms of immediate needs to be promptly met without sufficient time for recruitment of a legal labor supply.") Still other growers contended that children could harvest some crops better than adults and that the parents would not work without the children. A few farmers fell back on the ancient argument that they had not "hired" the children and that either the parents or the padrone should bear the legal responsibility.[42]

After 1948 the Labor Department expanded its program of farm inspection and reported some reduction in agricultural child labor, although until 1955, it must be emphasized, the department was still inspecting less than one-fifth of the seasonal farm workers in the state. While in 1948, 503 farm inspections had turned up 2,572 illegally employed minors, by 1952, 960 inspections revealed only 622 such children. It was clear that the Labor Department was pursuing enforcement through an educational campaign (growers were less likely to use child labor if they thought the Labor Department was checking) because the actual prosecutions for violations of the child labor statutes were few and far between: 7 in 1948, 1 in 1949, 11 in 1950, 7 in 1951, and 8 in 1952. In 1952 when the Consumers' League undertook its third full-scale investigation of migrant workers, its report recognized that the Labor Department had been only partially successful in forcing compliance with the agricultural child labor laws. The league suggested that a special division of migrant farm labor be created to centralize state control over all aspects of the migrant problem. The Labor Department was piqued by what it regarded as the league's lack of appreciation for what the department *had* accomplished. Late in 1953 Emily S. Marconnier, Director of the Labor Department's Division of Industrial Relations, advised that the league "recognize the great improvement which has been made and then point out that there is a great deal to be done."[43]

Throughout the 1950's Labor Department statistics showed a continuing decline in the number of agricultural child laborers. By 1959 the department's inspectors found only 174 illegally employed children in 2,141 inspections. After 1956 a part of this decline can be explained by the increasing use of a mechanical snap bean harvester. This machine, operated by two men, could pick an estimated 20,000 pounds of beans in an eight-hour day as compared to 600 pounds of beans which two pickers might hand-harvest in the same time. There were difficulties, of course: the machine cost about $11,000, it picked all the beans regardless of size in one tour, and some growers reported that it did not work well in wet weather. It was, nevertheless, far more efficient than hand-harvesting and the Labor Department predicted that "the mechanical bean picker . . . is here to stay." Experiments were under way in the late 1950's to develop a satisfactory tomato picker and cherry shaker and there appeared to be a possibility that mechanical pickle, blueberry, and raspberry harvesters might also be invented.[44] Just as the drive toward industrial efficiency in factories led to the replacement of many children by machines, so it appeared that the ultimate solution to the problem of child labor in commercial agriculture might lie on the drawing board.

Yet the 1950's were not a period when reformers sat idly by waiting for new machines to come forth. The Consumers' League, the N.A.A.C.P., church groups, newspapers, and other organizations continually forced public attention to the migrant problem and to the dangers faced by child laborers on all kinds of farms. The three Consumers' League migrant studies in 1944, 1945, and 1952 had helped to generate publicity. A small but steady residue of support for migrant reform came from some of the churches—the Home Missions Council of North America (a part of the National Council of the Churches of Christ in the United States) had been active since 1931 and during the 1950's sent out mobile units equipped with recreational, educational, and religious facilities to travel with the migrants. Admirable as this work was, in 1951 the Home Missions Council was able to send only one mobile unit to cover all of New York. Some ministers were quick to protest migrant conditions. The Reverend George Clarkson, Chairman of the Yates County Migrant Committee, told of going to protest the conduct of "a drunken driver who had returned [from the fields] about 8:30 P.M. with a truck load of workers jammed in like cattle with a rope across the back for a tail-gate." The driver had been stopping off at taverns on his seventy-mile trip and "when they arrived at the camp most of the passengers were nearly hysterical." The grower's wife advised Clarkson not to be concerned, for the migrants "were only 'cattle' after all!" But the churches were usually reluctant to fight openly for legislation. As a minister speaking for the Steuben County Migrant Committee told the Consumers' League in 1954, "we could not . . . sponsor a discussion of [a migrant bill] without destroying the position we are trying to establish with the growers . . . in this area."[45] It was the old problem of whether it was better to give piecemeal hand-outs or lobby for legislation. The newspaper reaction to the problem was mixed; some upstate journals pictured the migrants as essentially a group of happy banjo-strumming peasants. Thus the Geneva *Daily Times* announced in 1952 that "migrants are not slaving away un-happily under the yoke of ruthless exploitation as some do-gooders will have it." After conducting an investigation, that newspaper was convinced that the migrants were really quite contented and not anxious to be deluged by organized recreational programs. Most of them spent their free time reading comic books or drinking in a nearby town and greeted questions about their use of leisure time with puzzled stares. "Private philanthropic organizations are aflutter with missionary zeal to provide more dignified conditions for transient workers," commented the newspaper, but "the migrants themselves seem satisfied with things as they are."[46] In 1953, however, Allan Keller wrote a series of articles for the New York *World Telegram and Sun* pointing out once again atrocious camp conditions. One of the worst features of the system was the continuing exploitation of the workers by the padrone (crew leader or labor contractor) who often got the workers deeply in debt to the camp store by bringing them to the fields before the crops were ready and charging them high prices for food while the migrants sat "in their shacks, waiting to go to the fields and earning not a penny." Some padrones made additional money by supplying liquor and women to their workers.[47]

In the early 1950's the state legislature apparently decided that all this publicity might lead to legislation and that it would be better for such recommendations to come from the lawmakers themselves. The New York State Joint Legislative Committee on Migrant Labor was therefore established in 1952 under the chairmanship of Assem-blyman Alonzo L. Waters of Medina. Launching its own investiga-tion of migrants, this committee produced a 1953 report that took a middle position between the interests of the growers and the de-mands of the reformers. Although the report stated that "the annual incomes of seasonal agricultural workers . . . [are] reported to be such as not to enable them to achieve and maintain an acceptable standard of living" and that "most living quarters . . . [are] below a decent standard for health, protection, or normal family life," the Waters Committee devoted only eight lines to the migrant wage problem and made no recommendations regarding it, even though migrants were not covered by any minimum wage laws, state or federal. At the same time the Waters Committee cited problems faced by the growers. The migrants were unstable and unreliable. Growers faced a "lack of cooperation by migrants in the care and maintenance of camp facilities." Since a very large percentage of New York's interstate migrants were Negroes, the Waters Committee dedicated one section of its report to "the Negro family." However honorable the motives of the committee in doing this, its discussion of "the Negro family" was most unfortunate. It repeated as fact several notorious myths about Negroes. According to the Waters Committee the American Negro had been unable to develop "permanence in his family relations" because of "a lack of social control over sexual impulse"; hence, it was apparently logical for him to be a migrant. The committee did recognize that slavery had been a disadvantage to the Negro, although it was careful to point out that "children of working Negro mothers [at present] lack the advantages which such children had under slavery." (The advantages of slavery to children were not listed.) The tone of "The Negro Family" stressed the inevitability of Negro poverty and degradation: "From his earliest years the Negro child is culturally conditioned to farm labor." This assertion in the Waters Report could have been applied to any child, white or black, who had been born on a working farm.[48] One might conclude from "The Negro Family" that Negro migrants had problems far too deeply rooted and self-perpetuating for the state of New York to remedy. The Waters Report drew an immediate blast from the N.A.A.C.P. Herbert Hill, the association's Labor Secretary, described "The Negro Family" as "a shoddy collection of gross historical distortions and unmitigated falsehoods . . . [which] constitutes a vicious attack upon the entire Negro community under the imprimatur of the State of New York."[49] According to the N.A.A.C.P., the Waters Committee soon withdrew all the copies of its original report that it could find and reissued them with "The Negro Family" deleted. The real significance of "The Negro Family" was that it illustrated the most serious obstacle to migrant labor reform: the public tendency to regard such work as the natural and inevitable lot of those who engaged in it.

One of the principal recommendations of the Waters Committee led to the introduction in 1954 of the Van Lare-Waters Bill, which required all farm labor contractors (padrones) to obtain certificates of registration from the Labor Department. The Consumers' League felt that this measure did not go far enough because it empowered the Industrial Commissioner to revoke a contractor's registration only *after* he had violated the law. Consequently, the league persuaded Senator Dutton S. Peterson, a progressive farmer-minister-legislator from Odessa to introduce a broader bill which would have permitted the Industrial Commissioner to make a full investigation of the crew leader's character *before* a license was issued and thus prevent undesirable padrones from entering the state. This measure prohibited crew leaders from operating businesses which served migrants and also centralized responsibility for administering all migrant labor laws in a division of migrant farm labor within the Labor Department. In the end the less sweeping Van Lare-Waters Bill became law, but this was a step forward for as recently as 1950 Governor Dewey had vetoed a bill providing for the licensing of crew leaders.[50]

Another Waters Committee recommendation that became law in 1954 authorized the state Health Department to prescribe standards for living quarters at migrant camps occupied by ten or more persons. An extension of the state Sanitary Code set up new requirements for sleeping quarters, light and ventilation, fire safety, drinking water, sewers, and food storage. The Consumers' League was unhappy about this measure, pointing out that it did not "compel the establishment of any *new* standards" and left "the responsibility for the establishment of [health] standards, if any, in the hands of the Department of Health . . . which has permitted the disgraceful conditions which our studies revealed to continue unchecked." It was not long before the league received what it regarded as a typical illustration of the way in which the Health Department was going to enforce the law. In the late summer of 1954 a complaint reached the league about a migrant camp located near the town of Dresden in Yates County. This camp, it appeared, had an inadequate water supply. When the league forwarded the complaint to the state Department of Health they were told that "this camp has been under frequent inspection for many years and the District [Health] Office supervising this camp advises that the water supply is considered satisfactory." A. F. Allen, Chief of the Camps Sanitation Section, claimed that since the camp was the first area supplied from the public water supply system of the Village of Dresden any interruption in service or low water pressure would have affected the village as well. But according to a Consumers' League informant who lived near the area, the entire water supply for a camp of two hundred workers came from "small pipes running from a neighbor's cellar." A representative from the Yates County branch of the American Association of University Women reported being told by the local health officer "that he had fulfilled his part if there was a source of water on the grounds." Still, things were better than in 1952 when two hundred migrants at this same camp had been getting their water from a single faucet, but any improvement in the camp had been the work of "interested neighbors and not . . . public health personnel."[51]

Camp conditions continued to present serious problems throughout the 1950's. Consumers' League Inspection Reports for individual camps in 1959, although recognizing a number of excellent operations, contain frequent indications of trouble. "One room shacks—fire traps"; "the hot water shower did not function most of the summer"; "empty whiskey bottles lying around"; "privies on higher ground than single water spigot"; "showers and toilet don't work"; "no running water. No privy or toilet"; "buildings like chicken coops"; "cramped wooden structures, single-exit, inadequate water"; "poor wiring—kerosene stove in 2 story old house where 35 live"; and so on. Even the official figures of the state Department of Health for 1958 indicated that 34 per cent of the migrant camps in the state were either "fair" or "poor."[52] While a squalid camp did not necessarily employ child labor, the persistence of bad camp conditions did point up the futility of a multiheaded administration of the migrant problem. To the degree that unscrupulous padrones were allowed to operate, the task of the Labor Department inspectors would be that much more difficult. Although their official figures showed a reduction in child labor, the Labor Department was still inspecting less than half of the state's seasonal workers by 1960. Despite such incomplete enforcement, the legislature passed two regressive pieces of child labor legislation in 1954 and 1960. The State Board of Standards and Appeals has the power to adopt rules prohibiting or regulating employment of minors in dangerous occupations, but in 1954 farm work was taken out of their jurisdiction. The Consumers' League charged that this legislation had been "hastily drafted by the Assembly and rushed through the legislature with great speed . . . [with] no opportunity given to those organizations . . . concerned with the protection of children . . . to make known their views." According to the league, farmers were pleased; one upstate newspaper commented that the new law was "especially advantageous to farm operation as juniors can now operate farm tractors, milking machines and other farm machinery legally. [Previously] many instances of double compensation indemnity have been levied against farm operators when youths in this age group have been injured while operating farm equipment."[53] Farming *was* a dangerous occupation; between 1949 and 1955 twenty-seven farm children under eighteen met accidental death—most were caused by tractors. Fourteen- and fifteen-year-olds were now permitted to operate harvesters, threshers, hay balers, corn cutters, reapers, and other dangerous farm machinery. When the Joint Legislative Committee on Industrial and Labor Conditions held hearings in New York City in 1956, some of its members argued that the solution lay not in legislation but in education, and that regulation of dangerous machinery on farms would exclude children from employment and would result in idleness and juvenile delinquency. The Consumers' League replied that if it was necessary to expose children to dangerous machinery to stop them from becoming juvenile delinquents, *all* the dangerous machinery laws (including industrial) might as well be scrapped.[54] Throughout the rest of the 1950's the league strove without success to have the 1954 exemption repealed, but even their legislative counterproposals would have barred children only from operating dangerous farm machinery *for pay*, but would have offered no protection to children injured while operating tractors on their home farm. There is a general requirement that children working on their home farm be twelve years old, but this is not seriously enforced. Few would argue that children ought not to work around their home farms, for that is how they learn to be farmers, but tractor accidents continue to occur, injuring drivers as young as ten or eleven at home and away with fine impartiality.

The 1960 enactment permitted twelve- and thirteen-year-olds to work at harvesting berries, fruits, and vegetables for a maximum of four hours a day between 9:00 A.M. and 4:00 P.M. The 1958 Waters Committee report had stated: "Your committee . . . continues to receive information from growers concerning the problems of the migrant children over the age of 12 years in the camps." Moreover, the committee said, "the second most frequently mentioned law causing difficulty in recruiting labor for New York State are the existing child labor laws. Apparently crew leaders have difficulty in recruiting family crews who have children within the 12 to 14 age bracket." Actually this so-called berry-picking bill had been introduced on several occasions in the 1950's but had failed to pass during the Harriman administration.[55] Supported by the State Council of Churches and cosponsored by Assemblyman Alonzo Waters, the 1960 law was reasonable on the surface: four hours a day picking berries, fruits, or vegetables would presumably not harm a twelve-year-old who could qualify for a farm work permit. The danger as expressed to the author by Labor Department personnel lies in the ease with which the regulation can be violated. At least forty years before, the New York Child Labor Committee had discovered the difficulty of enforcing a restricted hours provision *within* a longer time period. It would be very difficult to prevent twelve-year-olds from working 9:00 A.M. to 4:00 P.M. if that is what the contractor, grower, or parent desired.

In many ways New York *was* attempting to adjust to, if not to solve, its migrant problem. In 1956 the Sanitary Code was extended to camps occupied by five persons or more (instead of ten or more), in 1957 farmers were flatly prohibited from using the services of a nonregistered crew leader (in 1960 certificates were denied to 23 crew leaders who had violated the Labor Law or the Penal Law), and in 1958 farm labor camp commissaries were required to obtain Labor Department licenses and post prices, while crew leaders had to keep payroll records and give workers written statements of wages earned and legal deductions made. A pilot program for the education of migrant children was conducted during the summer of 1956 and 1957, and in 1959 $40,000 was appropriated to carry this project forward. Child labor had clearly been reduced since 1948 although the berry-picking law showed signs of proving troublesome. Yet the fact remained that the average daily wage of the New York migrant worker in 1959 was only $5.40.[56] Few people appeared to be interested in the fundamental question of why the only workers who could bring New York's harvest to a successful conclusion were poor people who had to travel hundreds of miles in trucks, live in camps a third of which were *officially* described as inadequate, sacrifice their children's education, and expose them to the hazards of child labor.

The fundamental objection . . . to this proposal is that it establishes a bad principle. It takes the police powers of the state and lodges them in the federal government. It is another step in the undermining of the very structure of our government. It opens up a Pandora's box of evils which will fly out to plague us for all time to come.

—Buffalo *Post*, February 26, 1925

All that is necessary to marshal the wicked, money-grabbing vultures is to raise the banner of humanity. Of course this organized banditti opposed to the amendment offers some arguments for their dastardly cause. Some of the protests bear the stamp of falsehood on their face. Others are so crooked and misleading that they should defeat themselves, yet they do not.

—Port Chester *Item*, February 26, 1925

VIII. *The Child Labor Amendment in New York (1924-38)*

While the New York Child Labor Committee was struggling for child labor regulation within the state of New York, national child labor reform groups had obtained the passage of two federal child labor laws in 1916 and 1919. Both of these enactments were declared unconstitutional by the Supreme Court, but neither would have had any appreciable effect on New York had it remained on the statute books. According to the Federal Children's Bureau, New York was one of seventeen states whose child labor standards equalled or exceeded those set by the two federal laws. If the enactments had survived a court test, the federal child labor officials simply would have accepted New York employment certificates as evidence of compliance with the federal law and New York Labor Department inspectors would have been granted authority to conduct "federal" inspections.[1] George Alger and Manfred Ehrich of the NYCLC had both opposed the first federal law. Alger was in full agreement with *Hammer* v. *Dagenhart* and described the enactment as "an utterly ineffective piece of legislation at its best . . . [presenting] to the Supreme Court in the harshest, crudest and most imperfect form the Federal control of interstate commerce in child life."[2] Manfred Ehrich opposed the first act because "if Congress had the power to exclude goods from interstate commerce because they were made by children, it could likewise exclude goods because it disapproved of the lighting or toilet facilities of the factory." Such a broad grant of power might lead Congress to take "complete control of substantially all manufactures within the United States" and could put "an end to the reserve powers of the states." Alger supported the second federal child labor taxing law in principle (although disagreeing with some of its provisions), telling Roscoe Pound that while

> neither the control over interstate commerce nor the power to tax was intended as a means of supplanting the state in the regulation of its internal affairs . . . we are confronted with a condition and are trying not to bother with the technicalities of a theory.

Federal legislation, Alger thought, might ban child labor in broad terms but one could "never expect to centralize the control of children in Washington and we should not try to do it anyway. The States, in the main will have to work out their own child labor statutes."[3]

After the second federal child labor law was declared unconstitutional in 1922, the advocates of child labor reform concluded that the only way for them to obtain a federal law was through a constitutional amendment. Although divided in their views of what kind of amendment should be proposed and whether such a move should be postponed to a more favorable time, groups such as the National Consumers' League, the Women's Trade Union League, the League of Women Voters, the Women's Christian Temperance Union, the National Federation of Business and Professional Women's Clubs and the National Child Labor Committee began to press Congress for action. Under the leadership of Samuel Gompers, about two dozen national groups organized the Permanent Conference for the Abolition of Child Labor, which sent a large number of witnesses to testify before the Senate Judiciary Committee in January, 1923, on the need for a child labor amendment. The proponents of an amendment believed that they had a good chance of passing and ratifying a constitutional change because Congress had already accepted the principle of federal regulation (in the two rejected laws) and because it could be demonstrated that hundreds of thousands of children under the age of sixteen were still gainfully employed, some of them in states with abysmally low child labor standards. Senator Robert M. LaFollette was strongly in favor of a child labor amendment as were Secretary of Commerce Herbert Hoover, Senator Henry Cabot Lodge, and President Harding. "One need not be committed to the view that amendment is weakening the fundamental law," the chief executive said, "or that excessive amendment is essential to meet every ephemeral whim. We ought to amend to meet the demand of the people when sanctioned by deliberate public opinion."[4]

Early in 1924 the following amendment was put to a vote in Congress:

> Section 1. The Congress shall have power to limit, regulate, and prohibit the labor of persons under 18 years of age.
> Section 2. The power of the several States is unimpaired by this article except that the operation of State laws shall be suspended to the extent necessary to give effect to legislation enacted by the Congress.

The eighteen-year age limit was included at the request of Florence Kelley, who had been able to rally sufficient support for the idea that some seventeen-year-olds in hazardous occupations ought to be subject to federal legislation. However sound the principle, the eighteen-year limit enabled the opposition to caricature the amendment as designed to prevent seventeen-year-old "men" from helping with the supper dishes. There is little question that Section 1 *was* a very broad grant of *potential* power to Congress. The opposition, moreover, presented this *potential* power as power that would inevitably and immediately be put to use in order to nationalize American children. Section 2 of the proposed amendment was intended as an encouragement to the states to pass their own child labor laws, for to the degree that state laws equalled or exceeded federal standards, the state would avoid "federal" enforcement. Although opposition to the amendment had been expressed at congressional hearings by groups such as the National Association of Manufacturers, the American Farm Bureau Federation, the Sentinels of the Republic, and the Citizens' Committee to Protect Our Homes and Children, Congress was carried forward on what seemed to be a tide of favorable sentiment. The amendment, after all, was merely going to make possible congressional legislation that everyone except the Supreme Court wanted. The 1924 version of the child labor amendment passed the House of Representatives on April 26, 1924, by a vote of 297 to 69 and the Senate on June 2, 1924, by a vote of 61 to 23, with the chief opposition coming from Southern and border states whose generally low child labor standards would cause them to bear the brunt of federal regulatory activities. The Southern and border opposition was politically understandable considering the relatively large number of children employed there, particularly in agriculture, and the historic Southern aversion to federal "interference."

In the beginning there seemed little doubt that the amendment would quickly be ratified by the necessary number of states. Florence Kelley predicted ratification by 1925. Certainly the situation in New York appeared favorable, for the entire New York congressional delegation, with the exception of eight absent members and Republican Senator James W. Wadsworth, had voted for the proposal.[5] To Wadsworth the amendment was unnecessary "in view of the fact that all but three or four of the states of the Union already have child labor laws as strict or stricter than the one proposed in the amendment." (This statement was doubly inaccurate: the number of states with standards lower than those of the earlier federal laws was much larger, and, as Wadsworth must have known, the amendment did not contain any legislation.) In Wadsworth's opinion it was "entirely possible for the advocates of child labor legislation to persuade the few remaining states to toe the mark in the matter of progressive legislation"; all that was needed was "a little more education and a little more appeal to reason."[6] It soon became apparent that this point of view had a wide appeal and that the easy victory of the amendment in Congress was not to be duplicated in New York. While it might seem that there was no good reason for a state such as New York, whose child labor standards already exceeded any likely to be implemented by Congress under the amendment, to oppose federal action, substantive interests did lie behind the anti-amendment propaganda. New York businessmen, for example, were less impressed by arguments that they should favor the amendment in order to improve child labor conditions in Mississippi than by fears that the amendment might increase the risk of more federal labor legislation being passed. Large numbers of the state's Roman Catholic population, suspicious of moves in several other states to restrict the parochial school system and mindful of the increased financial burden on the parishes if children were made to stay in school longer, did not hesitate to fight the amendment. Some newspapers were acutely sensitive to legislative proposals which might bring about a stricter control of newsboys. New York farmers were one of the state's largest and least regulated employers of child labor and were natural opponents of the amendment. In addition to this core of interest opposition, a large reserve of emotional antagonism, both in New York and nationally, was just waiting to be tapped, for the amendment had been loosed upon a country weary of Wilsonian exhortations to do better, annoyed at the "big government" of the First World War, and prepared by the Red Scare to expect sensational revelations about almost anything. Some were already apprehensive about the efficacy of constitutional change as illustrated by the Prohibition Amendment. Others, whose sincerity cannot be doubted, were genuinely alarmed by what they regarded as a potential death blow to states rights. In short order a cloud of windy and bizarre rhetoric lay over the Empire State from the Battery to Niagara Falls. When the cloud lifted in 1926, proponents of the amendment had not even been able to get a vote in the legislature and the overwhelming endorsement of the amendment by the state's congressional delegation and by its Democratic and Republican party organizations had been demonstrated to have been far in advance of public opinion.

Although opposition to the amendment was national in scope and organizations such as the National Association of Manufacturers and the Citizen's Committee to Protect Our Homes and Children did work in New York to defeat the proposal, the most important grassroots work against the amendment was carried on by native New Yorkers. But the starting point for local opposition was often propaganda circulated by national groups. The American Constitutional League asked New York farmers whether they favored "the passage of a law prohibiting young men between the ages of fourteen and seventeen from working in gardens or on farms." Efforts to blunt the effect of such exaggerations on farmers proved unsuccessful. Thus, Congressman Hamilton Fish, Jr., hastened to "assure the farmers of New York State that there is not a single representative in Congress who has the slightest idea of interfering with the employment of children on farms," only to be met with editorial opinion that his "flights of oratory and his flood of invective against those whom he terms public misinformants do not serve to clarify in the minds of his farmer constituents the . . . exact effect that this proposed law may have upon them." Continuing the attack, the Middleport *Herald* admitted that it was "inconceivable" that Congress would try to prevent youngsters from helping around the farm but that once the lawmakers were "given the power to do so . . . there is no telling what might happen."[7] Dark predictions representing Congress as rubbing its hands in Machiavellian glee over the plans it was making to nationalize the nation's children the instant the amendment should be ratified were sometimes tied in with appeals to the farmers' sense of concern over the moral laxity of the twenties. The *Rural New Yorker* gave favorable attention to a speech delivered in the Ohio House of Representatives by Grace E. Makepeace. "Children of today do not listen to their parents," this legislator asserted; "instead they go over to a settlement house, learn a little dancing, and take part in some cheap dramatic performance, while father and mother . . . do the work these big boys and girls should be doing." The real need, as Representative Makepeace saw it, was for "more young men planting spuds and fewer making speed; . . . more young people painting fences and not so many painting faces; more following in the footsteps of their forefathers, rather than the steps of a dancing master."[8] The Jamestown *Journal* credited a local farmer, J. W. Whitford, with "expressing the farm opinion of New York" when he stated that the amendment was "a proposition to nationalize the children of the nation and a covert blow at the very foundation of the government." With a covert glance at the Prohibition Amendment, Whitford advised "that before adopting more constitutional amendments we enforce those we have already adopted."[9] And it did not require letters to the editor to reveal that most farmers instinctively opposed the amendment. The president of the State Farm Bureau Federation came out against the amendment and a poll taken by the federation of over two thousand farmers in thirteen counties during the spring of 1925 found them ten to one against the measure.[10]

Many upstate newspapers were against the amendment for reasons other than its supposed threat to farmers. "It is easy enough to comprehend the state of mind in which this proposal arose," sneered the Lyons *Republican,* "in the childless, sovietized, de-Americanized minds of overexcited feminists." But no matter. "A country that would brook no interference with its tea will not tamely submit to hand its children over to any political authority."[11] Speculating upon the adverse effect a child labor amendment would have had upon the careers of Abraham Lincoln, George Washington, James A. Garfield and Ulysses S. Grant, the Coxsackie *Union-News* observed that "for Americans to provide by the constitution that boys and girls must loaf on the old folks until they are 18 years old is one of the most preposterous pieces of blatherskiteism ever perpetrated on an unsuspecting public." The Monticello *Republican* asserted that "the country would be far better off if no amendments had been made to the original document beginning with the enfranchisement of the negroes down to the present day."[12] Attempting a more rational argument, the Whitney Point *Reporter* pointed out the difficulties of enforcing hours legislation on farm work because of the vagaries of the weather and advised some of the metropolitan area newspapers that were supporting the amendment to stop employing young children as newsboys. A majority of New York City papers did in fact support the amendment with only the *World* and the *New York Times* in opposition. Even the *World* had favored the proposal for a time, but in January, 1925, it came out against the amendment because of its "federal and not its substantive character," a states' rights position.

The *New York Times* believed that the process of reducing child labor on a national scale was already under way and "may be continued and completed without a Federal Amendment, provided the States of their own will set about the work."[13]

Catholic opinion on the amendment was divided. Precedents both for and against it could be found in Pope Leo XIII's encyclical *Rerum Novarum*. When the congressional hearings on the amendment had been held, there had been no public Catholic opposition, and Father John A. Ryan and Father Raymond A. McGowan of the National Catholic Welfare Conference had spoken in favor of it. Even Albany Bishop Edmund F. Gibbons, later a bitter opponent of the amendment, announced in 1924 that "no legislation of an antagonistic nature" had been passed during that year, an assertion which Father Ryan's biographer interprets as "a negative endorsement of the Amendment."[14] When the fight within the states began, Catholic journals were forced to choose sides. Proponents such as Father Ryan, Bishop Robert E. Lucey of Amarillo, Texas, and layman Frank P. Walsh of New York received a sympathetic hearing in the *National Catholic Welfare Conference Bulletin*, the *Catholic Charities Review*, the *Ecclesiastical Review*, and the *Catholic Worker*. The Jesuit *America* and the Catholic Central Verein were in opposition, as were most of the New York Catholic diocesan newspapers, among them the archconservative Brooklyn *Tablet*, the Buffalo *Echo*, the Syracuse *Catholic Sun* and the Albany *Evangelist*.[15]

By the time the amendment fight began in New York, most of the state hierarchy was in opposition and Charles J. Tobin, the Albany attorney who represented the bishops on legislative matters, was working steadily to defeat the measure. The principal reason for Catholic opposition was probably fear of the long-range effect on Catholic education that might be produced by the exceptionally broad grant of congressional power contained in the amendment. Once passed, the amendment might open the way for all manner of laws: to force parochial pupils into the public schools, to give federal aid to the public schools and not to the parochial schools, and to infringe upon parental control over children. If Congress were to pass a bill setting the school-leaving age at sixteen, parochial schools would be faced with heavy expenditures on plant and equipment (the same argument the Church was later to make against the New York State school-leaving age proposals). Irresponsible charges made by some opponents that the amendment was Communist-inspired may have had an effect upon Catholics of the rank and file, as did the continual editorializing by diocesan newspapers about the actions of the Mexican government against the Church during the 1920's and 1930's. "The educational institutions of Catholics have been crushed in the past," wrote Vincent A. McQuade, "and are subject to numerous unjust limitations in some countries of the world today. . . . Many [Catholics] hesitate to empower the Federal Government with authority which might, they fear, be abused."[16]

Many businessmen opposed the amendment, but realizing that they were vulnerable to the charge of special interest, they tried to keep their activities under cover. Hence actual business opposition was probably even greater than the work of their public organizations indicated. The National Association of Manufacturers, the New York Economic Council, the Associated Industries of New York State, the New York State Chamber of Commerce, the New York Manufacturer's Association, and the New York City Board of Trade and Transportation all openly opposed the amendment in New York State. James A. Emery, General Counsel of the N.A.M. prepared a pamphlet in which he charged that the amendment was inspired by Communists. "It is not without interest," said Emery, "to observe the relation between the philosophy of the Amendment, its obvious tendencies, and the plainly expressed purpose of modern Communism." Emery noted that the Communist Young Workers League advocated "the abolition of wage slavery for all young workers up to age 18," and resurrected an old statement made by the wife of Gregory Zinoviev, then president of the Young Communist International, which said: "We must nationalize the children. We must remove the children from the pernicious influence of the family." The fact that the Communist Daily Worker had advocated immediate ratification of the amendment helped opponents to document their charge, and Florence Kelley was well known as a socialist and had a "Russian-sounding" married name, Wishnieweski, which she no longer used.[17] But whenever possible, the manufacturers' groups tried to find persons who could attack the amendment from a disinterested position. Nicholas Murray Butler, President of Columbia University, and A. Lawrence Lowell, President of Harvard University, held very positive views against the amendment and lent the opposition cause considerable stature. "So far from protecting childhood," declared Butler, the Amendment is "a deliberate attempt to put forty-five millions of our population under the control of the Congress of the United States. . . . [It] might easily be made the entering wedge for a purely Communist attitude of the Government toward the people."[18] One of the most vocal independent opponents of the amendment who worked in close cooperation with the Associated Industries of New York State and with Louis A. Coolidge's Sentinels of the Republic was William R. (Daddy) George of Freeville, New York. George (1866-1936) was born in West Dryden, New York, but had moved to New York City to set up his own business of making jewelry cases. His interests lay elsewhere and soon he was working for the Charity Organization Society. George regarded himself primarily as a social worker and during the 1890's began to organize New York street toughs into Law and Order Gangs, taking the boys up to Freeville (near Ithaca) for the summer. In 1895 he returned permanently to Tompkins County, and started the George Junior Republic. The Junior Republic was a vocational school that boys and girls operated as a society in microcosm; the children were known as "citizens," currency was issued, cabinet officers appointed, and judicial proceedings held. As George himself described the project in 1925:

> The only conditions we make for admittance to the Republic are that a boy or girl must be sound mentally and physically and between the ages of sixteen and twenty-one. One third [of the citizens] are boys and girls who have come to the Republic of their own free will because they looked upon it as an opportunity to work their way through school. A second third are sent there by their parents because their parents believe in the Republic, and the last third are boys and girls who have been unruly and hard to manage at home. These are sent by parents and sometimes recommended by judges.[19]

The citizens of the Republic were required to work at various jobs and their type of lodging and meals depended upon how much Republic currency they could earn. Whatever its place in American social history, the Republic was not an experiment in communistic utopian living—rather it was a society in which economic differences were important and whose motto was "Nothing Without Labor." George believed that it was a mistake to give handouts; from his earliest days he had required the children he was helping to earn the food, clothing, and lodging he was providing. George was not an advocate of child labor; indeed, he had been one of the 1902 endorsers of the New York Child Labor Committee, but he was bitterly opposed to the child labor amendment. Not only was it "a slap in the face to everything which the Junior Republic exemplifies in the line of civic and economic responsibilities" but the eighteen-year age limit raised the possibility that the sixteen- and seventeen-year-olds at the Republic might be subject to some kind of federal inspection or control. George believed that it was more important for children to learn about the economic system under which they were living than to be prevented from working. "If they learn what it means to earn a dollar and have self-government," he wrote in 1924, "we are going to have less Bolshevists and fool ideas stated by welfare workers who are Socialists at heart, the 'parlor' type of Socialist." There was, he asserted, "one thing worse than child labor and that is child idleness."[20]

George became active in the fight against the amendment during the summer of 1924; soon he was writing to Mark Daly of the Associated Industries and to Louis A. Coolidge of the Sentinels offering his services as a speaker against the amendment. Addressing meetings in both New York and Massachusetts, most of George's speeches at first mirrored the standard opposition line. "The sentimental ideal of the little child working," he told a Buffalo audience, "takes hold of people's minds. There is a curse of underwork as well as overwork. All the doctors I have ever questioned . . . tell me that they have never had a case of a child being ill from overwork." As time went on, he began to lash out at labor unions, social workers, and college professors for being united in a conspiracy to inflict the amendment on the country. Frequently accused of being a paid propagandist for the textile interests, George himself said that "as between the Manufacturers' Association and the working groups [with their ostensible socialistic tendencies] he preferred to align himself with the former."[21] Working closely with Carleton A. Chase, President of the Syracuse First Trust and Deposit Company and later with Jerome D. Barnum, publisher of the Syracuse Post-Standard, George helped organize the New York State Citizens Committee for the Protection of Our Homes and Children whose members eventually included Dr. Livingston Farrand, President of Cornell University; Bishop William Burt of the Methodist-Episcopal Church; Bishop William Turner of the Roman Catholic Diocese of Buffalo; Rabbi Nathan Krass of Temple Emanu-el in New York City; Dr. Henry S. Pritchett, Chairman of the Carnegie Foundation; Alton B. Parker; and Judge Frank P. Irvine of Ithaca, the Chairman.[22]

In the background of all this activity were the New York businessmen who tried to avoid publicity by following the advice of the Associated Industries of Massachusetts, which in 1924 sent an elaborate set of campaign instructions into New York for the use of the industrial groups. The Massachusetts businessmen (then preparing for a referendum fight on ratification of the amendment in their own state) urged the New Yorkers to hold conferences with persons representing the state bar association, foreign language minorities, educational institutions, farm groups, women's organizations, and the clergy. "It is absolutely essential," the New Yorkers were warned, "in staging this preliminary conference that those invited should first be interviewed and if not informed as to the sinister purport of the Twentieth Amendment they should be educated by constructive argument." Otherwise spies from the proponents' camp might "become cognizant of the ways and means to be employed by the group opposed to legislative ratification." Moreover, the Massachusetts group advised, while "your [New York manufacturers'] organization is bound to be brought into the picture by the proponents . . . if it is not publicly active in the campaign work it will be difficult for the advocates of the amendment to establish their indictment against your organizations." Some manufacturers made their financial support of charitable and philanthropic organizations depend upon whether the latter opposed the amendment.[23]

Other opponents of the amendment scored points by calmly reiterating that the proposal was unnecessary since the Census of 1920 showed that child labor was decreasing (although the proponents claimed that this decline reflected the effect of the first two federal laws). Then the opponents would insist that the amendment was a very broad grant of power to Congress and if child labor was on the way out, why did the proponents want to give so much power to Congress? The answer was obvious: because the proponents had secret plans to bring child life completely under federal control. When those favoring the amendment replied that Congress would never use all the power available to it under the proposal, the opponents could ask with perfect reasonableness why so much potential power had been written into the amendment? William D. Guthrie, a former President of the New York State Bar Association and Professor of Constitutional Law at Columbia University, alarmed many people when he asserted that Section 1 of the amendment gave Congress "an unlimited power that could . . . be exercised to its utmost extent . . . not only as to the physical labor of children but likewise as to their mental labor . . . in school."[24] When such statements were combined with charges that the amendment was Communist in origin, the proposal began, indeed, to resemble a large-scale, insidious plot to take over the most important lever of control in any society—its educational system.

With the opposition's campaign gaining momentum during 1924, those who favored the amendment came to its defense in the hope that they could persuade the 1925 legislature to ratify it. Attempting to clarify the meaning of the proposal, George Alger asserted that it afforded "an opportunity which we should accept, of removing an illegitimate handicap upon New York business. It will enable the equalization of conditions of competition between low standard states and our own. . . . Under the . . . amendment . . . our own laws would not be suspended but remain in full force and the main effect of the federal law would be to remove inequalities which today work to the detriment of New York industry in competition with States whose standards are lower than ours."[25] Unfortunately for this argument, the growing consolidation of business into nationwide organizations had made state boundaries largely obsolete and many New York enterprises had interests in states with lower child labor standards. In September, 1924, the New York League of Women Voters took the initiative and organized the New York Committee for the Ratification of the Child Labor Amendment; composed eventually of forty-seven different organizations, this committee was the center of proamendment activities. At first the group used the offices of the New York Child Labor Committee as its headquarters and when it moved into a permanent location, the NYCLC continued to distribute ratification committee literature and to provide clerical assistance. Jeanie Minor became the executive secretary of the ratification committee and spoke for the amendment at meetings throughout the state. If the opposition had powerful friends, the proponents soon demonstrated that they, too, could rally influential persons and organizations to their support. The State Federation of Labor stood behind the ratification committee despite Catholic pressure upon some local labor leaders. State Labor Commissioner Bernard Shientag and State Health Commissioner Matthias Nicoll favored the amendment. Support was obtained from the four Railroad Brotherhoods, the State Association of Magistrates, the State Conference of Societies for the Prevention of Cruelty to Children and the American Legion of the State of New York. The National Child Labor Committee placed its secretary, Owen Lovejoy, at the disposal of the New York ratification committee. While the ratification committee had considerable difficulty in obtaining any unified support from the Protestant religious denominations, it did receive the endorsement of the Federation of Churches in Rochester and the Board of Christian Education of the Presbyterian Church as well as personal assistance from Dr. Harry Emerson Fosdick, Dr. Charles K. Gilbert, and Dr. Worth Tippy. With their help, some four thousand letters were sent out to Protestant ministers urging them to observe January 25, 1925, as Child Labor Sunday.[26]

In an attempt to counteract the opposition's success with the press, the ratification committee sent out sample editorials to over five hundred upstate newspapers, and claimed that by January 9, 1925, 120 of them had published favorable material on the amendment. Many of these editorials dealt with the question of the extension of federal power:

> Congress by the Amendment is to be given concurrent powers with the states in this field—no greater power, no different power, no new or unfamiliar power. Why should the manufacturers who are fighting this Amendment worry for fear Susie may be prohibited from washing the dishes? The state legislatures are not bothering with Susie. If they did, the Courts would upset the law as unreasonable interference with Susie's liberty guaranteed to her under the Bill of Rights. . . . And if Congress under this Amendment attempted anything so far fetched, the Courts would do the same with the Congressional enactment.[27]

Copies of a legal opinion endorsing the amendment by Dean Roscoe Pound of the Harvard Law School were sent to over 250 weekly papers and a letter signed by George Alger was distributed to every upstate chamber of commerce and to the editor of every newspaper in communities that had a chamber of commerce. These efforts had some success: certain upstate newspapers began to support the amendment. The Webster *Herald* urged its readers to check up on the child labor laws of backward states and then make a choice for the amendment. The Albany *Times-Union* took a similar position and the Jamestown *Post* remarked that "there has been more nonsense printed and spoken against the Child Labor Amendment than on any recent topic of public interest." The Baldwinsville *Gazette* thought that the state rights argument was "an absurd excuse for those who are afraid that they will lose the money gained from the employing of . . . child labor," while the Port Chester *Item* denounced the opposition as "wicked, money-grabbing vultures."[28]

The ratification committee organized a state-wide series of public speeches and debates in an effort to develop support for the amendment. More than forty public meetings were held in Westchester, Orange, Sullivan, and Rockland Counties. In Syracuse fifteen hundred persons came to see Owen Lovejoy of the National Child Labor Committee debate Joseph T. Cashman of the New York Bar Association; and in northern New York, Dr. L. F. Reed, a Baptist minister from Plattsburgh who had observed much child labor in Georgia, spoke in Glens Falls, Malone, Ogdensburg, Watertown, and Saratoga Springs. The ratification committee organized a special speaking tour for Julia Lathrop of the Federal Children's Bureau. In Buffalo, where Miss

Lathrop was scheduled to debate William R. George, feeling was so strong against the amendment that "it was impossible to get a group of representative citizens to sit on the platform with her." In presenting their case, the proponents stressed the necessity for a constitutional amendment; since the congressional enactments had been declared unconstitutional, an amendment was the only way child labor standards could be raised in backward states. They claimed that Congress would never use the broad grant of power to take over the educational system or to loose an army of federal inspectors on the states. The eighteen-year age limit had been included only to regulate hazardous industries, not to control education. Since New York's standards were already high, the amendment would have no effect on New York. Attacking the opposition's claim that the amendment was a Communist plot, those favoring it observed that if so, it had attracted some unusual supporters, viz. Warren G. Harding, Calvin Coolidge, and Herbert Hoover. Indeed, the principle of federal regulation of child labor had been urged by a host of blood-thirsty radicals such as Theodore Roosevelt, Albert J. Beveridge, and Henry Cabot Lodge.[29]

Both sides were hoping to influence the legislature. The ratification committee had assumed that it would have the support of Governor Alfred E. Smith because of Smith's record of favoring social legislation. This was a fundamental error. After the child labor amendment was overwhelmingly defeated in a Massachusetts referendum in November, 1924, rumor began to circulate that Smith was now committed to a similar test of popular will in New York. Members of the ratification committee, including Frances Perkins, Molly Dewson, Florence Kelley, and Grace Childs conferred with the governor but found him determined to insert a recommendation for a referendum in his annual message to the legislature. Proponents of the amendment were completely opposed to such a referendum because they feared a repetition of the Massachusetts debacle. Publicly, they asserted that a referendum would be meaningless because even if the amendment won, the badly apportioned legislature still would have to ratify it. The amendment might be favored by a majority of the state's voters but defeated in Albany by a majority of legislative districts. Consequently, the ratification committee made a gentlemen's agreement with Smith; according to this understanding, the amendment would be tabled in the legislature and would not be submitted for a vote to either the people or the lawmakers.[30] The supporters of the amendment interpreted Smith's stand on the referendum as having been caused by pressure from the Roman Catholic Church. It is significant that although Catholic opposition was less open in the 1920's than it was to be in the 1930's, the ratification committee was unable to persuade a single Catholic, other than those from organized labor, to join it in the fight for the amendment. Completely aside from the opposition of the New York Catholic hierarchy, Smith may have had misgivings about the prospect of federal control raised by the amendment, for he was in many ways a state-oriented progressive. (In the 1930's Smith came out openly against the amendment and was promptly charged with having betrayed his earlier ideals.)

Despite these developments, the proponents continued to prepare for the Albany legislative hearings on February 24, 1925. When the proceedings before the joint Judiciary Committees of the Senate and Assembly opened, the presiding officer announced that only three hours had been allotted for the hearing, but that the time would be divided equally. The opposition held the floor from 2:10 p.m. to 4:15 p.m., forcing the advocates of the amendment "to make their case with an audience already fatigued with long speeches and to carry on without some speakers who were compelled to leave to make trains." Feeling ran high at the hearing; one spectator screamed that the chairman of the ratification committee, Grace H. Childs, was a "damned Muscovite!" More such charges were levelled by Mrs. Florence Shumway of the Brooklyn Women's Club who stated that the amendment "came straight from Moscow." So much was said about the Communist origin of the amendment at the hearing that the *Herald-Tribune* reported that the opposition had no rational arguments but was relying entirely upon emotion. The newspaper correctly perceived that "the opposition to the child labor proposal is . . . almost always an opposition to something else." Charles J. Tobin, the Catholic lobbyist, charged that the amendment would make children the vassals of the state; William R. George, William McCarroll of the New York Board of Trade, and Russell Whitman of the New York Chamber of Commerce attacked the proposal because they felt that it violated state rights. Edward V. Terry of the American Constitutional League pointed out that three of the judges then sitting on the New York Supreme Court had begun life as newsboys on the Brooklyn Bridge; other speakers charged that the amendment implied that New York State was not competent to manage its own affairs.[31] When the proponents' turn came, they had only forty-five minutes to argue that the amendment was not the monster depicted by the opposition. Some two hundred supporters of the proposal heard Grace Childs praise New York's stringent child labor laws and ask why any state with such standards should fear federal legislation. By this time, however, the opposition had convinced many people that a state with such standards had no reason to cast a vote for federal intervention in other states.

In March, 1925, the New York State Senate passed the Fearon Bill calling for an autumn referendum on the child labor amendment. In the course of a stormy debate on the measure, Senator Nathan Straus, Jr., of New York City charged the Senate leadership with attempting to evade the issue and reminded his colleagues that the recent platforms of both the state Republican and Democratic parties had pledged ratification of the amendment. Senator George Fearon of Onondaga County replied that he had changed his mind about the amendment and would rather oppose it openly than "hide behind a party platform." The ratification committee denounced the Fearon Bill and declared that "any legislator who votes for . . . [it] is unfriendly to ratification and is simply hiding out in the woods when the chance has come to take a definite stand in favor of the children of this nation."[32] The ratification committee was counting on Governor Smith to carry out his part of the gentlemen's agreement and he apparently did, for shortly after the Senate action, Republican leaders in the Assembly emerged from a five-hour conference and announced that the Assembly would take no action on either the ratification or referendum proposals during the remainder of the 1925 session. Pro-amendment newspapers who were not in on the secret promptly excoriated state Republican leadership for repudiating "a measure which was passed by a Republican Congress, endorsed by two Republican presidents, and made a party issue by national and state Republican conventions." The Binghamton *Press* wondered just where "some of these machine-made Republicans . . . draw the line on loyalty to Republican principles." Nevertheless, the ratification committee had avoided a probable referendum defeat.[33]

By March, 1925, the child labor amendment appeared to be defeated nationally. Up to that time only four states had ratified it, while twelve had rejected it by a vote of both houses of their legislatures. The New York opposition rejoiced in pronouncing the amendment a dead issue. But it was not. Bills to ratify it were introduced in every session of the New York legislature after 1925, although for ten years they all died in committee. The Depression and the New Deal produced a sudden resurgence of national interest in the amendment and between January and September, 1933, nine more states ratified it. Encouraged, advocates of ratification in New York renewed their efforts, organizing the New York Child Labor Amendment Campaign Committee early in 1934 with George Hall as chairman and James E.

Sidel of the National Child Labor Committee as secretary. Eventually Mrs. Allan Coggeshall of the League of Women Voters headed the organization: Hall became Secretary; and Hilda S. Boyle of Schenectady, active in the State Federation of Labor and the League of Women Voters, became the legislative representative. Literally hundreds of philanthropic, charitable, religious, and labor organizations now supported the amendment.[34] Among the most active groups were the National and New York Child Labor Committees, the League of Women Voters, the Women's Trade Union League, the Women's City Club, the Consumers' League of New York, the New York State Federation of Women's Clubs, the Council of Jewish Women, and the Society of Congregational Women of New York State. Once again public meetings were organized throughout the state and literature was distributed to newspapers and radio stations, but the opposition soon demonstrated that it was still as effective as it had been in 1924-25. Indeed, it had added two arguments to its arsenal that effectively cancelled any advantage the proponents had gained as a result of the Depression. The steady growth of the "alphabet agencies" under the New Deal enabled the opposition to document its charge that the amendment would promote a federal bureaucracy. Proponents of the amendment had always claimed that if Congress should attempt to take advantage of the amendment's broad grant of power, the Supreme Court would put a stop to it. When the amendment came up for debate in the New York Legislature in 1937, the opponents refuted this argument by pointing to Franklin D. Roosevelt's "court-packing" scheme. Roosevelt himself was in favor of the amendment (Eleanor Roosevelt had been active in the ratification fight of the 1920's) as was Governor Lehman, but in spite of their vigorous support the proposal was not even forced out of its legislative committee until 1935. According to George Hall, members of the Judiciary Committees of both houses were all conservative lawyers or Catholics, who would not consider a favorable vote. The chairman of the Senate Judiciary Committee was Hyman Schackno, whom Hall blamed for the defeat of the NYCLC school-leaving bill and whom he regarded as subservient to Catholic pressure.[35]

After 1933 Catholic opposition had become more evident. "The Amendment in question is not a mere cloak to shelter little children," said the Brooklyn *Tablet*, "but a sentence of more schooling for youths and maidens of fifteen, sixteen, and seventeen." According to the Rochester *Catholic Courier* "Adoption of the amendment would . . . result in turning over young persons to the Federal Government until they have completed their eighteenth year." Referring to the stand against the amendment taken by the New York State Catholic Welfare Council (a group representing the Catholic Bishops of New York), the Albany *Evangelist* announced that "the position of every Catholic in this State should be evident. The Bishops, our divinely appointed leaders, have spoken. We need look no further."[36] Yet there were some Catholics who did not agree. Frank P. Walsh, Chairman of the Power Authority of New York, organized the Catholic Citizens' Committee for Ratification of the Federal Child Labor Amendment. "No man can speak for me as a Catholic against the Child Labor Amendment," he declared, "I have the right to speak as a member of the Catholic Church and I wish to stand here and resent publicly the hypocritical misrepresentation given the Church by some of its so-called leaders." Continuing his attack, Walsh asserted that "the basis of all opposition to the Child Labor Amendment is a desire for profit. I'd be ashamed to stand here and say that an effort to rescue children from factories would have anything to do with religious education." This stand drew immediate fire from the diocesan press; the Albany *Evangelist* called Walsh's Committee "misnamed and out of order" claiming that his guarantee that Congress would never use the power given it by the amendment was to "be taken for what it is worth—a personal opinion." Rumors began to circulate that Walsh sought an appointment to the Supreme Court and in the end his organization was able to make little headway against the combined opposition of the New York bishops.[37]

A host of other organizations again went on record as opposing the amendment, among them the New York State Grange, the State Conference of Farm Organizations, the State Farm Bureau Federation, the Merchants Association of New York City, the Catholic Daughters of America, the New York State Economic Council, the Knights of Columbus, and the Nassau County Bar Association. Coordinating the attack was a Voluntary Committee Opposed to Ratification of the Child Labor Amendment, identified by the New York Child Labor Committee as one of the three most powerful groups of opponents (the others being the Catholic leaders and the newspapers). Representing the voluntary committee, William R. George took to the hustings again. "You may . . . know," he wrote Syracuse publisher Jerome D. Barnum, "that that amendment has upon me the same effect that a red flag has upon a bull." In 1933, George and Barnum had started the League of Adult Minors, which was a group of people between the ages of sixteen and twenty-one who travelled to towns throughout the state telling audiences that *they* did not want to be controlled by Congress. Fearing the federal regulation of newsboys, Barnum's newspaper, the Syracuse *Post-Standard,* began such a venomous attack against the amendment that some Syracuse citizens set up a Committee of 100 to compel the newspaper to publicize some of the proponents' activities and "to give some prominence to letters to the editor and other releases which might otherwise . . . have been lost." According to the Child Labor Amendment Campaign Committee, the *Post-Standard* "had engaged in the most vicious and bitter opposition to the Amendment of all the newspapers of the state"; it particularly resented the newspaper's claim that the amendment "was the work of Communists led by the late Mrs. Florence Kelley." (She had died in 1932.) Once again prominent individuals such as William D. Guthrie, Nicholas Murray Butler, Elihu Root, and George W. Wickersham opposed the amendment because they felt it violated state rights. Ironically, Franklin Roosevelt himself provided a new argument for the opposition when he stated in 1934 that the NRA had eliminated child labor in the industries concerned.[38] Some less responsible individuals did not hesitate to add the Nazis to their list of "Red" bogeys and assert that the amendment would "Hitlerize" children. One widely circulated handout of Robert Edmonson's Edmonson Economic Service informed the public that the amendment was "mothered by a Marxian Apostle [Florence Kelley] . . . of the Jewish Communist Friederich Engels," that it was part of " 'Red' Roosevelt's Recovery Program" and that if passed, the government "could take children from their parents and establish them in colonies, as does the Soviet Government, and destroy their birth records so that the mother might never know her child."[39]

By April, 1935, proponents of the amendment finally succeeded in forcing it to a vote in the legislature. At the preliminary hearing, messages favoring the amendment from President Roosevelt, Frances Perkins, Senator Robert F. Wagner, Senator Royal Copeland, and James A. Farley appeared to increase its chance of ratification. New York City Mayor Fiorello H. LaGuardia was the principal speaker for the supporters, arguing in his own inimitable style that the federal government was not a foreign government and thus should receive a little more trust from the opposition. George Hall, however, was not optimistic; he predicted that "unless the church calls off its opposition, I am sure that we will fail in getting enough votes." Far from calling off its opposition, Charles Tobin, the lobbyist for the Catholic Church, became even more active behind the scenes and when the roll call came, the amendment was overwhelmingly defeated 102-35.[40] The next year the amendment was killed in both its legislative committees, but in 1937, after Governor Lehman had sent a special message to the legislature asking for ratification, the Democratic Senate voted 38-12 to ratify. The supporters could hardly believe the news. Charles Poletti, Lehman's Counsel, told George Hall that the outlook for ratification in the Republican Assembly was good, but Hall chose to interpret the vote as "an obvious attempt of one political party to out-do the other." Gertrude Zimand of the National Child Labor Committee believed final ratification was "almost a certainty," for everything had been cleared, she thought, with Roosevelt and Farley. But there was one ominous note. "All our advice from Albany," she wrote, "is that the opposition expressed by Catholics is the one thing that really matters."[41] This was true. When a delegation of several hundred supporters of the amendment went to Albany for the Assembly hearing on February 22, 1937, they found an equally large group of opponents present. Representatives of farm groups, parochial-school students, nuns, and priests were there in an unusual alliance to hear Edmund F. Gibbons, Bishop of Albany, read letters from the seven other New York dioceses that *officially* condemned the measure. In words whose effect was not lost upon the Catholic members of the Assembly or upon those non-Catholics who were going to face re-election in largely Catholic districts, the Bishop assailed the Senate's favorable vote as "not only an outrage but mighty poor politics." "We may be charged with ultra conservatism," he asserted, "but menaces of alarming proportions to religion and morality, the family, the home, the child, the workingman, the capitalist, the businessman, and the lawfully constituted government itself, demand that we be conservative." The Albany *Evangelist* reported that many Catholic Assemblymen "stormed" the Bishop with congratulations after his speech and gave themselves over to "open rejoicing" now that they had a reason for not yielding to the party leaders. The newspaper reported Catholic feeling throughout the state "at white heat at the thought of this dangerous measure being passed purely for political reasons."[42] On February 28 a letter from New York's Patrick Cardinal Hayes opposing the amendment was read in St. Patrick's Cathedral and in many other Catholic churches throughout the state. Friends of the amendment reported that at these religious services, printed post cards calling for the defeat of the youth control amendment were distributed with the ushers handing out and collecting the cards; each card bore the printed address of the local Assemblyman. This Catholic pressure combined with the resentment of the farmers brought the amendment down to a disastrous defeat in the Assembly on March 9, 1937, by a vote of 102-42. Over half the Democrats ignored Governor Lehman and other party leaders to vote against the measure, while the Republicans were almost entirely in opposition. The amendment's earlier victory in the Senate was now interpreted by disconsolate supporters as having resulted from a desire to rob Mayor LaGuardia of an issue in his forthcoming campaign for re-election and from the Catholic Church's having been caught by surprise without time to rally its forces.[43]

Although the amendment was reintroduced in the legislature in 1938, it was again defeated in the Assembly by a large majority and was, to all intents and purposes, a dead issue. Certainly, much of the New York Child Labor Committee's initial enthusiasm for the measure had been dampened. Contributions to the group fell off sharply because of the Depression and the members could not absorb the additional defection of contributors who stopped giving solely because of the NYCLC stand on the amendment. One former donor wrote that she was now giving her money "to other work for children which is not connected with socialism." As early as 1936 Hall had become concerned because he did not know which persons on the committee's list of contributors were for the amendment and which were against it; thus, he had advised the directors not to refer to the amendment in their appeals for funds. Manfred W. Ehrich, the committee chairman, believed that the proponents had made a great mistake by trying to have the amendment ratified in New York instead of working "quietly in the smaller states." Ehrich also stated that while he favored the amendment because of his lifelong child labor activities, he "feared its use as a precedent for further aggrandizement of Federal power." By 1938 Hall reported that the committee had discontinued all work for the amendment as "practically everyone agrees that complete ratification is now impossible to secure."[44] The Fair Labor Standards Act of 1938 finally established some federal regulation of child labor in interstate commerce, particularly in manufacturing, mining, and hazardous occupations and was upheld by the Supreme Court in 1941 (*United States* v. *Darby Lumber Co.*). The general age limit was sixteen, with eighteen the limit for hazardous occupations but several kinds of work are still exempted from the child labor provisions of the act: children employed in agriculture outside of school hours; children under sixteen employed by their parents in nonhazardous occupations other than manufacturing or mining; child actors; newspaper carriers; and homeworkers engaged in the making of wreaths.

Eventually, twenty-eight states ratified the child labor amendment, for Congress had not included a time limit for ratification. It would be simple to place the blame for its defeat in New York upon the shoulders of "reactionary" Catholics and farmers. Although it is true that Catholic pressure more than any other single factor brought about the defeat of the amendment in the legislature, the measure nevertheless was extremely vulnerable to opposition attacks that kept its supporters always on the defensive. The eighteen-year age limit and the power given Congress to limit, regulate, and prohibit labor seriously alarmed many people otherwise opposed to child labor. Consequently, the main burden of promoting the measure fell upon the original sponsors and their allies: the social workers, the women's organizations, the child labor committees and the philanthropic groups and these could not match the political leverage exerted by Catholics, farmers, and businessmen. The proponents occasionally reported polls showing a large percentage of New Yorkers in favor of the amendment, but if that is true, they failed to make a sufficient impression upon the legislators. The misgivings about the child labor amendment were similar to those aroused by Roosevelt's court reorganization plan, for the amendment seemed to threaten the constitutional balance of the American system. Although the barrage of propaganda laid down by the opposition affords some of the most striking examples of bizarre assertions and stupid reasoning in American history, the amendment's defeat must be ascribed principally to a serious miscalculation on the part of its framers. *They* knew that Congress would not exploit the grant of power, but the people apparently did not. The wording of the amendment gave the average person no particular reason to shake off apathy and fight for its ratification, while the "interested" opponents provided him with a wide choice of both rational and emotional reasons for rejecting it.

IX. Epilogue

By 1920 the New York Child Labor Committee had become an essentially conservative reform group whose principal aim was to consolidate its legislative gains on the state level by continuing to educate the public against the evils of child labor. The vast majority of the committee's members were not prepared to reconstruct society in order to abolish child labor; indeed, they regarded such abolition as a moral obligation of the existing society. Some of the early members such as Robert Hunter, Florence Kelley, and William English Walling had been socialists, but Hunter and Walling were gone and Miss Kelley was now General Secretary of the National Consumers' League. George Alger, who took over the chairmanship from Mornay Williams in 1920, believed firmly that capitalism could reform itself within a moral framework and was convinced

> that the professional and business life of America . . . has for its essential qualities, not decadence, but rather regeneration, in which moral forces have not lost ground but are receiving a sure and constant increase of power.

A distinguished lawyer, Alger had been one of the founding members of the Child Labor Committee in 1903 and was active in other areas of social reform as well. He had drafted New York's first Employers' Liability Act and served as associate counsel to the commission that drafted the state's first Workmen's Compensation Law. Governor Smith later appointed him a Moreland Commissioner to investigate the state prison system and its parole practices. Well acquainted with Theodore Roosevelt, Alger was a progressive Republican who felt that the states rather than the federal government should have the largest role in social reform.[1]

Serving with Alger as vice-chairman of the committee was Charles W. Appleton, a judge in the City Magistrates' Court who had been invited to join the committee in 1918 after he rendered a decision upholding the 1913 Continuation School Law. Additions from the metropolitan area to the original Board of Directors included Leonard W. Hatch, Chief Statistician of the Department of Labor and a member of the Industrial Board; Louis H. Pink, a member of the New York City Board of Education and later State Superintendent of Insurance;

Frances Perkins; Emily S. Marconnier, Director of the Labor Department's Bureau of Women in Industry and Minimum Wage; George J. Gillespie, a leading Catholic layman and member of the New York Board of Water Supply; and Abram I. Elkus, formerly Counsel to the Factory Investigating Commission, Ambassador to Turkey, and an important aide of Al Smith. The social workers included Pauline Goldmark of the Consumers' League; Nathalie Matthews of the Federal Children's Bureau; Lillian Wald; Owen R. Lovejoy, formerly Secretary of the National Child Labor Committee and later Secretary of the New York Children's Aid Society; Douglas P. Falconer, General Secretary of the Brooklyn Bureau of Charities; and Dr. S. Josephine Baker. Several prominent attorneys also served on the Board of Directors; Manfred W. Ehrich and Frederick A. O. Schwarz both held the chairmanship. Herbert H. Lehman ran the NYCLC Finance Committee during the early 1920's. Robert L. Hoguet, First Vice-President of the Emigrant Industrial Savings Bank, was often helpful in maintaining communications between the committee and the Roman Catholic Church on legislative matters, while Mabel Leslie of the Women's Trade Union League and Dr. E. H. Lewinski-Corwin, Secretary of the Public Health Committee of the New York Academy of Medicine, provided valuable assistance in their special fields.

The upstate representation on the board increased over the years; at various periods the active membership included Ansley Wilcox, a leading Buffalo attorney; Paul L. Benjamin, Secretary of the Buffalo Council of Social Agencies; Merle D. Thompson, an Elmira department store owner; Irving I. Goldsmith of Saratoga Springs, a State Supreme Court Justice and Deputy State Attorney-General; Frederick I. Daniels, the Syracuse Commissioner of Public Welfare; and Mrs. Henry G. Danforth, President of the Rochester Board of Education.[2] Attributing much of the committee's success to the active role taken by its Board of Directors, Fred Hall wrote that "these men and women were emphatically not honorary members." Jeanie Minor stressed that "the Committee, made up of individuals . . . who belong to Republican, Democratic, Socialist and Labor parties . . . always managed to keep the work . . . absolutely clear of any political affiliation or any question of preferring one political candidate over another."

Inevitably, the NYCLC became more highly organized; by the end of the 1920's its work was handled by eight standing committees: the Executive Committee, which acted for the Directors on a day-to-day basis (but could not spend more than one hundred dollars without calling a Directors' Meeting); the Finance Committee; the Committee on the Department of Labor, which kept tabs on the factories; the

Committee on the Department of Health, which watched the employment certification procedure; the Committee on the Department of Education, which monitored the Compulsory Education Law; the Committee on Newsboys; the Committee on Scholarships; and the Committee on Legislation.³ As secretary, George Hall ran the New York office and a field secretary handled most of the investigations and inspections. Jeanie Minor filled the latter post during most of her twenty-five years with the committee, but in 1932 she became a Depression casualty. The Depression had a disastrous effect upon the finances of the New York Child Labor Committee and contributions fell from $15,884.75 in 1929 to $7,227.08 in 1933. In 1932, 12,727 letters were sent out in an effort to raise money, but after the cost of the appeal was deducted, only $247.18 had been obtained. The committee could not afford to keep Miss Minor, and George Hall put it as best he could when he told her:

> Only those of us who have been consecutively on the job during this period can fully realize the many years of hard and effective work which you put in for the Committee. In this unfortunate readjustment the State, as well as the Committee, is losing one who has campaigned most successfully in the cause of working children. I am sure that . . . only the desperate financial condition of the Committee was responsible for its decision to reduce the staff and I am deeply sorry that the lightning struck in your direction.

The decision was not easy for the Board of Directors to make, and it had repercussions. An upstate member wrote that the board had "seriously weakened the effectiveness of work against child labor . . . and laid itself open to charges of ruthlessness more to be expected of a 'soulless corporation' than . . . an organization for social service." Some of the child labor reformers felt that Hall should have been the one to go, for Jeanie Minor's verve and sparkle often obscured Hall's solid administrative contribution to the committee, but he was senior to Miss Minor and had a family to support.⁴

For over thirty-five years Hall had worked tirelessly for the NYCLC. During part of 1931, for example, he was spending two days a week in Albany and one in New York City on legislative work; the remainder of the week he devoted to preparing for County Round Table meetings on the school-leaving age, the preparation of the annual report, the budget and financial appeals, a newsboy investigation, a radio talk, scholarship work, a conference with the National Child Labor Committee, and the drafting of a resolution on compulsory physical examinations for parochial school children for presentation to the annual meeting of the Roman Catholic Council of Bishops.[5] After Miss Minor's departure the committee considered the possibility of a financial merger with the National Child Labor Committee, but took no action and throughout the 1930's the NYCLC operated on "an irreducible minimum" of funds. Yet it was during this period that one of the committee's greatest gains—the Sixteen-Year School Leaving Law—was achieved. George Hall wangled help wherever he could and in 1936 he used workers from the New Deal's National Youth Administration to help in tabulating questionnaire results. The financial picture continued to deteriorate, and by 1940 contributions to the committee were barely paying Hall's salary. He told the directors that "some retrenchment will be necessary if the Committee is to continue as an independent organization."[6] Nothing was done until October 5, 1941, when Hall died suddenly in Montclair, New Jersey. His death made it unnecessary for the committee to continue its struggle with a dwindling budget. Feeling that much of the committee's original purpose had been achieved, Chairman Frederick A. O. Schwarz called a special Board of Directors meeting for November 14, 1941. At this meeting, attended by George Alger, Pauline Goldmark, Manfred Ehrich, and other members of long standing, a formal resolution dissolving the committee was prepared and on December 3, 1941, it was approved by the membership. Forty years of service thus came to an end—it had begun in the shadow of McKinley's assassination and ended a few days before the bombs fell on Pearl Harbor.[7]

What can be said of the campaign to end child labor in New York? It is apparent that the New York Child Labor Committee was largely responsible for the high standards of child labor legislation achieved in New York. It was the only organization in the state whose sole purpose was to end child labor through legislation; it rallied other groups, including organized labor, to the cause, and it opened and maintained communications with the state Departments of Labor and Education, even enlisting their personnel as members of the committee when necessary. Until the New York Child Labor Committee appeared in 1902, efforts to end the abuse had been notably unsuccessful. The committee pressed the idea that child labor was morally wrong until its constant lobbying and publicity made it a force that the legislators had to reckon with. The committee understood the difference between legislation and enforcement, and its inspection drives made it the bane of recalcitrant public officials who knew that sooner or later they would have to explain themselves to an irate Jeanie Minor or an impassive George Hall. Behind the committee stood newspapers and public opinion. The committee did not control large blocs of votes, but its constant tap on the legislative communications network was extremely important even though it defies quantitative measurement. In retrospect Jeanie V. Minor emerges as one of the more important, attractive, and hitherto neglected personalities of the progressive movement within the states. George A. Hall's colorless public personality has almost completely obscured his importance. He seldom lashed out at legislators and never blocked the doorways of sweatshops as did Florence Kelley, but his quiet conversations with legislators and his grasp of legislative detail made him indispensable as a balance to the mercurial Jeanie Minor. The committee could never have survived, certainly not beyond 1916, without the help of three of New York's most distinguished lawyers, Mornay Williams, George W. Alger, and Manfred Ehrich. These men helped to sustain the committee's finances through their own contributions and through their connections with some of the most affluent members of New York society. More importantly, they put their substantial legal talents at the disposal of a committee concerned with legislation. For it is clear that Williams, Alger, and Ehrich were deeply concerned about child labor. The committee was not just another "good cause" to them but a vehicle for removing both an affront to the public conscience and an indictment of their own responsibility as citizens. On this they could agree with the socialist members, Florence Kelley, William English Walling, and Robert Hunter, but after 1916 the socialist influence on the committee declined and the committee became largely what Alger and Ehrich chose to make it. Their subsequent achievement of fundamentally important measures such as the Double Compensation Law and the Sixteen-Year School Leaving Law shows that the chronological limitation of "The Progressive Era" had no meaning for them; they continued to work for child labor laws in the 1920's and 1930's just as they had at the turn of the century. This was their real, if unavoidable, limitation. For if it is important to establish the continuity of "progressivism" through the Second World War, it is even more important to assess the limitations such continuity placed on social reform within the states. Some of the most active members of the Child Labor Committee were lawyers, trained in the tradition of *stare decisis*: the slow organic growth of the law and society. This resulted not only in a patchwork quilt of legislation but in a tendency to view child labor as a series of different problems that could be solved through separate statutes. When the committee began its work, child labor was everywhere and it was understandable for them to feel that its sole mission was to stop children from working. In so doing it failed to recognize the need for an attack upon the total environment of the working child, upon the entire culture of poverty, but it would be unfair to blame the committee for its inability to see this. More than forty child labor laws testified to the committee's success in achieving its chosen aims. In 1939 George Alger said he knew of no further legislation the committee could suggest. Child labor had been the problem, and child labor had been dramatically reduced.

But what of school dropouts, the growing unemployability of minors legally entitled to work and that host of problems that reflect the disorganization of a large segment of modern society and are lumped under the rubric "juvenile delinquency"? While it would be illogical to charge the committee with failing to do something about these problems, it is necessary to emphasize their existence. This leads us to a more important consideration: the degree to which the committee and its associated organizations were responsible for reducing child labor. Although the New York reformers ended child labor in factories and department stores, they enjoyed only mixed success in tenement homework, the street trades, and agriculture. Symbols are of great importance in any society, for among their other functions they help to provide a sense of security and organization in a chaotic universe. As Alfred Hodder pointed out, it was important for people to *believe* that social problems were being attacked. It is not without significance that reasonably effective child labor legislation became acceptable as a public symbol during the period when more and more industrial innovations, the rising level of wages, and the activities of the craft unions were rendering child labor impractical in the largest and most efficient industrial plants. It is important to note that the most difficult areas of child labor reform were those hidden from public view (as in tenement homework) or protected by countersymbols as publicly acceptable as that of child labor legislation, viz. the sanctity of the individual entrepreneur (a vanishing breed and hence symbolically enshrined in the newsboy) and the virtue of the countryside (as embodied in the farm worker). As the idea of little children working became increasingly difficult for the public to accept, the task of the committee and the legislature in erecting the symbol of child labor legislation became easier. The reality of child labor law enforcement was another matter entirely, as this study has attempted to show. Symbolic legislation made it possible for the public to believe that child labor was being checked and to ignore a considerable body of evidence demonstrating that the existing laws were badly enforced and that children were still working in tenements, in the streets, and on farms. The Factory Investigating Commission in some ways only gave public sanction to the steadily decreasing factory and mercantile child labor (department stores also had a high public visibility); in tenement work and cannery labor the commission's recommendations were largely unenforced. Certainly the defeat of the child labor amendment points up the superior power of emotional symbols such as state rights, anticommunism, and family prerogatives over the symbol of child labor reform. One of the greatest challenges posed by the child labor laws was to the educational system, yet almost without exception the school superintendents failed to respond; instead they turned their offices into public echo-chambers, and when they were faced with the concrete problem of educating fourteen- and fifteen-year-olds in some meaningful way they took refuge in talk about "ineducability." The process of determining a child's fitness for the labor market—employment certification—was often a perfunctory and symbolic ritual. It is significant that the committee made no headway toward achieving the most fundamental of all the laws, that raising the school-leaving age to sixteen, until the Great Depression and its resulting New Deal made that reform publicly acceptable: the Depression by reducing the available jobs and the New Deal by its use of "crisis psychology" to achieve federal laws covering fourteen- and fifteen-year-olds.

That most child labor reform was purely surface in nature and failed to reach the basic problems of New York's youth can be seen in the crisis of today which, in cities like New York, probably exceeds the youth problem of 1900. But if the child labor reformers are to be charged with poverty-stricken imaginations, so are we. While a few organizations in New York, such as the Committee on Youth Employment of the old National Child Labor Committee and Mobilization for Youth are attempting an imaginative approach they are working with probably less public support than were the reformers of 1903. Time and again one hears the argument that delinquent youth ought to be put to work and that the child labor laws ought to be relaxed. Surely the final repudiation of the work of Hall, Minor, and Alger would be a public commitment to the idea that the only solution for juvenile delinquency is child labor. This is not to say that delinquent children cannot be helped by work or that finding work for dropouts is not a major problem. But if the child labor reform movement of the first half of this century has anything to teach us, it is the long-run futility of surface solutions, solutions that ignore the entire individual and attempt instead to deal with him as a series of separate problems. During the 1920's a perceptive children's court judge told Jeanie Minor something that made a deep impression on her. They had been discussing the problem of continuation-school truants—the problem of educating fourteen- and fifteen-year-olds who had left full-time school. The judge, Jeanie Minor wrote, "added wearily that to penalize boys for non-attendance upon a school which failed to meet their individual needs was . . . to inflame a just resentment into a fixed antisocial condition of mind."

One final word. If in many ways the committee was driven forward by events, so were the employers. One of the strongest impressions resulting from a study of the committee is that of employers and manufacturers pushed into employing children by costs, competitive pressure, a very human lack of imagination, and, of course, by ordinary greed. The exploiter of child labor for its own sake seldom existed; in his place stood a man not ordinarily given to philosophical worries about the future of the race but determined not to give his competitors an inch. The only fair way to deal with child labor was through federal legislation. This came permanently in 1938 although gaps remain. It is possible that if the child labor amendment had been ratified it might have encouraged broader programs to meet the grave problems of urban and migrant youth. However symbolic the New York laws, they did open a brighter world for some children. Even if child labor abuses were somewhat more subject to economic developments than to legislation, a great many children would have worked away their formative years if it had not been for the committee and its friends. The committee may have barred children from work only to have them buffeted by some other ill-conceived feature of their environment, but that does not alter the fact of its contribution. They achieved what it was possible to achieve on the state level for the working children of New York and no greater tribute could be given them. If their history has any value, more should be possible today.

Notes to Chapters

I. ORIGINS OF THE PROBLEM (1830-86)

1. New York State Department of Labor, *Report on the Growth of Industry in New York* (Albany: Argus Co., 1904), 5-6.

2. U.S., Department of the Interior, Census Office, *Statistics of the Population of the United States at the Tenth Census* (Washington, D.C.: U.S. Government Printing Office, 1883), pp. 705, 722, 839, 892; *New York Times*, December 26, 1882; State of New York, Bureau of Labor Statistics, *II Report* (1884), pp. 296-98. The population of New York City in 1880 was 1,206,299, an increase of 28 per cent over 1870.

3. Elizabeth S. Johnson, "Child Labor Legislation," in John R. Commons, *History of Labour in the United States* (4 vols., New York: Macmillan Co., 1918-35), III, 403-04. The states with a minimum age for employment were Massachusetts, New Hampshire, New Jersey, Pennsylvania, Rhode Island, Vermont, and Wisconsin. Those setting maximum hours were Connecticut, Indiana, Maine, Maryland, Massachusetts, Minnesota, Ohio, Pennsylvania, Rhode Island, South Dakota, Vermont, and Wisconsin. For the southern figures see *ibid.*, 405, and Elizabeth H. Davidson, *Child Labor Legislation in the Southern Textile States* (Chapel Hill: University of North Carolina Press, 1939).

4. W. W. Hening (ed.), *The Statutes at Large, Being a Collection of All the Laws of Virginia (1619-1792)* (13 vols., Richmond, 1809-23), II, 336.

5. Florence Kelley, "On Some Changes in the Legal Status of the Child Since Blackstone," *International Review*, XIII (August, 1882), 83-98; Edith Abbott, "A Study of the Early History of Child Labor in America," *American Journal of Sociology*, XIV (July, 1908), 17; New York, *Laws of 1826*, ch. 254; Elizabeth L. Otey, "The Beginnings of Child Labor Legislation in Certain States," in U.S., Senate, *Report on Condition of Women and Child Wage-Earners in the United States* (Senate Document 645, 19 vols., Washington: U.S. Government Printing Office, 1910-13), VI, 27-29 (hereafter cited as Senate Document 645).

6. For a full discussion of this point see Ralph H. Gabriel, *The Course of American Democratic Thought* (New York: The Ronald Press Co., 1940), chapter 18.

7. This point is developed by Rush Welter in his *Popular Education and Democratic Thought in America* (New York: Columbia University Press, 1962), pp. 103-05.

8. *Senate Journal*, 1853, pp. 898, 924; *Assembly Documents*, 1853, vol. IV, no. 94; *Assembly Journal*, 1853, p. 961; *Laws of 1853*, ch. 185. During the entire period up to the Civil War, New York passed only three laws which might conceivably apply to child labor: one in 1831 requiring the education of child paupers; one in 1850 providing for the payment of a child's wages directly to him if the parents did not request otherwise; and one in 1853 establishing a ten-hour day on public works. (*Laws of 1831*, ch. 277; *Laws of 1850*, ch. 266; *Laws of 1853*, ch. 641.)

9. Charles L. Brace, *The Dangerous Classes of New York and Twenty Years Work Among Them* (New York: Wynkoop and Hallenbeck Co., 1872), pp. 31,

90-93, 356-57; *New York Times*, December 25, 1868, January 26, 1873; U.S., Department of the Interior, Census Office, *The Statistics of the Population of the United States*, IX Census (1870) (3 vols., Washington: U.S. Government Printing Office, 1872), I, 793.

10. Brace, *Dangerous Classes*, pp. 362-65.

11. Stephen Smith, *The City That Was* (New York: Frank Allaben Co., 1911), pp. 20, 40.

12. *Harper's Weekly*, March 29, 1879, p. 246.

13. *Ibid.*, April 5, 1870, p. 266.

14. *Ibid.*

15. *Ibid.*, March 22, 29, 1879, pp. 246, 227.

16. Smith, *City That Was*, pp. 145, 166-67.

17. *New York Times*, October 6, 1869.

18. Brace, *Dangerous Classes*, p. 96; Henry F. May, *The Protestant Churches and Industrial America* (New York: Harper and Bros., 1949), p. 112. Brace later modified his view; by 1882 he had come out for a more equitable distribution of wealth.

19. Louis M. Hacker, Abraham Venitsky, and Dora Sandorowitz, "The Beginnings of Industrial Enterprise after the Civil War," Alexander C. Flick (ed.), *History of the State of New York* (10 vols., New York: Columbia University Press, 1933-37), X, 13-14.

20. Roy Lubove, *The Progressives and the Slums: Tenement House Reform in New York City 1890-1917* (University of Pittsburgh Press, 1962), pp. 12-20; Senate Document 645, II, 500-02.

21. There were two main classes of tenement labor: the tenement "sweat shop," which was, in effect, a factory in a tenement which employed workers from more than one family, and the tenement "homeworkers," usually from one family, who labored in their own tenement flat. Together, the two classes produced about one-half of the city's ready-made clothing.

22. Florence Kelley, "Report of the Committee on Child Labor," XII New York State Conference of Charities and Correction, *Proceedings*, in *Annual Report of the State Board of Charities for the Year 1911* (3 vols., Albany: Argus Co., 1912) I, 88.

23. *XII Annual Report of the Factory Inspector* (1897), p. 760. (All factory inspection reports, bureau of labor statistics reports, and labor department reports are from the state of New York unless otherwise identified.)

24. Jesse E. Pope, *The Clothing Industry in New York* (University of Missouri Studies, Social Science Series, Columbia [Mo.], 1905), pp. 30, 58.

25. Senate Document 645, II, 218, 230.

26. *XX Report Bureau of Labor Statistics* (1902), p. 70.

27. Commons, *History of Labor*, III, 411.

28. *Laws of 1874*, ch. 421; *Laws of 1876*, ch. 372.

29. *II Report Bureau of Labor Statistics* (1884), pp. 304-05.

30. Infra, p. 17; *New York Times*, December 26, 1882; *Tenth Census* (1880), pp. 705, 722, 839, 892.

31. *II Report Bureau of Labor Statistics* (1884), p. 305.

32. *New York Times*, February 16, 1882; Helen Campbell, *Darkness and Daylight, or Lights and Shadows of New York Life* (Hartford, Conn.: A. D. Worthington Co., 1892), p. 141.

33. Roger S. Tracy, M.D., "Hygiene of Occupation," *Buck's Hygiene*, vol. II,

reprinted in *II Report Bureau of Labor Statistics* (1884), (pp. 197-265), p. 201.

34. Fred R. Fairchild, *The Factory Legislation of the State of New York* ("Publications of the American Economic Association," 3rd Series, Vol. VII, No. 4, New York: Macmillan Co., 1905), p. 40; *Senate Journal*, 1882, pp. 871-72. One of the legislative techniques used by the New York Legislature for disposing of measures which the leadership does not want enacted, but for which enough public sentiment or lobby pressure has been aroused so that the proposal cannot be ignored, is to have one house pass the bill with the understanding that the other house will reject it. Each house does a certain amount of the other's "dirty work" in this fashion. This enables members of, say, the Assembly, to face their constituents, or the lobbyists, and "blame" the bill's failure on the Senate.

35. *Assembly Journal*, 1882, vol. II, 1126.

36. *New York Tribune*, April 12, 1882.

37. Howard L. Hurwitz, *Theodore Roosevelt and Labor in New York State, 1880-1900* (Columbia University *Studies in History, Economics and Public Law*, No. 500, 1943), pp. 20-26.

38. Fairchild, *Factory Legislation*, pp. 31-35.

39. Samuel Gompers, *Seventy Years of Life and Labour* (2 vols., London: Hurst and Blackett, Ltd., 1925), I, 189. There is disagreement on the number of persons employed in tenement cigar manufacture in New York City during the 1880's. Edith Abbott cites a Cigarmakers' Union circular giving 3,600 as the number (*Women in Industry*, New York: D. Appleton Co., 1913), p. 201; Howard Hurwitz gives a figure of 8,000 to 10,000 (*Theodore Roosevelt and Labor*, p. 79); the *New York Times* gave a figure of about 8,000 for 1884 (January 30, 1884); the Federal Census of 1880 reported 14,476 persons engaged in tobacco, cigars, and cigarette production, tenement and nontenement, in New York City (U.S., Department of the Interior, Census Office, *Report on the Manufactures of the United States at the Tenth Census,* Washington: Government Printing Office, 1883), p. 418. To complicate matters further, Hurwitz asserts that some 70,000 persons (tenement and nontenement) were working in cigars at the time. If Hurwitz' figures, based on Cigarmakers' Union sources, are accurate, it means that about one-seventh of the cigar labor force (those in tenements) produced just under one-half the total product.

40. Clare de Graffenried, "Child Labor," *Publications of the American Economic Association,* Vol. V (1890), 98-99.

41. *Ibid.,* p. 99.

42. *II Report Bureau of Labor Statistics* (1884), p. 146.

43. *Ibid.,* pp. 236-37; Hurwitz, *Theodore Roosevelt and Labor,* p. 80.

44. De Graffenried, "Child Labor," pp. 99-100.

45. Resolution of the New York City Board of Health, January 29, 1883, cited in Fairchild, *Factory Legislation*, p. 17; *Assembly Journal*, 1883, p. 167.

46. *II Report Bureau of Labor Statistics* (1884), p. 151.

47. Gompers, *Life and Labour*, I, 192; *Assembly Journal*, 1883, p. 167.

48. Gompers, *Life and Labour*, I, 192-94.

49. *Laws of 1883*, ch. 93.

50. *New York Times*, March 14, 1883.

51. Hurwitz, *Theodore Roosevelt and Labor*, p. 88.

52. Fairchild, *Factory Legislation*, p. 19; Gompers, *Life and Labour*, I, 196.

53. *Laws of 1884*, ch. 272.

54. *In re Jacobs,* 98. N.Y. 98 (1885). Adolph Strasser of the Cigarmakers'

Union retained Roscoe Conkling as attorney for the union in this case. Conkling failed to appear in court, and pocketed his fee of $1,000, refusing to refund it. Gompers and Strasser both reported that Conkling had tried unsuccessfully to get a postponement of the case because he had another case in Hartford, Connecticut, at the same time.

55. Gompers, *Life and Labour*, I, 197.

56. Edith Abbott reported only 775 persons authorized to manufacture cigars in tenements in 1901. (*Women in Industry*, p. 201.)

57. C. H. Parkhurst, *My Forty Years in New York* (New York: Macmillan Co., 1923), p. 126; Josephine Goldmark, *Impatient Crusader: Florence Kelley's Life Story* (Urbana: University of Illinois Press, 1953), pp. 72-73.

58. As William F. Willoughby, of the United States Department of Labor put it in 1901: "the same difficulty [in evaluating the work of state bureaus of labor statistics] is here met with as in the effort to show the good resulting from the work of a university. We know, nevertheless, that . . . [such bureaus] have accomplished a great deal of good." ("State Activities in Relation to Labor in the United States," *Johns Hopkins University Studies in Historical and Political Science*, XIX (1900), 11). Fairchild's judgment was that the New York bureau "furnish[ed] a certain official mouthpiece for the organized labor of the state." (*Factory Legislation*, p. 26.)

59. *Laws of 1883*, ch. 356; *I Report Bureau of Labor Statistics* (1883), p. 4; *II Report Bureau of Labor Statistics* (1884), pp. 20, 60. The police justice who affirmed the right of manufacturers to keep out state investigators later gave out the opinion that picketing was a form of assault. (Gompers, *Life and Labour*, I, 311.) By 1896 the bureau's annual appropriation had risen to over $25,000, as much as the federal Children's Bureau received in the first year of its operation.

60. *II Report Bureau of Labor Statistics* (1884), pp. 22-25; *First Annual Report of the Factory Inspectors of the State of New York* (1886) (Albany: Argus Co., 1887), p. 13.

61. All data and quotes from Peck's investigation are in *II Report Bureau of Labor Statistics* (1884), pp. 65, 67, 73, 77, 94, 98, 266-67, 277, 300, 302, 355-56.

II. LEGISLATION WITHOUT ENFORCEMENT (1886-1902)

1. *Tenth Census* (1880), p. 839.

2. My figure of 17 per cent applies to the six through fifteen age group. There were 1,129,808 children ages five through fourteen in New York in 1890. 832,498 of these attended school, leaving 297,310 out of school. (Department of the Interior, Census Office, *Report on Population of the United States at the Eleventh Census: 1890*, Washington, Government Printing Office, 1897), Part II, pp. 66, 138, 302. Unfortunately, the census breaks down the school figures in age groups of "five to nine," "ten to fourteen," and "fifteen to nineteen" to get the totals. I make the assumption that New York's 108,459 fifteen-year-olds were as likely to work as the 120,687 five-year-olds were not, and that these figures cancel out, leaving the school data for ages five through fourteen approximately valid for ages six through fifteen. Even so, my figures allow for 100,000 *idle* children (300,000 out of school minus 200,000 working).

3. Helen Campbell, *Darkness and Daylight,* pp. 139-40.

4. *Tenth Census* (1880), p. 614. The census reported that of over 47,000 persons working on men's clothing in New York City—an industry noted for its employment of entire families in tenement workrooms—only 231 were "children and youths." See *Tenth Census* (Report on Manufactures), p. 417.

5. Department of Commerce and Labor, Bureau of the Census, Special Reports, *Occupations at the Twelfth Census* (Washington: U.S. Government Printing Office, 1904), pp. clxxix, 634-40.

6. Herbert J. Bass, *"I Am a Democrat"*: *The Political Career of David Bennett Hill* (Syracuse, N.Y.: Syracuse University Press, 1961), pp. 47, 66-67.

7. *John Swinton's Paper,* October 18, 1885; Commons, *History of Labour,* II, 444-47.

8. Gompers, *Seventy Years of Life and Labour,* I, 277-78.

9. Charles E. Fitch (ed.), *Official New York from Cleveland to Hughes* (4 vols., New York: Hurd Publishing Co., 1911), I, 91.

10. Sydney H. Coleman, *Humane Society Leaders in America* (Albany: American Humane Association, 1924), pp. 71-75; *New York Times,* January 27, 1872.

11. *Laws of 1875,* ch. 130. This law actually made incorporated societies for the prevention of cruelty to children state agencies by providing that all fines imposed and collected under any act affecting children, where such a society was involved in the prosecution, should go to that society.

12. Fairchild, *Factory Legislation,* pp. 41-42.

13. *New York Tribune,* April 9, 1886.

14. *Senate Journal,* 1886, pp. 254, 575, 1028; *Assembly Journal,* 1886, p. 1534.

15. *Laws of 1886,* ch. 409. All factories in cities were subject to the law; those outside cities were regulated only if they employed more than five persons.

16. Bass, *"I Am a Democrat,"* p. 67.

17. Laws of 1886, ch. 409; *First Annual Report of the Factory Inspectors of the State of New York for the Year Ending December 1, 1886* (Albany: Argus Co., 1887), p. 6.

18. *I Report of the Factory Inspector* (1886), pp. 35-36.

19. *Laws of 1887,* ch. 462; *II Report of the Factory Inspector* (1887), pp. 24-25.

20. *II Report of the Factory Inspector* (1887), pp. 24-25.

21. *Laws of 1890,* ch. 298; Clara M. Beyer, "History of Labor Legislation for Women in Three States," U.S., Department of Labor, Women's Bureau, *Bulletin* (No. 66) (Washington: U.S. Government Printing Office, 1929), p. 69; *V Report of the Factory Inspector* (1890), pp. 90-92.

22. *V Report of the Factory Inspector* (1890), pp. 91-94.

23. *I Report of the Factory Inspector* (1886), pp. 17, 36; *III Report of the Factory Inspector* (1888), p. 67.

24. *X Report of the Factory Inspector* (1895), p. 25; *III Report of the Factory Inspector* (1888), p. 90.

25. Helen L. Sumner and Ethel E. Hanks, "Employment-Certificate System in New York," U.S., Department of Labor, Children's Bureau, *Administration of Child Labor Laws, Part 2* (Publication No. 17) (Washington: U.S. Government Printing Office, 1917), p. 52; *New York Times,* July 2, 1911.

26. *VIII Report of the Factory Inspector* (1893), p. 99 (The fines levied in the five cases totaled $65.); *II Report of the Factory Inspector* (1887), pp. 25-26.

27. Jacob A. Riis, *The Children of the Poor* (New York: Charles Scribner's Sons, 1892), p. 106.

28. *Laws of 1896*, ch. 991. The certificate also showed the child's name, description, place and date of birth.

29. For the investigation conducted for the New York State Assembly by Philip W. Reinhard see *Report and Testimony Taken Before the Special Committee of the Assembly Appointed to Investigate the Condition of Female Labor in the City of New York* (2 vols., Albany: Assembly Document No. 97, 1896); Florence Kelley, "Child Labor Legislation," *Annals of the American Academy of Political and Social Sciences*, XX (July-December, 1902), 156; Beyer, "History of Labor Legislation for Women in Three States," pp. 69-71.

30. *XI Report of the Factory Inspector* (1896), p. 20; *XII Report of the Factory Inspector* (1897), pp. 23, 712.

31. *Laws of 1889*, ch. 560. The new age limit was superior to that of any other state: New Jersey had a limit of twelve years for boys and fourteen for girls; Ohio, Maine, and Pennsylvania had a twelve-year limit; Massachusetts, a fourteen-year limit under specified conditions; Rhode Island, a ten-year limit; and Connecticut, a thirteen-year limit.

32. *I Report of the Factory Inspector* (1886), p. 15.

33. *Ibid.*, p. 16. This figure is probably high—it includes seventeen-year-olds.

34. *Laws of 1894*, ch. 671; *Laws of 1895*, ch. 988; *Laws of 1896*, ch. 606.

35. Florence Kelley Wischnewetzky, "A Decade of Retrogression," *The Arena*, vol. IV, no. XXI (August, 1891), 367.

36. Alfred Hodder, *A Fight for the City* (New York: Macmillan Co., 1903), pp. 62-63.

37. *Ibid.*, p. 188.

38. *Laws of 1889*, ch. 560.

39. *VIII Report of the Factory Inspector* (1893), pp. 27-28.

40. Florence Kelley, *Some Ethical Gains Through Legislation* (New York: Macmillan Co., 1905), pp. 74-75.

41. *I Report of the Factory Inspector* (1886), p. 23; Beyer, "History of Labor Legislation for Women in Three States," p. 68. For the view that child labor laws would lead to more legislation for adults see Felix Adler, "Child Labor in the United States and Its Great Attendant Evils," *Annals of the American Academy of Political and Social Science*, XXV, no. 3 (May, 1905), 14.

42. *IX Report of the Factory Inspector* (1894), p. 46. In 1894 the brickyard owners tried to have a law passed permitting children under fourteen to work, and to begin work before 6:00 A.M. The bill passed the legislature but was vetoed by Governor Roswell P. Flower.

43. *I Report of the Factory Inspector* (1886), pp. 29-30.

44. *XII Report of the Factory Inspector* (1897), p. 776; *New York Times*, December 17, 1896.

45. *Laws of 1889*, ch. 560; *Laws of 1899*, ch. 567.

46. For a brief discussion of the problems of enforcing safety legislation see Commons, *History of Labour*, III, 639-41; for workmen's compensation and the fellow-servant rule see *ibid.*, 564-77. I have personal knowledge of a case in which a workman in a well-run New York City printing plant about 1900 lost an arm to one of the machines. He regarded it as an act of generosity when the employer's insurance company settled with him for $300. Had the man gone to court, he probably would not have recovered a penny.

47. Senate Document 645, XVIII, 33-35.

48. *Ibid.*, 34, 247.

49. Helen Campbell, *Darkness and Daylight*, pp. 143-44.

50. *VI Report of the Factory Inspector* (1891), Part I, p. 30. Actually, legislation to deal with the injury problem was already on the statute books and could have been used if there had been any widespread desire to do so. An 1888 amendment to the Penal Code provided that any person who permitted a child under sixteen to work at an occupation where injury was likely to result was guilty of a misdemeanor. The factory inspector believed that it was not his "special duty" to enforce this provision. See *III Report of the Factory Inspector* (1888), p. 61.

51. *VI Report of the Factory Inspector* (1891), Part I, p. 29; *II Report of the Commissioner of Labor* (1902), I, 30-31.

52. *Laws of 1892*, ch. 673; *Laws of 1899*, ch. 375.

53. Hurwitz, *Theodore Roosevelt and Labor*, pp. 194-95, 203-06, 210-11.

54. Commons, *History of Labour*, III, 404-05. The nine states having a fourteen-year minimum age were Colorado, Connecticut, Illinois, Indiana, Massachusetts, Minnesota, Missouri, New York, and Wisconsin.

55. *I Report of the Commissioner of Labor* (1901), p. 110. For the Reinhard investigation see *supra*, p. 24.

56. *Ibid.*

57. *XV Report of the Factory Inspector* (1900), p. 53.

58. *VI Report of the Factory Inspector* (1891), Part I, p. 10.

59. New York *Herald*, June 12, 1890.

60. *III Report of the Factory Inspector* (1888), p. 48.

61. Florence Kelley Wischnewetzky, "White Child Slavery," *The Arena*, I (April, 1890), 595.

62. *IX Report of the Factory Inspector* (1894), p. 32.

63. Reinhard Committee, *Report and Testimony*, I, 5.

64. Fairchild, *Factory Legislation*, pp. 142-43.

65. *Eleventh Census* (1890), Part II, p. 347; *Tenth Census* (1880), p. 722; *Occupations at the Twelfth Census* (1900), pp. 348, 350; *XV Report of the Factory Inspector* (1900), pp. 12-13; *X Report of the Factory Inspector* (1895), p. 36; *I Report of the Commissioner of Labor* (1901), p. 135.

66. U.S. Labor Commissioner Carroll D. Wright admitted that the 1890 Census was "exceedingly unreliable." See H. L. Bliss, "Census Statistics of Child Labor," *Journal of Political Economy*, XIII (March, 1905), 246-48. Table 2 shows only a comparison between the census figures and the factory inspection figures for manufacturing and mechanical pursuits. When the census takers attempted to get figures on tenement, street, or agricultural child labor, they were entering a situation where parental evasion was much simpler, and statistics even more misleading.

67. Fairchild, *Factory Legislation*, p. 127.

68. U.S., Department of the Interior, Census Office, Twelfth Census, *Reports*, Vol. VIII, "Manufactures" (Part II, States and Territories), Washington: U.S. Census Office, 1902, pp. 580, 602; U.S., Department of Commerce and Labor, Bureau of the Census, Special Reports, *Occupations at the Twelfth Census* (Washington: U.S. Government Printing Office, 1904), pp. 348-51. According to the "occupations" report, New York had 14.4 per cent of her males ages ten to fifteen and 9.5 per cent of her females ages ten to fifteen engaged in gainful occupations of all kinds in 1900, an average of about 12 per cent. This compared with an average of about 10 per cent in Massachusetts, 20 per cent in Rhode Island, 15 per cent in New Jersey, and almost 40 per cent in North Carolina (p. lxx).

69. *XV Report of the Factory Inspector* (1900), pp. 12-13; *VI Report of the Factory Inspector* (1891), Part I, p. 10.

70. *Occupations at the Twelfth Census*, pp. 346, 350.

71. VI *Report of the Factory Inspector* (1891), Part I, p. 118; I *Report of the Commissioner of Labor* (1901), pp. 141-42.

72. *Twelfth Census* (1900), II, cxv-cxviii; IV *Report of the Factory Inspector* (1889), pp. 63, 74.

73. III *Report of the Factory Inspector* (1888), p. 33.

74. Riis, *Children of the Poor*, p. 93.

75. Adna F. Weber, "Labor Legislation in New York," New York State Department of Labor, *Monographs on Social Economics*, II (1904), 14.

76. II *Report of the Commissioner of Labor* (1902), I, 27.

III. THE NEW COMMITTEE AND THE BREAKTHROUGH OF 1903

1. Robert H. Bremner, *From the Depths: The Discovery of Poverty in the United States* (New York: New York University Press, 1956), pp. 213-14.

2. State of New York, Department of Public Instruction, *Forty-ninth Annual Report of the State Superintendent* (1902) (Albany: Argus Co., 1903), p. 112; I *Report of the Commissioner of Labor* (1901), p. 141; *Occupations at the Twelfth Census* (1900), pp. 346-52. Some estimates on the number out of school run as high as 450,000. See Commons, *History of Labour*, III, 416-17.

3. Annie S. Daniel, "Conditions of the Labor of Women and Children," *Journal of Social Science*, XXX (October, 1892), 78.

4. New York State Conference of Charities and Correction, "Proceedings" in *Annual Report of the State Board of Charities for the Year 1911* (3 vols., Albany: Argus Co., 1912), I, 88. The problem of reliable statistics on child labor in the slums is further complicated by the varying assumptions of investigators. During the 1890's Professor Franklin H. Giddings of Columbia's Department of Sociology made a study of some immigrant tenement areas. Finding in one block only 23 out of 196 school-age children at home or at work, and in others 27 out of 215 and 21 out of 354, he concluded that "the foreign-born population of the city is not, to any great extent, forcing children of legal school age into money-earning occupations." Giddings assumed (1) that the missing children were in school, when they might have been in street work and (2) that children who attended school were not child laborers. Actually it was not uncommon for children to be put to work on their return from school at the expense of their schoolwork, sleep, and health. (See Jacob Riis, *The Battle with the Slum*, New York: Macmillan Co., 1902, pp. 185-86.) In 1906-07 the State Labor Department checked tenements on Elizabeth, Mott, Mulberry, Baxter, Sullivan, Thompson, and Macdougal Streets, discovering 558 working children under sixteen, 512 of whom were under fourteen. 491 of these children said they attended school. Judging by these figures and other data compiled by the Labor Department, the Consumers' League, the Child Labor Committee, and the College Settlements Association showing (1) that the largest number of tenement child workers were concentrated in the trades most extensively carried on in tenement homes, (2) that these trades (such as clothing, artificial flowers, attaching pencils to dance programs, etc.) involved many unskilled operations easily performed by children, and (3) that there were between five and six thousand *licensed* tenements in New York City, Mary Van Kleeck concluded that "in home work in New York City there is an alarmingly extensive

employment of little children." See her "Child Labor in New York City Tenements," *Charities and the Commons,* XIX (January 18, 1908), 1412-13.

5. State of New York, Assembly, *Report of the Tenement House Committee of 1894* (Albany: J. B. Lyon Co., 1895), pp. 252-253; City of New York, Tenement House Department, *First Report* (2 vols., New York: M. B. Brown Co., 1902-03), I, 6.

6. *III Report of the Factory Inspector* (1888), p. 27; *Report of the Tenement House Committee of 1894,* p. 250.

7. *XII Report of the Factory Inspector* (1897), pp. 44-46.

8. Senate Document 645, II, 718-49; Mary Van Kleeck, "Child Labor in New York City Tenements," *Charities and the Commons,* XIX (January, 1908), p. 1407; *XII Report of the Factory Inspector* (1897), p. 52.

9. Kelley, *Some Ethical Gains,* p. 4.

10. Memphis *News Scimitar,* August 12, 1906, clipping in Eugene V. Debs scrapbook, vol. 7, p. 267, Tamiment Institute Library, New York City.

11. Senate Document 645, II, 297.

12. Consumers' League of the City of New York, *Report,* 1904, pp. 30-32.

13. Haryot H. Cahoon, "Children in Factory and Commercial Life," *New England Magazine,* XXV (December, 1901), 505.

14. For a full discussion of some of the semantic problems involved in the term "street trades" see Edward N. Clopper, *Child Labor in City Streets* (New York: Macmillan Co., 1912), pp. 4-6.

15. Frederick A. King, "Influences in Street Life," *Year Book of the University Settlement Society of New York* (1900), p. 32.

16. Unsigned article, *Charities and the Commons,* X (January, 1903), 55.

17. Elizabeth Oakes Smith, *The Newsboy* (New York: J. C. Derby Co., 1854), pp. 354-55. Even reformers like Jacob Riis expressed the hero point of view. See his "The New York Newsboy," *The Century Magazine,* LXXXV (December, 1912), 254-55.

18. Maud Nathan, *The Story of an Epoch-Making Movement* (New York; Doubleday, Page Co., 1926), p. 9.

19. Anna S. Walling et al., *William English Walling: A Symposium* (New York; Stackpole Sons, 1938), pp. 35-36. For a good discussion of New York settlement houses at the turn of the century see *XVIII Report of the Bureau of Labor Statistics* (1900), pp. 247-431.

20. I. N. Phelps Stokes, *The Iconography of Manhattan Island* 1498-1909 (5 vols., New York: Robert H. Dodd Co., 1895-1926), V, 2011.

21. Arthur M. Schlesinger, Jr., *The Coming of the New Deal* (Boston: Houghton Mifflin Co., 1959), p. 299.

22. Florence Kelley, "My Novitiate," *The Survey,* LVIII (April, 1927), 35. "Here was I," Miss Kelley said enthusiastically, "in the World of the Future."

23. Josephine Goldmark, *Impatient Crusader,* pp. 12-23, 36-47, 72.

24. Confidential statement to author, 1963.

25. Goldmark, *Impatient Crusader,* p. 78.

26. It was not incorporated as the New York Child Labor Committee until 1907.

27. Open letter, Association of Neighborhood Workers, Child Labor Committee, July 1, 1902, "Original Endorsers" folder, New York Child Labor Committee Papers, New York State Library, Albany, New York, hereafter cited as NYCLC.

28. Unsigned article, *Charities and the Commons,* X (January, 1903), 52-54.

Twenty-eight of the newsboys who were questioned made less than one dollar a week.

29. *Who's Who in New York* (1911), p. 501.

30. The phrase is Robert Bremner's. (*From the Depths,* ch. 9.)

31. *Ibid.,* p. 151.

32. N. Adler to Robert Hunter, Bath, England, September 11, 1902, folder 073, NYCLC; Contribution circular for 1930's, NYCLC.

33. John H. Rhoades to Felix Adler, New York, December 13, 1902, folder 073, NYCLC.

34. *Who's Who in New York* (1929), pp. 730, 1123, 1640, 1801; (1905), p. 832; (1911), p. 8.

35. George W. Alger to author, May 3, 1963.

36. Flier, "Child Labor in New York State" issued by committee, January, 1903, NYCLC; Memorial, 1902, NYCLC.

37. Report of the Child Labor Committee of the Central Federated Union of New York City, May, 1903, NYCLC.

38. Fred S. Hall to W. H. Baldwin, December 29, 1902, folder 073, NYCLC; Goldmark, *Impatient Crusader,* pp. 68-69; unsigned article, *Charities and the Commons,* XIX (March, 1908), 1721. The New York Committee correctly claimed to have been the first in the United States with a salaried staff. It hired Fred S. Hall as secretary. Formerly in industrial census work, Fred Hall was the older brother of George A. Hall, who would himself serve the committee as secretary for almost forty years.

39. Statement of receipts and disbursements, 1903-06, NYCLC.

40. Jacob Riis to the NYCLC, December 13, 1902, folder 073, NYCLC.

41. Pauline Goldmark, "Working Papers," *Annual Report of the State Board of Charities* (1911), I, 109. The Labor Department itself turned up 460 cases of children illegally employed in factories in 1903 (*III Report of the Commissioner of Labor,* I, 544-45).

42. Legislative Memorial, 1902, folder 073, NYCLC. This memorial was eventually signed by 171 New Yorkers, 84 of whom resided outside New York City. In addition to the persons already mentioned, Carl Schurz and Oswald Garrison Villard had signed it.

43. *Laws of 1897,* ch. 415; Summary of Educational Requirements for Employment Certificates made for Justice Collins (Children's Court, New York County), January 15, 1916, NYCLC.

44. *Ibid.*

45. Material for 1903 legislative campaign, folder 621.1, NYCLC.

46. New York *Tribune,* January 14, 1903; Albany *Express,* March 4, 1903; New York *World,* February 5, 1903; New York *Journal,* February 6, 1903; New York *Commercial Advertiser,* January 13, 1903; New York *Mail and Express,* February 16, 1903; New York *Evening Post,* March 11, 1903; Buffalo *Express,* February 27, 1903; Syracuse *Post-Standard,* March 9, 1903; Elmira *Advertiser,* March 7, 1903; Schenectady *Star,* January 30, 1903; Newburg *News,* February 3, 1903; material on 1903 legislative campaign, folder 621.1, NYCLC.

47. Thomas M. Mulry to the NYCLC, New York, March 3, 1903; Resolution, New York Monthly Meeting of the Society of Friends, March 7, 1903, folder 621.1, NYCLC; *New York Times,* February 1, 1903.

48. *New York Times,* February 2, 1903.

49. *III Report of the Commissioner of Labor* (1903), I, 54.

50. Material on 1903 legislative campaign, folder 621.1, NYCLC.

51. Report of the Child Labor Committee of the Central Federated Union, May, 1903, NYCLC.

52. Robert Hunter to Augustus N. Hand, New York, October 28, 1903, NYCLC; *The New York Red Book*, 1903, pp. 82-84, 134-35. Hill held a master's degree from the University of Vermont, had edited an ode of Horace, and had sponsored a bill to provide a building for the Buffalo Historical Society. As a member of the 1894 state constitutional convention he had secured the passage of an amendment requiring the use of voting machines in general elections.

53. *III Report of the Commissioner of Labor* (1903), I, 53.

54. *New York Times*, January 2, 12, 15, 1903. Brackett had also wanted to lead the Senate and was annoyed at the prospect of John Raines getting the job. Elsberg and Brown were dissatisfied with their original committee posts.

55. *Senate Journal*, 1903, p. 148; *Assembly Journal*, 1903, p. 267; *Laws of 1903*, ch. 184.

56. *Marino v. Lehmaier* (173 N.Y. 530).

57. *Laws of 1903*, ch. 184; Robert Hunter to Augustus N. Hand, New York, October 28, 1903, NYCLC.

58. *Laws of 1903*, ch. 184; *Laws of 1912*, ch. 333. No physical examination was required by law until 1912, although the 1903 law empowered health officers to ask for one.

59. *I Report of the Commissioner of Labor* (1901), p. 105.

60. New York City Consumers' League, *Annual Report*, 1901, pp. 6-7.

61. *Ibid.*, 1900, p. 14.

62. *Ibid.*, 1901, pp. 10-11.

63. Assembly Bill No. 530, reprinted in *III Report of the Commissioner of Labor* (1903), I, 132-35.

64. *New York Times*, April 16, 1903.

65. McClelland's motion carried by a vote of 25 to 9. *Senate Journal*, 1903, pp. 894-95, 1062; *Assembly Journal*, 1903, pp. 2580-81; *Laws of 1903*, ch. 255. No vacation work under fourteen was allowed in factories. A first-class city was one of over 250,000 population; a second-class city, one of over 50,000 but less than 250,000. All other cities were third class. At the time these laws were passed, the first- and second-class cities were New York, Buffalo, Rochester, Syracuse, Albany, and Troy.

66. Senate Bill No. 324. The penalties were: for a first offense, a fine of not less than $20 nor more than $100; for a second offense, a fine of not less than $50 nor more than $200; for a third offense, a fine of not less than $250, or imprisonment for not more than sixty days, or both.

67. *Senate Journal*, 1903, p. 1128; *Assembly Journal*, 1903, pp. 2128-29, 2873; *Laws of 1903*, ch. 380; *The City of New York v. The Chelsea Jute Mills*, 43 Misc. 266 (1904).

68. Senate Bill No. 426. The minimum attendance requirement for the night schools was six hours a week, sixteen weeks a year. The night schools were of greatest importance in New York City: during the school year 1903-04 a total of 15,864 children, ages fourteen to sixteen attended them, 12,081 of these in New York City. See State of New York, *First Annual Report of the Education Department* (1905), p. 66.

69. *Senate Journal*, 1903, pp. 1244, 1518; *Assembly Journal*, 1903, pp. 2714, 2859-60, 2915-16; *Laws of 1903*, ch. 459; Robert Hunter to Augustus N. Hand, New York, October 28, 1903, NYCLC.

70. *Senate Journal*, 1903, p. 148; Senate Bill No. 316.

71. Transcript, Hearing upon the various so-called Child Labor Bills before the Judiciary Committee of the Senate at the Senate Chamber, Albany, N.Y., March 4, 1903, NYCLC.

72. Confidential Report, "The Bootblack Industry of the City of New York," prepared by Francis H. Nichols, special agent of the Child Labor Committee, February 2, 1903, NYCLC.

73. Transcript of Hearing, NYCLC.

74. Ibid.; New York Evening Post, March 11, 1903.

75. Transcript of Hearing, NYCLC; Julius M. Mayer to Edgar T. Brackett, New York, March 4, 1903, "Street Trades" folder, NYCLC. The Children's Court was not made an independent tribunal until 1924.

76. Transcript of Hearing, NYCLC; New York Times, March 5, 1903.

77. Transcript of Hearing, NYCLC.

78. Open letter from Robert Hunter, Felix Adler, W. H. Maxwell, and Mornay Williams, New York Times, March 12, 1903.

79. Assembly Journal, 1903, pp. 965-66, 1545; Senate Journal, 1903, p. 765; Laws of 1903, ch. 151; Robert Hunter, Poverty (New York: Macmillan Co., 1904), p. 256. The provision on girls was added at the request of the SPCC; Gerry's opposition to the bill had been selective, and he was not, of course, opposed to the general principle of child labor regulation. Like many other state child labor reformers he saw the solution in terms of "patching" the existing legal codes rather than creating new ones.

80. By 1904 only five other states had a street trades law: Vermont, Ohio, Oregon, Washington, and Wisconsin. See William F. Ogburn, Progress and Uniformity in Child-Labor Legislation: A Study in Statistical Measurement (New York: Columbia University Press, 1912), p. 57. New York shared with Massachusetts the honor of having the strictest employment certificate law and it was the only state whose statutes declared that good health and normal development was necessary to obtain working papers. Continuation schools began in New York, with the education law changes of 1903. The 1903 laws made New York, with California and Illinois, one of three states with a maximum workday of less than ten hours for children. Although at the turn of the century some twenty-four states had factory child labor laws, and thirteen had mercantile laws, the New York laws were equaled in scope by only three states: Illinois, Minnesota, and Wisconsin. The New York minimum age of fourteen for employment in factories was generally established in the northern states by 1900. New York had been the first state to pass a law requiring that certain children go to school during the entire school year; by the end of 1903 thirteen states had such laws. For more data on the comparative standing of the states see Commons, History of Labour, III, pp. 410-37.

81. Edward Finch to Robert Hunter, n.d., NYCLC; Poverty, p. 238; material on 1903 legislative campaign, folder 621.1, NYCLC. The money came principally from contributions in response to 3,000 letters.

82. Theodore Roosevelt to Fred S. Hall, Oyster Bay, N.Y., September 15, 1903, folder 133, NYCLC.

83. William E. Walling, "Child Labor in the North: A Great National Evil," The Ethical Record, IV (December-January, 1902-03), 42.

IV. SUCCESS IN THE FACTORIES

1. Adna F. Weber, "The Growth of Industry in New York," New York State Department of Labor, *Monographs on Social Economics,* No. 4 (1904), pp. 25-35; *I Report of the Commissioner of Labor* (1901), pp. 105, 141. In 1900 the inspectors visited only 24,392 of New York's 78,658 industrial establishments. The leading industries were, in rank order: clothing and millinery; metals, machines, and conveyances; food, tobacco, and liquors; printing and paper goods; construction; wood manufacture; chemicals and paints; textiles; leather and rubber goods; stone and clay products. Sixty-three per cent of the state's manufactured goods came from New York City, whose manufactures exceeded those of every *state* in the Union except Pennsylvania. The metropolis ranked first in eight of the country's fifteen leading industries; even the smaller city of Buffalo was ahead of thirty states and territories in manufactured products. Eighty-one per cent of the state's manufacturing was concentrated in ten counties: New York, Kings (Brooklyn), Erie (Buffalo), Monroe (Rochester), Rensselaer (Troy), Albany, Onondaga (Syracuse), Oneida (Utica), Westchester (Yonkers), and Queens.

2. *I Report of the Commissioner of Labor* (1901), pp. 162-315. Working conditions in the factories left much to be desired; describing a study of the workroom conditions experienced by ten thousand factory workers in New York City, Pauline Goldmark told the Factory Investigating Commission in 1912 that only 7 per cent of the rooms were "clean and well-kept." Fifty-eight per cent were "fair" and 35 per cent "dirty and very dirty." (*Preliminary Report of the Factory Investigating Commission* (1912), III, 1634.)

3. *III Report of the Commissioner of Labor* (1903), I, 23; State of New York, *Preliminary Report of the Factory Investigating Commission, 1912* (3 vols., Albany: Argus Co., 1912), I, 612.

4. State of New York, Department of Labor *Bulletin,* (March, 1904), pp. 22-23; *IV Report of the Commissioner of Labor* (1904), I, 22-23. The Department of Labor was created in 1901 and administered the Bureau of Factory Inspection, the Bureau of Labor Statistics, and other bureaus.

5. *Ibid.,* p. 13.

6. *Preliminary Report of the Factory Investigating Commission, 1912,* I, 612.

7. *Ibid.,* I, 62; III, 1880 (testimony of Factory Inspector Ella Nagle).

8. *III Report of the Commissioner of Labor* (1903), III, xxxvii; *IV Report,* I, 283; Department of Labor *Bulletin,* (March, 1904), p. 24.

9. The quotation is from the New York *World* as cited in Hurwitz, *Theodore Roosevelt and Labor in New York,* pp. 210-11. George Alger claimed that Williams was one of the two commissioners of labor at that time "who were worth a damn" (the other was P. T. Sherman). (Alger to author, February 13, 1964.)

10. *Brooklyn Eagle,* December 12, 1904.

11. *New York Times,* December 19, 1904.

12. Open letter, "Child Labor in New York" by V. Everit Macy, J. W. Sullivan, and Robert Hunter, NYCLC.

13. John McMackin to Gov. Frank W. Higgins, Albany, February 8, 1905, reprinted in *IV Report of the Commissioner of Labor* (1904), I, 265-87; "Occupations at the Twelfth Census," pp. 302-05; 348-51. To prove that New York led the nation, McMackin claimed that of ten states New York had the lowest percentage of children under sixteen employed in textiles. A more general view of the statistics suggests that New York's percentage of children ages ten to fifteen em-

ployed in manufacturing and mechanical pursuits slightly exceeded that of Massachusetts (one of McMackin's ten states) in 1904.

14. McMackin to Higgins, *op. cit.*, pp. 268, 277-79, 282; see also *supra*, p. 32. The Eight Hour Law referred to work done for the State of New York.

15. *Ibid.*, p. 272; Open letter "Child Labor in New York."

16. *IV Report of the Commissioner of Labor* (1904), I, 21-22; *Preliminary Report of the Factory Investigating Commission* (1912), I, 65; statement of McMackin to the Albany *Argus* reprinted in "Child Labor in New York"; *New York Times,* December 8, 1904. McMackin's 30,000 poster-sized copies of the factory law averaged out to less than one poster for every two plants. They were written only in English, thus making it difficult for some immigrant workers to find out about their new benefits.

17. "Child Labor in New York"; *IV Report of the Commissioner of Labor* (1904), I, 271.

18. "Child Labor in New York."

19. *IV Report of the Commissioner of Labor* (1904), I, 111; *Laws of 1903,* ch. 459 (this provision imposed a fine of fifty dollars upon a person who employed a child under fourteen while school was in session); New York *Evening Post,* March 24, 1904. The case was tried on February 18, 1904, before Justice Roesch of the Fourth District Municipal Court. George W. Alger came as *amicus curiae* for the Child Labor Committee.

20. New York *Evening Post,* March 24, 1904.

21. *The City of New York* v. *The Chelsea Jute Mills,* 43 Misc. 266 (1904); New York *Evening Post,* March 24, 1904; "Child Saving Laws Sustained; Judge Roesch's Opinion," *Charities and the Commons,* XII (March, 1904), 309-10.

22. *New York Times,* March 25, 1904; Department of Labor *Bulletin,* (June, 1904), p. 177; Felix Adler, "Child Labor in the United States and its Great Attendant Evils," *Annals of the American Academy of Political and Social Science,* XXV (May, 1905), 8-9.

23. *II Report of the Commissioner of Labor* (1902), Section III, p. 29; *IV Report* (1904), Section III, p. 15.

24. "Child Labor in New York"; *IV Report of the Commissioner of Labor* (1904), Section III, pp. 9, 20; List of Organizations Condemning the Administration of Commissioner John McMackin, February 9, 1905, NYCLC.

25. *New York Times,* May 4, 1905. Sherman described himself as an independent reform Republican. In 1923 the acting secretary of the NYCLC recalled that "at that time [1905] the Committee established a procedure from which it has never deviated, i.e., no candidate was endorsed then or ever has been endorsed. . . . When a case of political appointment . . . concerning the enforcement of laws affecting children . . . [was] in question, the Committee's action . . . [was] always to outline qualifications which are desirable for such a position and to ask the appointing officials to regard these qualifications in determining their choice." (Address by J. V. Minor to 10th Annual Conference of the Association of Governmental Labor Officials, Richmond, Va., May 2, 1923, folder 610, NYCLC.)

26. G. A. Hall to the Legislative Committee, Women's City Club, March 2, 1906; circular letter to NYCLC members, March, 1906; Summary of Report of the NYCLC to the 3rd Annual Meeting of the NCLC, December 14, 1906, NYCLC. By urging its members to bombard George R. Malby, Chairman of the Senate Finance Committee, with letters and telegrams, the NYCLC succeeded in having the budget cut restored. Sherman immediately hired twelve new inspectors.

27. V *Report of the Commissioner of Labor* (1905), p. 18; *VII Report* (1907), I, Section II, pp. 11, 16, 23-24; *IV Report* (1904), I, Section III, pp. 14, 20; New York City Consumers' League, *Annual Report* (1906), p. 18.

28. Summary of Report of the NYCLC to the 3rd Annual Meeting of the NCLC, December 14, 1906, NYCLC.

29. George W. Alger to Paul M. Warburg, June 21, 1906, NYCLC. Fred Hall left to do social work in New Jersey. Although George Hall had studied at the New York School of Social Work he was still inexperienced. (Qualification sheet, George A. Hall, NYCLC) Fred Hall continued as a member of the NYCLC Board of Directors until the committee's demise in 1942; George Hall served the committee until his death in 1941, except for 1921-25 when he was on leave.

30. George W. Alger to G. A. Hall, September 5, 1905; Minutes of Meeting of NYCLC, November 15, 1907, NYCLC.

31. Constitution, New York Child Labor Committee, NYCLC.

32. Charter, Rochester Child Labor Association, April, 1910; Charter, Buffalo Child Labor Committee, 1910; Zenas Potter to G. A. Hall, Buffalo, March 22, 1912; Potter to Hall, October 14, 1910, NYCLC.

33. Mornay Williams to A. J. Boulton, November 25, 1914; Hall to Warburg, June 30, 1916; Financial statement, NYCLC, 1905; Treasurer's statement, 1909, 1912; Statement of Cash Receipts and Disbursements, 1920; Analysis of Financial Memorandum, 1915-26, NYCLC.

34. Statement of Scholarship Account, 1907, 1912; P. T. Sherman to Lillian Wald, Albany, August 30, 1905, Drawer 2, Wald Papers, New York Public Library; circular, "Scholarship Plan of the New York Child Labor Committee" (1909); G. A. Hall, "A Ten Years' War Against Child Labor in New York State, 1902-1912," NCLC Publication No. 17, n.d.; Hall to Mrs. M. L. Morrison, New York, December 5, 1917, NYCLC.

35. Memorandum, contributions received, 1929-37, "M. W. Ehrich" folder, NYCLC; Report of Scholarship Committee to the Board of Directors, October 6, 1932, folder 010; Report of Scholarship Committee to the Board, January 23, 1930, November 25, 1930, June 25, 1931; Memorandum, Child Labor Scholarships as Administered by the New York Child Labor Committee, 1929, folder 036, NYCLC. The committee sent undernourished scholarship cases to the Surprise Lake Winter Convalescent Camp, where they were kept until they gained enough weight to pass the physical examination for working papers. Maureen Cobbledick, the scholarship secretary, also arranged to have scholarship children whose bad teeth barred them from receiving working papers get dental treatment at twenty-five cents a visit.

36. Hall to Elizabeth R. Ogilby, October 11, 1935, NYCLC.

37. "Proceedings of the Annual Meeting of the National Child Labor Committee" (1905), *Annals of the American Academy of Political and Social Science,* XXV (May, 1905), 565-566; Goldmark, *Impatient Crusader,* p. 92; Elizabeth H. Davidson, *Child Labor Legislation in Southern Textile States,* pp. 122-24. Other charter members from the NYCLC were Robert Hunter and Paul Warburg.

38. J. V. Minor to Mrs. E. L. Holt, August 2, 1922, NYCLC. Even Edgar Gardner Murphy resigned from the national committee when it endorsed federal action.

39. Charles H. Hopkins, *The Rise of the Social Gospel in American Protestantism, 1865-1915* (New Haven: Yale University Press, 1940), pp. 34-35, 150-52, 247-48. Prominent New York Protestants, both lay and clerical, were taking strong

stands against child employment; among them Graham Taylor, Professor Henry C. Vedder, Rev. Charles Stelzle, Bishop Henry C. Potter, Rev. Edward A. Washburn and, of course, Walter Rauschenbusch.

40. "Action of Religious Bodies with Respect to Child Labor," NCLC Pamphlet No. 38 (1906). Unfortunately a complete list of the participants is not given.

41. Hall to Joseph F. Fletcher, May 17, 1929; Hall to John C. Bennett, January 29, 1908; circular letter, Hall to Greater New York Assemblymen, March 21, 1907, NYCLC; *Laws of 1907*, ch. 507.

42. *New York Times*, March 12, 1905.

43. Joseph L. Gitterman to Robert Hunter, June 9, 1906, folder 125, NYCLC.

44. J. K. Paulding to Joseph L. Gitterman, June 13, 1906, folder 125, NYCLC.

45. Letterhead, National Civic Federation, 1907; "Abstract of a Paper by Roland P. Falkner on the Extent of Child Labor in the United States as Shown by the Official Statistics," Box 136, National Civic Federation Papers, New York Public Library; New York City Consumers' League, *Annual Report* (1906), p. 42; Robert Wiebe, *Businessmen and Reform: A Study of the Progressive Movement* (Cambridge: Harvard University Press, 1962) points out that to the NAM the NCF was "part and parcel" of the AFL and was composed of "industrial doughfaces" (p. 31).

46. NCF Child Labor Commission, Report, n.d.; draft of article dated July 20, 1907, Box 136, NCF.

47. Ralph M. Easley to D. A. Tompkins, New York, February 13, 1907, Box 136, NCF; for the offending article see A. J. McKelway, "Child Labor in the Carolinas," *Charities and the Commons*, XXI (January 30, 1909); McKelway complained that Tompkins was one of only two North Carolina mill owners who had refused to let Lewis Hine, the NCLC photographer, into their mills; R. M. Easley to Editor, *Charities and the Commons*, February 1, 1909, Box 136, NCF.

48. S. M. Lindsay to R. M. Easley, May 18, 1907, Box 136, NCF. The third meeting of the National Child Labor Committee in December, 1906, heard reports from child labor groups in Missouri, the District of Columbia, Maryland, Wisconsin, Pennsylvania, Ohio, Iowa, Georgia, Alabama, Oregon, and North Carolina as well as New York.

49. Recommendations of the Committee on Legislation, 1908, NYCLC; *VIII Report of the Commissioner of Labor* (1908), Section II, pp. 98-121.

50. *Annual Report of the Factory Inspector* (1910), pp. 137-55.

51. Hall to W. W. Walling, March 29, 1909, NYCLC; *Laws of 1909*, ch. 299; *Laws of 1910*, ch. 155 (an amendment strengthening the accident-reporting law); *X Report of the Commissioner of Labor* (1910), p. 168. George Hall and Chief Factory Inspector W. W. Walling gave evidence on necessary industrial safeguards before a legislative hearing.

52. *Second Report of the Factory Investigating Commission*, 1913 (Albany: J. B. Lyon Co., 1913), I, 183-185.

53. *Preliminary Report of the Factory Investigating Commission*, II, 288-289; *Second Report*, I, 182-83.

54. *Laws of 1910*, ch. 674; *Laws of 1913*, ch. 464; *Ives v. So. Buffalo Railway Co.*, 201 N.Y. 271 (1911); State of New York, *Annual Report of the Industrial Commission* (1915), pp. 10-11; (1919), pp. 41-42; (1918), p. 21. The difficulty was that the Industrial Board had to investigate every occupation it proposed to add to the "dangerous" list and demonstrate that it was in fact hazardous. The efforts of the NYCLC to promote such investigations were, on the whole, un-

successful, except for one conducted in 1928. The inspectors could tag unguarded machinery as unsafe if it was supposed to have a guard under the law. The employer was then sent an official notice requiring him to install one.

55. George W. Alger to author, May 3, 1963; Historical Summary of the Double Compensation Problem, dated March 9, 1929, NYCLC.

56. G. W. Alger, Memorandum on Workmen's Compensation Amendment, March, 1923, NYCLC. The constitutionality of the 1913 New York Workmen's Compensation Law was also challenged, but the law was upheld by the New York Court of Appeals in *Jensen* v. *Southern Pacific Co.*, 215 N.Y. 514 (1915) and by the U.S. Supreme Court in *New York Central Railroad* v. *White*, 243 U.S. 188 (1917). For a discussion of Associated Industries see Belle Zeller, *Pressure Politics in New York* (New York: Prentice-Hall, Inc., 1937), pp. 49 ff.

57. *Laws of 1923*, ch. 572; J. V. Minor to Mark Daly, April 4, 1923; Daly to Minor, April 9, 1923; Historical Summary of the Double Compensation Problem, NYCLC; J. V. Minor to Charles D. Hilles, May 5, 1923, "Charles D. Hilles" folder; Minor to Alger, April 18, 1923, NYCLC; R. V. Ingersoll to Alfred E. Smith, May 17, 1923, in bill jacket for *Laws of 1923*, ch. 572, New York State Library. Notwithstanding the amendment, in 1932 the legislature passed the Gates Bill, which exempted employers from liability under double compensation if they had been deceived as to the child's age. Governor Franklin D. Roosevelt responded to NYCLC pressure and vetoed the bill.

58. *Brooklyn Citizen*, December 16, 1918, November 16, 1923; Historical Summary of the Double Compensation Problem; Minor to Shientag, January 11, 1924; Report of the Field Secretary to the Board of Directors, November, 1923, folder 052, NYCLC. In 1918 the Court of Appeals had not yet handed down its decision which would have required Mary Wolff to take the award under Workmen's Compensation.

59. Release, New York Child Labor Committee, 1933, folder 037.2, NYCLC; N.Y. State Department of Labor, *Special Bulletin* No. 168 (May, 1931), "The Social Aspects of the Administration of the Double Compensation Law in New York State," pp. 11, 68; *Industrial Bulletin* (July, 1938), p. 312.

60. News release, New York Child Labor Committee, 1933, folder 037.2, NYCLC.

61. *Laws of 1935*, ch. 603; Hall to the Board of Directors, October, 1938, folder 010, NYCLC; Harry Weiss, "Employers' Liability and Workmen's Compensation," in Commons, *History of Labour*, III (564-610), p. 609.

62. *IV Annual Report of the Commissioner of Labor* (1904), Section III, p. 43; *VIII Report* (1908), p. 9; *Annual Report of the Industrial Commissioner* (1915), pp. 63, 72; *Annual Report* (1920), p. 67. The factory inspectors, of course, did not find *every* legally employed child.

63. P. T. Sherman, "Enforcement of Factory Laws with Special Reference to Child Labor" in *Annual Report of the State Board of Charities for the Year 1905* (3 vols., Albany: Brandon Printing Co., 1906), I, 865; Report on Employers' Reasons for not Employing Children under Sixteen Years of Age, by S. M. Hartzmann, February 28, 1916, folder 010, NYCLC.

64. Statement of Abner M. Seeley, signed and approved by him, January 4, 1916, NYCLC; Joseph P. Murphy, "At What Age Should Children Enter Industry?" (Buffalo: Associated Industries, n.d.), pp. 8, 9, 16. In spite of the recurring argument that the earnings of child laborers were needed at home, a 1917 study in New York City showed that working children became juvenile

delinquents at a rate four times greater than their percentage in the population. See Mabel B. Ellis, "Child Labor and Juvenile Delinquency in Manhattan," *The Child Labor Bulletin*, VI (November, 1917), 173.

65. Memorandum on Child Labor, January 16, 1911, for submission to Governor John A. Dix, NYCLC. Sometimes the organizations worked at cross purposes. Florence Kelley complained that the charitable and philanthropic groups were not cooperating with the Labor Department; to her it was foolish to give charity to families whose children were not in school because the parents took the relief money and sent the children to work. One such society, she charged, had given a pension to a mother of six children for four years, during which time none of the children attended school a single day. (*Annual Report of the State Board of Charities*, 1905, I, 869.)

66. For the Triangle Fire see the reports of the Factory Investigating Commission and Leon Stein, *The Triangle Fire* (Philadelphia: J. B. Lippincott Co., 1962), pp. 12, 13, 23, 26, 28, 33, 80, 103, 205-07.

67. The important volumes of the commission's report for child labor data are: *Preliminary Report of the Factory Investigating Commission*, 1912 (3 vols., Albany: Argus Co., 1912); *Second Report of the New York State Factory Investigating Commission* (4 vols., Albany: J. B. Lyon Co., 1913; *Fourth Report of the Factory Investigating Commission*, 1915 (5 vols., Albany: J. B. Lyon Co., 1915). During its first year the commission held fourteen public hearings, heard 222 witnesses, and took 3,489 pages of testimony.

68. Historical Summary, Legislative Gains Year by Year (1913), NYCLC.

69. Flier, "Vicious Attack on Labor Law"; Report of Committee on Legislation to the Board of Directors, May 17, 1911, NYCLC; Beyer, "History of Labor Legislation for Women," pp. 80-82; *Laws of 1912*, ch. 539; Frances Perkins, *The Roosevelt I Knew* (New York: Viking Press, 1946), p. 13.

70. For examples of this testimony see *Preliminary Report of the Factory Investigating Commission*, 1912, I, 606-17.

71. Editorial, "The New York Factory Bureau," *The Survey*, May 11, 1912, pp. 266-68; New York *Globe and Commercial Advertiser*, February 28, 1914.

72. "The New York Factory Bureau," p. 268.

73. Hall to the Board of Directors, April 22, 1913, folder 010, NYCLC; New York *Globe and Commercial Advertiser*, February 28, 1914; David M. Ellis *et al.*, *A Short History of New York State* (Ithaca: Cornell University Press, 1957), p. 388. Glynn had been Lieutenant-Governor.

74. New York *Globe and Commercial Advertiser*, February 28, 1914. Pauline Goldmark, sister of Josephine Goldmark of the National Consumers' League, was formerly Associate Director of the Bureau of Social Research.

75. Copy of petition to Governor Whitman (1915), NYCLC.

76. *Preliminary Report of the Factory Investigating Commission*, 1912, I, 691.

77. George A. Hall, Memorandum on interview with James L. Gernon, August 20, 1915, NYCLC. Although Gernon's new title was First Deputy Industrial Commissioner, he actually ran the Bureau of Factory Inspection.

78. Circular letter, American Association for Labor Legislation, February 1, 1921, NYCLC. *The Roosevelt I Knew*, pp. 54-55. Shientag was appointed by Al Smith, Perkins by F. D. R., and Andrews by Lehman. Frances Perkins claims that she was, in effect, Industrial Commissioner during the tenure of James A. Hamilton (1925-28) because Smith asked her to bypass Hamilton and run the department.

79. Klingmann Bill, Assembly No. 623, NYCLC; *Laws of 1917*, ch. 689; Summary of Legislative Activity in 1917, New York Child Labor Committee, NYCLC; New York Times, February 18, 1918.

80. Summary of Accomplishments, 1917-18, New York Child Labor Committee, NYCLC; New York *Evening Sun*, February 13, 1919. This estimate of prewar wages was probably high. The wages in Rochester in 1913 for boys and girls ages fourteen to sixteen in shoe factories averaged $5.25 a week and about the same in men's clothing. Wages in paper box factories, cameras, printing, optical work, and button manufacturing in the same city all averaged under $10.00 weekly for the fourteen to eighteen group. (Rochester School Census Board, *Census Bulletin* No. 3, October 1, 1913.)

81. Recommendations of the Field Secretary to the Program Committee, May 17, 1926, folder 037.1, NYCLC. For an excellent discussion of labor's role see Zeller, *Pressure Politics in New York*, pp. 21 ff.

82. Report, "Child Labor Situations which Confront Labor Inspectors," dated October, 1930, NYCLC.

83. New York *World-Telegram*, April 22, 1936; Hall to Alger, February 9, 1938; Hall to the Board of Directors, 1937, May 16, 1940, NYCLC; Frances Perkins, *People at Work* (New York: The John Day Co., 1934), pp. 266-68. In 1937 George Alger complained vigorously to Governor Herbert H. Lehman and New York City Chief Magistrate Jacob Gould Schurman about the reluctance of the courts to enforce the child labor laws. He pointed out that while in 1936, 146 prosecutions had been started with 14 acquittals, 30 convictions, and fines totaling $304.50, fully 102 suspended sentences were granted. The upstate problem was even worse: only 13 of the prosecutions occurred there, with 10 suspended sentences and 3 fines totaling $22.50. "There is something missing in the tonic of enforcement," observed Alger. Either the child labor cases were weak or the lower courts were "out of sympathy with child labor enforcement." The Labor Department was discouraged. Interviewing Industrial Commissioner Elmer F. Andrews Alger found that he had "rather a defeatist attitude." Alger believed that the courts should help the Labor Department by imposing stiff penalties, a point with which Chief Magistrate Schurman agreed. "The vice of this situation," he declared, "lies in the fact that the law to which the suspended sentences relate is thus converted into an admonition which can be disregarded with impunity." But Schurman also criticized the Labor Department's policy of giving first offenders a warning instead of a summons. He promised to hear more labor cases personally and to send copies of Alger's letter to the other magistrates. During the next year 534 employers were convicted of child labor violations and 339 fined. (Alger to Lehman, December 10, 1937, NYCLC; New York *Sun*, October 14, 1937; Fred S. Hall, *Forty Years, 1902-1942: the Work of the New York Child Labor Committee*, Brattleboro, Vt.: E. L. Hildreth Co., 1943, p. 102.)

84. G. F. Zimand, "Wartime Child Labor in New York," *Better Times*, October 29, 1943; E. M. Corsi (Commissioner of Labor) speech at National Child Labor Committee luncheon, February 18, 1944, NCLC files; "The Effects of the War on Children," report of hearing held by the New York State Board of Social Welfare, May 9, 1943, in NCLC files. In New York City 6,938 children were found illegally employed in 1943, almost double the 1942 rate. Double compensation awards to injured minors shot up from 33 in 1941 to 289 in 1943. (Speech by Stanley M. Isaacs, President of United Neighborhood Houses of N.Y., February 18, 1944, files, NCLC.)

85. *Annual Report of the Industrial Commissioner* (1945), pp. 81, 88-89; *Annual Report of the Industrial Commissioner* (1955), p. 64; New York State Labor Department, *The Child Labor Laws and their Administration in New York State*, publication No. B-48, (July, 1952), pp. v, 27, 32-33. Following 1945 the Labor Department gave a steadily increasing percentage of its time to child labor inspections. Of the 320,000 inspected establishments of all kinds in 1945, only 10.4 per cent had been specifically checked for child labor violations. By 1950 21.4 per cent were being inspected for this abuse. While in 1945 of 33,400 establishments inspected for child labor, 24.6 per cent had violations, in 1950 of 81,165 such establishments only 3.0 per cent had violations. These figures included all types of business enterprises: manufacturing, amusement and recreation, hotels, laundries, restaurants, retail stores, dry cleaners, transportation and fruit and vegetable farmers. The Labor Department was materially assisted by the passage of the Coudert-Brook Law of 1945 which limited the after-school working hours of minors sixteen and seventeen years old to four hours a day and twenty-eight hours a week; fourteen- and fifteen-year-old minors were limited to a three-hour day and twenty-three–hour week.

V. EMPLOYMENT CERTIFICATES AND THE SCHOOL-LEAVING AGE

1. *Supra*, pp. 24-25.
2. Commons, *History of Labor*, III, 427-31 summarizes the situation in other states. Massachusetts was also the first state to require a promise of employment before a certificate would be granted. New York achieved this in 1921.
3. Goldmark, *Impatient Crusader*, p. 86; Jacob Riis to the NYCLC, December 13, 1902, folder 073, NYCLC.
4. Compilation of Number of Employment Certificates issued in New York City, 1901-17; Memorandum, The First Year's Work of Issuing Employment Certificates under the New Law (to the NYCLC Executive Committee-1904), NYCLC; *IV Annual Report of the Commissioner of Labor* (1904), Section I, p. 23; Pauline Goldmark, "Working Papers," II New York City Conference of Charities and Correction, *Proceedings*, 1911, p. 109. In 1903 the New York City Board of Health issued 23,591 employment certificates and refused 7,175 applicants, and it appeared that the new procedure was discouraging the use of false documentation. During the next year, however, the figures became ominous. In 1904 only 15,191 certificates were issued and the number of rejected applicants rose to 8,277. Children under sixteen who could not obtain evidence of age were now simply swearing that they were sixteen and presenting parental affidavits directly to employers as proof. Figures for the early part of 1904 reveal that 1,250 of 2,859 applications were denied because of insufficient evidence of age.
5. Lillian Wald to Dr. Abbott E. Kittredge, October 29, 1903, Drawer 1, Wald Papers; Julia Richman to Warburg, New York, November 23, 1906; Hall to New York City newspaper editors, October 13, 1906; Memorandum, The First Year's Work, NYCLC. In 1906 the first school census in nine years was finally taken. Considering the number of immigrants who had entered New York during that period it was about time.

6. *Laws of 1905*, ch. 518; Record of the 55th Street Office, New York City Board of Health, August 22, 1907, folder 343, NYCLC. The school record certifying graduation from the eighth grade was also required to show that the child was at least fourteen. Of 200 cases where "other" documentary evidence was used during 1907, 67 children offered Bar Mitzvah certificates; 47, the transcript of a relief society's record; 47, a graduation certificate from the eighth grade; 15, a transcript of a customs house record; and the remainder, other kinds of evidence.

7. George A. Hall, Report on Evidence of Age, October 26, 1906, NYCLC.

8. Memorandum regarding the Agnew Bill, June 11, 1907, NYCLC; *Laws of 1907*, ch. 585.

9. W. H. Maxwell, circular letter to school principals, September 10, 1908, NYCLC.

10. George A. Hall, Report to the Board of Directors, September 29, 1909, folder 356, NYCLC; S. Josephine Baker, "The Bureau of Child Hygiene of the Department of Health of the City of New York," Department of Health of the City of New York, *Monograph Series*, No. 4 (January, 1915), p. 154; J. V. Minor, "The Enforcement of an Educational Standard," in *Standards and Problems Connected with the Issuance of Employment Certificates* (Children's Bureau Publication No. 116, 1923); circular letter, Maxwell to principals, October 23, 1909, NYCLC. Working boys ages fourteen to sixteen in first- and second-class cities who were not elementary school graduates were required to attend these evening schools six hours a week.

11. George Hall, Report on Evidence of Age; *Laws of 1907*, ch. 291.

12. New York *World*, September 17, 1909.

13. J. V. Minor to Nellie G. Burns, October 23, 1930, NYCLC; 68th Commencement Program, New York University, June 7, 1900, in possession of Mrs. Geoffrey Ambrister, Darien, Conn.

14. Cohoes (N.Y.) *American*, September 28, 1932.

15. Report, J. V. Minor, 1907, 1908, 1911, 1913, NYCLC; U.S., Department of Labor, Children's Bureau, Publication No. 17, Helen L. Sumner and Ethel E. Hanks, "Employment Certificate System in New York," *Administration of Child Labor Laws*, Part 2 (Washington, 1917), p. 52. During the period October 22, 1907, to April 15, 1908, 280 children were so advised. Minor's initial results had not been very promising: of 102 requests to Russian cities only 6 certificates were received; of 80 Austrian requests 11 were received; of 74 Italian requests 16 were received; and of 11 Rumanian requests 3 were received.

16. Sumner and Hanks, "Employment Certificate System," p. 34; *Laws of 1904*, ch. 392.

17. Report, J. V. Minor, April 15, 1908, NYCLC; New York Child Labor Committee, "Annual Report" (1908) in *Annals of the American Academy of Political and Social Science*, XXXIII (May, 1909), 188.

18. Pauline Goldmark, "Working Papers," p. 117; *New York Times*, December 21, 1913; *Laws of 1913*, ch. 511.

19. G. A. Hall to R. C. Sheldon, December 8, 1917, NYCLC.

20. Baker, "The Bureau of Child Hygiene," pp. 150-53; *Preliminary Report of the Factory Investigating Commission* (1912), III, 176; Robert F. Wagner to G. A. Hall, October 9, 1912, NYCLC; Mary J. Morrison, "Employment Certificates," Department of Health of the City of New York, *Monthly Bulletin* (July, 1917), pp. 75-77.

21. Baker, "Bureau of Child Hygiene," p. 150; Morrison, "Employment Certificates," pp. 76-77. A limited employment certificate for cardiac children came into existence in 1928. The New York City Board of Health maintained close contact with relief organizations and the NYCLC scholarship program, and wherever possible attempted to help rejected applicants remove the reason for their rejection. The Health Department arranged to send some of the anemic children to country homes with the cooperation of organizations such as the Association for Improving the Condition of the Poor and the Children's Aid Society.

22. *New York Times*, June 2, 1914; June 7, 1914.

23. Compilation from New York City Health Department Reports, NYCLC; *Annual Report of the Industrial Commission* (1915), pp. 226-27. For the state as a whole in 1914, 30.6 per cent of all children granted certificates had American-born parents; 14.9 per cent, Russian-born; 14.5 per cent, German-born; 12.5 per cent, Italian-born; 8.2 per cent, Austrian-born; 7.5 per cent, Irish-born; 2.4 per cent, English-born.

24. Report of the work of the NYCLC from the year 1913 to date (November 14, 1921); Minor to Hall, May 1, 1916, NYCLC. This division had been created in January, 1915, and Miss Minor had been appointed its chief, pending a Civil Service examination. But although the heads of the Departments of Health and Education both attempted to give the NYCLC agent a chance to retain her job by making the examination open and competitive, the Civil Service Commission decided on a promotion examination limited to persons already officially employed by the two departments—Miss Minor had only been there as an unofficial agent of the NYCLC.

25. Table compiled by the NYCLC from Health Officer's reports; Sumner and Hanks, "Employment Certificate System in New York," pp. 109-10.

26. G. A. Hall, report of interview, August, 1915, folder 226.91, NYCLC.

27. H. M. Hicks to Commissioner of Labor, November 28, 1917, copy in folder 363, NYCLC.

28. Report of the Field Secretary to the Board of Directors, April 11, 1914, NYCLC.

29. Jeanie V. Minor to the Board of Directors, Report on Field Work for 1917, NYCLC.

30. *New York Times*, February 2, 1917; Wellington to Hall, June 2, 1916, NYCLC; *Laws of 1916*, ch. 465. The number of employment certificates issued in New York City fell from 47,033 in 1916 to 39,290 in 1917 as a result of this law.

31. Report on Vacation Permit Law, 1918; J. V. Minor to Dr. S. Josephine Baker, July 19, 1918, NYCLC.

32. J. V. Minor, Report to the Board of Directors, April 29, 1919, NYCLC.

33. *Thirteenth Census* (1910), IV, 73; *Fourteenth Census* (1920), IV, 440, 442 (The number of fourteen- and fifteen-year-old children had only risen from 305,664 in 1910 to 325,678 in 1920.); *Fifteenth Census* (1930), IV, 1, 90. According to the Federal Census of 1920 New York had the lowest percentage of employed males in the ten- to thirteen-year age group (0.6) of any state. In comparison, Mississippi had 26.1 per cent, North Carolina 14.7 per cent, Wisconsin 1.4 per cent, New Jersey 0.7 per cent, and Massachusetts 0.8 per cent. As for employed girls, New York tied with several other states at 0.2 per cent. In the fourteen-year-old age group New York was one of the best states, with only

6.0 per cent of the males employed and 3.7 per cent of the females. In the fifteen-year age group for males, however, twenty-seven states had a lower percentage employed than New York with its 28.3 per cent; in the fifteen-year-old female group thirty-nine states employed fewer children than New York with its 21.1 per cent. However as we have seen, the federal census was often misleading. In 1930, when New York State issued 47,350 employment certificates to minors fourteen and fifteen years old (see Table 6) for work in factories and commercial establishments, the census reported only 19,016 youngsters in that age group as gainfully employed in *all* occupations. While some of this discrepancy can be explained as consisting of youngsters who had taken out certificates and failed to use them, it is also true that after 1922 employers were required to notify employment certificating officers within three days whether a child had reported for work. Anyone familiar with New York's child labor problem would also view with a certain uneasiness the Census Bureau's bland pronouncement that it had excluded from its count children "working at home (presumably including industrial homeworkers) merely on general household work, in chores, or at odd times on other work." The NYCLC view of the situation is in "Has New York a Child Labor Problem?," circular, 1921, NYCLC.

34. Brief Outline Regarding Child Labor Conditions in New York State, September, 1926, prepared by the NYCLC for the Industrial Survey Commission; Memorandum regarding child labor in New York State, June 14, 1935, folder 351, NYCLC.

35. Figures compiled by the NYCLC from reports of the Attendance Division, New York State Department of Education.

36. *Laws of 1921*, ch. 386; Hall to Arthur S. Somers, February 25, 1918, NYCLC.

37. Alger to John Kingsbury, October 26, 1922; Investigation of Girls Obtaining Employment Certificates to do Housework at Home, report by Ethel H. Van Buskirk, October 5, 1922, NYCLC; *Laws of 1922*, ch. 464.

38. "Employment Conditions and Unemployment Relief," *Monthly Labor Review*, XXXV (July-December, 1932), 1269.

39. *Laws of 1921*, ch. 50, ch. 386.

40. Memorandum Regarding Need of Rewriting Present Compulsory Education Law, 1922, NYCLC.

41. Hall to Chairman of the New York State Industrial Survey Commission, February 1, 1928, NYCLC; *New York Times*, January 14, 1930; *Laws of 1928*, ch. 725, ch. 646.

42. Report of Upstate Investigation by Ethel H. Van Buskirk, December 13, 1921, folder 338, NYCLC.

43. J. V. Minor to the Board of Directors, April 16, 1931, folder 052; Upstate Work of the New York Child Labor Committee, 1927, folder 032, NYCLC. In Amsterdam, pleased at the new method being used to remove dust from a pearl button factory, Miss Minor suggested to the manager that this process "should . . . result in a pearly nimbus above the factory tower." Her humor elicited "the grave response that the dust was driven through several thicknesses of canvas . . . then duly packed in bags and sold for fertilizer." Jeanie Minor saw the point. "Obviously," she concluded, "pearl button dust is far too valuable a product to waste on the noses and throats of children."

44. Upstate Work of the NYCLC (Van Buskirk Investigation); Facts Relating

to the Issuance of Employment Certificates in Upstate Cities, report by J. V. Minor, August, 1927; Report of Field Secretary to the Board of Directors, May 21, 1929, NYCLC.

45. J. V. Minor to the Board of Directors, January 25, 1929, folder 052, NYCLC.

46. Field Secretary to the Board, May 21, 1929; January 25, 1929, NYCLC; *Laws of 1928*, ch. 646.

47. Minor to Gillespie, May 7, 1923, "Gillespie" folder, NYCLC.

48. Minor to the Board of Directors, October 1, 1931, NYCLC. During 1928, for example, 61,637 physical examinations were given in New York City and 15,248 children were rejected for physical defects. Only 605 were cases of permanent disability, mostly children with heart trouble, the remaining 14,643 were temporary rejections, the majority for bad teeth, vision, or tonsils. On reexamination all but 3,079 of the temporary rejections were granted certificates. In 1928 a special limited employment certificate for New York City cardiac children sixteen years of age was established. The certificate was valid for six months during which time the applicant was to receive treatment at the New York City Cardiac Clinic. This clinic, partly financed by the New York Heart and Tuberculosis Association, worked in close cooperation with the Employment Center for the Handicapped which was required to approve all prospective jobs for cardiac children. (Report on vocational adjustment of twenty-five sixteen-year-old cardiac children by I. E. Lamkin, December 18, 1930; Report of Field Secretary to the Board of Directors, September 30, 1930, NYCLC.)

49. G. A. Hall, Memorandum Regarding Present Status of Physical Examinations for Working Paper Children in New York City, June 18, 1929, folder 010, NYCLC.

50. J. V. Minor to the Board of Directors, September 30, 1930, May 21, 1929, folder 052, NYCLC. Jeanie Minor felt that the only way to tighten standards was to cut down the number of offices issuing certificates, somehow to create coordination between industry, the Labor Department, and the Bureau of Child Hygiene, so that examining physicians would know "what the children will be up against" in their new jobs. There should be periodic reexaminations of the working child up to his seventeenth birthday and he should be required to present his pledge of employment before taking his physical examination, so that the doctor might judge the youngster's capabilities.

51. Minor to the Board of Directors, April 25, November 25, 1930, NYCLC. In an effort to meet the NYCLC objections, Health Commissioner Wynne bypassed Dr. Blumenthal in 1930 by appointing an "acting" head of the Bureau of Child Hygiene, Dr. Thomas, whom Jeanie Minor praised for his "willingness to accept suggestions." She noted, however, that he had "inherited a crushing weight of departmental inertia and questionable political activity." See also Riegelman to Hall, May 13, 1933; Hall to the Board of Directors, May 19, 1933, folder 010, NYCLC.

52. Hall to S. Josephine Baker, March 11, 1938; Hall, *Forty Years*, pp. 43-44.

53. New York State Education Department.

54. *Ibid.*

55. Hall to Douglas P. Falconer, April 22, 1919; Arthur D. Dean to Hall, February 6, 1915, NYCLC; *Laws of 1913*, ch. 748; *Laws of 1919*, ch. 531; *Laws of 1924*, ch. 524.

56. Publicity Release, New York State Department of Education, November, 1926, NYCLC.

57. Circular on continuation schools compiled by Morris E. Siegal, Director of Evening and Continuation Schools, N.Y. State Department of Education, November 30, 1926, NYCLC.

58. G. A. Hall to the Board of Directors, April 22, 1931, NYCLC; *Thirty-Sixth Annual Report of the State Education Department* (1940), I, 112. In 1925-26 there were 51,081 enrollees in New York City, 3,224 in Rochester, 2,815 in Buffalo, and 1,067 in Syracuse.

59. Releases, State Education Department, June 17, 1929, June 24, 1929, January 30, 1930, folder 223; Circular, Onondaga Pottery Co., 1925, folder 222; Charles Woodward to Homer Folks, February 29, 1928, draft of reply, Folks to Woodward, folder 222, NYCLC.

60. Circular, "Child Labor News," New York Child Labor Committee, March, 1926, folder 123; Statistical Comparison of Number of Children 14-16 Enrolled in Continuation Schools with Number found at Work in Selected Cities by Labor Department Inspectors, October 5, 1927, NYCLC. The percentages of those found working varied from a low of .05 per cent in Lackawanna to a high of 45 per cent in Cohoes. While these figures illustrate the lack of inspection in some areas, it is also true that between fifty and sixty thousand factory inspections and some forty thousand mercantile inspections were being conducted each year in New York City at the time only 13 per cent of the continuation school population was found.

61. J. M. Johnson to Hall, December 20, 1933; E. Ehrlich to Hall, January 15, 1929, NYCLC.

62. Circular letter, City Division of the Anti-Red Society of America, folder 222, NYCLC.

63. *People* v. *Braunstein*, 162 N. E. Reporter 89 (1928); *New York Times*, May 6, 1928; New York *Sun*, April 30, 1935; *Thirty-Sixth Annual Report of the State Education Department* (1940), I, 112.

64. S. J. Baker to J. V. Minor, October 23, 1915, NYCLC.

65. Memorandum Regarding Conference with Education Department Officials, Albany, March 3, 1920, NYCLC.

66. Tabulation of Replies received from Questionnaires sent to Superintendents in 1923, NYCLC.

67. Florence Kelley to J. V. Minor, December 18, 1929, NYCLC. The NYCLC stressed that no fundamental change in the school-leaving age had been made since 1889, and that New York was now behind the states of Ohio and Montana, which had a sixteen-year limit, and Rhode Island, Maine, Michigan, Texas, and California, which had a fifteen-year limit.

68. George Alger to the *New York Times*, September 30, 1933; Minor to the Board of Directors, September 30, 1930, folder 052; Hall to John A. Fitch, November 8, 1930, folder "F"; Minutes of NYCLC Board Meeting, January 23, 1930, folder 042, NYCLC.

69. Signed article, Herbert H. Lehman, *United States Daily*, January 13, 1931, copy in Alfred E. Smith public papers, New York State Library.

70. Memorandum to NYCLC from Frances Perkins, Industrial Commissioner, May 8, 1931, folder 041, NYCLC.

71. J. V. Minor to the Board of Directors, December 17, 1931, folder 052;

Minutes of Special NYCLC Board Meeting, February 10, 1932, folder 042, NYCLC.

72. *New York Times*, March 16, 1933.

73. Hall to Alger, April 12, 1933, NYCLC.

74. Minor to the Board of Directors, December 17, 1931, folder 052, NYCLC.

75. Minutes of NYCLC Board Meeting, October 11, 1933, folder 042, NYCLC.

76. Rev. Joseph V. S. McClancy to Rev. James P. Hanrahan, July 12, 1933, February 27, 1934, files, Diocesan Superintendent's Office, Albany, N.Y.

77. Copy of telegram, Rev. William R. Kelley to Hyman G. Schackno, April 5, 1933; George Alger to the Board of Directors, December 7, 1932, NYCLC.

78. Hall to Maureen Cobbledick, April 5, 1933, "G. A. H." folder; Hall to Alger, April 12, 1933, "G. W. Alger" folder, NYCLC; McClancy to Steingut, April 12, 1935, files, Diocesan Superintendent's Office, Albany. The Buffalo *News* typified editorial reaction linking the sixteen-year bill with the Child Labor Amendment: "There is in the measure the suggestion of how the pending federal child labor amendment would be implemented. . . . Under the Feld bill minors between 14 and 18 years could be employed only at hours other than those during which schools are in session, and then only if requirements as to health and literacy were met. . . . Perhaps someone would add the requirement that home conditions must comply with certain rules and regulations of this or that bureau or department. There are those who would not stop at invasion of the home." (January 9, 1935.)

79. Outline of 1933-34 Campaign for Sixteen Year School-Leaving Bill, folder 037.2, NYCLC; Hall, *Forty Years*, p. 30.

80. Hall, *Forty Years*, p. 31; McClancy to Hanrahan, February 28, 1935, files, Diocesan Superintendent's Office, Albany. Of the 576 NRA Codes 527 established a sixteen-year minimum working age. Forty-nine set a minimum above eighteen years. Sixteen provided for exemptions from the sixteen-year age requirement for specific classes of workers, including newsboys and children who worked in retail trades after school hours. (See Office of NRA, Division of Review, Labor Studies Section, March, 1936, "Child Labor Control under NRA" by Solomon Barkin, p. 23.) New York also had its own "baby NRA," which was also declared unconstitutional in 1935.

81. McClancy to Hanrahan, February 13, 1935; McClancy to Steingut, April 12, 1935, files Diocesan Superintendent's Office, Albany; Hall to Alger, March 14, 1935; Hall to Clara Artus, March 25, 1935; Review of Child Labor Legislation before the New York Legislature of 1935, April 30, 1935, folder 010, NYCLC.

82. New York *World-Telegram*, May 1, 1935; Report of Survey of School Superintendents on the working of the new 16 year law; letters from superintendents, 1937, folder 253.1, NYCLC; *New York Times*, May 5, 1935. By 1938 ten states had a sixteen-year school-leaving age: Ohio, Montana, Wisconsin, Utah, Connecticut, New York, Pennsylvania, Rhode Island, North Carolina, and South Carolina. The NRA, to whose defeat in the courts Fred Hall attributed the passage of the Feld Bill, was not declared unconstitutional until May 27, 1935.

VI. COMMERCIAL ESTABLISHMENTS, TENEMENT
HOMEWORK, AND STREET TRADES

1. General Memorandum on Vacation Work, 1935, NYCLC.

2. *Thirteenth Census* (1900), IV, 496, 498; see also Table 5. In 1910, for example, the census listed 16,767 boys and girls ages ten through fifteen as employed in "trade" (including messenger, bundle, and office boys as well as store workers) throughout New York State, yet in that same year over 36,000 employment certificates for work in factories and commercial establishments were issued to fourteen- and fifteen-year-olds in New York City alone.

3. Kelley, *Some Ethical Gains*, pp. 30-31.

4. New York City Consumers' League, *Annual Report*, 1905, pp. 12-13.

5. Memorandum, "Suggestions for Legislation," December 6, 1906, NYCLC.

6. Florence Kelley, "Obstacles to the Enforcement of Child Labor Legislation," *Annals of the American Academy of Political and Social Science*, XXIX (January, 1907), 52-53; *IX Report of the Commissioner of Labor* (1909), pp. 30, 126.

7. Hunter, *Poverty*, p. 245.

8. *VII Report of the Commissioner of Labor* (1907), I, 75-76; U.S., Senate, *Final Report and Testimony Submitted to Congress by the Commission on Industrial Relations*, (Washington: Government Printing Office, 1916, Senate Document 415), III, 2218.

9. *Second Report of the Factory Investigating Commission*, 1913, I, 268, 271-72. Five thousand of the 20,000 women who worked over 54 hours a week were putting in between 57 and 60 hours a week.

10. *Commission on Industrial Relations*, III, 2337.

11. New York City Consumers League, *Annual Report*, 1901, pp. 15-17.

12. *Second Report of the Factory Investigating Commission*, 1913, I, 269-70, 281-82; *Commission on Industrial Relations*, III, 2344; George J. Kneeland, *Commercialized Prostitution in New York City* (New York: The Century Co., 1913), pp. 177, 212; The Committee of Fourteen in New York City, Department Store Investigation, *Report of the Subcommittee* (New York, 1915), p. 11.

13. *Laws of 1906*, ch. 490; *Laws of 1910*, ch. 387; *Laws of 1914*, ch. 331; *Laws of 1925*, ch. 622: New York *Evening Post*, December 8, 1906. The 1914 statute also set the closing hour for youngsters in stores at 6:00 P.M. In 1911 vacation work in stores by twelve- and thirteen-year-olds in second- and third-class cities was abolished. (*Laws of 1911*, ch. 866.)

14. "A Legislative Victory for Working Children," *Charities and the Commons*, (June 20, 1908), pp. 392-393; Hall to Fitzgerald, June 1, 1908, NYCLC; *Laws of 1908*, ch. 520.

15. See *Annual Report of the Industrial Commission* (1915), p. 81; (1920), p. 89. *Annual Report of the Commissioner of Labor* (1909), p. 38.

16. *Annual Report of the Industrial Commission* (1920), pp. 70, 89, 104; (1915), p. 86. The problem of statistics is again illustrated by the fact that 6,637 children under sixteen are reported as having been found employed in first-, second- and third-class cities for fiscal 1919-20 on page 89 of the 1920 Labor Department report and 8,584 are reported for the same period on page 26 of the report.

17. *Commission on Industrial Relations*, III, 2375. By 1920 the rate of illegally employed children was back up to 51 per cent—perhaps as a result of the stores in third-class cities coming under the law.

18. Report of Movie Investigation, 1915, NYCLC.

19. Poughkeepsie *Eagle News*, May 9, 1918; *New York Times*, June 25, 1921.

20. Report of J. V. Minor, October 16, 1916, folder 055; Minor to the Board of Directors, September 30, 1930, folder 052, NYCLC; *New York Times*, May 17, 1924.

21. J. V. Minor to the Board of Directors, September 30, 1930, October 6, 1932, folder 052, 010; Manfred W. Ehrich to Joseph V. McKee, September 16, 1932; Frank Gillmore to Jeanie Minor, January 15, 1932, NYCLC; New York *Herald Tribune*, September 19, 1932. To Jeanie Minor Buffalo had the highest standards of theatrical inspection in the state. The local SPCC under Douglas Falconer and Roy Woodbury—both members of the NYCLC—gave each applicant a mental and physical examination and checked his school record.

22. *Laws of 1921*, ch. 50; *Laws of 1924*, ch. 375; *Laws of 1925*, ch. 622.

23. J. V. Minor to John A. Fitch, July 31, 1928; Joseph A. McGinnies (Assembly Speaker) to Charles D. Hilles, February 10, 1927, NYCLC. Judge North was also a member of the committee.

24. Nicoll to Hamilton, July 16, 1928; Manfred W. Ehrich to Hamilton, July 18, 1928; Hamilton to Ehrich, July 23, 1928, folder 052, NYCLC. The figure was an NYCLC estimate.

25. *Laws of 1935*, ch. 640.

26. New York Child Labor Committee, Report of Vacation Work Survey, 1935 (mimeographed), NYCLC; *Annual Report of the Industrial Commissioner* (1955), p. 64.

27. *Annual Report of the Industrial Commissioner* (1950), pp. 70, 80, 83. As late as 1950 the Labor Department's Bureau of Enforcement—charged with carrying out the child labor laws—was inspecting a total of only 81,800 establishments of *all kinds* in New York State—23 per cent of the total number of establishments subject to the bureau's jurisdiction. Only about 33,000 of these were retail stores. Within that group of 81,800 establishments, only 2,467 were found to be employing children illegally, but 1,275 of these violators were retail stores and most of the others were commercial establishments. In 1955, 3,583 children were found illegally employed in New York State commercial establishments. The normal ratio of inspected establishments—about 100,000—to establishments under the child labor jurisdiction of the Labor Department—about 400,000— justifies the conclusion that during the 1950's at least eight or nine thousand children were still illegally employed in New York's commercial establishments.

28. For earlier discussions of this problem see *supra*, pp. 4-7, 10-13, 23, 39-41. In my discussion of tenement child labor I will be concerned with "homework." This is *not* synonymous with "sweatshop." A sweatshop is a fly-by-night factory; child labor occurred here but fell under the Factory Law rather than the homework legislation.

29. City of New York, Tenement House Department, *First Report* (2 vols., New York: M. B. Brown Co., 1902-03), I, 5-6; Lubove, *Progressives and the Slums*, pp. 133, 159, 162-63; Ruth E. Shallcross, *Industrial Homework: An Analysis of Homework Regulation Here and Abroad* (New York: Industrial Affairs Publishing Co., 1939), pp. 52-54; *Preliminary Report of the Factory Investigating Commission*, I, 84; *Laws of 1904*, ch. 550.

30. For a concise picture of the tenement population of Manhattan and its ethnic breakdown about 1900 see Lubove, *Progressives and the Slums*, Appendix III. Shallcross, *Industrial Homework*, pp. 27-28; *Second Report of the Factory*

Investigating Commission, 1913, II, 692. Between 1911 and 1932 the Italians comprised between 45 and 55 per cent of the homeworkers. By 1932 the Jews were down to 16 per cent. The number of tenement buildings in New York City rose to about 104,000 by 1916, but 26,000 of these were "new law," conforming to basic structural changes prescribed by the Tenement House Law of 1901.

31. Lubove, *Progressives and the Slums*, p. 94; *Second Report of the Factory Investigating Commission* 1913, II, 692-94; I, 95-99. Individual districts within New York and other cities had a higher density figure but on a city-wide basis New York appears to have had the highest known density of world cities.

32. *Second Report of the Factory Investigating Commission*, 1913, II, 681; Joel Seidman, *The Needle Trades* (New York: Farrar & Rinehart, Inc., 1942), p. 63; *Second Report*, I, 92-93; II, 677-79.

33. "Report of the Committee on Child Labor" in *Annual Report of the State Board of Charities for the Year 1911*, p. 88; *Preliminary Report of the Factory Investigating Commission*, I, 90; Kelley, *Some Ethical Gains*, pp. 6-7; New York City Consumers' League, *Annual Report*, 1903, p. 38.

34. *Second Report of the Factory Investigating Commission*, I, 107; *Preliminary Report*, I, 89-90.

35. *Second Report of the Factory Investigating Commission*, 1913, II, 692-94; I, 95-99.

36. The cities visited were Auburn, Buffalo, Lockport, Niagara Falls, Tonawanda, Rochester, Syracuse, Utica, Troy, Yonkers, Little Falls, Dolgeville, Herkimer, Gloversville, and Cohoes.

37. *Second Report of the Factory Investigating Commission*, II, 708-23.

38. For a discussion of the Cigar Laws see *supra*, pp. 10-13, *Laws of 1892*, ch. 673. The prohibited articles for which outsiders must get a permit included coats, vests, trousers, kneepants, overalls, cloaks, hats, caps, suspenders, jerseys, blouses, waists, waistbands, underwear, neckwear, furs, fur trimmings, fur garments, shirts, purses, feathers, artificial flowers, cigars, and cigarettes. Tenement homework inspections were the responsibility of the Labor Department. See also *Laws of 1899*, ch. 192; *XI Report of the Factory Inspector* (1896), p. 25. The prevailing legal opinion was that parents who used their children in homework were not "employers" and hence could not be prosecuted even though their children were working on factory material. In theory the manufacturer who gave out homework might be prosecuted, but he could effectively deny having "hired" the child.

39. Elizabeth S. Sergeant, "Toilers of the Tenements," *McClure's Magazine*, XXXV (July, 1910), 238; Shallcross, *Industrial Homework*, p. 130; Mary Van Kleeck, "Child Labor in New York City Tenements," *Charities and the Commons*, XIX (January, 1908), 1408; *XIV Report of the Factory Inspector* (1899), pp. 37-38; *I Report of the Commissioner of Labor* (1901), pp. 121-22. The figures on tenement licenses refer, of course, to *rooms* rather than buildings. In 1904 room licenses were abandoned and licenses for the entire tenement building began to be issued.

40. Adeline E. Simpson to Hall, January 26, 1911, NYCLC.

41. *Second Report of the Factory Investigating Commission*, 1913, II, 729-31; *Preliminary Report of the Factory Investigating Commission*, I, 86; *Laws of 1904*, ch. 550.

42. *People* v. *Balofsky*, 167 N.Y. Appellate Division 913 (1915). A Homework Division was also established in the Labor Department.

43. Louis Levine, *The Women's Garment Workers* (New York: B. W. Huebsch Inc., 1924), pp. 144-57, 168, 194, 226-28, 473-74; Charles E. Zaretz, *The Amalgamated Clothing Workers of America* (New York: Ancon Publishing Co., 1934), pp. 43-44; Shallcross, *Industrial Homework*, p. 40.

44. Senate Document 645, II, 317; Goldmark, *Impatient Crusader*, pp. 128-31.

45. *Annual Report of the Industrial Commission* (1918), pp. 39-42.

46. State of New York, Department of Labor, *Industrial Bulletin* (June, 1920), pp. 162-63.

47. *Annual Report of the Industrial Commission* (1920), pp. 32-35, 45, 47. A study of 500 homeworkers in New York City during 1919 revealed that 47 per cent earned less than five dollars a week and 42 per cent less than ten dollars a week. (See *Monthly Labor Review*, February, 1921, p. 187.) For the legal background on what constituted an "employer" see *People ex rel. Price* v. *Sheffield Farms Co.* 225 N.Y. 25 (1918) and *People ex rel. Flannery* v. *First American Natural Fern Co.* 230 App. Div. 502 (1930).

48. *Third Annual Report of the New York Commission to Examine Laws Relating to Child Welfare* (Legislative Document No. 88), 1924, p. 12; *Annual Report of the Industrial Commissioner* (1923), p. 83; *New York Times*, January 11, 1924; U.S., Department of Labor, Children's Bureau, Publication No. 234, Mark Skinner, *Industrial Homework Under the National Recovery Administration* (Washington: Government Printing Office, 1936), pp. 4-5. The Bureau of Women in Industry was created in 1918. The Subcommittee found 535 children at work, 445 of whom were illegally employed; in the same year (1923) the Labor Department had found only 183 illegally employed homework children in the entire state. See also J. V. Minor to the Board of Directors, March 24, 1924, folder 010, NYCLC. Miss Minor described the opposition to the 1924 measure as "a powerful lobby of flower and feather manufacturers." For the later bills see Senate Bill No. 1459 (1924); Assembly Bills No. 1655 (1925) and No. 1546 (1928). The NYCLC also introduced unsuccessful bills to abolish all homework in the sessions of 1924, 1925, and 1928. The rise of racketeering in the New York garment industry following the IGLWU strike of 1926 diverted public attention from the plight of the homeworker.

49. Children's Bureau Publication No. 244 (1938), Mary Skinner, *Prohibition of Industrial Homework in Selected Industries Under the National Recovery Administration*, p. 12. Of the 576 NRA codes 101 eventually barred homework; in addition most of the codes (527) prohibited children under 16 from engaging in homework. By the early 1930's some estimates placed the number of the state's homeworkers at 300,000. The NRA homework codes of most importance to New York were in men's clothing, neckwear, medium- and low-priced jewelry, and tags.

50. Shallcross, *Industrial Homework*, pp. 59-62; Solomon Barkin, "Child Labor Control Under N.R.A.," p. 23.

51. *Laws of 1934*, ch. 825; Memorandum on Neustein-O'Brien Bill for Governor H. H. Lehman from Elmer F. Andrews, bill jacket file, New York State Library.

52. *Laws of 1935*, ch. 182; *Industrial Bulletin* (March, 1938), p. 124; (August, 1938), p. 354; *Annual Report of the Industrial Commissioner* (1950), pp. 75-76; Hall, *Forty Years*, p. 86; *Annual Report of the Industrial Commissioner* (1955), p. 77. For an analysis of the national effect of the Fair Labor Standards Act

see Golda Stander, "Child Labor in Industrial Homework under the Fair Labor Standards Act," *The Child* (January, 1943).

53. For earlier comments on the street trades see *supra*, pp. 41-42, 57-61.

54. "Newsboy" is used to mean a boy *selling* papers to passersby in the street and is not to be confused with "carrier boy," who *delivers* papers to customers on a fixed route.

55. E. N. Clopper, *Child Labor in City Streets* (New York: Macmillan Co., 1912), pp. 128-29.

56. Memorandum on messenger boys prepared by J. K. Paulding, 1904, NYCLC.

57. Rev. John P. Peters, "The Story of the Committee of Fourteen of New York," *Social Hygiene* (July, 1918), pp. 347-53, 376.

58. *Laws of 1893*, ch. 692.

59. *The Social Evil in New York City: A Study of Law Enforcement by the Research Committee of the Committee of Fourteen* (New York: Andrew H. Kellogg Co., 1910), pp. 127-29.

60. Report of Edward F. Brown, agent, March 2, 1910, NYCLC.

61. Letter to editor from NYCLC, New York *Evening Post*, October 6, 1910; *Evening Post* editorial, October 5, 1910.

62. *Laws of 1910*, ch. 342; *Laws of 1934*, ch. 741; Kelley, *Some Ethical Gains*, p. 19; U.S., Department of Commerce, Bureau of the Census, *Prisoners and Juvenile Delinquents in the United States*, 1910 (Washington: Government Printing Office, 1918), p. 159.

63. *Laws of 1928*, ch. 646; Fred S. Hall to NYCLC membership, October 27, 1903, NYCLC.

64. *II Annual Report of the Education Department* (1906), p. 8; Myron S. Adams, "Children in American Street Trades," *Annals of the American Academy of Political and Social Science*, XXV (May, 1905), 41-42.

65. *Laws of 1907*, ch. 588; Minutes of NYCLC meeting, February 24, 1906; Report of Committee on Newsboys to the Board of Directors, October 1, 1908, NYCLC.

66. Clopper, *Child Labor in City Streets*, pp. 52-60; Report of Secretary, NYCLC, April 16, 1908, NYCLC; Hall, *Forty Years*, pp. 78-79; Circular, NYCLC, January, 1910. The NYCLC estimated that one out of every two newsboys under fourteen was violating the age, hours, or badging provisions of the Street Trades Law during 1909. The committee claimed 2,500 violations by the metropolitan area's 5,100 newsboys who were under 14. It is interesting to note that the federal census reported only 977 newsboys under fourteen in the entire state in 1910. (See *Thirteenth Census* (1910), IV, 496.)

67. Clopper, *Child Labor in City Streets*, pp. 134-35; Senate Document 645, VIII, 86-87; Mabel B. Ellis, "Child Labor and Juvenile Delinquency in Manhattan," *The Child Labor Bulletin* (November, 1917), p. 193.

68. George A. Hall, "A Fifteen Years' Fight for Working Children (1902-1917)," typed copy, NYCLC.

69. Myron E. Adams, "Municipal Regulation of Street Trades," National Conference of Charities and Correction, *Proceedings* (1904), p. 299.

70. Summary of Work of Glen Edwards, Field Secretary, November 1, 1913, to March 1, 1914, "G. Edwards" folder, NYCLC; *Child Labor News* (October, 1926). The Buffalo Children's Aid Society found that 71 per cent of them were

twelve- and thirteen-year-old boys earning $1.50 a week. Fifty-five per cent of them were retarded in school—twice the average rate—and 73 per cent had one or more physical defects.

71. Report of Glen Edwards from Syracuse, May 20, 1914, NYCLC. In Syracuse there was only one truant officer for every thirteen thousand children.

72. Albany *Evening Journal*, April 21, 1916; Marcia P. Johnson to J. V. Minor, November 8, 1917; Summary of Replies to Questionnaire, New York Child Labor Committee, 1919, NYCLC. Among the cities not enforcing the law were Troy, Binghamton, Albany, and Yonkers.

73. *Laws of 1913*, ch. 618; *Laws of 1928*, ch. 646. The Gerry Society's opposition to newsboy regulation had been vociferous during the 1903 legislative debates (See Ch. III). The best case that can be made for their position was their belief that their society could do a better job of ministering to street children than could the police. Raising the age limit would create more children who would sell illegally and thus be prey for the police and the reform schools. William H. Maxwell, however, believed that the Gerry Society "has assumed the attitude of doing nothing itself, and endeavoring to prevent any other party from doing anything, to alleviate the condition of the newsboys." (Maxwell to Frank C. Hooper, April 9, 1907, NYCLC.)

74. Hall, *Forty Years*, pp. 80-81; *Laws of 1914*, ch. 21; Hall to L. W. Wilgus, January 9, 1911; J. V. Minor, circular letter to state school superintendents, February 16, 1924, NYCLC.

75. Typed confidential report, "The Bootblack Industry of the City of New York," by Francis H. Nichols, February 2, 1903, NYCLC. Clopper, *Child Labor in City Streets* has a discussion of the Greek-padrone system, pp. 83-96.

76. James Lee to Principals, School Districts 1 and 9, New York City; Hall to William J. O'Shea, September 24, 1918; Report of J. V. Minor, July, 1918, NYCLC.

77. Report of NYCLC Law Enforcement Committee, April 16, 1931, folder 033; Report of Law Enforcement Committee to the Board of Directors, December 7, 1932, folder 010, NYCLC; Hall, *Forty Years*, p. 79; J. V. Minor to the Board of Directors, April 27, 1928, April 16, 1931, folder 052, NYCLC. Enforcement of the Street Trades Law had been the responsibility of the police and the educational authorities since 1907. Following 1921 it was centered in the Education Department but cities under 200,000 population might request police aid.

78. J. V. Minor to the Board of Directors, November 23, 1928; May 21, 1929, folder 052; Hall to the Board of Directors, May 19, 1933; Table, "Cities Where Street Trades Law is Applicable and Number of Badges Issued in Each," folder 010, NYCLC.

79. Bernard M. Knight to Harry W. Wagner, n.d. copy in J. V. Minor to the Board of Directors, April 16, 1931, folder 052, NYCLC.

80. Figures from NYCLC table and State Education Department. The decline after 1950 was partly due to the raising of the street trades age from twelve to fourteen.

81. *Ibid.*

82. Hall, *Forty Years*, pp. 29-30; M. W. Ehrich to Hugh Johnson, July 13, 1933; Alger to Rogers, September 19, 1933, NYCLC.

83. For the code provisions see Barkin, "Child Labor Control under N.R.A.," p. 9; *Editor and Publisher*, November 18, 1933.

84. Hall to Ehrich, June 26, 1934, "M. W. Ehrich" folder, NYCLC; New York *Daily News,* June 28, 1934; New York *Post,* June 25, 1934.

85. Copy of amendment to Article V, Section 1 of NRA Newspaper Code, NYCLC; Barkin, "Child Labor Control under N.R.A.," pp. 14-15, 19; Hall to the Board of Directors, July 12, 1934, folder 010; Hall to the Board of Directors, October 25, 1938, folder 051, NYCLC.

86. Advance Report of the Secretary on the Street Trades, October, 1938; Summary of Remarks of Frieda S. Miller to NYCLC Board of Directors, February 24, 1939, folder 010; Report of Secretary to the Board, March 13, 1940, folder 010, NYCLC. For the present provisions of the law see Secs. 3219-a and 3219 of the New York State Education Law. At present the minimum age for a newspaper carrier is twelve; he may not work before 6:00 A.M. nor after 7:00 P.M., nor more than four hours on days when school is in session and five hours on other days. The minimum age for bootblacks and other street workers is also fourteen. The street-selling situation was apparently still quite serious immediately after the Second World War. In 1946 Walter O'Leary, Director of the Bureau of Attendance of the New York City Board of Education, told the New York Consumers' League that although there had been a sharp drop in the number of badges issued this did not mean that fewer boys were engaged in street selling. He believed that the situation was "deplorable and out of hand." He blamed public apathy, the lack of sufficient attendance officers to work at night, and the lack of shelters for boys who were picked up at night. (Consumers' League of New York, Minutes of Board Meeting, October 29, 1946.) In 1952 a bill passed the legislature which made newspaper carrier boys "independent contractors" in order to relieve newspapers of having to carry workmen's compensation insurance for them. Governor Dewey vetoed it.

VII. DILEMMA IN AGRICULTURE

1. For a full discussion of this point see Richard Hofstadter, *The Age of Reform* (New York: Vintage Books, 1960), ch. I.

2. State of New York, Department of Labor, "Child Labor on New York State Farms, 1948," *Special Bulletin* No. 227 (1949), p. 8.

3. *Second Report of the Factory Investigating Commission,* 1913, I, 125; Mabel L. Hopper, *Migrant Farm Workers in New York State* (Consumers' League of New York, 1953), p. 1. The Canners' Association claimed that the number employed sometimes ran as high as 40,000.

4. *Second Report of the Factory Investigating Commission,* 1913, I, 124-125; *VIII Annual Report of the Commissioner of Labor* (1908), Section II, p. 361. As far as can be determined the first migrant workers from outside the state did not come until after the First World War. One survey conducted by the State Labor Department in 1908 revealed that of 2,546 women employed in canneries fully 766 had been regularly working more than twelve hours a day.

5. For the text of the bill see *III Annual Report of the Commissioner of Labor* (1903), Section II, p. 147. The bill was reported out of committee favorably after an eleven-year age limit was inserted but did not get to a second reading.

6. *III Annual Report of the Commissioner of Labor* (1903), p. 57; *Second Report of the Factory Investigating Commission,* 1913, II, 762. Sometimes there was a fourth building: the vinery.

7. *VIII Annual Report of the Commissioner of Labor* (1908), pp. 336-41.

8. *Ibid.,* pp. 343-45.

9. *Ibid.,* pp. 352-53.

10. Mornay Williams to C. K. Marlatt, April 25, 1910; T. C. Sweet to Hall, April 26, 1910; Hall to Mrs. Horace Eaton, April 28, 1910; NYCLC News Release, March 29, 1910, NYCLC; Beyer, "History of Labor Legislation for Women," p. 85. For the New York City Consumers' League study see Pauline Goldmark, "Women and Children in the Canning Industry: An Investigation in New York State" (1908).

11. Hall to Zenas L. Potter, February 16, 1911; flier, "Objections to Long Hours for Women and Young Girls in Canning Factories," April 15, 1911, NYCLC. The canneries tried to get this exemption in 1911 as well.

12. Hall to Potter, July 5, 1911; Potter to Hall, August 30, 1911, NYCLC; *Second Report of the Factory Investigating Commission,* I, 126-28, 133. Potter wrote most of the commission's cannery report.

13. *Second Report of the Factory Investigating Commission,* I, 133-36; II, 785, 787.

14. *Ibid.,* 789.

15. *VIII Annual Report of the Commissioner of Labor* (1908), pp. 413-14. The largest number of families appear to have come from Buffalo; others came from Rochester, Syracuse, and Utica. In areas where "local" labor was used, a considerable number of children came to the cannery alone and obtained employment. The Factory Investigating Commission found that of the 1,259 children under sixteen employed in the sheds, 754 were working by themselves and not as part of a family group.

16. Half of the foreign families in a group of forty cannery "colonies" checked by the Factory Commission returned to their homes more than forty days after school had begun.

17. *Second Report of the Factory Investigating Commission,* II, 773, 790-98; *Laws of 1913,* ch. 529; *New York Times,* January 10, 1913.

18. Norman Hapgood and Henry Moskowitz, *Up from the City Streets: Alfred E. Smith* (New York: Grosset and Dunlap, 1927), pp. 71-72. For a slightly different version of this incident see Henry F. Pringle, *Alfred E. Smith: A Critical Study* (New York: Macy-Masius Publishers, 1927), p. 168. During the pea crop season (June 25-August 5) the Industrial Board was authorized to permit work up to twelve hours a day and sixty-six hours a week.

19. *New York Times,* April 1, 9, 17, 18, 22, 1915; New York *Tribune,* April 30, 1915; Beyer, "History of Labor Legislation for Women," p. 87.

20. Amsterdam *Sentinel,* April 24, 1915.

21. Beyer, "History of Labor Legislation for Women," p. 87.

22. *New York Times,* March 7, 1915; Fred S. Hall to G. W. Alger, December 8, 1915, NYCLC.

23. *Annual Report of the Industrial Commission* (1915), pp. 218-19.

24. *Annual Report of the Industrial Commissioner* (1914), p. 132; for the 1929 investigation see Consumers' League of New York, *Behind the Scenes in Canneries* (New York, 1930).

25. Nellie F. Burns to J. V. Minor, October 10, 1930, "N. F. Burns" folder,

NYCLC; Frances Perkins, *People at Work,* pp. 274-76; Commons, *History of Labor,* III, 487. During the winter of 1929-30 the NYCLC conducted an investigation of Suffolk County (Long Island) scallop sheds and found children as young as eight working after school until 10:00 P.M. opening scallop shells. Scallop sheds were not covered by the Cannery Shed Law, but in response to the committee's findings, Industrial Commissioner Perkins issued an order placing such sheds under the labor law.

26. "Child Labor on New York State Farms, 1948," pp. 8-9; Hall, *Forty Years,* p. 90; Remarks of F. S. Miller to the Board of Directors, February 24, 1939, folder 010, NYCLC.

27. Report of the Plan and Scope Committee, October 6, 1930, folder 037.1; George Hall, Special Report to the Board of Directors, July 12, 1934, folder 010, NYCLC.

28. There are four kinds of seasonal field agricultural workers (as distinguished from year-round farm labor): (1) those who have their homes near the commercial farm and walk to work; (2) those who are trucked out each day from nearby cities—the "day-haul" workers; (3) those who come from cities within New York but live in work camps for the season—the "intrastate" migrants; (4) those who come from outside the state.

29. Use of Child Labor in Commercialized Agriculture: Excerpts from report by Roy F. Woodbury, Director, Juvenile Protective Department of Children's Aid Society, Buffalo, copy in folder 010, NYCLC.

30. *Moreno* v. *Halstead Canning Co.,* 258 App. Div. 832 (1939); Minutes of Board Meeting, October 25, 1938, folder 042; Hall to membership, November 16, 1939; Hall to the Board of Directors, December 19, 1939, March 13, 1940, folder 010, NYCLC.

31. Transcript of discussion on farm labor at NYCLC Board Meeting, February 24, 1939, folder 010, NYCLC. Children who work on their home farm are still not required to have an employment certificate.

32. Draft of Report, "New York's Migrant Problem" prepared by G. A. Hall, March, 1940, NYCLC, pp. 3, 15-16. Hall reported that some of the workers were afraid to talk to him because they feared that data on their earnings might reach welfare officials in their home cities. Eighty per cent of the workers covered by the study had been trucked out to the fields for the summer from Utica and Syracuse. Hall estimated the number of migrant workers in the state (both intrastate and interstate) at twenty to thirty thousand, a figure which was probably accurate. There are some indications, however, that Hall was including "day-haul" labor in his estimate. Judging from later figures it is probable that the total "seasonal labor force" (including day-haul, interstate and intrastate migrants) was about eighty thousand.

33. *Ibid.,* pp. 17-25.

34. Overcrowding on Trucks, 1937-39, Report by State Committee on Summer Farm Labor Problems, bill jacket file (*Laws of 1940,* ch. 334), New York State Library. Hall to the Board, December 19, 1939, NYCLC.

35. Hall to the Board of Directors, December 19, 1939; March 13, 1940; May 16, 1940, NYCLC; Mark Graves to H. H. Lehman, April 4, 1940; Thomas J. L. Corcoran to Lehman, April 5, 1940, bill jacket file (*Laws of 1940,* ch. 334), New York State Library.

36. Hall to the Board of Directors, May 16, 1940, November 19, 1940, NYCLC; *Annual Report of the Industrial Commissioner* (1940), p. 89.

37. State of New York, Interdepartmental Committee on Farm and Food Processing Labor, *New York's Harvest Labor* (report covering 1943-48, Albany, n.d.), p. 6; Hopper, *Migrant Farm Workers*, pp. 3-4. According to the league about 110,000 workers helped in the harvesting and processing of New York's crops during 1951. Of these about 2,000 were intrastate migrants from Buffalo, Syracuse, and New York City, about 3,500 were white families from Pennsylvania and a few neighboring states, about 4,000 were single men from Puerto Rico and the British West Indies, and about 25,000 were Southern Negroes. The remainder were "day-haul" or local laborers.

38. Hopper, pp. 88-91. The nine agencies were: the State and County Health Departments, the State Department of Agriculture and Markets, the State Department of Social Welfare, the State Employment Service, the State Education Department, the State Department of Labor, the State Police, the State Youth Commission, and the State Extension Service.

39. Consumers' League of New York, "The Joads in New York," (January, 1945), pp. 3, 8-9, 14; Consumers' League, Minutes of Board of Directors Meetings, March 25, 1947, April 29, 1947, files, New York Consumers' League. These files were lent to the author by Henry B. Herman, formerly president of the New York Consumers' League, and are now available in the State Historical Society of Wisconsin, Madison, Wisconsin.

40. Consumers' League of New York, "What Next for New York's Joads?" (January, 1946), pp. 6-7.

41. Hopper, *Migrant Farm Workers*, pp. 76-77; New York State Interdepartmental Committee on Farm and Food Processing Labor, "Migrant Farm Labor in New York State," (Albany, 1961), p. 7. Between 1946 and 1951, for example, the number of child care centers in the state declined from twenty to ten (by 1960 the number had risen to fifteen).

42. Consumers' League of New York, Statement on the Proposed Budget for the Department of Labor Presented to the Fiscal and Tax Committees of the New York State Legislature by Janet R. Davis, Executive Secretary, February 11, 1948, Consumers' League files; "Child Labor on New York State Farms, 1948," pp. 1-2, 18, 20-23, 32, 34-35. "Hourly" wage rates for farm work are computed from the piecework rate. All such figures tend to be misleading because a few days of rain can stop the income of a migrant group; a poor crop season because of dry weather will also reduce the group's earnings. It is interesting to note that the seven growers and contractors who were convicted of child labor violations in 1948 received maximum fines of fifty dollars. Two of the seven received suspended sentences.

43. Hopper, *Migrant Farm Workers*, pp. 90-91; Emily S. Marconnier to Minna F. Kassner, November 12, 1953, files, Consumers' League of New York. The statistics and prosecution figures are from Labor Department summaries prepared by Mrs. Marconnier. See also Minna F. Kassner to Marconnier, December 19, 1953, files, Consumers' League of New York. Anywhere from a third to a half of the illegally employed child laborers who *were* discovered were under fourteen years of age. In some parts of the state the State Employment Service had helped to enforce the labor law by refusing to supply workers if a farmer appeared to be using child labor. However the Employment Service affected only day-haul workers, not migrants.

44. New York State Department of Labor, "Labor Laws in Action on New York State Fruit and Vegetable Farms, 1960," *Special Labor News Memorandum* No.

89 (July 7, 1961), p. 28; "Survey of Effects of the Mechanical Bean Harvester in New York State, 1958," *Special Labor News Memorandum* No. 82 (July 1, 1959), pp. i, 1-3, 5, 10.

45. *New York Times,* July 25, 1951 (the Home Missions Council had only ten mobile units to cover twenty-seven states); Rev. H. Norman Sibley to Minna Kassner, March 10, 1954; "First Class Citizens," address by Rev. George Clarkson before American Association of University Women, Keuka College, March 25, 1952, files, Consumers' League of New York.

46. Geneva *Daily Times,* July 19, 1952.

47. New York *World-Telegram and Sun,* September 8, 1953. Naturally not all camps were bad. The 1953 Consumers' League study made particular mention of two excellent operations: the H. J. Heinz camp in western New York and the Stephen W. Blodgett camps in the Hudson Valley.

48. State of New York, *Report of the New York State Joint Legislative Committee on Migrant Labor,* March 3, 1953, pp. 19, 22-25.

49. Herbert Hill, *No Harvest for the Reaper* (New York: N.A.A.C.P., n.d.), p. 5.

50. Peterson Bill, Senate Intro. No. 1856, Senate Print No. 1986 (1954); Analysis of Four Bills Sponsored by the Joint Legislative Committee on Migrant Farm Labor, March, 1954, files, Consumers' League of New York.

51. A. F. Allen to Minna F. Kassner, November 8, 1954; Louise Kipp to Kassner, September 29, 1954, November 18, 1954, files, Consumers' League of New York.

52. File of 1959 camp inspection reports, Consumers' League of New York files; State of New York, *Report of the New York State Joint Legislative Committee on Migrant Labor,* 1959, (Legislative Document No. 28), p. 20.

53. Minna Kassner to Editor, *New York World-Telegram and Sun,* April 5, 1954, files, Consumers' League of New York.

54. New York State Department of Labor, "Work Injuries in New York State Agriculture," Publication No. B-123 (December, 1961), p. 5. For the nation as a whole, farm injuries were sustained by 5,210 out of every 100,000 employed persons. For all industries combined the rate was only 3,140 per 100,000. See also Statement to the Joint Legislative Committee on Industrial and Labor Conditions submitted by the Consumers' League of New York, December, 1956, League files.

55. State of New York, *Report of the New York State Joint Legislative Committee on Migrant Labor,* 1958, pp. 20-21.

56. "Labor Laws in Action on New York State Fruit and Vegetable Farms, 1960"; New York State Education Department, "A Report on the State Education Department Pilot Project: Summer School Education of Migrant Children," (September 25, 1957); New York State Department of Labor, "Employment and Earnings of Migrant Farm Workers in New York State," Publication No. B-116 (August, 1960), p. 11.

VIII. THE CHILD LABOR AMENDMENT IN NEW YORK (1924-38)

1. The first federal law of 1916 barred from interstate commerce (1) the product of any mine or quarry produced in whole or in part by children under sixteen; (2) the product of any mill, cannery, factory, or manufacturing establishment

produced in whole or in part by children under fourteen or (3) by children in the fourteen to sixteen group working more than eight hours in any one day or more than six days a week, or after 7:00 P.M. or before 7:00 A.M. This law was declared unconstitutional by a 5–4 decision of the Supreme Court in 1918 on the grounds that the commerce clause did not permit control of the states in their exercise of the police power over local trade and manufacturing. See *Hammer* v. *Dagenhart*, 247 U.S. 251 (1918). The second federal law of 1919 provided for a ten per cent tax on the net profits from the products of a mining or manufacturing establishment in which children were employed in violation of standards identical with the first law. The second law was declared unconstitutional by an 8–1 decision of the Supreme Court in 1922 on the grounds that it embodied an improper use of the taxing power. See *Bailey* v. *Drexel Furniture Co.*, 259 U.S. 20 (1922). See also U.S., Department of Labor, Children's Bureau, *Administration of the First Federal Child-Labor Law* (Bureau Publication No. 78, 1921), pp. 109-12; U.S., Department of Labor, Bureau of Labor Statistics, *Proceedings of the Seventh Annual Convention of the Association of Governmental Labor Officials of the United States and Canada* (Bureau Bulletin No. 266, 1921), pp. 141-43. The states considered to have standards equal or superior to the federal laws were Oregon, Montana, North Dakota, Kansas, Oklahoma, Minnesota, Wisconsin, Illinois, Indiana, Ohio, Kentucky, Tennessee, Alabama, West Virginia, New York, Massachusetts, and Connecticut.

2. G. W. Alger, signed article, "Tax Child Labor to Death," New York *Herald Tribune,* July 6, 1918.

3. M. W. Ehrich to editor, New York *Herald Tribune,* June 13, 1937; Alger to Roscoe Pound, September 25, 1918, NYCLC. Alger supported NRA but grew increasingly cool toward the child labor amendment. Ehrich was opposed to many features of the Fair Labor Standards Act.

4. For surveys of the forces promoting the amendment on the national level see Clarke A. Chambers, *Seedtime of Reform: American Social Service and Social Action, 1918-1933* (Minneapolis: University of Minnesota Press, 1963), pp. 32-37 and Richard B. Sherman, "The Rejection of the Child Labor Amendment," *Mid-America,* Vol. 45 (January, 1963), 3-5. The national campaign to ratify the amendment is treated in Ned Weisberg, "The Federal Child Labor Amendment: A Study in Pressure Politics," unpublished doctoral dissertation, Cornell University, 1942. See also *New York Times,* December 9, 1922. Resolutions calling for an amendment had been introduced in Congress as early as 1922 by Representative Roy G. Fitzgerald of Ohio and Senator Hiram Johnson of California.

5. For the congressional hearings see U.S., Congress, Senate, *Child Labor Amendment to the Constitution, Hearings Before a Subcommittee of the Committee of the Judiciary,* 67th Cong. 4th sess. (1923). The text of the amendment is in House Joint Resolution 184 (68th Cong., 1st sess., *Congressional Record,* Vol. 65, Part 7, 7176); see also p. 7295 and (Part 10) p. 10142. Of the 69 dissenting votes in the House, 55 were from Southern or border states, and of the 23 dissenting votes in the Senate, 15 were from Southern and border states. The Senate refused to agree to a proposal that the amendment must be ratified within five years.

6. James W. Wadsworth to Mrs. J. Kennedy Todd, May 8, 1924, NYCLC.

7. Circular, American Constitutional League, 1924, NYCLC; Brewster *Standard,* February 27, 1925; Middleport *Herald,* February 24, 1925.

8. Lyons *Republican,* April 10, 1925, reprints the entire piece from *The Rural New Yorker.*

9. Jamestown *Journal,* February 27, 1925.

10. Newburgh *News,* March 21, 1925.

11. Lyons *Republican,* March 20, 1925.

12. Cocksackie *Union-News,* March 12, 1925; Monticello *Republican,* February 19, 1925; Buffalo *Truth,* December 20, 1924.

13. Whitney Point *Reporter,* February 19, 1925; Herbert Bayard Swope to Alfred E. Smith, June 10, 1927, "1927 legislation" folder 200-6-4, Smith Papers, N.Y. State Library; *New York Times,* January 29, 1925. Among the other upstate journals opposing the amendment were the Catskill *Mail,* Albany *News,* Carthage *Republican,* Buffalo *Post,* Troy *Times,* Carmel *Courier,* Patchogue *Advance,* Ogdensburg *News,* and *Rural New Yorker.*

14. Vincent A. McQuade, *The American Catholic Attitude on Child Labor Since 1891* (Washington, D.C., Catholic University of America, 1938), pp. 130-31; Francis L. Broderick, *Right Reverend New Dealer: John A. Ryan* (New York: Macmillan Co., 1963), pp. 155-56.

15. Tom Ireland, *Child Labor As a Relic of the Dark Ages* (New York: G. P. Putnam's Sons, 1937), p. 109; Broderick, *Right Reverend New Dealer,* p. 156. Senator Thomas J. Walsh of Montana, one of the amendment's sponsors, was a Catholic as was the man who was perhaps its leading national opponent, James A. Emery, General Counsel of the N.A.M.

16. McQuade, *American Catholic Attitude,* p. 170.

17. James A. Emery, *An Examination of the Proposed Twentieth Amendment to the Constitution of the United States* (New York: N.A.M., 1924), p. 21; *The Daily Worker,* December 1, 1924.

18. N. M. Butler to William T. Byrne, April 5, 1935, Smith Papers.

19. For an account of George's early life see William R. George and Lyman Beecher Stowe, *Citizens Made and Remade* (Boston: Houghton Mifflin Co., 1912); W. R. George to Mark O. Prentiss, August 26, 1925, George Junior Republic Papers, Cornell University, hereafter cited as GJR with box number; W. R. George, radio broadcast script, November 18, 1925, GJR-24. Tuition was charged at the Republic; in 1925 it was six hundred dollars a year.

20. George to Henry W. Thurston, June 9, 1924, GJR-23; George to Charles Dawson, August 7, 1924, GJR-60; Buffalo *Truth,* December 25, 1924, January 8, 1925.

21. Buffalo *Evening News,* October 24, 1924; Ithaca *Journal-News,* December 11, 1924; September 23, 1924; W. R. George to Thomas F. McGuire, October 27, 1924, GJR-23.

22. W. R. George, draft of article, February 7, 1925, GJR-23; George to James A. Emery, September 10, 1924, GJR-60; *New York Times,* December 5, 1924; Syracuse *Post-Standard,* January 10, 1925.

23. "Suggestions for Campaigns in Opposition to the Ratification of the Twentieth Amendment to the U.S. Constitution," Associated Industries of Massachusetts, 1924, GJR-74.

24. William D. Guthrie, "Radio Address on the Child Labor Amendment," New York State Bar Association, *Bulletin* (April, 1934), pp. 179-80.

25. Memorandum on Federal Child Labor Amendment by G. W. Alger, "G. W. Alger folder," NYCLC.

26. "Report of the Work of the New York Committee for the Ratification of the Child Labor Amendment," Grace H. Childs, Chairman, April 6, 1925, NYCLC. Among the organizations belonging to the ratification committee were the Ameri-

can Association for Labor Legislation, the New York Branch of the American Association of University Women, the Girl Scouts, the Salvation Army, the New York City Federation of Women's Clubs, and the New York Congress of Mothers and Parent-Teachers Associations. William R. George could not understand the American Legion's endorsement of the amendment, which was probably due to its extensive youth program. "There is too much of the Communistic and Socialistic element favoring the amendment to click with their ideas of Americanism," George observed to Jerome D. Barnum on November 25, 1933 (GJR-30).

27. Sample editorial, "May Susie Wash the Dishes?" by R. J. Plimpton, 1924-25, NYCLC. The ratification committee spent $2,359.95 on the campaign between October 22, 1924, and April 9, 1925.

28. Webster *Herald*, April 3, 1925; Albany *Times-Union*, March 12, 1925; Jamestown *Post*, March 11, 1925; Baldwinsville *Gazette*, February 13, 1925; Port Chester *Item*, February 26, 1925; New York *World*, February 26, 1925. Also supporting the amendment were the Binghamton *Press*, Watertown *Times*, Newburgh *News*, Syracuse *Telegram*, Rochester *Journal* and Utica *Press*. The farm press was uniformly hostile although the amendment did get some support in its early days from the *American Agriculturalist*.

29. Report of Work of the Ratification Committee.

30. *Ibid.;* "Shall we Have a Child Labor Referendum?" *The Reform Bulletin*, XVI (February 27, 1925), 1. The precise date of the "gentlemen's agreement" is not clear, but it was described in a private report of the ratification committee written on April 6, 1925. There is some evidence that the committee was still working on Smith as late as February 13, so the actual agreement may have come after the hearing of February 24.

31. Report of Work of the Ratification Committee; New York *Herald Tribune*, February 26, 1925.

32. Troy *Times*, February 25, 1925; Albany *Times-Union*, February 24, 1925; Syracuse *Herald*, March 10, 1925; Syracuse *Post-Standard*, March 11, 1925.

33. Buffalo *Courier*, March 12, 1925; Binghamton *Press*, March 16, 1925.

34. The four ratifying states were Arkansas, Arizona, California, and Wisconsin. The states that rejected it by a vote of both houses were Connecticut, Delaware, Georgia, Kansas, Massachusetts, North Carolina, South Carolina, South Dakota, Tennessee, Texas, Utah, and Vermont. An extensive list of these groups is in the NYCLC papers. They included everything from the Rabbinical Assembly of the Jewish Theological Seminary to the Social Service Department of the Hospital for Joint Diseases. See also Minutes of NYCLC Board Meeting, December 15, 1933; Minutes of Meeting of Child Labor Amendment Campaign Committee, December 6, 1934; Hall to Courtenay Dinwiddie, October 6, 1934, NYCLC.

35. Hall to Leo Eisen, March 15, 1934; Hall to John H. Farley, April 6, 1934; Hall to Clara Artus, August 16, 1933, NYCLC.

36. Brooklyn *Tablet*, December 1, 1934; Albany *Evangelist*, February 22, 1935.

37. McQuade, *American Catholic Attitude*, p. 43; Gertrude Zimand to Walsh, March 17, 1937, Frank P. Walsh Papers, New York Public Library; Albany *Evangelist*, February 21, 1936.

38. Albany *Evangelist*, February 26, 1937; Form letter, League of Adult Minors, GJR-30; George to Barnum, October 26, 1933; GJR-30; Minutes of Meeting of Child Labor Amendment Campaign Committee, January 19, 1934, March 5, 1934; Hall to Frederick I. Daniels, January 18, 1934, NYCLC; F. D. Roosevelt

to Courtenay Dinwiddie, November 8, 1934, facsimile copy, NYCLC; Courtenay Dinwiddie to trustees, National Child Labor Committee, June 17, 1938, Walsh Papers; S. I. Rosenman (ed.), *The Public Papers and Addresses of Franklin D. Roosevelt*, III, 415.

39. Flier issued by the Edmonson Economic Service (New York City), 1936, Walsh Papers.

40. Mrs. Horace Eaton to Hall, January 22, 1935; Hall to Eaton, February 25, 1935; Hilda Boyle to Hall, April 15, 1935, NYCLC; Syracuse *Herald*, January 24, 1935. Roosevelt wrote Lehman and several other Governors asking them to promote ratification. See *Public Papers*, V, 657.

41. Hall to members, NYCLC, February 4, 1937, NYCLC; Zimand to Walsh, February 4, 1937, Walsh Papers; Gertrude Zimand, interview with author, April 11, 1963. Every Democrat in the Senate except Erastus Corning of Albany voted for the amendment. Corning was eulogized in the Catholic press.

42. New York *Daily News*, February 24, 1937; Albany *Evangelist*, February 26, 1937.

43. Ireland, *Child Labor As a Relic*, pp. 213, 219-21; New York *Daily News*, June 23, 1937; G. F. Zimand, A Study Outline on Pending Federal Child Labor Legislation, September 15, 1937, NYCLC.

44. Hall to Gertrude S. Thomas, March 5, 1935; Hall to Charles H. Foster, March 10, 1936; Ehrich to Hall, December 23, 1936; Hall to Alger, April 13, 1938, NYCLC.

IX. EPILOGUE

1. George W. Alger, *The Old Law and the New Order* (Boston: Houghton Mifflin Co., 1913), p. 268; G. W. Alger, signed article, "Tax Child Labor to Death," New York *Herald Tribune*, July 6, 1918. Alger was a graduate of the University of Vermont (1892) and of the New York University Law School. In addition to his other activities he was an arbitrator in the cloak and suit industry, helped reorganize RKO Pictures Corporation, and served as a member of President Truman's Loyalty Review Board.

2. Membership and Board of Directors lists, NYCLC.

3. Address of Jeanie V. Minor to Association of Governmental Labor Officials, Richmond, Va., May 2, 1923, folder 610, NYCLC; NYCLC Constitution and By-Laws, folder 071; Hall, *Forty Years*, p. 10.

4. Hall to Minor, July 1, 1932; Hall to the Board of Directors, December 7, 1932, NYCLC. Hall's salary was $5,000 a year and Miss Minor's $4,750.

5. Program of Activities for January, February, March, 1931 (January 8, 1931), folder 010, NYCLC. In 1926 Grace Abbott, Chief of the Federal Children's Bureau, urged Hall to take the civil service examination for social economist so that he could head the Social Service Division of the Children's Bureau (Abbott to Hall, January 27, 1926, NYCLC). Jeanie Minor died in 1957 at the age of eighty-six "mentally alert and interested in world events to the last." (Mary K. Armbrister to author, May 23, 1958.)

6. Hall to F. E. Desmond, January 9, 1936, "NYA" folder; Hall to the Board of Directors, November 19, 1940, folder 010, NYCLC.

7. *New York Times,* October 6, 1941; Minutes of Special Meeting of the Board of Directors, November 14, 1941, folder 041; F. A. O. Schwarz to the Board of Directors, December 5, 1941, folder 041, NYCLC.

Note on Sources

The sources I have relied on in this study are fully detailed in the notes. Works by three earlier writers on child labor in New York were most helpful to me, and I should like to make special acknowledgment of my debt to Fred R. Fairchild, Mary Stevenson Callcott, and Fred S. Hall. My most important source by far was the files of the New York Child Labor Committee in the New York State Library at Albany. Comprising roughly eighty thousand items, housed partly in filing cabinets and partly in unorganized bundles and cartons, this collection contains all manner of correspondence, reports, investigations, surveys, and publications relating to child labor in New York. The papers of the Consumers' League of New York covering the 1940's and 1950's were of value on the migrant labor problem; they will shortly be housed in the State Historical Society of Wisconsin. Other Consumers' League papers on the 1920's are in the Cornell University Library, and some of the correspondence between the New York and National Consumers' Leagues will be found in the Library of Congress. The papers of the National Child Labor Committee in the Library of Congress contain relatively little material related to New York. The George Junior Republic Papers at Cornell are a mine of information on the child labor amendment fight in New York. They contain letters, pamphlets, and a large number of newspaper clippings related to that struggle. The New York Public Library's magnificent pamphlet collection provided me with indispensable background material. To a lesser extent I found the following collections useful: National Civic Federation Papers, Lillian Wald Papers and Frank Walsh Papers (New York Public Library); Nicholas Murray Butler Papers (Columbia University—only published material in the papers is available); Alfred E. Smith Public Papers (New York State Library). Frances Perkins has a lengthy memoir in the Columbia University Oral History Project, but it is closed to scholars. I was permitted to use some of the current files of the New York State Labor Department in New York City and to examine material in possession of the National Child Labor Committee. The official publications of the State of New York, particularly of the Labor Department, were indispensable. The earlier reports of the Labor Department, particularly those of the Factory Inspector, must be used with caution because of their occasional statistical errors and because of the department's tendency to see the child labor problem as limited to the children it actually discovered. Nevertheless, the reports provide an unusual insight into the attitudes, problems, and arrangements of state bureaus.

Index

Abbott, Lyman, 46
Accidents: and courts, 28, 52; to children, 28-30; number of, 70, 79, 81, 83; in factories, 79-80; on farms, 180-81, 192-93. *See also* Commercial farms
Addams, Jane, 44, 78
Adler, Felix, 46, 57, 60, 69, 74
Age. *See* Minimum age; Proof of age; School-leaving age
Agrarian Myth, 77-78, 169, 170
Agriculture: child labor in, 77-78, 169; and First World War, 92; N.Y. production, 169; mechanization of, 175, 179, 187-88. *See also* Commercial farms; Growers; Migrant workers
Alabama: child labor committee in, 45
Albany: truants in, 16; employment certification in, 113, 114, 116; newsboys in, 162, 164-65
Alger, George W.: 46, 72, 91, 114, 221, 143 n. 83; on double compensation, 81-82; on employment certification, 110; on NRA, 166; on federal child labor laws, 195-96; on Child Labor Amendment, 205-06; career of, 217, 265 n. 1
Altgeld, John P., 43
Amalgamated Clothing Workers of America, 147
American Association for Labor Legislation, 91-92
American Federation of Labor, 78
Amsterdam: employment certification in, 106-07
Andrews, Elmer F., 92, 152
Appleton, Charles W., 217
Apprenticeship, 2
Artificial feathers, 8
Artificial flowers, 40, 49, 152
Associated Industries of Massachusetts, 204-05
Associated Industries of New York State, 81

Association for Improving the Condition of the Poor, 5, 42
Association of Neighborhood Workers, 44, 71
Astor, William B., 4
Attendance. *See* Compulsory education law; School attendance; Truancy

Baker, Dr. S. Josephine: 105, 114, 120; and employment certification, 102, 103, 104
Baldwin, William H., 46, 74
Barnum, Jerome D., 204, 212-13
Beacon: employment certification in, 113
Beans: mechanical harvest of, 187-88
Belmont, August, 4, 77, 78
Bergh, Henry, 18
Binghamton: newsboys in, 165
Birth certificates, 23, 53, 97-103
Births: number of in N.Y., 23
Blair, George, 5-9
Blumenthal, Dr. J. L., 114
Boards of Health: defects in, 24-25, 47-48
Bootblacks, 17, 57-61, 163
Box-making, 29
Brace, Charles L., 1, 3, 5, 6, 8
Brackett, Edgar T., 51, 57
Brickyards, 28
Brooklyn: tenement sweatshops in, 40
Buffalo: 28, 72; employment certification in, 107, 116; homework in, 143; newsboys in, 143
Butler, Nicholas Murray, 77, 202

Canneries: 88, 171, 175, 176, 177-79; in Second World War, 94; wages in, 170, 175; child labor in, 172, 173-75; and Factory Commission, 173-76
Canners, 170-71, 172-73, 175, 176-77, 178, 179
Cannery sheds: 172, 175-76; child labor in, 171-72, 173-75

269

72, 74, 219; organization of, 44-47, 50, 71-72, 217-19; activities of, 46-62, 65-70, 71, 77, 86, 91, 92, 111, 112, 114, 115, 116, 129-30, 133, 134, 135, 136, 137, 138, 150-51, 155, 157-58, 163, 167-68, 172-73, 176-77, 181-83, 184; and scholarships, 72-74; and NCLC, 74-75; and double compensation, 81-84; and employment certification, 98-103, 110, 112-16; and school-leaving age, 120-27; and Child Labor Amendment, 206, 215; evaluation of, 220-21, 224; end of, 220

New York City: death rate in, 40; employment certification in, 114-15; population density of, 141

New York City Board of Education, 8, 121

New York City Board of Health, 4, 10-11, 101, 102, 129-30, 150, 154

New York City Bureau of Attendance, 164

New York City Bureau of Child Hygiene, 114-15

New York City Charities Organization Society, 5, 42

New York City Children's Court, 59

New York City Consumer's League, 24, 42, 53-54, 88, 132, 150, 184-93

New York City Court of Special Sessions, 59

New York City Retail Dealers Association, 130

New York City Tenement House Department, 39

New York Committee for the Ratification of the Child Labor Amendment, 206, 207

New York State: industrial growth of, 1, 17, 237 n. 1; class city system in, 54-55; agriculture in, 169

New York State Bureau of Factory Inspection, 20-25, 30, 32, 33, 35-36, 64-65, 86

New York State Bureau of Labor Statistics, 7, 9, 13-15, 19

New York State Charities Aid Association, 5

New York State Citizens Committee for the Protection of Our Homes and Children, 204

New York State Commission to Examine Laws Relating to Child Welfare, 81, 150

New York State Committee on Summer Farm Labor Problems, 180, 183

New York State Council of Catholic School Superintendents, 123, 124, 125

New York State Council of School Superintendents, 110

New York State Department of Health, 191

New York State Education Department, 120-21, 123

New York State Federation of Labor: origins of, 18; and NYCLC, 46-47; and legislation, 88, 123, 134, 138, 177, 206

New York State Federation of Women's Clubs, 125

New York State Industrial Board, 89, 91

New York State Industrial Commission, 91-92

New York State Interdepartmental Committee on Farm and Food Processing Labor, 184

New York State Joint Legislative Committee on Migrant Labor. See Waters Committee

New York State Labor Department: 66-68, 91; organization of, 30, 35-36, 70, 89-91, 92, 151; inspection activities of, 67-70, 133-35, 138, 139-40, 152, 177-78, 179, 184, 186, 187, 244 n. 85, 252 n. 27

New York State Legislature, 8-9, 11-12, 19, 21, 31, 51-52, 55, 88, 121-26, 133-35, 151, 152, 208, 209, 210, 213-15

New York State Medical Society, 19

New York State War Council, 94

Niagara Falls, 113

Nicoll, Mathias, 139

Night schools, 15, 36, 56. See also Continuation schools

Night work, 28, 32

Nine-hour day, 88

North, Luella R., 138